# The Guru Guide™ to the Knowledge Economy

## The Best Ideas for Operating Profitably in a Hyper-Competitive World

Joseph H. Boyett
and
Jimmie T. Boyett

John Wiley & Sons, Inc.
New York • Chichester • Weinheim • Brisbane • Singapore • Toronto

This book is printed on acid-free paper. ♾


Published by John Wiley & Sons, Inc.
Published simultaneously in Canada.



Library of Congress Cataloging-in-Publication Data

Boyett, Joseph H.
The Guru guide to the knowledge economy : the best ideas for operating profitably in a hyper-competitive world / Joseph H. and Jimmie T. Boyett.
p. cm.
Includes index.
ISBN 0-471-39085-2 (cloth : alk. paper)
1. Information technology—Economic aspects. 2. Electronic commerce. I. Boyett, Jimmie T. II. Title.
HC79.I55 B69 2001
658—dc21 2001017639

Printed in the United States of America.

10 9 8 7 6 5 4 3 2 1

To Maria Carvainis,
our agent, our advocate, and our friend.

Her dedication, professionalism, and tenacity
keep the rest of us on our toes.

# Contents

# Introduction

You need quick access to state-of-the-art management information, right? Of course you do, particularly when it comes to gaining access to ideas that could help you navigate the treacherous waters of today's economy. If you are like most people, however, you simply have too much to do and too little time to sift through hundreds of books and thousands of articles and Web sites to find the advice you need. Which books should you read? What articles could provide you with insight into emerging issues? Whose writings should you seek on the Internet? Who are the authorities when it comes to business today? What advice do they give? How do the ideas of one authority complement or conflict with those of another? You need a guide to answer these questions. Congratulations. You have just found it.

*The Guru Guide™ to the Knowledge Economy: The Best Ideas for Operating Profitably in a Hyper-Competitive World* has been designed to provide you with a clear, concise, and informative digest to the best thinking about what it takes to survive and succeed in the new global, high-tech and knowledge-intensive world of business. You are holding in your hands a highly opinionated but informative guide to the ideas of the world's top business advisors. Like the original *Guru Guide™* (Wiley, 1998), we have designed this guide to be more than just an overview of current thinking. We go further to link and cross-link the ideas to show where the experts agree and disagree. We show how the gurus' ideas have evolved. Finally, we provide an evaluation of their strengths and weaknesses.

## OUR GURUS

In selecting our gurus, we began by making a list of what we thought were some of the most important issues businesspeople are facing today. After much discussion and debate, we finally settled on six topics that would complement and expand on the topics of leadership, managing change, learning organizations, teamwork, strategy, managing people, and organizational design that we covered in *The Guru Guide™*. Here they are:

**The changing economy.** How have economic conditions changed, and what do these changes portend for the future?

**Electronic commerce.** How can businesses leverage the Internet and e-commerce for profit and competitive advantage?

**Knowledge management.** How should businesses manage their knowledge assets?

**Customer-relationship management.** How can businesses leverage computing and communications technology to build more-enduring relationships with their customers?

**Globalization.** How can companies exploit the global opportunities for business that are now possible because of the computing and communications revolutions of the last two decades?

**Business ethics.** How should business leaders balance their responsibilities to employees, stockholders, and society as a whole?

Once we had our topics, we started looking for our gurus. We focused our search primarily on the most significant books and articles that had been published over the last three years. We checked the best-seller lists to see what people were reading, and we asked our friends, clients, and associates to recommend people they thought had unique insights. In total, we considered the writings of over 300 people. We ultimately narrowed our list down to the 115 gurus listed here.

Verna Allee
Daniel Amor
Douglas Armstrong
Doug Bandow
Christopher A. Bartlett
Michael Berry
Keki R. Bhote
Annie Brooking
Stanley A. Brown
Lowell Bryan
Jeffrey H. Coors
Jay Curry
John Dalla Costa
Thomas H. Davenport
Frank W. Davis Jr.
Stan Davis
George S. Day
Peter Drucker
Leif Edvinsson
Farid Elashmawi
John Elkington
Juanita Ellis
Ralph Estes
Philip Evans
Walter Forbes
Jane Fraser
Cyrus F. Freidheim
Hilary F. French
Milton Friedman
Thomas L. Friedman
Richard Gascoyne
Bill Gates
J. Russell Gates
Sumantra Ghoshal
Blair Gibb
James H. Gilmore
Seth Godin
Ian Gordon
Vijay Govindarajan
C. Jackson Grayson Jr.
Alan Greenspan
Anil K. Gupta
John Hagel III
Philip R. Harris
John M. Hood
Michael J. D. Hopkins
Frances Horibe
Joel Hyatt
Jean-Pierre Jeannet
Rolf Jensen
Thomas O. Jones
Bruce Judson
Ravi Kalakota
Rosabeth Moss Kanter
Guy Kawasaki
Kevin Kelly
Rushworth M. Kidder
Philip J. Kitchen
Steffano Korper
David Kosiur
Philip Kotler
Dorothy Leonard
Peter Leyden
Gordon Linoff
Alex Lowy
Edward Luttwak

Michael S. Malone
Karl B. Manrodt
Chuck Martin
Regis McKenna
Christopher Meyer
John Micklethwait
Mary Modahl
James Moore
Tom Morris
Walid Mougayar
Frederick Newell
Ikujiro Nonaka
Carla O'Dell
Jeremy Oppenheim
Jeff Papows
Don Peppers
Jeffrey Pfeffer
B. Joseph Pine II
Laurence Prusak
James Brian Quinn
Wilhelm Rall
Frederick Reichheld
Marcia Robinson
Martha Rogers
Jonathan Rosenoer
W. Earl Sasser
Don E. Schultz
Evan I. Schwartz
Peter Schwartz
Jeffrey L. Seglin
Patricia Seybold
Carl Shapiro
David Siegel
Marc Singer
Robert C. Solomon
Ruth Stanat
Thomas A. Stewart
Robert I. Sutton
Karl Erik Sveiby
Hirotaka Takeuchi
Scott I. Tannenbaum
Don Tapscott
David Ticoll
Amrit Tiwana
Hal R. Varian
Manuel G. Velasquez
Chris West
Adrian Woolridge
Thomas S. Wurster

Our gurus are drawn from leading research and teaching centers, such as the Wharton School of the University of Pennsylvania, International Management Development Institute (IMEDE), Switzerland, Harvard, Massachusetts Institute of Technology (MIT), and the London Business School. Our gurus also represent some of the world's largest and best-known management consulting firms, including McKinsey & Company, Booz-Allen, Ernst & Young, and Arthur Andersen. And they include pioneers in the high-tech industry such as Bill Gates of Microsoft and Seth Godin of Yahoo!

Our gurus are the best and/or most popular business writers and thinkers of today. You won't agree with everything they have to say—we don't either—but we are confident that they will stimulate your thinking, point you in new directions, and challenge many of your best-loved assumptions about what makes today's economy work, what's ahead, and what it will take for you and your company to succeed.

## ORGANIZATION OF THIS BOOK

We have designed this book to be your reference manual to today's hypercompetitive economy. It is organized around key business issues. We cover each issue in a separate chapter and present a summary of the best thinking of a panel of gurus about that issue. We show where the gurus agree and disagree. When our gurus offer different approaches—such as a different sequence of steps to follow in addressing an issue or solving a problem—we use exhibits to illustrate the similarities and differences.

We have organized our gurus' ideas into six chapters.

**Chapter 1: The Knowledge Economy** investigates how information technology and the Internet have changed the world of business. In this chapter, we explain why our gurus say that knowledge is the new wealth of organizations. We examine what our gurus have to say about why a knowledge-intensive economy has emerged and how it differs from the industrial economy of the past. We conclude this chapter with some speculation from our gurus about what may come next. Some say even more revolutionary changes in the economic foundation of business will occur soon. We will tell you in this chapter what they say about why and how these changes will occur and what they portend for your business.

**Chapter 2: Electronic Commerce** examines what our gurus have to say about both business-to-business and business-to-consumer e-commerce. We outline the reasons they believe so many high-flying dot.coms have crashed, and we review their recommended steps for implementing e-commerce business models that work. We reveal our gurus' "secrets" for building a Web site that attracts lots of visitors, keeps them coming back, moves products and sells services, and most important, makes money. We conclude with an overview of what our gurus say are seven critical success factors for doing business via the Internet.

**Chapter 3: Knowledge Management** covers one of the hottest management topics of the day. In this chapter, we present three "realities" that our gurus say make knowledge hard to manage, and we outline 10 steps that they say you should follow in implementing knowledge management in your company. We conclude with a discussion of the human aspects of knowledge management and tips our gurus have for creating a culture that supports the growth and sharing of knowledge within a company.

**Chapter 4: Customer-Relationship Management** is all about marketing in the postindustrial world. In this chapter, we explain why our gurus say that mass marketing is dead and one-on-one customer-relationship management is now critical. We list 20 ways our gurus say customer-relationship management is different from traditional marketing and outline four key concepts that our gurus say provide the justification and intellectual underpinnings of customer-relationship management. We conclude with a discussion of the basic steps and six cultural "conditions" that our gurus say are necessary for making the transition to customer-relationship management.

In **Chapter 5: Globalization,** we identify three forces that our gurus say are driving the creation of a truly global economy, and we compare and contrast the views of opponents and proponents of this trend. We then examine reasons our gurus give for taking a company global. We conclude with a review of the key arguments in a debate between two well-known international consulting firms over the best strategies for taking a company global.

In **Chapter 6: Business Ethics in the Knowledge Economy,** we explain why our gurus say that business ethics, corporate social responsibility, and a focus on what they call the "triple bottom line" are critical today. We review seven revolutions that our gurus believe are forcing global companies to pay more attention to the environmental and social impact of their operations. We present the key arguments for and against company involvement in environmental and social issues. We summarize four international codes of ethics that our gurus maintain are the ones knowledge-economy companies are adopting. We conclude with a discussion of three classic approaches the gurus recommend you follow in resolving ethical dilemmas.

Finally, in an appendix, we provide biographies for all of the gurus, including in many instances postal addresses, phone numbers, and e-mail addresses where they can be reached.

## SOME GUIDANCE ON WHAT FOLLOWS: HOW THE CHAPTERS ARE ORGANIZED

Throughout *The Guru Guide™ to the Knowledge Economy:The Best Ideas for Operating Profitably in a Hyper-Competitive World,* we have tried to summarize as clearly, succinctly, and objectively as possible the gurus' key ideas. Our personal opinions are expressed in sections entitled "Our View" and preceded by the following icon:

At the beginning of each chapter, we use the icon below to identify the gurus whose ideas are covered in that chapter. For example, the chapter on knowledge management begins as follows:

KNOWLEDGE MANAGEMENT—The Gurus

At the end of each chapter, we provide a summary of the key ideas presented in that chapter. Key ideas are identified by the following icon:

KEY POINTS

You can read this book straight through, from beginning to end, covering the topics in the order we present them, or you can go directly to a topic that interests you. You can read the chapters in any order you wish because each has been designed to stand on its own. Therefore, we encourage you to start with whichever topic is of most interest to you at the moment. If you are interested in specific gurus, check the index or the guru lists at the beginning of each chapter to find out where they appear in the book, and proceed accordingly. You are in control of how you read this book. In fact, this advice is a good summary of the message contained herein. You are in control, or at least you had better be.

So here it is—an unbiased but highly opinionated look at the best and worst the most notable knowledge-economy gurus have to offer. We wish you good reading and success. If you have comments about *The Guru Guide™ to the Knowledge Economy: The Best Ideas for Operating Profitably in a Hyper-Competitive World* or would like to learn about other *Guru Guides™* as they become available, please visit our Web site at http://www.jboyett.com or e-mail us at Boyett@jboyett.com.

Joseph H. Boyett
Jimmie T. Boyett

## THE KNOWLEDGE ECONOMY—The Gurus

**Stan Davis,** senior research fellow with Ernst & Young Center for Business Innovation and author of eight books, including *Blur: The Speed of Change in the Connected Economy,* which he coauthored with Christopher Meyer

**Philip Evans,** consultant with the Boston Consulting Group and coauthor of *Blown to Bits: How the New Economics of Information Transforms Strategy*

**Bill Gates,** cofounder of Microsoft, Inc.

**James H. Gilmore,** cofounder of Strategic Horizons LLP, member of the faculty of The Institutes for Organization Management for the U.S. Chamber of Commerce, and coauthor of *The Experience Economy*

**Alan Greenspan,** chairman of the Federal Reserve Board

**Joel Hyatt,** cofounder and spokesperson for Hyatt Legal Services and coauthor of *The Long Boom: A Vision for the Coming Age of Prosperity*

**Rolf Jensen,** director of the Copenhagen Institute for Future Studies and author of *The Dream Society: How the Coming Shift from Information to Imagination Will Transform Your Business*

**Kevin Kelly,** executive editor of *Wired* and author of *Out of Control: The New Biology of Machines, Social Systems, and the Economic World* and *New Rules for the New Economy*

**Peter Leyden,** former managing editor of *Wired,* journalist and coauthor of *The Long Boom: A Vision for the Coming Age of Prosperity*

**Alex Lowy,** cofounder of the Alliance for Converging Technologies and coauthor of *Digital Capital*

**Chuck Martin,** author of *The Digital Estate: Strategies for Competing, Surviving, and Thriving in an Internetworked World*

**Christopher Meyer,** consultant with Ernst & Young and coauthor of *Blur: The Speed of Change in the Connected Economy*

**James Moore,** founder and chairman of GeoPartners Research, columnist for *Upside,* and author

**Jeff Papows,** former chief executive officer of Lotus Development Corporation and author of *Enterprise.com*

**B. Joseph Pine II,** cofounder of Strategic Horizons LLP, guest lecturer, award-winning author of *Mass Customization: The New Frontier in Business Competition,* and coauthor of *The Experience Economy*

**Peter Schwartz,** cofounder and chairman of Global Business Network, author of *The Long View,* and coauthor of *The Long Boom: A Vision for the Coming Age of Prosperity*

**Carl Shapiro,** professor, University of California, Berkeley, and coauthor of *Information Rules: A Strategic Guide to the Network Economy*

**Don Tapscott,** author of *Creating Value in the Network Economy,* cofounder of the Alliance for Converging Technologies, coauthor of *Digital Capital,* and regular contributor to *Computerworld*

**David Ticoll,** cofounder of the Alliance for Converging Technologies (now Digital 4Sight) and coauthor of *Digital Capital*

**Hal R. Varian,** professor, University of California, Berkeley, and coauthor of *Information Rules: A Strategic Guide to the Network Economy*

**Thomas S. Wurster,** consultant with the Boston Consulting Group and coauthor of *Blown to Bits: How the New Economics of Information Transforms Strategy*

1

# The Knowledge Economy

As the United States entered the last few years of the twentieth century—the century that has been called "America's century"—almost everyone was convinced that this country's economy had changed in fundamental ways. Old ideas about unemployment and inflation, the stock market and shareholder behavior, market share and business cycles, and much much more seem to be just that—old, outdated ideas. Unemployment in the United States fell to record lows in the late 1990s, but labor costs didn't skyrocket, and inflation stayed low. The Asian economy went into free fall but somehow the U.S. stock market kept on climbing. Predicted economic disasters didn't occur, or at least weren't as severe as predicted. Then in the year 2000 it all seemed to begin to unravel. High-flying dot.com stocks tumbled. Venture capital that had flowed so freely for most of the 1990s dried up. What was going on? Had the U.S. economy really changed, or had the excitement that drove the explosion of dot.com start-ups truly been irrational?

In fact, U.S. Federal Reserve chairman Alan Greenspan had been asked to address that very question as far back as 1998, near the high point of the "new economy" excitement. His answer was "Yes . . . maybe . . . no . . . well, we'll see," or something like that. In part, Greenspan said:

> Our economy, of course, is changing every day, and in that sense it is always "new." The deeper question is whether there has been a profound and fundamental alteration in the way our economy works that creates discontinuity from the past and promises a significantly higher path of growth than we have experienced in recent decades.
>
> The question has arisen because the economic performance of the United States in the past five years has in certain respects been unprecedented. Contrary to conventional wisdom and the detailed historic economic modeling on which it is based, it is most unusual for inflation to be falling this far into a business expansion.

> Many of the imbalances observed during the few times in the past that a business expansion has lasted more than seven years are largely absent today. To be sure, labor markets are unusually tight, and we should remain concerned that pressures in these markets could spill over to costs and prices. But, to date, they have not.[1]

Greenspan acknowledged the impact of technological innovations and the breakthroughs in globalization that have raised productivity and moderated price fluctuations, but he added a caveat to the notion that we live in a new economic order:

> The same enthusiasms and fears that gripped our forebears, are, in every way, visible in the generations now actively participating in the American economy. . . .
>
> Hence, as the first cut at the question "Is there a new economy?" the answer in a more profound sense is no. As in the past, our advanced economy is primarily driven by how human psychology molds the value system that drives a competitive market economy. And that process is inextricably linked to human nature, which appears essentially immutable and, thus, anchors the future to the past. . . .
>
> Perhaps, as some argue, history will be less of a guide than it has been in the past. Some of the future is always without historical precedent. New records are always being made. Having said all that, however, my experience of observing the American economy day by day over the past half century suggests that most, perhaps substantially most, of the future can be expected to rest on a continuum from the past. Human nature, as I indicated earlier, appears immutable over the generations and inextricably ties our future to our past. . . .
>
> In summary, whether over the past five to seven years, what has been, without question, one of the best economic performances in our history is a harbinger of a new economy or just a hyped-up version of the old, will be answered only with the inexorable passage of time. And I suspect our grandchildren, and theirs, will be periodically debating whether they are in a new economy.[2]

Has the U.S. economy and by implication the economy of the rest of the world fundamentally changed? Greenspan may be uncertain, but by in large, our gurus are not. They echo *Wired* magazine's executive editor, Kevin Kelly, in his certainty that a new economic order, rooted in electronic networks, is producing "tectonic upheavals" in the marketplace and society.[3] Not only are our gurus certain that there is a new economic order; they are also convinced that they know exactly how the new economic order differs from the old and what those differences mean to business and society. The primary differences, say our gurus, are these. The keys to competitive success in the industrial economy of the past were control over physical and financial assets. In contrast, the keys to competitive advantage in today's economy can be found primarily in the control of information and knowledge assets. The industrial economy that created wealth by creating things is dead or dying. The old economic order has given way to a new one based on information and ideas. In short, we now have a "knowledge economy."

**Business at the Turn of the Century**

As the century closed, the world became smaller. The public rapidly gained access to new and dramatically faster communication technologies. Entrepreneurs, able to draw on unprecedented scale economies, built vast empires. Great fortunes were made. . . . Every day brought forth new technological advances to which the old business models seemed no longer to apply. [The year was 1899.][4]

In this chapter, we have gathered our gurus' answers to why the knowledge economy has emerged and what it means. We conclude with thoughts about what comes next. At least three of our gurus think that the information-centric, knowledge economy may already be in decline. They see evidence of a *post*–knowledge economy on the horizon. Before we get to that, however, let's take a look at what our gurus say about the growth of the knowledge economy and how it has changed the rules of business.

We begin with the work of three gurus—Peter Schwartz, Peter Leyden, and Joel Hyatt—who propose to explain why the knowledge economy evolved in the first place and perhaps more important, what it portends for the long term. Schwartz is the cofounder and chairman of the Global Business Network and author of *The Art of the Long View.* Leyden is a former editor of *Wired* magazine. Hyatt is a member of the California Public Utilities Commission. You probably know him better as the cofounder and television spokesperson for Hyatt Legal Services. Schwartz, Leyden, and Hyatt lay out what they call their "vision for the coming age of prosperity" in their 1999 book *The Long Boom.*

## THE ORIGIN OF THE LONG BOOM

Remember 1980? Okay, we know. You were just a kid back then, not even out of kindergarten. Well, ask your parents or consider how Peter Schwartz and his *Long Boom* colleagues describe the period. (Also see Exhibit 1.1.)

> The world in 1980 was filled with much agony and soul-searching. In America, the economy was in shambles. The inflation rate was 14 percent, and the unemployment rate was 10 percent; combined, they created what

EXHIBIT 1.1. **The World in 1980**

**14% inflation rate**

**10% unemployment rate**

**21% interest rate**

Americans called the misery index. On top of that, interest rates were 21 percent. Europe was in worse shape, with the added problem of militant labor wreaking more havoc. The communist USSR, too, had an anemic economy, but we didn't find out until later because they put out phony statistics. What we could see was that they had invaded Afghanistan the year before and seemed bent on expanding their empire. Meanwhile, the United States couldn't get Iranian revolutionaries to release American hostages held for more than a year. Jimmy Carter was the president in 1980, running against Ronald Reagan, whose campaign slogan was "Are you better off today than you were four years ago?" The resounding answer was no, and Reagan won in a Republican landslide. . . .

This was a time before music CDs, compact discs, were introduced. The CD came along in 1981—and now they make up everyone's music collection. This was a time before the FAX machine. There were no faxes until 1985. By 1987, they were nearly ubiquitous in business. This was a time before VCRs and video stores got off the ground. The VCR was still in an experimental phase and in a standards battle between VHS and Betamax. This was before cable television really got started. The very earliest stations like HBO were playing to small audiences, but there was no CNN or MTV. Mobile phones did not exist—businesses had to use radios with dispatchers. For that matter, the world of telephones in the United States was still controlled by a monopoly, Ma Bell, and state companies in other countries. The Walkman was not even around. Mobile music was in the same place as mobile telephony. And most important of all, the world lacked the personal computer.[5]

Technically, of course, as Schwartz, Leyden, and Hyatt admit, the last sentence isn't really true. Personal computers did exist in 1980. Steven Jobs and Stephen Wozniak, cofounders of Apple Computer, had produced the first personal computer way back in 1977. But personal computers weren't being widely used in 1980. They were still somewhat of a novelty and would remain so until IBM introduced its version of the personal computer in 1981. From that point on, personal computers grew in popularity. By the early 1990s, they were a staple in practically every business. Along the way, they became more and more powerful, proving the truth of Moore's Law—an observation made by Gordon Moore, a cofounder of Intel—that the power of microprocessors, and thus the speed and power of personal computers, would double every 18 months. By the early 1990s, the most common personal computers were far more powerful than the multi-million-dollar mainframe computers of the early 1980s.[6]

By the early 1990s, personal computers were beginning to change the world, just as Apple cofounder Steven Jobs had predicted they would. The authors of *The Long Boom* maintain that the introduction of the personal computer has turned out to be as important as the introduction of the printing press.

> The personal computer, like the printing press, had the potential to change almost everything. The personal computer was the key tool that allowed the "centralisms" of bureaucratic corporations and Welfare states and communism to be undermined. We had had computers long before—ever since World War II—but they had been huge mainframe computers that centralized all tasks and were run by elite engineers and technicians. The significance of the personal computer was that it decentralized computer-processing power—and thus facilitated the decentralization of decision making and raw power itself, which had previously tended to move toward the center. The personal computer was the key tool that began to reverse that trend and to allow the spread of power to the periphery. It would become The Great Enabler [of the new economy].[7]

Then, say Schwartz and his coauthors, something happened in the early 1990s that gave the Great Enabler even more power:

> By the early 1990s, . . . the isolated personal computers began to be tied together in networks. At first, they were in small local networks within offices, but soon they were networked between offices and within larger organizations. Ultimately they began getting tied together in even larger public networks. Until then, the personal computer had essentially been a glorified typewriter or number cruncher. Through networking, the personal computer became a communicator, and that shift from calculator to communicator made all the difference in the world. Calculators are useful, but limited. Most people don't really want to sit around and crunch numbers. They want to communicate, and communication is at the heart of everything

> we humans do. So with a change in the way we communicate comes a change in the way we do almost everything else.[8]

By 1993 the first Web browsers were being introduced, and as the *Long Boom* authors note, the computing and communications revolution took off. The number of microprocessors sold, the feet of fiber-optic cable laid, the number of cell-phone subscriptions, the number of Internet hosts and servers, and the number of Internet users were all beating Moore's Law and doubling every year instead of every 18 months. "Personal computers . . . saturated the business world, . . . moved from business into the home, and . . . [began] spreading from the developed to the developing world."[9] The knowledge economy was on its way.

Of course, personal computers and the Internet weren't the only enablers of the knowledge economy. Schwartz and his coauthors point to other significant developments in the 1980s and early 1990s, including the following:

- **Technological openness.** When it brought out its version of the personal computer (PC), IBM, the near-monopoly and proponent of proprietary standards that stifled competition, decided to outsource the development of its PC's operating system to Microsoft and to allow Microsoft to sell the operating system to others, even IBM's competitors. This commitment to technological openness led to wave after wave of competitive innovation in the personal-computer field.

- **Breakup of Ma Bell.** In 1982 the U.S. government entered into a consent decree with AT&T that led to the breakup of the Bell telephone system, launching an explosion of entrepreneurial zeal, investment, and innovation in the telecommunications industry.

- **Dismantling of the post–World-War II "welfare" state.** Throughout the 1980s, a wave of conservative politicians, led by Ronald Reagan in the United States and Margaret Thatcher in Great Britain, began to dismantle systematically many of the key features of the industrial economy "welfare" state built up after World War II. Among other things, they attacked labor unions, deregulated businesses, tightened monetary policy, and allowed unemployment rates to rise in order to fight inflation. Partially as a consequence of these actions, argue the *Long Boom* authors, the relatively static and slow-moving industrial economy was forced to become more entrepreneurial and innovative. Corporations began to downsize and outsource work to smaller businesses. Full-time workers, many in midlife, were forced to become contract workers or temporaries with no job security and few, if any, benefits. Schwartz and coauthors note, "Many people were hurt by these transitions, and Reagan and Thatcher were insensitive to their plight."[10]

- **Evolution of a new business model.** Near San Francisco, in what was to later be called the Silicon Valley, a group of young, highly entrepreneurial companies began to experiment with a new business model. Much less hierarchical than traditional American firms, these start-up companies made speed in everything they did, from design to manufacturing and getting products to markets, their hallmark. Schwartz and his coauthors compare what these companies were doing to a football strategy introduced in the early 1980s by San Francisco 49ers head coach Bill Walsh:

> Walsh created what became known as the West Coast offense, which was based in great part on speed. Other teams might grind up the field by running for short gains up the middle, or protect the quarterback while he threw long passes that were occasionally caught. The 49ers darted up the field with quick short passes to the sidelines that were very difficult to defend against and that brought consistent mid-range gains. The West Coast offense was also about smarts. The key player was the quarterback, who had to act independently and make split-second decisions in reaction to the defense. Other players also had to play with their heads and exploit unforeseen opportunities. The West Coast offense was also about constant innovation. Every week the team came up with different plays and strange combinations of players that the other teams, with more static strategies, did not know how to cope with. And finally, the offense was dynamic. It changed approaches not just week to week but during the game. Walsh would purposely run a preordained set of twenty-five plays at the start of the game so that he could immediately adapt to the reactions of the defense.
>
> Using that strategy, the 49ers became phenomenally successful, winning their first Super Bowl championship in 1981, and eventually adding another four. . . . By the 1990s, virtually all the best teams in pro football were running the West Coast offense and racking up Super Bowl championships. The strategy had spread through the heartland of America to Denver, Green Bay, and Minnesota, among other teams. The West Coast offense was now just the winning one.[11]

The Silicon Valley companies developed a business model that eerily paralleled Walsh's football strategy, particularly in their emphasis on speed and innovation. And like Walsh's strategy, their business model began to catch on. Companies in the high-tech centers of Boston, Austin, Seattle, Minneapolis, and elsewhere began to adopt it. Like the West Coast football offense, the West Coast business model began to be seen as a winning one.

• **Emergence of true globalization.** Finally, say our gurus, the 1980s marked the beginning of true globalization. Deng Xiaoping grabbed control of power in the People's Republic of China in the late 1970s. In 1980 Mikhail Gorbachev became a member of the Soviet Union's Politiburo. Both men began moving their respective countries toward market economies. During the cold war, the economies of free-world countries had become integrated into a global economy. Now, the former communist countries would be joining them. Such truly global economic integration was historically unprecedented.

All of these events, write our gurus, were enablers of the knowledge economy, but they weren't the Great Enablers—a title reserved for the personal computer and the communications revolution. The question is, "Why?" What is it about the computing and communications revolution that made such a difference? Two Boston Consulting Group consultants, Philip Evans and Thomas S. Wurster, offer one possible explanation in their 1999 book *Blown to Bits.* They argue that the underlying economics of information blew apart traditional business models and made the knowledge economy not only possible but inevitable.

## BLOWN TO BITS: HOW THE ECONOMICS OF INFORMATION MADE THE KNOWLEDGE ECONOMY POSSIBLE

Evans and Wurster start with a rather bold statement:

> *Every* business is an information business.[12]

"Wait a minute," you say, "I run a hospital. I'm not in the information business." Think again, instruct our gurus. One-third of the cost of health care in the United States is attributed to capturing, storing, processing, or retrieving information such as patient records, accounting records, and insurance files. You may not think you are in the information business, but you are.

"Well, what about manufacturing?" you ask. "I make things. Surely your gurus don't claim that I'm in the information business, do they?" Yes, they do. Think about it; chances are that your products contain information. For example, some automobiles today contain as much computing power as a midrange computer. And even if your products don't contain information, your processes do. Think about how dependent you are on information-rich functions such as market research, logistics, and advertising. Accurate and timely information is critical for your control of work in process and inventory. The same is true of every business.

Information is critical whether you are talking about value chains (the sequence of activities that a business performs to design, produce, market, deliver, and support a product), supply chains (the personal, contractual, electronic, and other channels that link businesses together in an industry), consumer franchise (brands and the tools such as advertising, promotion, and so on that are used to build brands), or formal organizational structures and ways people work together and communicate within your business (see Exhibits 1.2–1.5). Businesses are designed the way they are and function they way they do because of the way information must flow through them.

The logic that transcends the business models designed by the titans of American industry such as Andrew Carnegie, Henry Ford, and Alfred P. Sloan is essentially informational—a working out of what types of information can be shared

EXHIBIT 1.2. **Value Chains**

EXHIBIT 1.3. **Supply Chain**

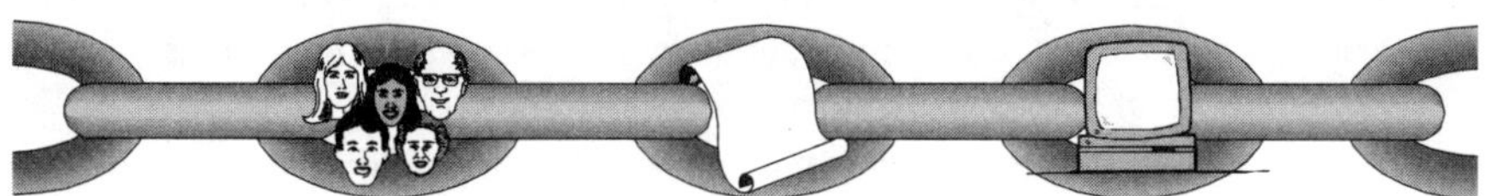

EXHIBIT 1.4. **Consumer Franchise**

EXHIBIT 1.5. **Formal Organizational Structures**

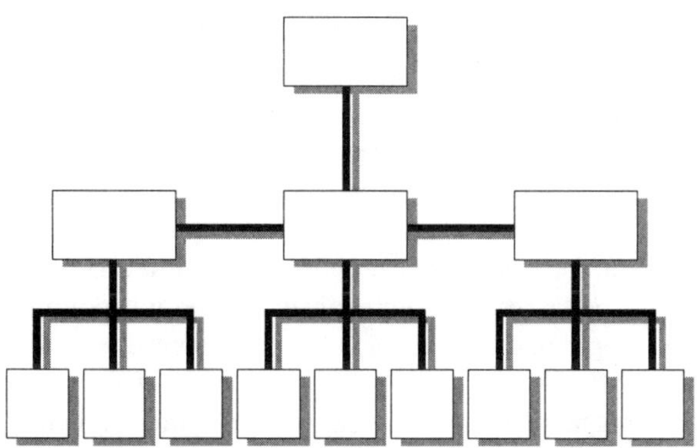

most efficiently within the boundaries of a company rather than across them. "Fundamentally," explain Evans and Wurster, "information and the mechanisms for delivering it are the glue that holds together the structure of businesses."[13] It follows that the computing and communications revolution begun in the 1980s is the great enabler of the knowledge economy because it is melting that glue: "When everyone can communicate . . . with everyone else, the narrow, hardwired communications channels that used to tie people together simply become obsolete. And so do all the business structures that created those channels or exploit them for competitive advantage."[14]

Chuck Martin, author of *The Digital Estate,* states that, at a minimum, the computer and communications revolution and the rise of the knowledge economy, which he calls the Digital Estate, results in a radical shift of power from businesses to customers and from managers to employees:

> The Digital Estate gives new meaning to *customer empowerment.* On the Net, individuals can be the authors of their own worlds, both literally and metaphorically, and this assertion of authority has interesting implications, in both the home and the office. Leading companies in the Digital Estate have found ways to creatively tap into this sense of individualism, so that customers and employees achieve even more control, while the companies also benefit.
>
> When on the Net, people are already interactive participants. While they are in this frame of mind, they might be willing to get their own information, create their own products, and search the enterprise databases themselves. The increase in user control increases their sense of responsibility and their desire to contribute. People go on the Net because it is interactive. So it makes sense that, while there, they will take every opportunity to interact. All they need are the tools.
>
> Similarly, the internal extensions of the Internet, the corporate intranets, give employees a new way to participate in the mission of the company. Intranets remove many of the restrictions that have pushed companies toward bureaucratic organization. Centralized control of information is inefficient in a digital environment because it is unnecessary. Formerly, the *control* of information was power. In the Digital Estate, the *distribution* of information is power. In the network-centric world, the more a company gives away, or pushes out, to consumers or end users, the more widespread and powerful a company can become.[15]

Evans and Wurster insist that you must understand two fundamental principles to appreciate fully the power of the communications and computing revolution and what is driving the rapid move to the knowledge economy:

1. There is a fundamental difference between the pure economics of a physical "thing" and the pure economics of a piece of information.
2. As long as information requires a physical mode of delivery (e.g., a letter requires a mail-delivery person, and a book requires a distributor), then there is a necessary trade-off between the amount of information you can convey (richness) and the number of people to whom you can convey the information at one time (reach).

Let's examine each of these rather intriguing ideas more thoroughly.

## The Economics of Information versus the Economics of "Things"

Evans and Wurster remind us that information and physical things are fundamentally different. Consider the following:

- You can sell a physical thing, such as a car or watch, and you can sell information, such as directions or "how-to" advice, but there is a fundamental difference between the two transactions. When you sell the thing, you no longer own it. The watch, car, television, golf club, and so on are no longer yours. When you sell information, however, you retain ownership and can sell it again and again.
- You can reproduce physical things and you can reproduce information, but again, there is a difference. When you reproduce a physical thing, the second copy is almost as expensive to make as the first. However, the cost of producing a second copy of information is nearly zero. The initial costs of producing information—research, development, experimentation, testing, and so on—do not carry over to subsequent copies, so you can reproduce the information without limit for almost no cost.
- No matter how well they are made, physical things eventually wear out. Information may become dated, unfashionable, or obsolete, but it never wears out. Information doesn't deteriorate with use. In fact, it can actually become more valuable. Consider the following example. You know the lowest price dealer "X" will take for a particular make and model of car. I know the lowest price dealer "Y" will take for that same make and model. When we share our information, that is, use it, we both gain. Your information becomes more valuable, and so does mine.
- Things exist in time and place. You can find them, count them, time them, store them, or tax them. Information obeys no such laws. It's anywhere and everywhere at anytime.

Evans and Wurster make one final point about information and things. Until the emergence of the knowledge economy, they say, information and things were linked—information depended on a physical thing or carrier. For example, the greeting (information) in your letter could travel only as far and as fast as the postal-delivery person (physical thing or carrier). All along the value and supply chains, information in the old industrial economy flowed in a slow, linear fashion, captive to the physical things that carried it. As Evans and Wurster describe it, "the economics of information and the economics of things [were] tied together like participants in a three legged race."[16] Consequently, all business models in the old economy were built on a compromise or trade-off. That's where the second principle comes into play.

## The Trade-Off between Richness and Reach

Evans and Wurster note that, because information has been historically embedded in or linked to physical things, businesses have always had to make a trade-off between the richness (quality, quantity, accuracy, timeliness) of information they provided consumers or others and the reach of that information (the number of people who could receive it). They write, "Until recently, it has been possible to share extremely rich information with a very small number of people and less rich information with a larger number, but it has been impossible to share simultaneously as much richness and reach as one would like."[17] This trade-off, they note, is at the heart of the way most companies conducted business in the old economy. The automotive industry is a good example.

If you were in the market for a new car during the days of the old economy, you would visit your local dealerships to get information about the various makes and models of cars they were selling. Assuming you were able to find a knowledgeable salesperson, you could engage that person in a dialogue and consequently get a lot of rich (detailed, customized, and, you hoped, accurate) information about your prospective purchase. The problem, both for you and for the automotive company, was that there were only so many hours in the salesperson's day, and he or she could talk to only a limited number of people. In other words, the automotive company's reach through the salesperson was limited.

In contrast, if the automotive company ran an advertisement during the Superbowl, it could send its message to a lot of people—that is, its reach was great. However, the amount and quality (richness) of information it could send was limited. There is just so much you can say in a 30-second advertising spot, and by necessity, what you say can't be tailored to individual interest. In other words, the Superbowl ad was not very rich. Examples of this kind of trade-off, suggest Evans and Wurster, can be found throughout the old economy:

> Within a corporation, traditional concepts of span of control and hierarchical reporting are predicated on the fact that communication cannot be rich and broad reaching simultaneously. Jobs are structured to channel rich communication among a few people standing in a hierarchical relationship to one another (upward or downward), and broader communication is effected through the indirect routes of the organizational pyramid.
>
> "Relationships," among and within corporations, as well as with retail customers; "loyalty" to a product or an employer; and "trust" of a person or a brand are all the products of *rich* exchanges of information among people who by doing so have narrowed the reach of their options. The marketing mix, searching and switching behavior, branding, retail franchises, supply chain relationships, organization—indeed even the boundaries of the corporation—all are built on this pervasive, universal, and obvious trade-off between richness and reach.[18]

The power of the computing and communications revolution, according to Evans and Wurster, is that it "blows up" the trade-off between richness and reach. We now have connectivity through the Internet and other sources, and we have computing and other technical standards, such as HTML formats for Web pages, that allow us to share rich information efficiently over great distances. Instead of being forced to choose between richness *or* reach, we can now have richness *and* reach. Suddenly, say our gurus, everything changes.

> It is connectivity and standards together that displace the trade-off between richness and reach. They allow advising, alerting, authenticating, bidding, collaborating, comparing, informing, searching, specifying, and switching, with a richness that is constrained only by the underlying standards and a reach that is constrained only by the number of players connected and using that standard. . . .
>
> As the trade-off between richness and reach blows up, economic relationships, in all their manifestations, will change radically. A sales force, a system of branches, a printing press, a chain of stores, or a delivery fleet—which once served as formidable barriers to entry because they took years and heavy investment to build—will suddenly become expensive liabilities. New competitors will come from nowhere to steal customers. . . .
>
> When everyone can exchange rich information without constraints on reach, the channel choices for marketers, the inefficiencies of consumer search, the hierarchical structure of supply chains, the organizational pyramid, asymmetries of information [differences in knowledge among people or companies that affect their bargaining power], and the boundaries of the corporation itself will all be thrown into question. The competitive advantages that depended on them will be challenged. The business structures that had been shaped by them will fall apart.[19]

The auto consumer is no longer dependent on the dealership for rich information, and the automobile company has virtually limitless reach for its message. Traditional business structures and models are dismantled. A knowledge economy with new business models can be born.

## THE RISE OF VALUE NETWORKS

Kevin Kelly, executive editor of *Wired* magazine and author of *New Rules for the New Economy,* reminds us that the business models of the industrial, richness, *or* reach world weren't exactly simple or efficient. It could take a lot of effort from a lot of people to accomplish the most basic task. Kelly uses the simple example of buying a banana to illustrate his point.

Let's say you wanted to buy some bananas in the old economy. Simple, you say. You would get in your car—or even better, walk—to your local produce stand or grocery store and buy a bunch. Right? Sure, but a lot had to happen before the bananas you just bought appeared at the produce stand. A whole complicated system was in place and operating behind the scenes to make those bananas available for you to purchase.

Long before you arrived at the store, the local grocer or produce-stand operator had anticipated your order, along with the orders for bananas he expected to get from other customers. He then sent his request for bananas he thought you and his other customers would want to buy to a wholesaler, who aggregated that request with other requests for bananas and relayed the combined order to various buyers or shipping intermediaries. These intermediaries contacted farmers' cooperatives, who parceled out the orders to planters in Honduras. The planters filled the orders and sent the bananas on their way to you through a complicated chain of reverse links. Such was the banana value chain.

Kelly notes that similar value chains existed for just about every other product or commodity.

> Between the author of a book and you there needed to be a chain of editors, bankers, printers, distributors, wholesalers, and booksellers. Between you and good health care were doctors, nurses, insurance behemoths, and hospital staff. Between you and the car of your dreams stood a line of miners, smelters, engineers, manufacturers, railroad yards, showrooms, and salesmen. Each one of these agents moved the good or service along; some by completing the product (the car engineer) or customizing the service (the hospital staff), and some simply by physically moving it toward you (the banana boat). . . . Each intermediate link in the long chain of creation added some measure of extra value, justifying the cost the link added to the good's final price. Companies competed to insert themselves into a value chain, then to expand their control of greater lengths of the chain.[20]

Kelly explains many of these classic value chains were crowded with intermediaries and that the prime value that many of these intermediaries added for the customer was informational. For example, while the banana wholesaler handled the product and even stored it for a time in inventory, the primary value it added was collecting and passing along the information on who needed bananas, how many they needed, and where the bananas could be found. As Evans and Wurster might say, information was the glue holding together the banana value chain.

Now imagine, says Kelly, how much simpler it would be if you could go directly to the producer for the item you wanted. Reconsider your banana order under those circumstances. "In theory," Kelly writes, "small bunches of bananas could be wrapped and sent directly to your home from a particular plantation with fewer intermediaries involved in warehousing and storage, and thus at lower costs. You would place an order directly to Best Bananas in Honduras for one bunch per week, except during the school holidays, and they then would mail them out to you."[21] But, Kelly continues, think of what you would need in order to place your order directly with Best Bananas:

> To do that effectively . . . would require network technology capable of a) finding a plantation you like; b) getting the right bunch to you at the right time; c) shifting to a cooperating planter if the first planter's fruit was not yet ripe; d) tracking the account payable for such a tiny buyer as yourself; and, e) dealing with all the millions of ordinary exceptions and screw-ups that any system as complex as this would entail.[22]

Such technology didn't exist in the industrial economy. Thanks to the great computer and communications enabler, however, it does now. Of course, Kelly admits that it may be a while before bananas skip the industrial value chain, but that's not true of other goods and services. The great enabler is causing a lot of classic value chains to unravel: our gurus call this unraveling of value chains "deconstruction" or "disintermediation."

## Disintermediation: The Unraveling of the Value Chain

On the surface, disintermediation doesn't look like anything new. After all, direct marketers have been "disintermediating" retailers for some time. As Evans and Wurster note, when Sears introduced its catalog in the nineteenth century, it disintermediated hundreds of local general stores. However, the disintermediation in the knowledge economy is different. Call it "Disintermediation Plus," if you wish, but there are differences.

Evans and Wurster point out that, when Sears disintermediated the small-town stores, it didn't offer a superior value proposition, just a different one. In their terms, Sears with its catalog offered a different trade-off between richness and reach. The customer got more reach, for example, more styles of clothes to choose from, at the cost of some richness—not being able to touch the clothes and get personal advice from the store owner.

Now, consider a different and more modern example. When Michael Dell started assembling and selling personal computers by mail order from his college dormitory room in the mid-1980s, he was disintermediating CompUSA and other computer retailers in much the same way Sears had disintermediated small-town merchants. Dell's customer gave up some richness—the opportunity to spend time talking to a "techie"—in return for some reach, in this case, more configuration options. Like Sears, Dell's value proposition wasn't necessarily superior to that of the computer retailers. It was just different. Contrast that form of disintermediation with what happened when Dell started selling computers via the Internet in the mid-1990s. Dell's customers retained the reach they had before when ordering by phone or fax while simultaneously gaining richness through truly individualized configurations, an extremely wide range of price combinations, on-line technical support, and so on. This time around, the value proposition Dell offered wasn't just different; in many respects it was actually better.

Kelly notes that the banking industry was one of the first in the United States to feel the effects of disintermediation.

> They noticed quite rightly, that as information technology infiltrated the banking industry, and as the industry was deregulated, nobody seemed to need banks anymore—at least not banks as bureaucratic intermediaries. You could get easier loans at Sears, higher interest from a mutual fund, and better service at an ATM. Banks functions were being "*dis*intermediated" the bankers cried! For the typical neighborhood bank this was especially true. The disintermediation of the financial systems continues unabated; every week another bank branch shuts down.[23]

Ultimately, argue Evans and Wurster, when electronic home banking takes off, as it is expected to do in the next few years, the entire retail-banking value chain may be dismantled. Here is the scenario they paint:

> Today's business model [for retail banking] is a vertically and horizontally integrated value chain: multiple products are originated, packaged, sold, and cross-sold through a common set of proprietary distribution channels. These channels have high fixed costs and substantial economies of utilization and scale. These factors determine the rules of engagement and competitive advantage. The fundamental unit of value is the customer relationship. Distribution systems are optimized around servicing that relationship. . . .
>
> Electronic home banking looks at first glance like another, but cheaper, distribution channel. . . . Many banks see it that way, hoping that widespread adoption of home banking might enable them to scale down their high-cost physical channels. Many offer proprietary software to support home banking and even free electronic transactions. But electronic home banking is much more than the emergence of a new distribution channel for incumbents. Customers now can access information and make transactions in a variety of fundamentally new ways.
>
> One way is through personal financial software . . . such as Intuit's Quicken or Microsoft Money. . . . Customers can [already use these programs to] pay bills, make transfers, receive electronic statements, reconcile their checkbooks, and integrate account data into their personal financial plans. . . . But customers are still largely locked into dealing with their own bank, albeit by a nonproprietary route.

> However, there is yet another way. Most major financial institutions maintain Web sites. [Soon we will have software] bridges between personal financial software and the Web sites of financial institutions, combined with advances in reliability, security, digital signatures, and legally binding electronic contracts, [with] the Web to support the full range of banking services. . . .
>
> When that happens, the trade-off between richness and reach in retail banking will be broken. Customers will be able to contact any financial institution for any kind of service or information. They will be able to maintain a balance sheet on their desktop, drawing on data from multiple institutions. They will be able to compare alternative product offerings and sweep funds automatically between accounts at different institutions. They will be able to announce their product requirements and accept bids. They will be able to make sophisticated comparisons between product and service offerings. . . .
>
> As it becomes easier for customers to compare and switch from one supplier to another, the value, indeed the meaning, of the primary banking relationship will become problematic. The competitive value of one-stop shopping and established relationships will drop. Cross-selling will become more difficult. Available information about the customer's behavior and preferences will become more evenly distributed among competing institutions. The winner in any contest for a consumer's business is less likely to be the primary bank and more likely to be whoever makes the best offer for that particular product or service. Competitive advantage will be determined product by product, and therefore providers with broad product lines will lose ground to focused specialists.[24]

If such a scenario happens, say Evans and Wurster, the traditional retail-banking value chain will be destroyed. Banks won't disappear, but their business model will be shaken badly.

How likely is such a scenario for retail banking? Evans and Wurster admit that most bankers see it as unlikely, arguing that most banking customers will not put their checking accounts out for frequent bid since the cost of switching from one account to another is still too high. (See Exhibit 1.6 for more information on the concept of switching costs.) Some of our gurus agree with the bankers. Jeff Papows, author of *Enterprise.com,* asserts that banking is one of the industries least affected by the Web and is likely to remain so for some time.[25] Certainly, writes Papows, banks have been and will continue to be less affected, at least in the short term, by the computing and communications revolution than booksellers, stock traders, personal-computer retailers, auto dealers, and travel agents. (See Exhibit 1.7 for a discussion of five non-cost-related factors for determining an industry's vulnerability to the Web's impact.)

## EXHIBIT 1.6. **Switching Costs and the Knowledge Economy**

Here is how Carl Shapiro and Hal R. Varian, coauthors of *Information Rules*, explain switching costs.

*Like it or not, in the information age, buyers typically must bear costs when they switch from one information system to another. Understanding these costs of switching technologies, or even brands, is fundamental to success in today's economy.*

*Compare cars and computers. When the time comes to replace the Ford you've been driving for several years, there is no compelling reason to pick another Ford over a GM or a Toyota. Your garage will hold a Chevy just as well as a Ford, it won't take long to learn the controls of a Toyota, and you can haul the same trailer with either vehicle. In short, you can easily transfer your investments in "automotive infrastructure" to another brand of car. In contrast, when the time comes to upgrade the Macintosh computer you've been using for years, you are going to need a mighty good reason to pick a PC or a Unix machine instead of another Mac. You own a bunch of Mac software, you are familiar with how to use the Mac, your Mac printer may have years of good service left in it, and you probably trade files with other Mac users. You are facing significant costs if you decide to switch from one information technology to another.*

*With the Mac you have made significant durable investments in complementary assets that are specific to that brand of machine. These investments have differing economic lifetimes, so there's no easy time to start using a new, incompatible system. As a result, you face switching costs, which can effectively lock you into your current system or brand. When the costs of switching from one brand of technology to another are substantial, users face lock-in. Switching costs and lock-in are ubiquitous in information systems, and managing these costs is very tricky for both buyers and sellers.*

*Source:* Carl Shapiro and Hal R. Varian, *Information Rules: A Strategic Guide to the Network Economy,* (Harvard Business School Press, 1998), pp. 103–104. Also see pages 170–171 for the gurus' advice on how to manage switching costs and minimize lock-in.

While there may be some debate about the impact of the Web on banks, it is clear that many industries, such as those mentioned by Papows, have been significantly effected by the technology and that many more will be similarly effected in the future. To those industries, our gurus offer their sage advice. Bill Gates, cofounder of MicroSoft, suggests that the most important thing you must do in preparing to survive and thrive in the knowledge economy is to find a new way to add value.[26] The value of "pass-through" middlemen, such as the travel agent who simply books airline reservations, is rapidly approaching zero. So, how can you add value in the knowledge economy? One way, say our gurus, is to become a "navigator."

EXHIBIT 1.7. **Five Noncost Features that Determine the Impact of the Web on an Industry**

| Noncost feature | Most-affected Industries | Least-affected industries |
|---|---|---|
| | Books | Food |
| | Stocks | Consumer durables |
| | Personal computers | Clothing |
| | Automobiles | Local services |
| | Travel | Banking and insurance |
| Choice | Offers products or services with great variety/options. | Offers products or services with limited variety/options. |
| Customization | Accommodates high degree of product/service customization. | Provides mostly standard versions. Customization is the exception and costly. |
| Convenience | Transactions on the Web provide real and practical convenience to the consumer. | Transactions on the Web are possible but offer only limited improvement over current options. |
| Community | Product or service generates a strong community activity and affinity. For example, people who enjoy the same type of books or music feel a strong sense of identification with each other. | Product or service generates little sense of community. People who buy the same type of oven or refrigerator don't necessarily identify with each other because of their choice. |
| Change | The product or service changes frequently. For example, stock prices change every minute, and books can rapidly go out of print or stock. | The product or service changes slowly. For example, the features of refrigerators haven't changed that much over the last 10 years. |

*Source:* Jeff Papows, *Enterprise.com: Market Leadership in the Information Age* (Reading, MA: Perseus Books, 1998), pp. 98–100.

## Reintermediation: The Rise of Navigators

What is a "navigator"? Let's begin by revisiting Evans and Wurster's retail-banking scenario (see Exhibit 1.8). Banking customers in the old economy were essentially captive to the long banking value chain. Their banks offered a limited number of products (loans, investments, checking and savings accounts, etc.); developed, acquired, and operated transaction-processing hardware and software; built and staffed branches; manned 1–800 customer-service numbers; and provided automatic teller machines (ATMs) and tellers to interface with customers and provide these services.

In contrast, the computer and communications revolution would make electronic banking more cost effective and convenient (see Exhibit 1.9). Banking customers in the knowledge economy would be able to bypass traditional retail banks and go electronically to the vendor or vendors who could provide them with the most customized financial services at the lowest cost. In the knowledge economy, these same customers would be set free to roam within an entire network of financials services, picking and choosing the services that were exactly right for them. The linear retail-banking value chain would be replaced by a complex, and often confusing, banking value network. And, say our gurus, people will require assistance to navigate this network.

Network navigators are essentially the middlemen of the knowledge economy, whose function is to assist people in finding their way through these complicated networks. Many of our gurus refer to the emergence of navigators as "reintermediation"—the opposite of "disintermediation" (don't you just love these terms?). Many more think that navigation—or reintermediation, if you prefer—is going be the source of employment and profit for a lot of people and companies in the future. Kevin Kelly concludes that, to the extent you are on the Internet—and he believes that someday everyone in the world will have e-mail—you are going to be involved with intermediation either by using navigators to find what you want or by acting as a navigator to help somebody else:

> I don't want six billion emails a day as everyone shares what's on their mind. Since half the world will probably have their own businesses, and half of those will be start-ups, I will do everything I can to insert intermediaries between my mailbox and their mail senders, to sort out, route, and filter

EXHIBIT 1.8. **Retail-Banking Scenario**

EXHIBIT 1.9. **Banking Value Network**

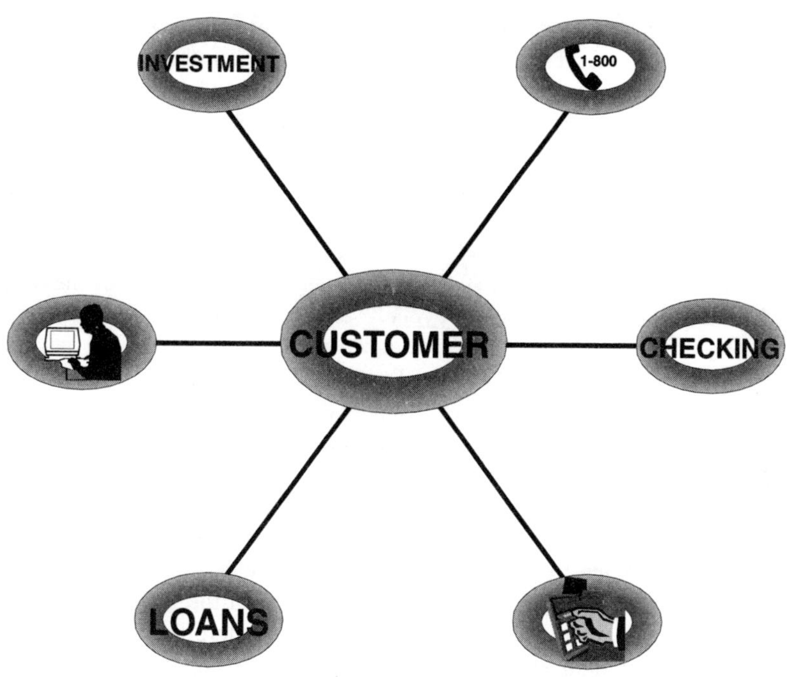


> my incoming mail. By the same token when I go to email old Mohammed Jhang, someone whom I have not met, who lives in Chinese Turkestan, to let him know about my latest gene therapy cure for arthritis, I'll need an intermediary to find him and then to reach past his blocking filters. I probably won't get through so I'll need more intermediaries (An advertiser? A lottery? A locating agent?) to lure him into the open, perhaps a pigeon-racing club, or the cineplex where he gets his movies from, to make him aware of my discovery. Sure, anyone can type "new gene therapy cure for arthritis" and turn up 32,000 hits. But you need intermediaries to vouch for their medical worthiness. You need intermediaries to compare my price and the others. The marketspace of the new economy can hold far more intermediaries than the marketplace of the old could.[27]

At least two things appear certain, according to our gurus. First, as the old industrial value chains get blown up, almost everyone will be forced to do at least some business through a value network. Second, everyone doing business in a value network will find themselves either being served by a navigator or acting as one. Consequently, say our gurus, everyone needs to learn what good navigators already know: that value networks are quite different from value chains.

## The Economics of Value Networks

Kevin Kelly illustrates a fundamental difference between the economics of the old industrial economy and the new network economy as follows. Imagine, he says, that you owned a milk factory where 10 people bought milk from you once a day. How much could you expect your revenues to increase if you added one new customer? If you said 10 percent, you're right! Congratulations.

Now, says Kelly, imagine that you sell the milk factory and buy a small telephone network of 10 customers who talk to each other once a day and pay you for each call they make. Suppose you again add just one new customer. How much could you expect your revenues to increase? 10 percent? Wrong. 12 percent? Still wrong. 15 percent? No, says Kelly, you could expect your revenues to go up a whopping 20 percent.

What's going on here? you ask. Network economics. And here is what makes network economics different from industrial economics. Assuming each of your telephone customers talked to every other customer once a day, they would make not 10 calls but 100 calls ($10^2$ or $10 \times 10$). Therefore, when you increase your customer base by one, your new expanded network makes not just 11 calls but 121 calls ($11^2$ or $11 \times 11$). That is, in fact, 21 percent more calls and presumably 21 percent more revenue to you. In fact, suggests Kelly, the value of your network might increase even more.[28]

Suppose, in addition to talking in pairs, your customers could have three-way, four-way, and multiway conference calls and you could charge not by the call but by the number of people connected and sharing information. The addition of just a few people could send the value of your network skyrocketing, both for you and for your customers, which is exactly what Kelly says happens in value networks. It's called Metcalfe's Law, named for Bob Metcalfe, the inventor of a network technology called the Ethernet. It goes like this:

> The sum value of a network increases as the square of the number of members. In other words, as the number of nodes in a network increases arithmetically, the value of the network increases exponentially. Adding a few more members can dramatically increase the value of all members.[29]

As a result, it is preferable to be part of a large network because the number of possible connections one can make increases dramatically as the size of the network grows. For some examples, see Exhibit 1.10.

> Any network has two ingredients: nodes and connections. In the grand network we are now assembling, the size of the nodes is collapsing while the quantity and quality of the connections are exploding. These two physical realms, the collapsing microcosm of silicon and the exploding telecosm of connections, form the matrix through which the new economy idea flows.
>
> *Kevin Kelly*[30]

EXHIBIT 1.10. **Connections as a Function of the Size of a Network**

| Size of the Network | Number of Connections |
|---|---|
| 4 | 12 |
| 5 | 20 |
| 6 | 30 |
| 7 | 42 |
| 10 | 100 |
| 100 | 10,000 |
| 1,000 | 1,000,000 |

*Note:* The actual formula for calculating the number of connections, where $n$ equals the size of the network, is $n \times^{(n-1)}$ but can be approximated by $n^2$ when $n$ is large.

## The Power of Increasing Returns

Carl Shapiro and Hal R. Varian are two business professors at the University of California, Berkeley. In their 1999 book *Information Rules,* they explain that the "bigger-is-better" aspect of networks gives rise to a phenomenon that is highly characteristic of the knowledge economy, a phenomenon that economists call "increasing returns."[31] In other words, because it is better to be connected to a large network than to a small one, the larger your network becomes, the more attractive it will be. That's what happened to Microsoft and Intel in their battle with Apple. "As Wintel's [Windows/Intel] share of the personal computer market grew, users found the Wintel system more and more attractive," write Shapiro and Varian. "Success begat more success, which is the essence of [increasing returns]."[32]

Of course, increasing returns can have results that aren't so positive, as Apple experienced, at least for awhile. As more people bought Wintel, fewer wanted to buy Apple computers because they didn't share the Wintel technical standards, that is, they weren't part of the Wintel network. If Wintel experienced the "virtuous" part of increasing returns, Apple experienced the "vicious" part. In its most extreme form, this virtuous-cycle/vicious-cycle aspect of increasing returns can lead, explain our gurus, to a winner-take-all market in which the strong get stronger and the weak get weaker until a single firm or technological standard eventually vanquishes all others. It may appear to happen overnight but rarely does.

Our gurus say that the typical pattern of increasing returns is a long lead time followed by explosive growth. The network is established and starts growing. The value to network members grows exponentially, as we described earlier. Then suddenly a critical mass is reached (our gurus call it a "tipping" point), and the network takes off. It seems that everyone wants to be a part of it. Shapiro and

Varian cite fax machines and the Internet as two good examples of increasing returns in action:

> The Scottish inventor Alexander Bain patented the basic technology for fax machines in 1843, and AT&T introduced a wire photo service in the United States in 1925, but faxes remained a niche product until the mid-1980s. During a five-year period, the demand for and supply of fax machines exploded. Before 1982 almost no one had a fax machine; after 1987, the majority of businesses had one or more.
>
> The Internet exhibited the same pattern. The first e-mail message was sent in 1969, but up until the mid-1980s e-mail was used only by techies. Internet technology was developed in the early 1970s but didn't really take off until the late 1980s. But when Internet traffic did finally start growing, it doubled every year from 1989 to 1995. After the Internet was privatized in April 1995, it started growing even faster.[33]

Kelly notes that the concept of increasing returns may seem at first glance to be almost identical to the old industrial concept of economies of scale: "The more of a product you make, the more efficient the process becomes. Henry Ford leveraged his success in selling automobiles to devise more productive methods of manufacturing cars. This enabled Ford to sell his cars more cheaply, which created larger sales, which fueled more innovation and even better production methods, sending his company to the top."[34] However, explains Kelly, there are two important differences, the first of which we have already seen. In network economies, value increases exponentially, and once a critical mass is reached it can skyrocket. Industrial economies of scale tend to build value more slowly and in a linear fashion. Kelly likens the difference to the difference between a piggy bank and compounded interest.[35]

A second and more important difference, writes Kelly, concerns the way value is created under the two systems and the extent to which it is shared.

> Industrial economies of scale stem from the Herculean efforts of a single organization to outpace the competition by creating value for less. The expertise (and advantage) developed by the leading company is its alone. By contrast, networked increasing returns are created and shared by the entire network. Many agents, users, and competitors together create the network's value. Although the gains of increasing returns may be reaped unequally by one organization, the value of the gains resides in the greater web of relationships."[36]

In short, while Microsoft and Intel benefit enormously from the Wintel network, so do all the people who are members of the network. Much of the value of the network, maybe even most of it, never winds up in Bill Gates's bank account. It remains in, or perhaps more precisely is created by, the massive number of connecting points and complex relationships within the network itself.

## Value Flows from Connectivity

If most of the value in a network economy resides in the networks themselves, you might think that the best strategy would be to own and tightly control a network, that is, have what our gurus call a "closed system." If you could own and operate a proprietary/closed network and keep it growing long enough to reach critical mass, then increasing returns would really kick in and you would become richer than Bill Gates. That's exactly what some have tried to do. For example, Kelly notes that, when Citibank pioneered the use of ATMs in banking in the 1970s, it initially blanketed New York with machines that wouldn't work with those of any other bank. The other banks found it hard to compete because their proprietary networks of ATMs weren't as big. Then, writes Kelly, something happened that Citibank never expected. The competing smaller banks decided to cooperate. They agreed on a common standard and linked their ATMs in an "open" network called Plus. Suddenly, this open system of networks was much bigger than Citbank's proprietary network. The law of increasing returns kicked in for the small banks rather than for Citibank. Eventually, Citibank was forced to give up its proprietary ways and join with the other banks.

The knowledge economy favors open over closed systems, because, argues Kelly, "the more networks a thing touches, the more valuable it becomes. The value of an invention, company, or technology increases exponentially as the number of systems it participates with increases linearly."[37] Value is a function of connecting points. Every additional node added to a network increases the value of all of the nodes because it increases opportunities for making connections. And you always get more connecting points with open systems than with closed ones. Consider Kelly's example of the opportunities sparked by e-mail:

> While it is true that every additional email address in the world increases the value of all previous email addresses, . . . the increase in value happens because each email address is a node of opportunity, not just an artifact. An email address is more than a way to exchange memos. Because email is rooted in a network, opportunity runs in several directions at once. For instance, once it was realized that mail addresses could be archived easily (opportunity number one), it occurred to someone that they could be collected automatically (opportunity two). They could also be mailed to in bulk (opportunity three). The domain part of the address could be analyzed and used to detect patterns of usage (opportunity four). Addresses in a Rolodex could be updated automatically by the addressee (opportunity five). The address artifact itself could contain more than just a name; it could also hold other facets of interests that the owner was willing to exchange in certain circumstances (opportunity six).[38]

Networks, particularly networks connected to networks through open standards, writes Kelly, spew opportunities for everyone. "By connecting everything to everything, they increase the number of potential relationships, and out of relationships come products, services, and intangibles. . . . A connected object, one that is a node in a network that interacts in some way with other nodes, can give birth to a hundred unique relationships that it never could do while unconnected. Out of this tangle of possible links come myriad new niches for innovations and interactions."[39] And, out of this tangle comes totally new business models.

> We have observed that there is indeed an underlying logic and order to the emerging digital organizational form. This form is network-enabled, inter-enterprise, and core competency based. Customers are integrated; knowledge is actively and freely created and exchanged. What we are witnessing is the emergence of a new kind of blueprint; perhaps hard to decipher, but no less essential.
>
> *Don Tapscott*[40]

## THE CREATION OF NEW BUSINESS MODELS

Don Tapscott, David Ticoll, and Alex Lowy are cofounders of the Alliance for Converging Technologies and coauthors of *Blueprint to the Digital Economy.* They argue that a key characteristic of the knowledge economy is the emergence of new network-based business models that "are as different from the traditional Industrial Age corporation as the latter was from the feudal craft shop of the penultimate agrarian economy."[41] Tapscott, Ticoll, and Lowy call these new business models Business Webs, or B-Webs. Whereas the model corporation in the industrial age was a megacorporation that did everything from product creation to distribution and sales itself, B-Webs rely on an elaborate network of suppliers, distributors, service providers, and customers who come together to conduct business on the Internet and through other digital means in order to create value for customers and shareholders. (For a slightly different way of conceptualizing these new business models, see the boxed quote "James Moore on Business Ecosystems.")

Tapscott, Ticoll, and Lowy identify five types of B-Webs that can be found in the knowledge economy, although they admit that their typology isn't very pure. "As with most such models," they write, "these are guidelines; in the real world, most e-business situations will blend features of multiple types."[43] As you review each of the models described below,[44] note how each type of B-Web is, in effect, not a single company but a complex network of companies. As we noted in the last section, the value flows from that connectivity. What matters is the digital network and how it is used. The network of relationships enhanced and maintained through computer and communications technology is the key feature distinguishing these knowledge-economy business models from their industrial-age counterparts.

**James Moore on Business Ecosystems**

More and more, companies are realizing that they cannot innovate alone. Any truly revolutionary advances in serving customers, in creating and transforming markets, in introducing new products or processes, or in restructuring the enterprise requires complementary adaptations—"coevolution"—on the part of many other organizations....

Enabled by network technologies, we have entered an age of organizational plasticity where the key to growth is found in the forging of business community relationships....

Networks of complementary functions—some provided by companies themselves, but most contributed by others—are being established. These networks comprise synergistic communities, or what I call "business ecosystems." "Business ecosystems" ... are made up of customers, suppliers, lead producers, and other stakeholders—even competitors—interacting with one another to produce complementary goods and services in a particular market segment space. These ecosystems form around early species of products, technologies, and business models. In the best situations they flourish and spread across broad market territories.

*James Moore*[42]

### Open Market (Agora)

The open-market, or Agora, type of B-Web facilitates a complex exchange in which prices are "discovered" in real time through negotiations between buyers and sellers.[45] E-Bay and Priceline.com are two examples.

Exhibit 1.11 illustrates the way open-market B-Webs work.

### Aggregation

The aggregation type of B-Web is led by a single company that positions itself as a value-adding intermediary between producers and customers. Aggregation is similar to the concept of navigation discussed earlier. Amazon.com and E*Trade are examples of aggregation B-Webs. See Exhibit 1.12 for an illustration of an aggregation B-Web.

### Value Chain

We know value chains aren't supposed to exist anymore. But that's what Tapscott, Ticoll, and Lowy call this type of B-Web. By their definition, value-chain B-Webs are partnered companies that use their individual competencies to produce a product tailored to a customer's individual needs. The price of the product is usually negotiated

## EXHIBIT I.11. **An Open-Market B-Web**

**Charlie** decides to sell his automobile using an on-line auction. He uses a search engine to find webgavel.com.

**Webgavel.com** allows Charlie to present his automobile to its registered users in return for a percentage of the profit from his sale.

**George** decides to put a bid on a car using an on-line auction. He finds webgavel.com and places a bid on Charlie's car, basing his price upon the competing postings.

Since his bid is the highest, George gets the car. Webgavel.com takes its percentage, and Charlie gets what's left.

EXHIBIT 1.12. **An Aggregation B-Web**

**Emma** has no experience with purchasing electronics but wants to buy a basic stereo system.

**Joe** is an audiophile and is looking for a top-rated system at an affordable price.

**Stereo.com**'s Web site offers a large, diverse inventory of stereo systems and includes a wide variety of information about stereo systems, together with independent ratings. It also provides links to MP3 databases and stereo discussion groups.

EXHIBIT 1.12. **(continued)**

Emma and Joe access the Stereo.com site. Although they have different needs Stereo.com is able to provide them information they need to make informed purchases . . .

. . . at reasonable prices

or based on the amount of customization required. A primary company in the partnership leads and manages the production process to ensure operational effectiveness. Cisco Systems, which provides routers and other products needed for the Internet and corporate computer networks, is an example of a value-chain B-Web. Unlike traditional integrated manufacturers, Cisco produces only a small fraction of the products it sells itself. Most functions are performed by a network of distributors, manufacturers, and suppliers. Cisco primarily handles marketing and customer relations. Most important, it carefully controls the flow of information from customer order until delivery. Dell Computer is another example of a value-chain B-Web.

Exhibit 1.13 shows how the business model for a value-chain B-Web works.

## EXHIBIT 1.13. A Value-Chain B-Web

**Ellen** owns a twenty-first-century auto plant that produces customized cars from a diverse collection of parts and integrated technologies.

**Carl** partners with Ellen to produce safety glass. He buys glass from a partner/supplier in the B-Web and adds a patented coating. Carl takes customized orders from a variety of companies and not just from Ellen.

**Louie** is another specialized producer in partnership with Ellen. His company buys glass from the same supplier/partner Carl uses and turns the raw glass into headlights.

**Ellen** combines the technologies and components supplied by her partner/specialists to produce a high-value customized product for her customers.

### Alliance

The alliance type of B-Web is the most "virtual" of the B-Webs. It attempts to produce a high-value product, like Ellen does in the value chain, but without having any single partner exercise overall control. Instead, the alliance partners agree on a set of facilitative rules and standards and then cooperate as equal partners to create value. The Java Alliance between Sun, IBM, Oracle, and Netscape that sought to create a new computing platform to compete with Microsoft is an example of an alliance B-Web.

An alliance B-Web is illustrated in Exhibit 1.14.

EXHIBIT 1.14. **An Alliance B-Web**

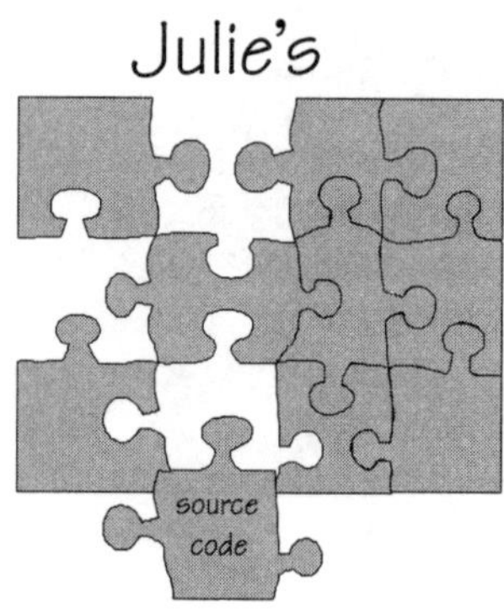


**Julie** produces a unique piece of source code that can be used to speed up certain types of applications. She publishes it free on the Internet.

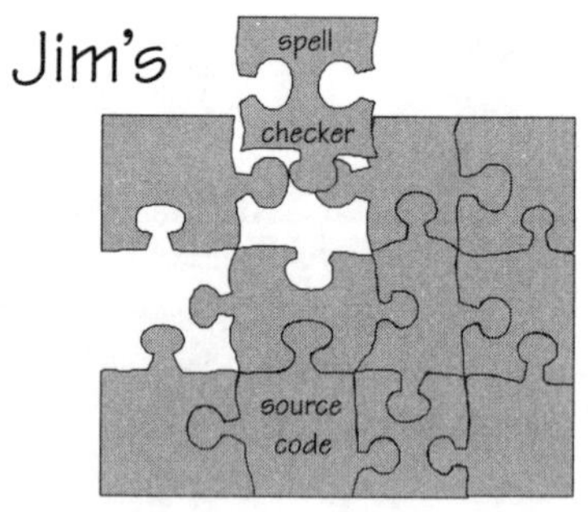


**Jim** creates a new and improved spell checker for word processors. He also publishes it free on the web.

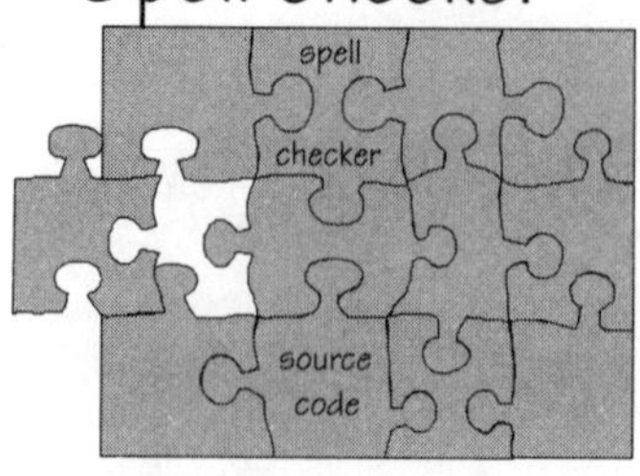


**Luke** takes Julie's source code and uses it to make Jim's spell checker work faster. Like Luke and Julie, he publishes on the Internet. Again, the product is free.

### *Distributive Network*

The distributive-network B-Web serves the other types of B-Webs "by allocating and delivering goods—whether information, objects, money, or resources—from providers to users."[46] Gas pipeline, logistic companies, postal services, banks, power distributors, and telcom operators are all examples of possible distributive-network B-Webs (see Exhibit 1.15).

Tapscott, Ticoll, and Lowy argue that the emergence of these new business models will force all businesses to rethink the value proposition or end-customer experience that they offer. They suggest that this reexamination must proceed in two steps—"disaggregation" followed by "reaggregation."

> **Step #1: Disaggregation.** The industrial-age company reexamines the end-customer experience (value proposition) it offers and separates that experience into its component parts. What goods, resources, business processes, and organizational structures does it now use? These become the "molecular elements" for rethinking the business.
>
> **Step #2: Reaggregation.** The company then reassembles, redesigns, adds to, and generally reconfigures the molecular elements discovered in step one to take advantage of the opportunities for value creation offered by new networked digital technologies. Ultimately, the company ends up participating in one or more of the five new business models.

If "disaggregation" and "reaggregation" sound a little like the "disintermediation" and "reintermediation" that we discussed earlier, that's because they are similar.

EXHIBIT 1.15. **A Distributive-Network B-Web**

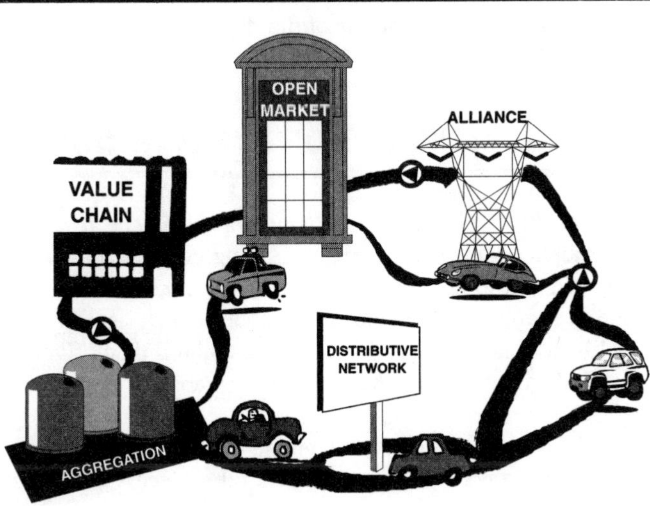

The latter are part of the former. One of the things companies do when they "disaggregate" is rethink the need for and role of intermediaries.

Tapscott and his coauthors provide the following illustration of the way the disaggregation/reaggregation process might work in practice, using the *Wall Street Journal* as their example.

> The *Wall Street Journal,* published since 1889, spent its first century as an aggregated collection of content (news, listings, advertising), context (the physical newspaper), and infrastructure (printing, physical distribution). These elements were bundled together into a single, tightly integrated offering. With the arrival of the Internet, The *Journal* has been disaggregated into its component parts, and reaggregated into an entirely new value proposition. The content is now available through a variety of contexts, including the publication's own online service, The Wall Street Journal Interactive. It is also available through a variety of third party online contexts, including Microsoft's Web Channels and the PalmPilot wireless network.
>
> These services all share a common underlying infrastructure—the Internet—but each also depends on unique infrastructure components that enable different kinds of customer value proposition. The *Journal's* own Website provides the entire contents of the printed newspaper, with a rich set of enhancements and customization features, for the serious reader. The Microsoft channel provides quick news updates for desktop users. The PalmPilot version is like the Microsoft channel, but for users on the run. In each case, The *Journal* has profoundly redefined and enhanced its value proposition to meet a particular set of customer needs.
>
> And in each case, a different cast of players—not only Microsoft and Palm Computing, but also network companies such as BellSouth—participates in The *Journal* community of electronic business value creation. They are all collaborating and competing in the creation of value, with an eye to the changing needs and expectations of the digital end-customer.[47]

## THE BLURRING OF EVERYTHING

In their 1998 book *Blur: The Speed of Change in the Connected Economy,* Stan Davis and Christopher Meyer, two Ernst & Young consultants, maintain that no company today can act alone.[48] And that truth, declare our gurus, is at the heart of the knowledge economy and new business models, such as Tapscott's B-webs. Whether they like it or not, everyone is forced to embroil themselves in economic webs. Davis and Meyer assert that these economic webs aren't really new.

> Economic webs have always existed in elementary form. They spring up wherever one company's well-being hinges on the success of others. In the

> past, this was usually the result of geography. Think of a shopping mall. The Sharper Image would seem to have nothing in common with Talbot's next door, but each depends heavily on the traffic generated by its neighbor. Colocation also means shared labor pools. Companies starting up today in Silicon Valley or in North Carolina's Research Triangle Park benefit from the critical mass of local talent. Critical mass within a region also boosts market awareness. Dozens of biotech start-ups got more attention—and undoubtedly more capital—when they were clumped together and called "the Massachusetts Miracle." The same phenomenon often happens in the arts. Impressionists made a splash because there was a school of them. Similarly, thanks to a thriving Chicago theater scene, even small repertory companies can be profitable in the Windy City. And a band like Pearl Jam might still be playing dive bars if it weren't part of the "Seattle sound."[49]

However, say Davis and Meyer, economic webs of the knowledge economy are different in at least two respects:

1. The ideal knowledge-economy web is often a temporary one involving "a constellation of players coalescing quickly around an emerging business opportunity, *and* dissipating just as rapidly once it runs its course."[50] (See Exhibit 1.16 for one explanation of the temporary nature of these webs.)
2. Many, if not most, of the knowledge-economy webs are global. "Global connectivity is stretching linkage to the far corners of the economic world. Companies can be oceans apart and still climb into the same boat."[51]

Being involved in economic webs means that "you have to place your fate more squarely in the hands of companies and management teams outside your jurisdiction. . . . You must give up the idea of control and rely instead on your ability to influence."[52] The challenge of managing, thriving, and indeed even surviving in such an economy can be daunting, write the gurus. How do you know when to enter a web and which webs to enter? How do you pick the right partners? How do know when the web has run its course—as it surely will—and when to exit? According to Tapscott, Ticoll, and Lowy, organizations that get the answers to these types of questions right will "have a hope of survival. Punishment will be swift for those that don't."[53]

These are the challenges and uncertainties of the knowledge economy. What's certain, if anything? Davis and Meyer cite the John Donne poem:

> No man is an island, entire of itself; every man is a piece of the continent, a
> part of the main. If a clod be washed away by the sea, Europe is the
> less, . . . any man's death diminishes me, because I am involved in mankind;
> and therefore never send to know for whom the bell tolls; it tools for thee.[54]

"So good luck finding the point where you stop and the market begins," they write. "The distinction between a company and the environment it exists in is becoming

### EXHIBIT 1.16. The Temporary Nature of Economic Webs

Kevin Kelly notes that tight connectivity in the emerging network economy makes it behave much like a biological ecosystem that is "chock-full of opportunities, which are in constant flux, appearing and disappearing as species jockey for their niches." Think of the knowledge economy as a fast-moving jungle in which all the commercial organisms are both competing and co-evolving. In the jungle, "biologists describe the struggle of an organism to adapt . . . as a long climb uphill, where uphill means greater adaptation." The most perfectly adapted is said to have reached a peak. In the knowledge economy, we can think of companies arranging and rearranging themselves into economic webs all in an effort to find better ways to adapt to changing consumer demands, all in an effort to reach their economic peak. The problem for biological organisms and knowledge-economy companies is that in a jungle, whether ecological or economic, it is often hard to determine from the jungle floor what is a peak and what is just a hill. "The . . . landscape is 'rugged,' disrupted by gulfs, precipices, and steep slopes. Trails are riddled with dead ends, lead to false summits, and made impassable by big-time discontinuities." Like organisms, companies may find themselves just at the top of a hill, or at best a "suboptimal" peak. Suddenly, the landscape has changed. The only thing the company or organism can do is come down from the hill, devolve, and start over. "The harsh news," writes Kelly, "is that 'getting stuck on a local peak' is a certainty in the new economy. Instability and disequilibrium are the norms; optimization won't last long. Sooner, rather than later, a product will be eclipsed at its prime." When that happens—and in the knowledge economy it will happen suddenly and often—a company will have to practice what economist Joseph Schumpter calls "creative destruction." It will have to abandon products, services, and economic webs that once worked but which no longer work as well and move on to something new.

*Source:* Kevin Kelly, *New Rules for the New Economy: Ten Radical Strategies for a Connected World* (New York: Viking, 1998), pp. 83–86.

hazier. Your agenda is all tangled up in mine. It's a BLUR."[55] What is more, the economy just keeps on reinventing itself. The good news or bad, depending on your viewpoint, is that some of our gurus maintain that the knowledge economy may no longer be so new. In fact, a new post–knowledge economy may be emerging.

## THE NEXT ECONOMY

Rolf Jensen is director of the Copenhagen Institute for Future Studies, which has been described as the world's largest future-oriented think tank. In his 1999 book entitled *The Dream Society,* Jensen declares that the new information-centric economy is dying. "The sun is setting on the Information Society," he suggests, and it is doing so "even before we have fully adjusted to its demands as individuals and as companies."[56] The knowledge economy, he says, even now is being replaced by a post–knowledge economy, one based not on the exploitation of information but rather on stories. That's right—stories! Jensen declares that the market for stories will gradually eclipse the market for tangible products.

Jensen argues that the market for stories already exists. He cites as an example the market for eggs in Denmark. The egg is a traditional product with a long history and has been in everyone's diet for centuries. It is a commodity. Yet in Denmark, eggs from free-range hens have taken half of the market, even though they cost 15 to 20 percent more than regular eggs. Why are the people of Denmark willing to pay more for eggs from free-range hens? Simple, answers Jensen: Eggs from free-range hens have a better story.

> Consumers do not want hens to live their lives in small, confining cages; they want hens to have access to earth and sky. Consumers want what could be called "retroproducts"; they desire eggs to be produced under the technology and methods of our grandparents—the old-fashioned way. This means that the eggs become more expensive—more labor-intensive—but consumers are happy to pay an additional 15 to 20 percent for the story behind the egg. They are willing to pay more for the story about animal ethics, about rustic romanticism, about the good old days.[57]

Jensen admits that the "story" attached to the egg is an irrational element. After all, it doesn't reflect any difference in the quality of the product, but that's the point. It *is* an irrational element. It's feeling. It's emotion. And, it's worth 15 to 20 percent more.

Jensen predicts that products will become secondary in the future. Only the story attached to the product will matter. We will move from a data- and knowledge-rich information society to a story- and emotion-rich dream society. But why now? you might ask. To answer that question, says Jensen, we have to take a "sprint through the history of humanity."[58]

## A Sprint through the History of Humanity

If you look at history over the last 100,000 years, writes Jensen, you will find that it is largely about our struggle to find increasingly more sophisticated ways for machines to do our work.

> It all began the first time we used a stone to crush the nut we had decided to eat. It continued when we let horses and oxen do our ploughing for us or hoist our water from the well. Later, we proceeded to let the might of the rivers and the winds alleviate the hard toil of grinding down our corn to flour and irrigating our fields. By the time we reached the eighteenth century, our knowledge of the laws of physics had reached a level enabling

> us to construct steam engines that were able to transport people and products over great distances. In the present century, oil has been the most important source of energy. Today, only a small part of our energy needs rely on muscle power.
>
> Muscle power has, by and large, been supplanted by machines. In affluent countries, muscle work is more likely to be done for fun than out of need. Most of us are more likely to experience physical exhaustion at play than at work. Our brow becomes more sweaty outside the workplace than inside.
>
> In the second half of the present century, our brains and our senses become next in line to have their tasks automated. Computers and intelligent machines no longer simply perform routine chores; they get a crack at even the most advanced assignments. Computers have freed the weather watchers from the tedious parts of forecasting; scanners have taken over an ever-increasing number of doctors' tasks, and our highways are lined with automatic patrols, video cameras that observe, record, and keep track of the speed demons—even issuing them tickets. The automation of brains and senses will have more in store for us that is yet to be seen, but we can begin to imagine the shape of things to come.[59]

Jensen insists that 100,000 years of history can bring you to only one conclusion: "For much of the world, the focus on acquiring more and more of the material aspects of life is drawing to an end. Instead, we have a growing interest in humankind's emotional side."[60] First, machines replaced brawn. Most recently, more intelligent machines have begun to replace brain power. The agrarian and industrial societies have been automated nearly out of existence, and fewer and fewer people make their living on the farm or in factories. Now, suggests Jensen, we are beginning to see the same thing happen to the information society—a hypothesis that may come as a surprise to many high-tech companies that are struggling to find skilled workers.

The result of these changes, argues Jensen, is that, while our material needs will remain considerable, "the material aspect of our living will receive less attention—we will cease to define ourselves through physical products, relying instead on stories and feelings."[61] When machines took over for our muscles in the industrial age, the market for sports, athletic, and exercise equipment—the muscle-work-for-fun market—exploded. Now, as machines take over more of the cerebral and sensory work, Jensen expects to see the growth of a new market centered around cerebral and sensory experiences.

## Six Emerging Emotional Markets

Jensen admits that the dream society is uncharted territory and that the emotional markets he envisions are just emerging, but he offers profiles of six such markets that exist or likely will emerge soon:

1. **Adventures for sale.** Here, the market is for thrills and excitement, whether actual or vicarious. Mountain-climbing expeditions, hot-air-balloon rides, and expeditions to the South Pole all fall within the market for adventures. So do most sporting events. "Sports has come a long way from being the meeting place of amateurs, to become the great, commercial market for adventures."[62] Sports stars become wealthy as much from selling their stories as from playing their games. When Nike hires an athlete to endorse its product, it isn't selling shoes; it is selling the excitement of the athlete's story. When Harley-Davidson sells a motorcycle, it is selling much more than a means of transportation; it is selling an adventure. But, you might ask, isn't this just marketing? Not exactly. Jensen would argue that, in the information and industrial societies that we are leaving, advertisers use adventures to sell products or services. In the dream society, companies will use products or services to sell adventures. The motorcycle will be secondary. The Harley-Davidson adventure is what people will buy.
2. **The market for togetherness, friendship, and love.** This is a market concerned with interpersonal relationships—romance, family, friendship, neighbors. A telecommunications company can be a firm that provides telephone lines and connections, but it can also be in the business of *bringing people closer together,* if only symbolically. When it does the latter, the telephone company is in the togetherness/friendship/love market. Bars and clubs sell beer, wine, and liquor, but the smart ones know that they are really selling togetherness, conviviality, and social contact—i.e., a place where everybody knows your name. Many other businesses can or will be primarily in the togetherness market—restaurants, coffee shops, and theme parks, for example. Jensen argues that brand identity for many businesses in the dream society will be as much about togetherness, solidarity, and interpersonal feelings as it is about quality, dependability, and reliability. "More and more companies," he says, "will need to think about how their own brand identity can be focused on the idea of drawing people together."[63]
3. **The market for care.** This is the market for giving and receiving compassion, comfort, healing, help, and happiness. The Red Cross, Salvation Army, nursing homes, hospitals, and pet stores are clearly in this market, but so are toy manufacturers when they produce dolls and electronic pets that require care. Makers of the Tamagotchi electronic egg warned purchasers that the egg had to be played with and lavished with tender loving care or it would turn into a horrid, ill-behaved monster.
4. **The who-am-I market.** This market is about identity. Jensen cites Louis Vuitton as a typical dream-society company squarely in the who-am-I market. "Louis Vuitton . . . sells travel gear—bags and suitcases. But it does so with an added dimension. You get a story along with the suitcase, a story many customers value more highly than the practical utility of the suitcase. . . . I am an exciting person, gliding with perfect ease through posh hotels all over the world, and I do it in style."[64] Moet & Chandon, Ralph Lauren, Giovanni Versace, Gucci, and the Swiss watchmaker Swatch are all in

the who-am-I market. The clothes manufacturer Esprit, explains Jensen, has a story that says "I'm anti-consumer and environmentally aware. I buy for my vital needs, not for my ego." "Marlboro Country" isn't about cigarettes. It's about an image.

5. **The market for peace of mind.** From Jack Daniel's whiskey to Lands' End chinos ("So easy going it's hard to believe they are descended from a starchy British officer in the Punjab"), some companies will appeal to the market for stories about peace of mind and permanence. Jensen lists the following most commonly revisited peace of mind stories from the past. Dream-society companies will turn to these to find narratives and myths from which to construct their stories.

- The classic England of the nineteenth century. In the wealthy English manor house, tradition and good taste are the order of the day. Existence and values are fixed and accepted by all. There is plenty of time for a spirited conversation about art or for big-game hunting in Africa and plenty of time to meet around the tea table in the beautiful garden in a stress-free, idyllic existence.
- The Wild West with small, comprehensible cities, where the sheriff, the undertaker, the editor, the bartender, and the local beauties meet the cowboy riding into town. Here, values are fixed; justice may be summarily executed, but good prevails over evil. The task is to create a whole new life surrounded by spectacular scenery with buffalo, wild bears, and wolves.
- Paris in the 1920s. The Moulin Rouge, the artistic milieu, red wine, and round-the-clock joie de vivre, unfettered by obligations—all bespeak resplendent beauty and amity in the bistros. It's a dream of the carefree life with romance, love, and art. Take a walk through the streets of Paris in the early hours after a long night at the Moulin Rouge.
- The ancient world of Greece. Here, Aristotle wanders the plaza among Doric columns, expounding on the meaning of life and death with intellectual rigor while his doting pupils listen. The white buildings, the blue skies, the olive trees, and a sea of jumping dolphins complete the idyllic picture.
- The Japanese samurai period, with its codes of honor, loyalty, and brotherhood. It is a bellicose period, but battles are fought with swords and according to rules of chivalry. Good prevails over evil. It is also about beautiful Asian architecture and tea ceremonies, about women in kimonos and green rice fields.
- Man of the great outdoors, outside the reach of civilization's corrupting influences. People live in harmony with nature, the forests, and the animals. Water is drawn from clear, billowing brooks, and only the most necessary animals are killed. Joy is to be found in an unspoiled existence with no change and no problems. Back to nature.
- The Vikings of the north, who venture out to distant lands to pillage and plunder, yet preserve their purity of mind. The quiet living off the land,

the love-filled home life is interrupted here and there by family feuds. The thralls know and accept their place in life with a smile. All values are fixed and permanent.

- The Great Moguls period in India. Mighty yet just princes live lives of refined luxury listening to music that appeases the soul and speaks to romance and unrequited love. Here, power is just, beautiful, and everlasting.[65]

6. **The market for convictions.** This is the market for values—position statements on everything from ecology to the environment to human rights to ethics to animal welfare to genetic engineering to whatever. Dream-society companies in the market for convictions extol firmly held beliefs. Their story says, "We have a heart. We have feelings. We are more than just a rationalistic, profiteering machine." The Body Shop doesn't just sell cosmetics. It stands for something. Again, the product or service itself (its content or utility) becomes secondary to the emotion. The purpose of the product or service is to embody the story. It is the story, the emotion—this time the emotion tied to a value or belief—that is being sold.

Are Jensen's ideas just the fanciful notions of a crazed futurist? Maybe. Then again, maybe not. Other gurus are beginning to present somewhat similar arguments. Some are even beginning to suggest what might come after the dream society.

## THE EXPERIENCE ECONOMY

In *The Experience Economy,* B. Joseph Pine II and James H. Gilmore argue that experiences are becoming an economic offering as distinct from services as services are from products. "Companies," they write, "stage an experience whenever they *engage* customers, connecting with them in a personal, memorable way."[66] While Pine and Gilmore's experiences aren't exactly the same as Jenson's emotional markets, they are similar because the product or service becomes only the mechanism for delivering what is really being sold—the story, the emotion, the *experience.*

Our gurus note that restaurants have been in the experience business for some time. Eating establishments such as Hard Rock Café, Planet Hollywood, Medieval Times, and the Rainforest Café don't just serve food; they stage an experience. Pine and Gilmore believe that all businesses will be forced to follow these restaurants' lead in the future. The only way a company will be able avoid having its products and services turned into commodities, bought solely on the basis of price, is to turn them into experiences that engage customers and connect with them in a personal and memorable way; that is, the eggs must have a story or they are just eggs.

For diehard manufacturers, caution Pine and Gilmore, leapfrogging to the experience economy will be quite a feat. Manufacturers and product designers will be forced to stop focusing so much on the internal mechanics of their products and turn their attention to the total experience a person receives while using them.

Goods will have to be, in the authors' terms, *experientialized.* Automakers already focus on the *driving experience.* Publishers focus on the *reading experience.* Furniture makers focus on the *sitting experience.* Now, appliance manufacturers will have to focus on the *washing experience, drying experience,* and *cooking experience.* Apparel manufacturers will have to focus on the *wearing experience,* the *cleaning experience,* the *hanging experience,* and the *drawering experience.*

## The Progression of Economic Value

Pine and Gilmore argue that staging experiences is the future for almost all companies because experiences provide greatly increased economic value for customers. They offer the example of a common event most people experience while growing up—a birthday party. In the 1950s, when it was time for Johnny or Susie to have their birthday party, their moms went to the grocery store, purchased flour, sugar, eggs, milk, cocoa, and so on and made their birthday cake. Companies provided the commodities—the flour, sugar and so on. Moms provided the experience.

In the 1960s and 1970s, companies like General Mills and Procter & Gamble began packaging cake mixes and canned frostings. Moms still provided the birthday experiences, but they got a lot more help—and they were willing to pay for it. The packaged mixes cost more than the commodities, but they also saved time. That alone added value.

In the 1980s, supermarkets began opening bakeries. Now, they were able to offer not just packaged cake mixes but cakes, baked and frosted to individual taste. Mom and Dad only had to pick the cake up on the way home from work. The supermarket-prepared cake was 10 times the cost of packaged mixes, but it added value. Moms and Dad could let the supermarket take care of the baking so they could save their time and energy for planning and throwing the party.

In the 1990s, companies like Chuck E Cheese, McDonald's, and the Discovery Zone decided they could go the supermarkets one better. They could stage the entire experience. Of course, the experience could cost hundreds of dollars, but it added still more value. Now, all Mom and Dad had to do was show up and bring their checkbook.

This simple saga of the birthday party, write Pine and Gilmore, perfectly illustrates the progression of economic value that is leading us to the experience economy. "Each successive offering—pure ingredients (commodities), packaged mixes (goods), finished cakes (services), and thrown parties (experiences)—greatly increases in value because the buyer finds each more relevant to what he truly wants (in this case, the giving of a fun and effortless birthday party)."[67]

A company that offers experiences wins in two ways. First, it differentiates its offerings. Second, it can charge a premium price because what it is offering has distinctive value. Such companies will prosper. In contrast, "those businesses that relegate themselves to the diminishing world of goods and services will be rendered *irrelevant*" [emphasis ours.][68]

## The Four Realms of Experience

How will companies go about constructing experiences? Pine and Gilmore believe they will draw on four realms of mutually compatible experiences—entertainment, educational, escapist, and aesthetic. Ideally, they will use several of these at once to create unique personal encounters.

1. The *entertainment realm* refers to the realm of actors, comics, singers, and dancers. The focus of the experience is on helping people smile, laugh, and otherwise enjoy themselves.
2. The *educational realm,* as its name implies, is about learning—helping people become more informed, increasing their knowledge, or enhancing their skills.
3. The *escapist realm* is the province of theme parks, casinos, virtual reality headsets, chat rooms, and paint ball in the local woods. It's entertainment where the individual being entertained becomes the actor.
4. Finally, the *aesthetic realm* involves a kind of passive immersion. "While guests partaking of an educational experience may want to *learn,* of an escapist experience to *do,* of an entertainment experience want to . . . *sense,* . . . those partaking of an esthetic experience just want to *be* there."[69] When you stand on the rim of the Grand Canyon, visit an art gallery, or sit at the Café Florian in Old World Venice, say our gurus, you are having an aesthetic experience.

In designing your experience offerings, Pine and Gilmore recommend that you draw from all four realms so that your experiences are rich, compelling, engaging, and most of all, unique. Ask yourself the following:

- What can be done to improve the aesthetics of the experience? The aesthetics are what make your guests want to come in, sit down, and hang out. Think about what you can do to make the environment more inviting, interesting, or comfortable. You want to create an atmosphere in which your guests feel free "to be."

- Once there, what should your guests do? The escapist aspect of an experience draws your guests further, immersing them in activities. Focus on what you should encourage guests "to do" if they are to become active participants in the experience.

- The educational aspect of an experience, like the escapist, is essentially active. Learning, as it is now largely understood, requires the full participation of the learner. What do you want your guests "to learn" from the experience? What information or activities will help to engage them in the exploration of knowledge and skills?

- Entertainment, like aesthetics, is a passive aspect of an experience. When your guests are entertained, they're not really doing anything but responding to (enjoying, laughing at, etc.) the experience. Professional speakers lace their speeches with jokes to hold the attention of their audience, to get them to listen to the ideas. What can you do by way of entertainment to get your guests "to stay"? How can you make the experience more fun and enjoyable?[70]

Address these design issues, advise our gurus, and you will be well on your way to participating and thriving in the experience economy. You won't, as they say, be rendered irrelevant.

## BEYOND THE KNOWLEDGE ECONOMY

So, there you have it. The industrial economy gives way to the new information economy. The information economy gives way to the dream society or the experience economy. Where else can we go? Can there be anything after dreams? Rolf Jensen says no, that "the Dream Society is the ultimate societal type,"[71] but Pine and Gilmore disagree. They insist that there is something more. After we have fed them (the agrarian society), lavished them with material things (the industrial society), connected them and given them knowledge (the information society), and catered to their every emotion (the dream society/experience economy), we could transform them. Sounds a little scary, doesn't it? But here is how Pine and Gilmore see the birthday experience we discussed earlier when it is turned into a birthday transformation:

> As more and more companies compete with the staged birthday events offered by . . . Chuck E Cheese, and the like, . . . this genre of experience will undergo commoditization, resulting in lower prices for single birthday events. Eventually, some experience stager will realize that shifting to birthday transformations would increase customer value and thereby forestall commoditization. What might such a company—a transformation elicitor—do? Well, rather than focusing simply on just this year's party, it might guide parents through multiple birthdays as the child grows, and it might concern itself not only with staging the party but also with selecting gifts, inviting guests, and encouraging post-party behaviors. Gifts, for example, could be aimed at a child's developmental needs. Guests might serve as professional role models, from spheres of life in which the child already shows interest or in which the parents wish to encourage him. Thank-you notes, with preengineered templates and pre-stamped envelopes, might accompany the transformational birthday offering, to help birthday children become more conscious and appreciative. And most important: Each year's birthday party would be treated as an incremental event in the overall management of childhood development. Such birthday guides may or may not emerge from the current birthday experience circuit, but they may just as well come from a toy manufacturer (leveraging its child development expertise), par-

enting magazine (which understands child rearing as a parenting issue), or sports management firm (with a portfolio of potential role models).[72]

Pine and Gilmore suggest that similar transformations could be offered by other industries. For example, restaurants could offer diet transformations and nutrition management, thereby ending up competing with Weight Watchers and Jenny Craig. In addition to offering a reading experience, Barnes and Noble could offer reading transformations along with their espresso. You would pay them to guide you through your intellectual pursuits, identifying books and articles you should read, consulting with you on your reading progress, and maybe even testing you to make sure you are absorbing the right ideas.

All of this could be a little scary if you are convinced that our gurus are correct in their predictions, but they can't predict the future any better than you or I. Back in 1980, how many of them predicted that a computer and communications revolution would set off a long boom? How many foresaw the blowup of richness and reach? How many predicted the unraveling of value chains and the creation of value networks? How many warned the intermediaries of the coming of disintermediation? How many were aware of the value of connectivity or that there could be such a thing as increasing returns? And who among them understood B-Webs or thought they were even possible?

How many? None. So, the next time your kid is due for a birthday party, get on the Internet, go to your favorite search site, and type in "birthday transformations." Who knows? It just might return the name of a business right down the street.

## KEY POINTS

- Most gurus insist that there is a knowledge economy and that it can be expected to produce—in fact is already producing—"tectonic upheavals" in the marketplace and society.
- The knowledge economy is the result of the computer and communications revolution that occurred during the 1980s and 1990s. The development of the personal computer and the opening of access to the Internet are two key events.
- Every business is in the information business. The logic that transcends the business models designed by the titans of American industry, such as Andrew Carnegie, Henry Ford, and Alfred P. Sloan, is essentially informational, or a working out of what types of information can be shared most efficiently within the boundaries of a company rather than across them.
- Information is the "glue" that holds together the structure of businesses. Therefore, anything that alters the flow of information drastically impacts that structure. The computer and communications revolution altered the flow

of information and melted the glue that held industrial-age businesses together.

- Prior to the computing and communications revolution, information was embedded in physical modes of delivery; for example, the information in a letter could only travel as far and as fast as the mail carrier who delivered it.
- The pure economics of a physical "thing" and the pure economics of a piece of information are fundamentally different. The economics of both are compromised when they are linked, as they were before the computer and communications revolution.
- When information is embedded in physical modes of delivery, a basic law governs its economics: There is a universal trade-off between richness (the quality, accuracy, timeliness) of information and its reach (the number of people who can receive it). All business processes in the past were designed on the basis that such a trade-off was a necessity.
- The computer and communications revolution makes the trade-off between richness and reach unnecessary. It is now possible to have richness and reach.
- The computer and communications revolution, because of its impact on the trade-off between richness and reach, is unraveling industrial economy value and supply chains.
- Pass-through middlemen (intermediaries), who essentially serve as connecting points for the physical flow of information, are becoming unnecessary. Many businesses are being disintermediated.
- Value chains are being replaced with value networks that are more efficient and that provide customers with substantially greater options and bargaining power.
- A new type of intermediary, sometimes called a navigator, is emerging to help people negotiate their way through the value networks.
- Large networks are much more valuable than small networks. The "bigger-is-better" characteristic of value networks makes them subject to "increasing returns." Because large networks are more valuable than small ones, the larger a network gets, the more desirable it becomes; therefore, success begets success in a network economy.
- Value flows from connectivity. Open systems are favored over closed systems in the new network economy because they typically provide more connecting points.
- New business models that rely on an elaborate network of suppliers, distributors, service providers, and customers who come together to conduct business on the Internet and through other digital means are being developed. At

least five new business models can be discerned: open market, aggregation, value chain, alliance, and distributive network.

- Value networks and the new business models are blurring everything. The distinction between a company and the environment it lives in is becoming hazy.
- A new post–knowledge economy may be emerging that is based not on the exploitation of information but on stories. This market for feelings may gradually eclipse the market for tangible products. Six such emotional markets can be discerned now: adventures for sale, the market for togetherness, friendship, and love, the market for care, the who-am-I market, the market for peace of mind, and the market for convictions.
- An alternative post–knowledge economy is one based on experiences. Companies in such an experience economy generate value by building unique personal encounters from four experience realms: entertainment, educational, escapist, and aesthetic.
- Ultimately, we may see the development of an even newer post–knowledge economy in which the chief value that companies deliver won't be food, material things, information, connectivity, emotional satisfaction, or experiences but individual or personal transformations.

## ELECTRONIC COMMERCE—The Gurus

**Daniel Amor,** author of *The E-Business (R)evolution*

**Douglas Armstrong,** coauthor of *The Clickable Corporation*

**Peter Drucker,** professor of social science and management at The Clairmont Graduate School and author of numerous business books

**Juanita Ellis,** coauthor of *The E Commerce Book*

**Walter Forbes,** venture capitalist and author of *The Future of the Electronic Marketplace*

**Richard Gascoyne,** author of *The Corporate Internet Planning Guide*

**J. Russell Gates,** coauthor of *The Clickable Corporation*

**Seth Godin,** vice president for direct marketing at Yahoo! and author of *Permission Marketing*

**John Hagel III,** coauthor of *Net Worth: Shaping Markets When Customers Make the Rules*

**Bruce Judson,** cofounder of Time Warner's Pathfinder Web site and coauthor of *Hyper Wars*

**Ravi Kalakota,** coauthor of *E-Business*

**Guy Kawasaki,** CEO of garage.com

**Steffano Korper,** coauthor of *The E Commerce Book*

**David Kosiur,** author of *Understanding Electronic Commerce*

**Mary Modahl,** author of *Now or Never: How Companies Must Change Today to Win the Battle for Internet Consumers*

**Walid Mougayar,** author of *Opening Digital Markets*

**Marcia Robinson,** coauthor of *E-Business*

**Jonathan Rosenoer,** coauthor of *The Clickable Corporation*

**Evan I. Schwartz,** author of *Digital Darwinism: Seven Breakthrough Business Strategies for Surviving in the Cutthroat Web Economy*

**Patricia Seybold,** coauthor of *Customers.com*

**David Siegel,** author of *Creating Killer Web Sites* and *Futurize Your Enterprise*

**Marc Singer,** coauthor of *Net Worth: Shaping Markets When Customers Make the Rules*

# 2

# Electronic Commerce

Reflecting on the impact of electronic commerce (or e-commerce), Peter Drucker offered the following observation in the October 1999 issue of *The Atlantic Monthly:*

> The truly revolutionary impact of the Information Revolution is just beginning to be felt. But it is not "information" that fuels this impact. It is not "artificial intelligence." It is not the effect of computers and data processing on decision-making, policymaking, or strategy. It is something that practically no one foresaw or, indeed, even talked about ten or fifteen years ago: *e-commerce*—that is, the explosive emergence of the Internet as a major, perhaps eventually *the* major, worldwide distribution channel for goods, for services, and, surprisingly, for managerial and professional jobs. This is profoundly changing economies, markets, and industry structures; products and services and their flow; consumer segmentation, consumer values, and consumer behavior; jobs and labor markets. But the impact may be even greater on societies and politics and, above all, on the way we see the world and ourselves in it.[1]

In his article, Drucker compares the computer and communications information revolution of today to the industrial revolution of the early 1820s and finds many parallels. The steam engine, he notes, had been first applied to an industrial operation (the spinning of cotton) in 1785. It triggered the industrial revolution just as the computer triggered the information revolution. By the early 1800s, the steam engine had been employed to mechanize the production of everything from textiles to paper, glass, leather, bricks, iron, and even cannons and muskets for warfare. Its application to ginning cotton, says Drucker, "created a huge demand for low-cost labor and made breeding slaves America's most profitable industry for some decades."[2] The steam-driven mechanization of industry led to the rise of the factory, the creation of a "working class," and the breakup of the nuclear family as industry took the worker out of the home. And yet, writes Drucker, the application of the steam engine toward the production of goods wasn't the seminal event that transformed the world.

> [The application of the steam engine to industry] . . . only mechanized the production of goods that had been in existence all along. It tremendously increased output and tremendously decreased cost. It created both consumers and consumer products. But the products themselves had been around all along. And products made in the new factory differed from traditional products only in that they were uniform with fewer defects than existed in products made by any but the top craftsmen of earlier periods.[3]

Then in 1829, writes Drucker, the steam engine was applied to create a product that was truly without precedent. It was that product, not the mechanization of industry, that set off the biggest economic boom in history until that time. The product that revolutionized the world, says Drucker, was the railroad.

> The railroad was the truly revolutionary element of the Industrial Revolution, for not only did it create a new economic dimension but also it rapidly changed the *mental geography*. For the first time in history human beings had true mobility. For the first time the horizons of ordinary people expanded.[4]

The parallel to the information revolution, writes Drucker, is that, "like the Industrial Revolution two centuries ago, the Information Revolution so far—that is, since the first computers, in the mid-1940s—has only transformed processes that were here all along. . . . The processes have not been changed at all. They have been routinized, step by step, with tremendous saving in time, and often, in cost."[5] Until recently, like the steam engine, the computer helped us to do things faster and cheaper, but it hadn't helped us to do *new* and transformative things. But *e*-commerce is different, declares Drucker.

> E-commerce is to the Information Revolution what the railroad was to the Industrial Revolution—a totally new, totally unprecedented, totally unexpected development. And like the railroad 170 years ago, e-commerce is creating a new and distinct boom, rapidly changing the economy, society, and politics. . . .
>
> In the new mental geography created by the railroad, humanity mastered distance. In the mental geography of e-commerce, *distance has been eliminated. There is only one economy and only one market* [our emphasis].[6]

Every village, town, and hamlet touched by the iron rails and trains that rode over them in the 1800s was permanently transformed. Every business touched by e-commerce is equally transformed. And no business is immune, say our gurus.

## A NOTE TO THE READER

Most of our e-commerce gurus are academicians or consultants and as such enjoy creating new jargon and debating its proper use. The debate over e-commerce is a good example. Most of our gurus agree that, at a minimum, e-commerce refers to shopping over the Internet. Buying a book from Amazon.com, a toy from e-Toys, or a computer from Dell.com are all e-commerce activities. However, many gurus maintain that e-commerce encompasses more than just transactions between businesses and consumers. They add to the definition Internet-enabled electronic transactions between businesses themselves. For example, Steffano Korper and Juanita Ellis, authors of *The E Commerce Book,* divide e-commerce into two main categories:

- *Business-to-consumer e-commerce:* interactions and transactions between a company and its consumers,[7] such as the purchase of the Dell computer.
- *Business-to-business e-commerce:* the selling of products and services between corporations and the automation of systems,[8] such as the Chrysler Corporations Supply Partner Information Network, which allows the company's suppliers to share software applications, databases, procurement analyses, and other information via the Internet.

David Kosiur, author of *Understanding Electronic Commerce,* goes even further. He states that "electronic commerce is a system that includes not only those transactions that center on buying and selling goods and services to directly generate revenue, but also those transactions that *support* revenue generation, such as generating demand for those goods and services, offering sales support and customer service, . . . or facilitating communications between business partners."[9]

Other gurus disagree with such a broad definition of e-commerce. They prefer to restrict it to Internet-based sales and use a different term for the broader business applications of the Internet. For example, Ravi Kalakota and Marcia Robinson, authors of *E-Business,* say that we are moving beyond e-commerce to something called "e-business," which they define as "the complex fusion of business processes, enterprise applications, and organizational structure necessary to create a high-performance business model"[10] all presumably using the Internet. IBM Corporation was one of the first to use the term *e-business* instead of *e-commerce.* They define it as "a secure, flexible and integrated approach to delivering differentiated business value by combining the systems and processes that run core business operations with the simplicity and reach made possible by Internet technologies"[11]—whatever that means.

In his book *The E-Business (R)evolution,* Daniel Amor adds that there are at least 13 types of e-businesses, only one of which is e-commerce. According to Amor, e-business includes the following:[12]

1. E-auctioning: auctioning on the Internet.
2. E-banking: Internet-enabled electronic banking.

3. E-commerce: Internet retailers such as Amazon.com that offer books, CDs, and other products and services for sale direct to consumers.
4. E-directories: telephone and other directories offered on the Internet.
5. E-engineering: electronic collaboration between engineers over the Internet.
6. E-franchising: affiliation programs such as those between large booksellers on the Internet that allow franchise partners to distribute their products on their Web sites.
7. E-gambling: gambling via the Internet.
8. E-learning: Internet-based training.
9. E-mailing: correspondence via the Internet.
10. E-marketing: One-to-one marketing over the Internet.
11. E-operational resource management: acquisition and management of operational resources such as capital equipment (such as computers), maintenance, repair and operating supplies (such as office supplies), and travel and entertainment (such as travel services) over the Internet.
12. E-supply: linkage of manufacturers, logistics companies, senders, receivers, and retailers to coordinate order generation and order taking over the Internet.
13. E-trading: buying and selling stocks over the Internet.

## OUR VIEW

As you can see, our gurus find it quite easy to get e-carried away. The whole e-commerce versus e-business debate has gotten out of hand, and as Walid Mougayar, author of *Opening Digital Markets* says, "E-commerce? E-business. Who E-cares?" He writes: "Attempting to define e-commerce or e-business is guaranteed to generate Byzantine debates with meaningless origins. . . . [It's like] trying to answer the . . . question: 'If one synchronized swimmer drowns, would the others follow?'"[13] Who knows? Who cares?

In this chapter, we will use the term *electronic commerce,* or *e-commerce,* in its broadest sense, encompassing what some of our gurus describe as e-business, e-trading, and a host of other e-activities. We agree with the way Patricia Seybold, coauthor of *Customers.com,* defines electronic commerce:

> Today's electronic commerce isn't limited to shopping over the Internet. It's also not confined to supply-chain transactions between large trading partners. Electronic commerce (also known as electronic business) is doing business electronically—*all* the aspects of doing business. It embodies the entire business process—from advertising and marketing, through to sales, ordering, manufacturing, distribution, customer service, after-sales support, and replenishment of inventory—managing the entire customer and product life cycles.[14]

## E-COMMERCE IS A THREAT TO TRADITIONAL BUSINESSES

Think you are safe from the impact of e-commerce? Forget it, say our gurus; e-commerce is a threat to every traditional business. Drucker cites the case of one midsize company in the American Midwest. Founded in the 1920s, the company manufactured inexpensive dinnerware for restaurants, school cafeterias, and hospitals. Its owners, the grandchildren of the founder, were confident they were reasonably immune from competition. Because the type of china they sold was heavy and fragile, it wasn't cost effective to ship it long distances. Consequently, it was traditionally sold within a short distance from the manufacturer. The company dominated 60 percent of the market within a hundred-mile radius of the factory. Suddenly in the late 1990s, everything changed. The Midwest china factory was touched by e-commerce. Drucker explains: "One of its customers, a hospital cafeteria where someone went 'surfing' on the Internet, discovered a European manufacturer that offered china of apparently better quality at a lower price and shipped cheaply by air. Within a few months the main customers in the area shifted to the European supplier."[15] Thanks to e-commerce, the china company lost half its market share.

Bruce Judson, cofounder of Time Warner's Pathfinder Web site and coauthor of *Hyper Wars,* provides an interesting perspective on how quickly e-commerce has become a threat to a wide range of traditional brick-and-mortar businesses.

> Five years ago, if local retailers were asked to list their major competition, the local bookstore would mention great concern about the chain superstore being built in a nearby mall; the car dealer would tell you tales of how the dealer down the street snatches customers away from him; and the funeral director might scratch his head when asked about competition on casket sales, and then he might mention the one or two other funeral homes in town. The same was true of many financial services: Local banks were the primary sources of mortgages in each town, and local insurance agents competed among each other.
>
> Many businesses have thrived in part because of geographic protection. Customers—even corporate ones—have always liked doing business face-to-face with people they know, and if a product is involved, the consumer is always happy if he or she can walk out with the exact item desired.[16]

E-commerce permanently changes the business dynamics. If you are a local retailer, bookstore owner, car dealer, funeral director, or bank manager, suddenly you have lots of new competition. It's the 1800s again and the railroad that Drucker describes has just come to town. Judson cites the mortgage industry as just one example of a once geographically protected business that is now highly vulnerable, due largely to e-commerce:

> Until recently, mortgages were essentially a local business. Now, lower-cost national, online providers are actively competing in this arena. For example, the American Finance and Investment Company (AFI), a subsidiary of Virginia First Savings Bank, and other banks are transforming the home mortgage business by offering competitive loan rates to out-of-region customers and simplifying the application process: The customer fills out and submits an application online, which then triggers the electronic retrieval of the applicant's credit report; these are forwarded to a "decision engine" to quickly determine eligibility. The customer receives approval notification quickly, usually in less than five minutes.
>
> Since the process is entirely automated, AFI has two advantages over traditional competitors: (1) Its cost to process a loan is far lower than banks that rely principally on loan officers. It is, therefore, typically able to offer better rates than local competitors. (2) The company is able to provide the customer with a convenience that was previously unknown. Just a short time ago, it would have been impossible to imagine that from one's own home, in under five minutes, one could obtain a new mortgage.[17]

Automotive manufacturers and dealers have felt similar pressure from e-commerce. Judson notes that, prior to the rise of the Internet, car buying through dealers remained fundamentally unchanged since the 1950s. Then in the span of just three years in the late 1990s, a host of auto buying sites were launched on the Internet, and the whole industry changed. E-commerce in car buying brought about more change in the auto industry, says Judson, than had occurred in all of the previous 40 years combined. The same is true in practically every other business sector. If you are in retail, warn our gurus, you are particularly vulnerable.

> Here at the turn of the century, many companies are beginning to smell the toast burning. Americans have been putting up with Detroit's cars, Hollywood's movies, Nashville's songs, Silicon Valley's computers, and New York's financial products the way they put up with encyclopedias. In the Old World, the customer had little choice. In the New World, customers will have the power. Just as a tsunami sweeps the landscape, the Customer-Led Revolution will sweep away businesses that still cling to Old World strategies.
>
> *David Siegel*[18]

Here is how Walter Forbes, a venture capitalist interested in e-commerce, describes the future of retail in his 1998 book *The Future of the Electronic Marketplace:*

Let us take a drive down whatever "Miracle Mile" of retailing might exist in the vicinity of any American city in the year 2008. The sprawling malls of asphalt and concrete are now only secondarily centers for shopping. Theme restaurants and specialty shops still exist, depending in part on the draw of passing customers on their way to the cinemas and virtual reality gaming arenas now anchoring the malls, where once stood the mega-stores of the preceding century. Some of the land once paved to provide parking for the malls has been reclaimed for green space. Some of the largest parking garages have been converted into training facilities for Olympic skateboarders and mountain rollerbladers; smaller ones stand empty or have been razed. . . .

Way back in the 1990s there were 18.6 square feet of retail space for every man, woman, and child in the United States—twice the amount of two decades earlier. And whereas every square foot generated an average of $175 in sales in 1975, 20 years later it generated $166. At the same time, expenses were skyrocketing. Even the superstores were not looking so super in comparison with cyber retailers, who populated a market no less competitive yet far more immediate and omnipresent than any physical shopping district. A cyber retailer could slash its expenses to barely 14 percent of revenues, while operating costs relative to sales were rising at almost every downtown or suburban retailer. . . . With no inventory, no display space, and no old-fashioned stores to service, sales per square foot had become irrelevant for the cyber retailers of 2008. And the new generation of shoppers in cyberspace found no full parking lots, no jostling crowds, and no "sold out of size 14." Parking lots had been replaced with bandwidth, jostling crowds with server consumption and transaction speed, lack of inventory with just-in-time manufacturing and next-day drop shipping.

On the shop floor in the late twentieth century, there were perhaps 30 models of portable stereos on display—ten brands, with three- or four-speaker configurations. Buying such a stereo in 2008, you simply suggest to your personal agent that you want the speakers to be separable. In a flash, all those models with stationary speakers disappear from the "shelves." Say you want a twelve-disk CD changer. Gone in the blink of an eye are all the one- or six-disk models. You want a built-in graphic equalizer. Suddenly, there in front of you—from 3800 models available on your doorstep tomorrow morning—are five, displayed with brands and prices. The entire process has taken 5 minutes of your time. Before you could even have gotten the attention of a harried clerk with five other pushy customers waiting to elbow you out of the way, you have found the portable stereo system that suits you best, and your family will be listening to it at tomorrow evening's barbecue.

Not only will your purchase be delivered promptly to your doorstep; it will be there at a price 20 percent below the best price on the shelf of a national discount store. Why? No rent and no salesclerk to pay, no heating

> bills or parking lot attendants, and no inventory to float. No inventory, yet total availability. Instead of a salesperson, the cyber retailer becomes an information and mediating agent. The manufacturer becomes an assembler. This is the shape of the new "mall" of cyberspace.[19]

How likely is it that Forbes's vision of the future will become a reality? Bruce Judson reports that, when he originally began talking about the Internet's probable impact on retailing, he took a moderate, even conservative position. At the time, he argued that it was premature to sound the death toll for physical stores and that sales at brick-and-mortar outlets would decrease at the margins only. By 1999, after witnessing a surge of electronic shopping, he changed his mind. "I now anticipate a major shakeout among retailers," he says. "The brick-and-mortar shopping world will not go away, but the number of viable companies in it will shrink significantly."[20]

Forbes and Judson may be right, but you couldn't tell it by what we see going on around us in Atlanta, Georgia, as we write this. Rather than plowing up asphalt and turning mall parking decks into rollerblade training facilities, developers in our area are busy building new shopping malls. And rather than being devoid of shoppers, Atlanta's existing malls are filled to the brim with eager buyers. Still, we have to admit that some shakeout is likely. Some retailers undoubtedly are going to find themselves in real trouble. Which ones? Judson expects three types of retail businesses to be most affected:

> First, businesses that provide a limited social experience are at risk. If most consumers don't enjoy a particular shopping task, such as buying pool-cleaning supplies, then brick-and-mortar businesses that specialize in that area are likely to be vulnerable to online shopping.
>
> Second, . . . smaller, local businesses [are vulnerable]. These businesses have long struggled to survive in a world dominated by large chains. Unfortunately, low-price shopping on the Internet adds yet another reason they may have difficulty remaining viable.
>
> Third, large chains with inefficient operations or those saddled with the high overhead costs related to maintaining a brick-and-mortar business will face price pressure that could well endanger their ongoing operations.[21]

We think Judson is pretty much on target.

> If you think you are safe from the Internet, join the ice factories that thought refrigerators would never sell.
>
> *Guy Kawasaki*[22]

If e-commerce is a threat to traditional businesses, as most of our gurus think it is, the question is: Why? Our gurus suggest three reasons:

1. On-line shopping offers consumers several distinct advantages that traditional businesses cannot easily match.
2. E-commerce changes pricing models in ways that are disadvantageous to traditional companies.
3. E-commerce makes many aspects of traditional branding obsolete.

Let's look at each of these challenges to traditional businesses in greater detail.

## Threat #1: E-commerce Offers Distinct Advantages to Consumers That Traditional Businesses Cannot Easily Match

In their 1999 book *The Clickable Corporation,* Jonathan Rosenoer, Douglas Armstrong, and J. Russell Gates list six distinct advantages e-commerce offers consumers that traditional companies have difficulty matching.[23]

**Advantage #1: E-commerce companies provide consumers with instant access to detailed information about products and services.** In a traditional business, customers who want information about a product or service have only a few options. They can wait in line to talk to a salesperson (and hope the person is knowledgeable) or hunt through a company catalog or brochure. In contrast, savvy e-commerce companies can make a wealth of detailed information available to customers instantaneously, and they can make it possible for customers to access this information in a variety of ways—by product model, style, color, and so on. Rosenoer, Armstrong, and Gates note that "today's consumers have grown accustomed to instant responses from all kinds of computerized devices, ranging from automated teller machines to microwave ovens. The Web conditions people to expect the same from virtually all businesses."[24] E-commerce companies can meet those expectations. Traditional companies can't, or at least they can't do so as easily or as well.

**Advantage #2: E-commerce companies provide consumers with a much wider range of choice in products and services.** All traditional businesses have space and inventory restrictions. There is a limit to the variety of products and services they can offer. In contrast, e-commerce companies can offer, if not an unlimited range, at least a much wider range of products and services. Additionally, by building a database on their customers' preferences and previous purchasing behavior, e-commerce companies can help customers make the right choice from a dizzying range of options.

**Advantage #3: E-commerce companies offer consumers the convenience of 24-hour shopping.** "A century ago," write the authors, "the [local] apothecary, haberdashery, and general store had the convenience advantage [over competing businesses] if you could walk to them in ten minutes. Later they had the convenience advantage if you could drive to them in ten minutes."[25] Now, e-commerce companies have the convenience advantage. They are literally one click away—as close as the tip of your finger. Plus, they are always open.

**Advantage #4: E-commerce companies can offer products and services customized to match individual preferences.** "In the movie *Field of Dreams,*" write Rosenoer and his coauthors, "Kevin Costner plays a baseball-loving farmer, who hears a disembodied voice instructing him to build a big ballpark in the middle if his Iowa cornfield. 'If you build it, they will come,' the voice repeats."[26] Our gurus note that this could well be the mantra of traditional businesses—build the product and hope the customers will come. E-commerce turns this "build-it-first" notion upside down. Companies like Dell Computer let customers come on-line, choose from a wide array of options, and build exactly the product they want. The mantra of e-commerce, say Rosenoer, Armstrong, and Gates, might well be "Let *them* build it, and they will come." (We will discuss this approach to "mass customizing" products and services in greater detail in Chapter 4.)

**Advantage #5: E-commerce companies have lower operating costs than their brick-and-mortar counterparts and can pass these savings along to customer in terms of lower prices.** In many cases, e-commerce companies can use technology to streamline processes, eliminate overhead, and more effectively manage their supply chains. Consequently, their operating costs are usually less than their traditional counterparts. For example, note our gurus, e-commerce banks can often keep their overhead to as little as 1 percent of assets, compared with 2 or 3 percent for traditional brick-and-mortar banks. E-commerce companies can pass along these savings to customers and gain an advantage.

**Advantage #6: E-commerce companies can bring together people with similar interests and create a sense of community.** "In the past," write our gurus, "community was a function of geography, centered in the churches, schools, and living rooms of your hometown. The automobile and telephone changed that, and now the Internet is transforming it as well. Suddenly, people from all over the world with a common interest in estate planning, women's rights, or nursing homes are meeting and creating new communities online."[27] Recognizing this insatiable desire for communities of every shape and kind, alert e-commerce companies are seeking to establish and nurture communities as a great way to connect with customers.

## Threat #2: E-Commerce Makes Both Supply and Demand More Apparent and Thereby Changes Pricing Models

In his book *Digital Darwinism,* Evan I. Schwartz states that e-commerce is profoundly changing the pricing models for most businesses.

> [E-commerce] creates a market in which the value of each piece of merchandise will fluctuate freely and continuously, and buyers and sellers will wield every tool available to them in their struggle to prevail over one another.
>
> This is very different from walking into a store, or any marketplace, seeing a price tag, and deciding whether you want to buy at the posted price. We tend to take this notion of *fixed* retail pricing for granted, as if this was the only way to do things. But fixed pricing, as a practice, is fairly recent and very Western. In the United States, fixed pricing dates back only 125 years, when mass retail pioneers such as Aaron Montgomery Ward and Frank W. Woolworth popularized the practice. And in the marketplaces and bazaars of Turkey, Indonesia, and India, things haven't change much over time—if there is any posted price at all, it's usually just the starting point for a negotiation.[28]

Schwartz notes that developments in transportation and communication have always affected pricing schemes. The growing network of railroads and canals in the mid-1800s, for example, made the mass distribution of mass-produced goods feasible and Ward and Woolworth's fixed pricing schemes plausible. "Meanwhile," writes Schwartz, "the telegraph became a pervasive business-to-business medium among traders, bankers, investors, merchants, entrepreneurs, and captains of industry. Whereas prices for retail goods became fixed, products such as coal, wheat, and pork bellies became dynamically priced commodities because information about them, especially current prices, could be relayed quickly for the first time."[29]

Now, communications technology is allowing a shift in pricing schemes once again. Haggling, bidding, custom costing, and rapid-response pricing are becoming fixtures of e-commerce. While Schwartz and our other gurus don't expect fixed pricing to go away, at least for less-expensive mass-produced merchandise, they expect dynamic pricing in which buyers and sellers negotiate in real time to become much more prevalent. As a consequence, our gurus believe, in market after market there will be a tendency for prices to fall to their lowest competitive point. E-commerce is creating a business environment that is much more competitive and fluid. Mary Modahl and her colleagues at the e-commerce research firm Forrester Research call this new competitive environment *dynamic trade* and warn that companies that fail to understand and adjust to it "will lose control of their prices, revenue streams, and profits as more consumers shop on-line."[30]

In dynamic trade, writes Modahl in her book *Now or Never,* both the supply and demand for products and services become more apparent. As a result, prices tend to fall to their lowest competitive point and vary as demand shifts. According to Modahl, the Internet has two key impacts on price:

1. It increases the consumers' perception of the available supply of goods and services.
2. It allows e-commerce companies to collect more accurate and timely information about demand.

Let's look at each of these two impacts.

### *Pricing Impact #1: The Internet Increases Apparent Supply*

Modahl points out that in the traditional marketplace there is a difference between actual supply and that apparent to the customer.

> When a buyer seeks a product, whether it is information such as news or hard goods like groceries, they go to the market. But the market is only as large as the one that a consumer can reasonably address. To an isolated villager, the "market" is limited to what is piled up in the stalls of local merchants. Similarly, when a woman drives in her sedan to the mall, she chooses a blouse from among the stores in the mall. If she wants to, she can drive another forty-five minutes to a discount store like TJ Maxx or Frugal Fannies, where it is possible (though she can't be sure beforehand) that she'll find the exact same blouse at 50 percent off. But most women won't take the time to go find out.
>
> In the cases of both the villager and the mall shopper, the actual supply of whatever they were seeking is many times larger than the supply around which they must make their purchase decisions. However, it simply isn't practical for consumers to locate and include all of the actual supply when making their decisions. Instead, consumers make their purchases from the supply they can easily find—the apparent supply.
>
> While there is no evidence that the Internet increases the actual supply of goods in any consumer market, it clearly increases the apparent supply. . . . Once on-line, . . . consumers can visit both upscale shops and discounters without moving an inch. In addition, new price-comparison engines sift through hundreds of Web sites, searching for the best price on a given item. As a result, the Internet is driving up the quantity of goods that consumers can see and driving down prices.[31]

And, notes Modahl, the actual difference in prices for identical products charged by e-commerce and traditional retailers can be considerable. For example, she reports on an experiment undertaken by Forrester in which the researchers used price-comparison software readily available to consumers to check prices on a CD, a kitchen appliance, and a personal digital assistant. On average, the e-commerce sites quoted prices 15 percent below their brick-and-mortar counterparts. The CD was available on-line for 37 percent less. Price differences such as these and more important, the ease with which consumers can discover these differences is certain, writes Modahl, to "cause real problems for companies whose products are sold at different rates in markets separated by geography or information. . . . Price differences based on poor information or geographic distance won't stand up very well in the Internet economy."[32]

### Pricing Impact #2: The Internet Makes It Possible for Companies to Tie Prices Closer to Demand

According to Modahl, most traditional companies have sought to measure demand for their products and services. For example, grocery stores and other retailers regularly collect point-of-sale data in an effort to monitor what is selling and what is not. The problem for traditional businesses has always been one of getting such information in a timely manner. In many companies, even today, point-of-sale data may not show up in printed reports until weeks after the sales have occurred.

In contrast, many or most e-commerce companies collect and make available to decision makers point-of-sale data as the sales occur. Companies like Amazon.com actually measure demand in advance of sales by taking prepublication orders for books and music CDs. Others, such as Priceline, let consumers submit a kind of "request for proposal"—I would like to purchase a one-way coach ticket from New York to Los Angeles on this airline for $$$$—and allow companies to respond: At this airline we have a seat available on this flight for $$$$. Modahl predicts that the availability of such current information will force all companies to change the way they measure demand and set prices:

> In the past, suppliers set the market agenda, determining which products to sell and at what price. The successful companies were those that did a good job of estimating future demand. Of course, no company ever estimated demand exactly right, so gaps existed. Sometimes, companies missed the opportunity to sell, when demand ran higher than available supply. Other times, they made more than the market wanted and had to write off inventory. Using primitive tools like monthly retail reports, companies tried to adjust to demand, but their ability to react was limited. . . .
>
> On the Internet, companies will measure and respond to current demand: what consumers want now. As they do, they will change the dynamics of competition. When consumers set the agenda, it is more important for companies to be able to respond quickly than it is for them to predict well. In Dynamic Trade, companies that can adjust the prices and quantities of goods—their supply—more closely to consumers' current demand will succeed. This eliminates the gaps between what consumers want and what companies can offer them.[33]

Modahl predicts that the consumer industries most vulnerable to these demand affects will be the ones that deal with temporary "hits" or fads (such as movies and music), focus on events (such as sports and entertainment), or operate on a seasonal pattern (such as fashion and toys). Consider, she says, what opportunities might have been presented to Hasbro, maker of the Furby toy, if e-commerce had been in full swing in 1998, when Furby became the hottest toy of the holiday season. Although fewer than 10 percent of consumers were on-line shoppers at the time and only 1 percent of toys were sold on-line, those who did go on-line to bid for a Furby drove the price of the toy up to more than $300 compared with its typical brick-and-mortar retail price of $30 to $40.

Imagine what will happen, writes Modahl, when e-commerce accounts for a quarter of the toy market, as it is expected to do soon. Presented with another Furby hit and the availability of current information on demand, Hasbro might decide to raise prices rather than make more Furbys. Alternatively, it might produce more of the product. Either way, the market-driven price for the toy would provide Hasbro with new ways to maximize its profits. The implications, declares Modahl, are clear: "Retailers that have managed gaps between supply and demand using blunt tools such as end-of-season sales and layaway plans will adjust their prices far more often in response to Internet competition."[34] And, say our gurus, companies shouldn't feel immune to the price pressure of dynamic trade simply because they have an established brand. E-commerce is also affecting branding.

## Threat #3: E-Commerce Negates the Value of Conventional Branding

In their 1999 book *Net Worth,* McKinsey consultants John Hagel III and Marc Singer predict that e-commerce will undermine the value of conventional brands by removing two constraints that have made brands viable in the past. First, brands previously were a substitute for the limited information consumers had about vendors and product/service options. "Rather than over invest in collecting difficult-to-find information, customers rely on brands to assure them of a predictable product experience. McDonald's may not offer the best meal experience, but it does offer a predictable meal experience relative to a no-name restaurant where the consumer may experience either a gourmet treat or food poisoning."[35]

Second, brands compensated for the limited shelf space vendors had for displaying products.

> From a vendor's viewpoint, brands help "pull" customers into retail stores. In the process, they help the vendor persuade the retailer to dedicate some of its scarce shelf space to the vendor's products. Similarly, retail brands help customers decide which retail stores to frequent. Given the limited selection that scarce shelf space affords, customers look to brands for assurance that the limited selection will be consistent with their buying preferences. If the customer's primary consideration is fashion and he isn't sensitive to price, he may frequent an upscale men's clothing boutique. On the other hand, if he's looking for durable work clothes at a low price, he's more likely to frequent a well-known discount mass merchant.[36]

E-commerce removes both constraints. On-line vendors like Amazon.com can provide almost unlimited product choice while simultaneously providing detailed information about product functionality, pricing, and so on. Consequently, write Hagel and Singer, much of the traditional value of brands is negated. Does that mean that brands will disappear? Our gurus don't think so. However, they do believe that the role of brands will change.

Hagel and Singer note that brands today are largely product-centric: "They are statements about the vendor or the products offered by the vendor. Brands say: Buy this product because the vendor has a reputation for high-quality products or excellent service or because the product itself is a reliable or low-cost product."[37] Such branding was valuable in an environment wherein selections were limited and information was scarce. That is no longer the case. In an e-commerce world, argue our gurus, the constraint that customers face isn't selection or information, but time. There are only 24 hours in a day, and today's customers want assurance that, in return for their attention, they will be rewarded with customized bundles of products and services—just the selection and information they want, when they want it. In such an environment, write Hagel and Singer, a new type of brand will emerge that is more customer-centric rather than product-centric:

> Customer-centric brands have two components—they assure the customer that the vendor knows and understands that individual customer better than anyone else does, and they promise the customer that the vendor can tailor products and services to meet that individual customer's needs better than anyone else can. These brands thereby assure customers that they will receive a very high return on any attention they focus on the owner of the brand. They also offer the promise of increasing returns—the more attention the customer gives to a brand, the more the brand owner will learn about the customer, and the stronger the value of the brand becomes to the customer.[38]

## MOVING FROM BRICK-AND-MORTAR TO E-BUSINESS

If you own or work in a traditional brick-and-mortar business, you are probably a little nervous by now. If our gurus are right, all those e-businesses springing up on the Internet are going to steal your best customers, upset your pricing schemes, destroy your brand name, and generally make you as obsolete as a buggy-whip manufacturer. What can you do? The obvious answer is to take the plunge and get into e-commerce yourself. But how? Don't worry. Our gurus have plenty of advice. In fact, they have tons upon tons of advice. Would-be e-commerce gurus have churned out literally hundreds of books and thousands of articles in just the last few years, purporting to offer you tried-and-true "roadmaps" and "cyber rules for success" for putting your business on the Internet. It is impossible for us to cover here the entire range of tips, tricks, and techniques the e-commerce gurus offer. If we tried, we wouldn't be able to get to any other topic in this book. Instead, we have pulled together some of the latest and best thinking from the most popular and prolific e-commerce gurus concerning three topics:

1. **Basic steps of implementing e-commerce.** Our gurus warn that there is a lot more to successful e-commerce than just hiring a techie to design a Web site and put your product catalog on-line.
2. **Designing a Web site.** While a good Web site isn't all there is to good e-commerce, it doesn't hurt. We will consider what our gurus have to say about creating a Web site that attracts lots of visitors, keeps them coming back, and perhaps most important, moves products and sells services.
3. **Critical success factors.** We will conclude with a discussion of some important tips for success. Think of these as the lessons our e-commerce gurus have learned the hard way.

## Basic Implementation Steps

All e-commerce gurus have their own recommended 5-step, 8-step, or 10-step roadmap to success. After all, most of them are consultants, and consultants always have ready-made implementation plans. As you might expect, the plans vary considerably in quality and completeness. Some are so simple as to be practically useless. Others are laden with jargon and are so short on detail that they require "expert" interpretation—which maybe was their author's intention. Two of the better plans offered by the e-commerce gurus are those presented by Richard Gascoyne in his 1997 book *Corporate Internet Planning Guide* and by David Siegel in *Futurize Your Enterprise.* We first summarize Gascoyne's ten steps for building an internet strategy. You can find a summary of Siegel's series of six meetings for designing a customer-led Web site in Exhibit 2.1.

### EXHIBIT 2.1. David Siegel's Six Meetings to Design a Customer-Led Web Site

David Siegel, author of *Creating Killer Web Sites* and *Futurize Your Enterprise*, recommends that you begin your e-commerce journey by appointing a chief net officer (CNO) to lead an on-line business unit. You should establish this on-line business unit as a separate organization with a separate budget and the freedom to act independent of the rest of the organization. Once you have created the on-line business unit and appointed its initial staff, gather key executives and the CNO's staff for a series of meetings. Each meeting should take a couple of days and should be held at an off-site location where the participants can focus on the task at hand.

Siegel envisions that the on-line unit led by the CNO will eventually become the company as more and more customer groups are served by the company's e-commerce efforts. He writes:

**The transformation begins when the CNO establishes the new online business unit, hiring a small team of new people to help get it started. The web team quickly forms customer divisions, . . . the divisions continue to grow as more and**

(continued)

EXHIBIT 2.1. **(continued)**

**more employees join the online business unit, and . . . the CNO adds new customer groups. Finally, the old company is left with only stragglers, who get left behind as the company enters the New World. At that point, the CNO is out of a job—she either stays on in a new capacity or goes to her next company.**

| Meeting | Key Questions to Answer |
|---|---|
| **Meeting #1: Commitment** | What would happen if we put every person in our company right on our customer's desktop?<br>Which business areas are we open to exploring, and which are we going to avoid?<br>Which parts of our industry are going on-line fastest?<br>What changes do we expect from competitors?<br>Which start-ups are going to put us out of business?<br>Which of our customers would make good partners?<br>Who are our leading-edge customers?<br>Who will our most-profitable customers be in three to five years? |
| **Meeting #2: Customer Segmentation** | Who are our top 50 customers?<br>Which individuals are working their way toward top-50 status?<br>Who are our most-important customer groups whose needs should be satisfied first on-line?<br>(Siegel advises that you should clearly identify at least 10 customer groups and then decide which of those you can really satisfy 110 percent. Agree on one to four groups to target with your initial Internet efforts. You will need to staff your on-line business unit with at least 10 full-time employees for each customer group you are targeting.) |
| **Meeting #3: Active Listening** | How are our on-line customers going to change our company?<br>What can we offer our customers on-line to get their attention? What would astonish and delight them?<br>What are the online habits of our customers—prospective, new, and committed? Where do they surf? How many hours do they spend on-line? What engages them? What turns them off?<br>(Siegel says you should engage in a dialogue with actual customers as you seek answers to these questions. He warns that you should not take your clues from what your competition is doing. Do your own research.) |

(continued)

EXHIBIT 2.1. **(continued)**

| | |
|---|---|
| **Meeting #4: Measuring Success** | How will we measure the success of our on-line efforts? Possible measures include the following:<br>• Number of page views.<br>• Number of unique visitors.<br>• Number of visitors who register.<br>• Number of page views per visit.<br>• Amount of time visitors stay on the site.<br>• Number of repeat visitors.<br>• Average order size.<br>• Time of day that gets the highest orders.<br>• Errors.<br>• Returns.<br>• Relation between amount of information provided and size of purchase.<br>• Estimated number of customers who would be upset if your site went down for (1) an hour, (2) a day, or (3) a week.<br>• Sales to repeat customers. |
| **Meeting #5: Customer Modeling** | What are the profiles of our top three customer groups? (Construct an elaborate profile of a representative member.)<br>How will they find our site?<br>What key words might they type into a search engine?<br>How much time will they have when they reach our site?<br>What is likely to draw their attention?<br>What can we offer them on-line?<br>What will entice them to visit our site a second time?<br>(Siegel suggests constructing a feature matrix identifying the features of your site that will be attractive to your ideal customer as a beginning, intermediate, and experienced user of your site. The deliverable from this meeting is a prioritized list of desirable features, broken down by release, for each customer group you want to satisfy.) |
| **Meeting #6: The Plan** | What are the key steps/phases in our design efforts?<br>Which features will be added to our site, and in what order?<br>What is our time frame for moving from one release to another?<br>Which customers' needs and expectations will be met at each stage/release? |

*Source:* David Siegel, *Futurize Your Enterprise: Business Strategy in the Age of the E-Customer* (New York: Wiley, 1999), p. 114.

Gascoyne lists 10 steps for building your Internet strategy:

1. Embrace the Internet strategically.
2. Develop and accept new business assumptions.
3. Envision complete customer-centric solutions.
4. Predict points of entry.
5. Redefine relevant core competencies.
6. Experiment with innovative solutions.
7. Define your value proposition.
8. Explore profit models.
9. Identify points of departure.
10. Plan a phasing approach

Let's look at each of these steps in some detail.

### Step #1: Embrace the Internet Strategically

The biggest mistake most companies make in their first efforts with e-commerce, says Gascoyne, is to launch a Web site without first developing a strategy for integrating the Internet with their overall business objectives. At least initially, most companies view the Internet as little more than just another marketing vehicle or distribution channel. Consequently, they miss its real significance and the opportunities it presents for fundamentally redefining business rules and relationships with customers. If you want to succeed in e-commerce, declares Gascoyne, you must embrace the Internet as a strategic opportunity. That means getting senior members of the management team involved in the effort.

Gascoyne suggests that your first step should be to create an Internet team composed of executives and line managers from your operations, marketing, and technology groups. This team's primary task will be to look beyond an on-line presence to assess and define how the company can employ the Internet to change your business fundamentally. Your Internet team should seek answers to the following types of questions:

- Who are our customers and what are their profiles? (See more about customer profiles later in this chapter and in Chapter 4.)
- What are our customers' needs? (See Chapter 4 for a full discussion of how our gurus recommend that you determine customer needs.)
- What overall solutions are our customers seeking? Gascoyne suggests that you revisit current customer "scenarios" and predict future ones. He defines a scenario as "the process the customer goes through to solve a problem or fill a need."[39] Ideally, he says, you should "understand your customers' needs, values and expectations so well that you can predict *exactly* what steps they will take to solve the problem or fulfill the need."[40]

- What are your core competencies? What part of your customers' solution can you best provide?
- Who are your current business partners? How do they help you provide a total solution to your customers' problems? Gascoyne states that you should revisit current business partners and define new ones "in areas where your business cannot differentiate itself or maintain necessary core competencies."[41]
- Is your business moving in the wrong direction as the Internet changes the assumptions of business?
- Do you have the business and technology skills to understand where you need to be going?
- Do you have the appropriate team in place to guide you?
- Is senior management willing to offer strategic direction as you launch your e-commerce efforts?
- Have you embraced the Internet strategically?

Although Gascoyne doesn't discuss it, an issue that you might want to consider at this stage if you are a traditional brick-and-mortar business is how you will mix your "bricks" and "clicks." Are you going to integrate your Internet business with your traditional business, or are you going to keep the two separate? Different companies have adopted different strategies, as Ranjay Gulati and Jason Garino point out in their article "Get the Right Mix of Bricks & Clicks." For example, Office Depot fully integrated its Web site with its retail stores. On the other hand, Barnes & Noble spun off Barnesandnoble.com as a totally separate company. Other companies have adopted something in between total separation and total integration. How do you decide whether separation or integration is the best strategy? Gulati and Garino suggest that you should fully integrate your "bricks" and "clicks" if the following statements are true:[42]

Your brand extends naturally to the Internet.

Your current executives have the skills and experience to pursue the Internet channel.

Your current executives are willing to judge the Internet initiatives by a different set of performance criteria than is used for the traditional business.

Your distribution systems translate well to the Internet.

You information systems provide a solid foundation for your activities on the Internet.

Either your distribution or information systems provide you with a significant competitive advantage.

On the other hand, Gulati and Garino recommend that you should keep your "bricks" and "clicks" separate if the following statements are true:

You will target a different customer segment or offer a different product mix over your Web site compared with what you offer in your stores.
You will need to price differently on-line in order to stay competitive.
You recognize that the Internet will fundamentally threaten your current business model and that you will have channel conflict.
You are having trouble attracting or maintaining talented executives for your Internet division.
You need outside capital to fund your Internet venture.
Separate ownership of your "bricks" and "clicks" will offer you greater flexibility in developing partnerships with other companies.

### *Step #2: Develop and Accept New Business Assumptions*

Once your Internet team has secured a genuine commitment from senior management to approach e-commerce as a strategic opportunity, their next step, says Gascoyne, should be to examine your current business models and assumptions in light of the unique capabilities the Internet offers. In particular, your Internet team should discuss how the following Internet capabilities could be exploited to develop new products and services your customers might value.[43]

- If the corporate information systems are sufficiently flexible, integrated, and networked, Internet technology can be used to generate and retrieve information from a variety of existing corporate systems such as customer and prospect databases, billing and expense databases, and existing application systems.
- Internet technology can be employed to create rich customer interfaces combining video, audio, images, and text. Virtual-reality interfaces can be deployed that allow users to visually navigate through virtual 3-D environments.
- Information presented to the customers can be personalized based on an individual customer's profile or other conditions.
- The customer interface can be frequently updated with relevant and real-time information.
- Unlike traditional systems and paper processes (fax, carbon copies, etc.), Internet technology can provide degrees of security to protect customers' privacy and restrict access to sensitive data.
- Internet technology makes it possible to easily link the Internet sites of global business partners in order to offer customers more-complete solutions. These links can be transparent to the user.
- The Internet may change the user interface paradigm. The customer can now pull for information or businesses can push information.
- The Internet provides a unique ability to bring together people with similar interests into virtual communities for business or social experiences.

As the Internet team reviews the new capabilities offered by Internet technology, says Gascoyne, it should be developing a new set of business assumptions, like those illustrated in Exhibit 2.2.

EXHIBIT 2.2. **Example of New Business Assumptions**

| Old Business Assumptions | New Business Assumptions |
|---|---|
| Access to markets is limited due to geographic and other constraints. | Access to markets is significantly increased. |
| Barriers to entry are significant. | Barriers to entry are low. |
| Agility is important. | Agility is essential. |
| A focus on core competencies provides strategic insight. | A focus on core competencies is paramount due to increased competition and the need to partner with others. |
| The value proposition for the customer changes slowly. | The value proposition for the customer changes constantly in response to innovations in products and services. |
| Companies need the ability to change. | Companies must continuously change in order to grow. |
| Marketing drives the business strategy. | A combination of technology and marketing drives the new business strategies. |
| Product quality is important. | Time to market and product quality are both important. |
| The Internet is a piece of the business solution. It is seen as another marketing-and-distribution channel. | The Internet is essential. It is a complementary business design that requires managers to rethink their business processes and create new kinds of customer solutions. |
| The company has a moderate number of competitors. | The company has a large number of competitors and many of them are global and/or come from different industries. |
| Products are regionally customized. | Products must be individually customized. |
| The company designs its products. | Customers design their own products. |
| Formal alliances, mergers, and acquisitions are common. | New types of business-partnership arrangements emerge in which the alliances are opportunity based and less formal, and involve linking Web sites to deliver value. |
| The key to software success is ease of use. | The key business success factor is flexibility in systems architecture. |
| Customers' needs change slowly. | Customers' needs, expectations, and priorities change constantly as new services, virtual products, and choices become available. |

*Source:* Adapted from Richard J. Gascoyne and Koray Ozcubukcu, *Corporate Internet Planning Guide: Aligning Internet Strategy with Business Goals* (New York: Van Nostrand Reinhold, 1997), pp. 107–142.

These new business assumptions should in turn, writes Gascoyne, lead the Internet team to redefine the business model. See Exhibit 2.3 for an example of the way an Internet team for a newspaper might redefine its business model on the basis of the changing business assumptions listed in Exhibit 2.2.

### *Step #3: Envision Complete Customer-Centric Solutions*

With its new business model in hand, the Internet team should next turn to considering new products and services. "The most successful Internet strategy," writes Gascoyne, "offers a more complete, convenient, and timely solution for the customer than available today."[44] He suggests that the best way for the Internet team to envision new customer solutions is for it to develop scenarios of the company's typical customers in their daily practices. The teams should ask questions such as the following:

EXHIBIT 2.3. **Example of Redefined Business Model**

| Old Business Model | New Business Model |
|---|---|
| Editions of the paper are produced at regular, predefined intervals. | Editions of the paper are produced progressively as the news evolves. |
| Distribution of the news to end users is time consuming and labor intensive. There may be significant delays between production and consumption. | Distribution of the news is instantaneous. Immediacy enhances the relevance and value of the news content. |
| The same product is sold to all customers. | Published material can be tailored to the subscriber's interest. |
| Content is static and constrained by page size, layout, and advertising requirements. | Content is dynamic and includes video, audio, 3-D images, photo and news libraries, in-depth analyses, tutorials, reference aids, and historical data. |
| Readership is geographically limited. | Readership is global. |
| Reader interaction is limited to letters to the editor. | Reader interaction can be extensive, with readers engaging in facilitated discussions on a news story or with a particular journalist, author or subject-matter expert. |
| Advertising is static. | Advertising is dynamic and interactive, with links to advertisers' own Internet material. Advertising can be specifically targeted. |

*Source:* Adapted from Richard J. Gascoyne and Koray Ozcubukcu, *Corporate Internet Planning Guide: Aligning*

- What problems are the customers trying to solve?
- What needs are they seeking to meet?
- How can our Internet-enabled products and services or new ones be harnessed to provide our customers with a more complete solution?
- What new business partners do we need to make that happen?

### Step #4: Predict Points of Entry

Gascoyne defines "points of entry" as "all the possible routes potential customers might use to get to your site."[45] For example, they might come to your site via a link from a business partner's site, another related product or service site, a search engine, on-line or off-line advertisements, and so on. If you have done a good job of developing customer scenarios in step three, says Gascoyne, then points of entry should be obvious.

### Step #5: Redefine Relevant Core Competencies

In step 5 the Internet team rethinks the core competencies the company will need from the perspective of the Internet customer. As the company moves from the old non-Internet-enabled business model to the new Internet-enabled business model, relevant core competencies will likely change. For example, Gascoyne notes that a relevant core competency for traditional newspaper customers might be the newspaper's ability to print and distribute the daily paper in a timely manner, whereas a relevant core competency for Internet customers might be the ability of the paper to provide in-depth coverage and analysis of news events. The key to this step, explains Gascoyne, is for the Internet team to discern a differentiable solution based on its company's strategic core competencies. In short, what makes your company unique?

### Step #6: Experiment with Innovative Solutions

Gascoyne writes, "There are business problems that Internet technology can solve, and, more important, business opportunities it can create. For example, the Internet facilitates communication with suppliers, but it also creates new opportunities by offering more personalized and complete solutions to a global audience. It is important to recognize the difference between these two concepts, because you need to experiment with solutions to optimize and reengineer your business as well as with new solutions that customers will value."[46] This is the step in which the Internet team should be proactive. What can the company do, using the capabilities of the Internet, that will be truly innovative and most important, deliver significant new value to the customer?

### Step #7: Define Your Value Proposition

The value proposition is what the customers get in return for their attention. Gascoyne notes that "the processes for creating value in the physical and virtual worlds

EXHIBIT 2.4. **On-Line Customer Needs and Expectations**

| Customer Need / Expectation | Meaning |
|---|---|
| **Convenience** | Products and services are available all the time. |
| **Transparency** | The customer isn't bothered with the details of how an end product, service, or solution is achieved. |
| **Simplicity** | Interfaces are intuitive, comfortable, and easy for the customer to use. |
| **Guaranteed fulfillment** | Products and services are delivered on time and as promised. |
| **Security** | The customer doesn't have to worry about loss of privacy or improper access to sensitive information. |
| **Education** | Information that the company provides is concise, relevant, timely, well presented, and genuinely informative. |
| **Personalization** | Products, services, and Web content are customized to fit individual preferences. |
| **Timeliness** | The company responds immediately to customer needs and problems. |
| **Choice** | The company provides a wide range of options for meeting customer needs. |
| **Interaction** | Customers have the opportunity to join with others in a community of interests. |

*Source:* Adapted from Richard J. Gascoyne and Koray Ozcubukcu, *Corporate Internet Planning Guide: Aligning Internet Strategy with Business Goals* (New York: Van Nostrand Reinhold, 1997), pp. 26–28, Table 2.1.

are not the same. The most successful Internet value propositions take into account four components: (1) relevant core competency (in your customers' eyes) and compelling solution differentiation; (2) the value of interlinked business partners; (3) customers' changing needs and expectations; and (4) Internet-enabled business capabilities."[47] (See Exhibit 2.4 for a list of needs/expectations of on-line customers.) The unique combination of these four components creates value. It is important that the nature of the value proposition is clear both to the customer and to the company.

### *Step #8: Explore Profit Models*

So far, few companies have made a lot of money on the Internet, but Gascoyne sees no reason why your company shouldn't. In this step, the Internet team has the task of determining how profits will be generated from your on-line presence. Will it be through the payment you receive for the innovative solutions you offer and expert advice you provide, compensation for leads you generate for others, cost savings, advertising, subscriptions, or some other vehicle? In exploring ways to generate profits from the Internet, Gascoyne warns that you shouldn't assume that old profit models will work:

> The Internet is still a new economic model. Do not look to traditional profit models for comfort and solutions; experiment with new ones. For example, Internet newspaper subscriptions may not be an appropriate (value recapture) model because the Internet newspaper is not a newspaper in the traditional sense. People do not use online newspapers for the same purposes as a hard-copy paper. Reading online newspapers is usually done with a specific purpose in mind. . . .
>
> [Consequently,] a pay-per-view model may be more appropriate that a subscription-based approach. . . . Perhaps customer needs would best be met by setting up a search service for news articles relating to a specific subject, or by offering the option of ordering a single paper rather than a regular subscription.[48]

### *Step #9: Identify Points of Departure*

"Points of departure" are the locations customers may want to go after they have visited your site. You will want to develop business-partner relationships with other companies that can help to complete your vision of the total solution for the customer and link to their Internet sites. Gascoyne suggests that your Internet team answer the following questions to determine relevant points of departure:

- What can't you provide, or what can someone else provide better to complement your service or product?
- To complete the solution, where would users naturally want to go next after they received value from your site?
- What new partners or interlinkers do you need to develop?
- Do you want transparent (the customer doesn't recognize the link as a link to another site) or nontransparent linking from your site?
- What customer information, if any, will you forward to your interlinking partner?

### *Step #10: Plan a Phasing Approach*

Gascoyne recommends a phased approach for implementing your Internet strategy. He suggests that the Internet team begin with a clear definition of the end result you are seeking and then break down implementation into a series of small phases. Each of these phases, he warns, should be implemented in quick succession to minimize the risk of being beaten to the market by a competitor or making unwarranted assumptions. You want to test your solutions and assumptions on the Internet as quickly as possible, evaluate what you have learned, and incorporate those lessons into your next phase. In defining your phased approach, Gascoyne says your Internet team should spell out, at a minimum, the business assumptions; business, marketing, and technology objectives; and methods of measuring the success of each phase. For example, the plan for the first phase might read something like this:

### E-Commerce Implementation: Phase One

- Business Assumptions

  A and B will be the most relevant customer values.
  Technology Z will be matured by Z date.
  The key business partners for this phase are D, C, and E.
  Our relevant core competency is Z.

- Business, Marketing, and Technology Objectives

  Generation of marketplace awareness.
  Development and testing of new marketing, business, and technology models.

- Success Criteria

  Twenty leads per month.
  Operationally robust system.
  Flexible software architecture.
  High-usage volume from links from new business partners.

## Web-Site Design

Whether you follow Richard Gascoyne's 10 essential steps, hold David Siegel's six meetings, or accomplish your e-commerce planning in some other fashion, much of what you will be discussing will have to do with the style, content, and functionality of your Web site. Web sites are the storefronts of the knowledge economy and, like physical storefronts, can be attractive or dull; they can help your business or turn potential customers away. If you have spent any time at all on the Internet, you know how widely Web sites range in quality. You probably have bookmarked a few you love for their style, content, and overall friendliness. You probably know of many more that you stumbled on by chance and promised yourself that you would never visit again. Getting Web sites right can be tricky, but never fear, our gurus are here to help. Here is a list of the most-important "Dos" according to Daniel Amor, author of *The E-Business (R)evolution,* followed by some "myths" of Web-site marketing that Seth Godin, vice president for direct marketing at YAHOO! says you should avoid.

### *Daniel Amor's "Dos" of Web-Site Design*

Amore recommends that, in designing your company's Web site, you should be careful to do the following:

1. **Take Web site design seriously.** Amor compares your Web site to your company's business card. You want to make sure it presents the image you want to convey about your company.
2. **Remember that content is king.** Visitors should never leave your Web site without taking away some useful information. Content is much more important than fancy graphics. (Although see Seth Godin's cautions about content in the next section.)
3. **Make your documents Web friendly.** Unlike paper documents, documents on the Web are not read in linear fashion. Imbed links in documents you post on your site to allow users to navigate easily to related material or a more in-depth discussion of a subject.
4. **Provide a summary of the contents of each Web page in the title and in the URL.** Make it easy for visitors and search engines to discover the contents of each page.
5. **Limit the number of links on a single page to 10 or less, unless the page contains a link list.**
6. **Check every Web page to ensure that it downloads fast even on the slowest connections.**
7. **Have your Web site checked by Bobby (*http://www.cast.org/bobby/*) to ensure that it is accessible to people with disabilities.** Your site should be compatible with the W3C Web Accessibility Initiative (http://www.w3.org/WAI/).
8. **Provide a summary of the content of each Web page at the top of each page.**
9. **Provide the capability for visitors to download information in a variety of different formats, such as HTML, ASCII, Postscript, Acrobat, Word, and so on.**
10. **Concentrate on providing information about your products and services.** Most visitors are more interested in those topics than in your company.
11. **Provide a separate page where visitors can provide you with feedback on your Web site and express their interests and concerns.**
12. **Conduct surveys on your Web site to learn more about your customers needs and interests.** Offer a prize or gift to encourage people to respond to your survey and to reward them for their effort. (See Chapter 4 for our gurus' recommendations concerning the types of questions you should ask customers to determine their needs.)
13. **Create a page of frequently asked questions (FAQs) containing questions asked most often by your customers together with your responses.** Consider creating a separate FAQ page for each product and service you offer. Update your FAQ pages frequently to include new questions you receive.

14. **Provide visitors an easy way to e-mail you their questions and concerns.** Establish a customer-care department to respond quickly to e-mail you receive. Use an auto-reply system to notify visitors that their e-mail has been received and will be responded to promptly.
15. **Adopt and use a consistent format for all company e-mail, news-group posting, and Web-page design.** Your customers should be able to recognize at a glance that the e-mail, posting, or Web page is coming from your company.
16. **Adopt a company policy forbidding "spamming"—the sending of information to people who do not ask for it.**
17. **Provide a clear and simple-to-use interface.** Navigation bars should be intuitive and easy to use. All graphical navigation buttons and bars should be reproduced as textual links for browsers that don't support graphics.
18. **Provide a navigation scheme that is consistent throughout your site.** Always provide users with the ability to jump directly back to your home page or the beginning of a channel from every page.
19. **Make it easy for customers to contact the right people in your company to respond to needs.**
20. **Put the most important and useful information at the top of each Web page.** Most users never scroll down to see more than the top 20 percent of each page.
21. **Limit your color selections to two or three colors, and use them consistently throughout your site.** Choose a color scheme that supports the message of your Web pages and the image you want to convey for your company. For example, blue is tranquil, intuitive, and trustworthy. Orange conveys happiness, courage, and success. Check http://www.myth.com/color or http://www.artomatic.com/color/ for a discussion of the meanings most people attach to different colors. Make sure that each of your Web pages is clearly readable if printed out in black and white. If they are not, you should change your color scheme.
22. **Limit the use of large graphics or videos that take more than a few seconds to download.** Always provide a text alternative for visitors who wish to switch off automatic image loading.
23. **Use "infortainment" and "edutainment" special events to attract people to your site.**
24. **Provide links to sites where your visitors can download plug-ins or special software they might need to view documents or files on your site.**
25. **Keep your Web site's content up-to-date so that people will come back regularly.** Update your site frequently so that you can offer something new each time a visitor comes back.
26. **Offer free information, products, or services to encourage people to visit your site.**
27. **Collect information from your visitors about their needs and preferences, and then use that information to personalize your Web site as much as possible.**

28. **Try to create a sense of community on your Web site for people with common interests, and then arrange your content to make it easy for them to access the information that interests them.** For example, if your Web site is designed to appeal to pet owners, you might create segments of your site to appeal to dog owners or even owners of a specific breed.
29. **Display a privacy notice and ensure that it is followed.** (See Chapter 4 for a discussion of customer-privacy issues and some suggestions about the content of your privacy statement.)
30. **Provide a simple search engine for your site that visitors can use to find information fast.**
31. **Ensure that every piece of information on your Web site can be accessed with three or fewer clicks of the mouse button.**
32. **Think globally and act locally.** Develop country- or region-specific Web sites in local languages that cater to local business practices and customs.
33. **Choose a domain name that fits your business and needs.** If your company is well known, use the company name. Otherwise, select a name that matches a keyword your target customer would use in a search engine.
34. **Register your site with all search engines and on-line directories.**
35. **Display your domain name everywhere you display your company logo**—that is, in traditional media advertising, on business cards and letterheads, and so on. Either display the domain name such as www.mycompany.com/ or the complete URL, http://www.mycompany.com/. Always include the "/" at the end.
36. **Avoid the use of "Under Construction" signs.** Visitors should not be invited to your Web site until you are sure that nothing is missing and all links are working correctly.
37. **Make sure that the image of your company conveyed by your Web site is consistent with the image you convey through traditional communication methods such as television, radio, magazine, and newspaper advertising.**
38. **Follow the following rules if you use banner advertising:**

- Keep the banners small.
- Use a concise and professional design.
- Avoid complex animations.
- Make sure all text is legible.
- Make sure all links work.
- Most important, make sure the message in the ad is short but compelling.

### *Seth Godin's Myths about Marketing on the Web*

Here are a dozen myths that Seth Godin says have developed about the Web. Think of them as the "Don'ts" of Web design and maintenance.[49]

**Myth #1: Traffic (hits!) is the best way to measure a Web site.** A "hit" is a single ping on your Web site. Godin notes that the number of hits tells you nothing about how well your Web site is working. There is just no correlation between hits and sales.

**Myth #2: If you build great content, people will return over and over.** Godin says there are only two kinds of great content that will bring people back to your Web site again and again: (1) providing news, which is extremely expensive to do well, or (2) providing truly customized data, such as the tracking tool on Federal Express's Web site. If you want people to come back to your site, advises Godin, you have to remind them to do so. You can't count on them to return on their own. That means you have to promote your Web site like you promote the other aspects of your business.

**Myth #3: You can sell stuff on the Web if you invest enough in a secure server.** Selling isn't about technology, writes Godin; it's about selling. If you invest all your effort into acquiring or building infrastructure, you'll just end up with a great store but no sales.

**Myth #4: The search engines are the key to traffic on your site.** Don't count on random visits from search engines to build traffic to your site, says Godin. Just remember that half of all searches are failures and the one hundred most-searched words are off-color or pornographic. You will need some other vehicle for attracting attention. In short, your site will need marketing.

**Myth #5: You need Java and Shockwave to be at the cutting edge.** Godin asserts that most people don't want the latest technology. They want technology that is easy to use and that works. Remember, 85 percent of people who go on-line say they are smarter than average. When your site screams at them that they don't have the right plug-ins or that their modem is too slow, you're telling them they're stupid. That's not what you want to do. At least it isn't if your goal is to sell products and services.

**Myth #6: The Web is like TV.** The Web isn't TV. Godin cites Bill Gates as an example of someone who believed in this myth. Gates has spent over a half a *billion* dollars trying to build traffic to Web sites with TV-like programming. None of his efforts have been successful. Godin says we may see a merging of the Web and TV sometime in the future when fiber/cable network access is available to most homes. However, right now a TV-like content business just will not work on the Web.

**Myth #7: Lots of people surf the Web.** Not true, says Godin. Actually, the average person has been to only 100 sites and bookmarked only 14 of them. You can't count on the volume of Web surfers to make your site a success.

**Myth #8: If you don't experiment now, you will lose later.** Wrong, says Godin. If you don't run *good* Web experiments now, you will lose later. Poorly designed Web experiments, like any poorly designed experiments, yield bad data. In short, give the same care and attention to the design of your marketing experiments on the Web as you would to any other marketing test you might run.

**Myth #9: Your site should be a complete on-line experience.** Godin notes that a few companies such as Netscape, AOL, and YAHOO! have attempted to build complete experiences, so-called portal sites. But, he warns, portal sites are difficult to build and expensive to maintain. A poorly designed and maintained portal site is worse than none at all.

**Myth #10: Anonymity is good for the Net.** It is true, writes Godin, that today people can surf the Net without being recognized. A number of companies today offer anonymous accounts. But, he says, such anonymity is bad for your business. An anonymous visitor to your Web site is like a customer visiting your brick-and-mortar store wearing a ski mask. Such visitors are rarely good citizens, and they almost never buy anything. You don't want visitors to your site to keep their anonymity. You want to reward them for giving it up. You want their permission to get to know them better. (See Chapter 4 for a discussion of how our gurus say you can get such permission from your customers and prospects.)

**Myth #11: You can make money selling banner ads.** Wrong, writes Godin. Even the largest Web sites have found it difficult to make money from banners. As much as 85 percent of their banner space goes unsold. That's like trying to make money running a magazine in which five out of six of your ad pages are unsold every issue. It just won't work.

**Myth #12: Activity is good.** Just because you can put something on your Web site doesn't mean that you should. Large companies in particular have been prone to this mistake, writes Godin. Because they can build the site themselves, they put everything on it that any executive can think up, mistakenly believing that they are doing marketing. Don't make that mistake. Think it through. How will that new feature help serve customers?

## The Critical Success Factors

A common theme runs through all of the "Dos" and "myths" of Web-site design that our gurus preach. Perhaps Patricia Seybold, author of *Customers.com,* puts it best:

### It's the Customer, Stupid!

Whether you are making it easier for your Web-site visitors to contact the right people in your company, making sure your graphics load fast, protecting your site visitors' privacy, doing any of the other "Dos," or avoiding getting trapped by the "myths," the common theme running through it all is to take care of the customer. Seybold says she learned that lesson in 1995 while researching best practices in 16 companies that, unlike many of their counterparts, seemed to be getting e-commerce right. These companies were the true e-commerce pioneers, and they were succeeding because they were putting the customer first. More specifically, explains Seybold, these companies were succeeding because they were doing seven things in their e-commerce initiatives that other companies weren't.[50] Seybold calls these seven things the seven critical success factors in e-commerce:

1. Target the right customers.
2. Own the customer's total experience.
3. Streamline business processes that impact the customer.
4. Let customers help themselves.
5. Help customers do their jobs.
6. Deliver personalized service.
7. Foster community.

## Critical Success Factor #1: Target the Right Customers

Seybold cites American Airlines and National Semiconductor as two companies that early on targeted the right customers in their e-commerce initiatives—those customers who could make the biggest difference to the bottom line. In the case of American Airlines, the "right customer" was the AAdvantage frequent flyer. The company designed its initial e-commerce efforts, starting in 1995, to cater to the needs of its frequent flyers—planning travel, booking flights, applying for upgrades, and locating hotels and restaurants offering AAdvantage miles. In the case of National Semiconductor, the right customers were design engineers—those people who do the technical evaluation of National Semiconductor's products that they will build into cellular telephones and other electronic products. The National Semiconductor Web-site design team focused its initial efforts on providing these engineers with easy access to product data sheets, samples, pricing information, detailed technical specifications, product search facilities, and other resources. The site became so popular that it went from zero visitors to over 500,000 per month in the first two years of existence.

How do you discover the right customers to target? Seybold suggests the following four steps:

### Step #1: Know who your customers and prospects are.

Even if you sell through indirect channels, says Seybold, you should try to learn as much as you can about your end customers' needs and expectations.

> You may feel that there's no reasonable way to accurately find out who your customers are, particularly if you sell through indirect channels. But that's no longer true, as we've seen from Hallmark (which offers customers a reminder service), Quaker Oats (which lures customers to its Rice-A-Roni site for recipes), and many, many others. With today's cost-effective customer out-reach technologies—ranging from Web sites to e-mail to member cards—you can identify at least a reasonable subset of your customer base.[51]

**Step #2: Find out which customers are the most profitable.**

American Airlines targeted its frequent flyers because they fly more often than other travelers and are therefore more profitable. Wells Fargo Bank focused on its high-net-worth customers because they used many fee-based services that generated additional revenues for the bank. AT&T targeted small-business customers for its initial e-commerce efforts because they used products and services that were standard across the country and thus cost effective to provide. In determining which customers are most profitable, cautions Seybold, be sure to look at what it costs you to service the customer group, as well as the revenues they generate. Also, consider the lifetime value of the customer.

**Step #3: Decide which customers you want to attract (or keep from losing).**

Both the *Wall Street Journal* and *Reader's Digest* directed their initial e-commerce efforts at young adults because those were the people who were less likely to subscribe to their print editions. Bell Atlantic targeted residential customers with its initial efforts on the Web as a way of counteracting increased competition from cable companies, cellular companies, and long-distance providers for residential business. (See Chapter 4 for guidance from our gurus on how to calculate the lifetime value of a customer.)

**Step #4: Know which customers influence key purchases.**

As in the case of National Semiconductor, the person who influences the buyers may be a more-important target for your e-commerce efforts than the actual buyers themselves. For example, Community Playthings, a manufacturer of day-care equipment and specialized furniture for children, built its Web site to cater to the needs and interests of physical therapists. Although physical therapists normally do not actually purchase day-care equipment or furniture, they do recommend the equipment that should be bought. Seybold notes that, because a single physical therapist often works with multiple day-care centers, Community Playthings found that it could generate multiple sales by pleasing just one physical therapist.

## Critical Success Factor #2: Own the Customer's Total Experience

"Above all," writes Seybold, "customers like to have a well-orchestrated, well-designed, predictable experience of doing business with you. Yet, they also want to feel in control. The need to have the ability to call the shots, to tailor their own experience to fit their individual circumstances."[52] Customers want you to save them time and irritation, offer them peace of mind, deliver consistently, and respect their individuality. In short, says Seybold, customers want you to take responsibility for their total experience and then deliver an experience that is not just satisfying but delightful. No e-commerce company does that better, she argues, than Amazon.com, "Earth's Biggest Bookstore." What are the lessons we can learn from Amazon.com? What do they do so well that other companies don't? What should you be doing in your e-commerce efforts to imitate them? Seybold lists eight things:

1. Focus on the customer's total experience of doing business with you. Identify each step or business event in the customer's most-likely interactions with your firm, and streamline each of those steps.
2. Reassure customers at each step with features like near-real-time order confirmations and shipping notifications.
3. Capture customers' profile information and offer them the opportunity both to change their profiles at any time and to select a set of profile defaults for "fast-path" dealings with your firm (like Amazon.com's One-Click purchasing).
4. Give customers access to their entire transaction history with your firm.
5. Let customers specify what, if anything, they'd like to receive proactive notifications about.
6. Recruit thousands of business partners who can represent your firm to their customers by making it very easy for them to sell your products and receive commissions.
7. Make it so easy for your suppliers to deal with you that they're eager to do so. Help them present their products to your customers in the most effective way.
8. Focus on excellence in the customer experience and in execution of customer service to keep your customers loyal and to stimulate referrals. Combine that with aggressive marketing to bring in new customers who will be seduced by the customer experience as well as the products you offer.[53]

### *Critical Success Factor #3: Streamline Business Processes That Impact the Customer*

One of the things you will quickly learn as you put up a Web site and begin to engage in e-commerce, writes Seybold, is that your existing business processes may need a major redesign.

> Once you begin to experiment with a customer-facing Web site, you'll discover that customers will tell you exactly what they want and need with great precision. And you'll probably learn, to your dismay, that in order to really streamline tasks from the customer's point of view, you'll have to do major rework on your existing enterprise systems and business processes. What your Web site highlights, in an unflattering way, is all the black holes that exist in your company's operations. Today you have people who know where the problems in your processes are. They do workarounds. They fill the gaps. They do their best to provide your customers with seamless service. Yet behind the scenes there are usually a number of handoffs back and forth between departments: information is passed along verbally or informally. Someone will make adjustments to a standard process or product in

order to accommodate a customer's needs. Someone else will ensure that the order is filled, the billing problem resolved, the delivery expedited. Yet once customers begin interacting with you via the Web, that safety net falls away. Your company is left standing naked in front of its customers and channel partners. Every wrinkle shows; every blemish spoils the customer's ability to help herself to information and transactions.[54]

If you want your e-commerce efforts to succeed, you will have no choice but to redesign your business processes. However, warns Seybold, don't think of it as just another round of 1990s-style reengineering:

Back in the heyday of reengineering, many companies focused on the wrong things. They streamlined business processes, all right. They reengineered their businesses to make them more cost-efficient. But they left out the most important piece of the equation. They didn't start from the outside—the end customer—and work in. Instead, they worked from the inside out, streamlining administrative processes, manufacturing operations, procurement processes, and so forth. These were all valuable initiatives. Many of them saved companies a great deal of money and made them leaner and more productive. But they haven't affected the revenue side of the equation. Most of the reengineering efforts that took place in the 1990s didn't involve the end customer, so they didn't focus on the key priority of making it easy for customers to do business with the firm. They haven't made a difference in keeping customers happy and loyal, coming back for more, and telling their friends about your great products and service.[55]

This time around, advises Seybold, the customer must be the focal point of your redesign. That requirement will present your design team with both business and technical challenges.

The biggest business challenge will be resolving the issue of who "owns" customer information. Seybold notes that, in most traditional businesses, customer information is spread across product lines, particularly if your business is organized along product lines. In order to create a customer-friendly e-business, you will need a consolidated set of customer-profile and transaction information, and you will need to redesign processes to ensure smooth handoffs across all of the functional departments (marketing, sales, order entry, customer service, billing, manufacturing, fulfillment, etc.) that interact with the customer. Ideally, says Seybold, you will want someone or some group (global sales or marketing vice president, a customer steering committee, "customer czar," etc.) to have clear ownership and control of both customer information and all business processes that affect the customer.

The chief technical challenge your design team will face will be to link all of the customer information that resides in different databases electronically in order for work to flow smoothly from one application to another across functions (order entry to credit check to accounting to inventory, etc.). Although there is no one "right" way to link applications, maintains Seybold, there are four conceptual building blocks that many companies have found useful:

1. **Customer profiles.** These are customer preferences and other personal information you have learned about a customer. For example, an airline might collect information on customers' seating and meal preferences, the airport from which they usually fly, weekend travel, and so on. Seybold notes that "these aren't just 'nice-to-know' features that a customer service representative would see when on the phone with the customer; they're actionable pieces of information that can be used to launch applications."[56] For example, an airline might use information about its customers' weekend travel to send them targeted e-mails promoting special bargain weekend fares to destinations they frequent. (See Chapter 4 for a list of information our gurus say you should collect and maintain in your customer profiles.)
2. **Business rules.** Business rules specify practices to be followed under different conditions. They may be explicit—if the customer orders a quantity of 100 or more, then give him a 10 percent discount—or implicit: If a long-term customer needs expedited shipment, waive the extra freight charges. By combining customer preferences and business rules, you can create automated systems that provide customers with information, products, and offers that are customized for them.
3. **Business events.** Business events are the steps in a business process that trigger interactions between people and applications, such as placing an order, checking credit, checking inventory, shipping product, and so on. You must identify all of the key business events to ensure that information and tasks flow smoothly from one system to another for each event.
4. **Business objects.** Business objects are entities with a common and explicit definition, such as "customer," "order," and "account." Along with business events and business rules, business objects provide a common language technical and nontechnical people can use to describe the business. For example, a "checking account" is defined as an account that does such-and-such whereas an "investment account" is an account in which such-and-such occurs.

The concepts of customer profiles, business rules, business events, and business objects will help your design team meet the business and technical challenges we mentioned earlier. Seybold explains as follows:

> From an organizational stand-point, you can collect customer profile information, business rules, and business events from each group within your company that owns a piece of the customers. Then, by pulling this information together into a common business model, each group will be able to see where its information fits. . . .
>
> From a technical standpoint, you'll be able to use the business events that each group has identified to create interfaces among the applications

EXHIBIT 2.5. **A 360-Degree View of the Customer Relationship**

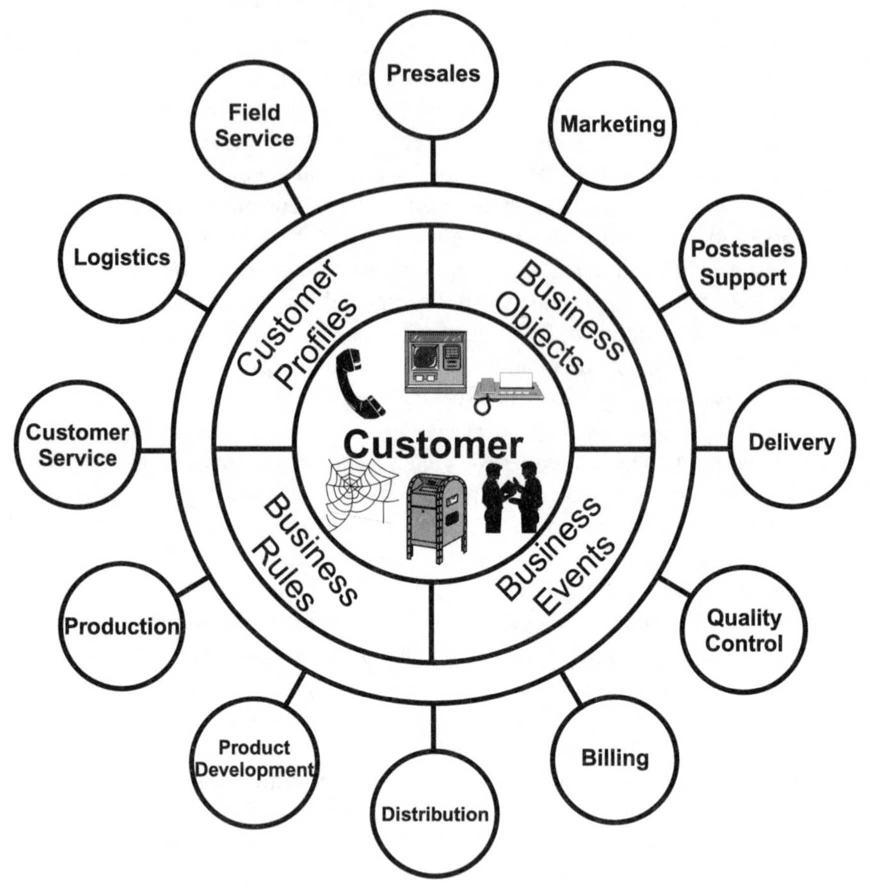


> that need to interact with one another. You'll use the business rules and customer profiles to develop front-end applications that will respond appropriately to each customer. And you'll use the business object definitions to design the components of your new applications.[57]

Your ultimate objective, says Seybold, should be to provide a 360-degree view of the customer relationship in which everyone who interacts with a customer in any way sees the total picture of that customer's relationship with your company (see Exhibit 2.5). Your company electronically "remembers" everything about the customer and consequently can offer the customer one-stop shopping across all of its product lines. The customer can access information, perform transactions, place orders, and request services across all product lines while never having to be bothered with the complexities of information flows necessary to make that happen.

### Critical Success Factor #4: Let Customers Help Themselves

"Your customers want more than a good Web site," writes Seybold, "they want a seamless web of interactive applications that will let them help themselves to information, perform transactions, check on the status of things, make inquiries, and get information that's relevant to their particular situation. They'll want to be able to perform all of these functions more or less interchangeably, by phone, fax, or e-mail or via the Web. And, when appropriate, they want a person integrated into the process."[58] Seybold cites Dell Computer as one of the most successful e-commerce companies in terms of allowing customers to help themselves. Here are some Dell practices that Seybold says all companies should be emulating:

- Dell makes it possible for customers to browse product marketing and technical information about various models of computers, configure and price systems, place orders, and check on the status of orders electronically without assistance.
- Dell has integrated its telephone-based sales, order entry, and service functions with its self-service Web site. Consequently, customers who begin a transaction or inquiry on Dell's Web site and find, for some reason, that they need assistance from a person can switch to a telephone call. The person they call will have access to the information they have entered via the Web site. Dell reports that customers who begin placing an order on its Web site and then switch to a phone call to complete the transaction are 1.5 times more likely to place an order than regular callers. Also, Dell reports that self-configured systems tend to have a higher selling price than the average systems sold by the company. In short, when allowed self-service, Dell's customers tend to upsell themselves.
- Customers who purchase a computer from Dell are given a special service-code number. By entering that code number on Dell's Web site, these customers can gain access to an on-line diagnostic and troubleshooting program customized for the make and model computer they are using. If they still need assistance, they can switch to a telephone call, and the Dell technician will have access to the self-service troubleshooting session they were running.
- Dell makes it possible for business customers to create password-protected Web sites called Premier Pages that can be accessed through their internal company intranets. Through their Premier Pages, Dell's corporate customers can access custom catalogs showing predetermined configurations of computers with account-specific pricing based on volume purchase agreements. Premier Page users can also get customized on-line technical support, purchase history reports, and more.

## Critical Success Factor #5: Don't Neglect Business-to-Business Electronic Commerce

Business-to-business (B-to-B) e-commerce is the fastest-growing segment of e-business, and for many companies, it is the most profitable. It is also more demanding than other forms of e-commerce. The tips to successful B-to-B e-commerce, says Seybold, are as follows:

### B-to-B Success Tip #1: Develop a deep understanding of the way your customers do their jobs.

In designing its Web site to support design engineers, National Semiconductor [NCR] surveyed the engineers themselves in order to determine the steps they followed in deciding on the chips to procure. The company then incorporated the results of the survey into its Web site.

> [National Semiconductor's team] . . . discovered that most designers started by surveying the field researching the capabilities of the current products on offer. To do this, they relied on the volumes of material they had already been given by each of the major suppliers. Most said they began with the binders of data sheets they had on their shelves. A few used CD-ROM catalogs. Many of them said they'd then check with the vendors' sales reps to make sure they had the latest information, and a few said they would look on the Web for product up-dates. This information told National Semi where to start: it needed to make it easy for design engineers to get the most current information about its products without worrying about keeping loose-leaf binders up to date or having to pick up the phone to call a sales rep. The fact that a few customers were already looking on the Web pointed them in the right direction.
>
> Next [the NCR team] discovered that when engineers look for a part, they want to be able to search based on the parameters they are seeking: low voltage, a certain price point, a particular function, or a minimum clock speed, for example. Finding something that met all the criteria was time-consuming if a customer had to leaf back and forth through catalogs. So National Semi scoured the countryside for a parametric search engine it could use on its Web site. The company found one, but it had to be rewritten (in Java) to do the job.
>
> Then [NCR] learned that once engineers had pinpointed a few products with the right specs, the next things they needed were the information and tools required to evaluate the chips for their project: detailed technical specifications, software simulations they could run against their own data, and samples of the chips they could test in the lab. So National Semi made it easy for engineers to download detailed data sheets, download software simulations, and order sample chips, each with a single click.[59]

Once you understand your customers' requirements and have incorporated them into your initial site design, says Seybold, don't stop there. Continuously refine and improve your Web site and business processes to make it even easier for your customers to do their job. For example, National Semicondutor monitors what customers do on its site and uses that information, among other things, to take steps out of the searching and ordering process, thus reducing the typical number of "clicks" required for customers to access the information they needed. Between 1995 and mid-1997, they were able to cut the average number of clicks from 8 to 2.5.

***B-to-B Success Tip #2: Give customers direct access to your inventory.***

Boeing gives customers access to its spare-parts inventory so they can see what parts are in stock, what they will cost, and even where they are warehoused. A small print shop in Palo Alto places a unique twist on the "access-to-inventory" concept. This shop provides a feature on its Web site that allows customers to view the press time available on its various types of printing presses. Users see a calendar for each press, with available hours in green and booked hours in red. Customers use the feature to schedule their printing to arrive at the print shop when press time is available on the equipment they require. The print shop, in turn, uses the feature to do some unique scheduling of its on, as Seybold explains:

> When I complimented the owner on this feature, he laughed and explained that there was more to the application than met the eye. He said that his customers all had different styles when it came to meeting deadlines. Some would call on Tuesday and say that a job would be ready on Thursday, but it was never actually ready till the following Monday. Others were always accurate in their estimates. So, he explained, each customer who logs in sees a different version of the press availability calendar. The customer whose estimates are accurate will see the real schedule. The customer whose estimates are always off by three days will see a schedule that has been "doctored" to induce them to get their work in sooner.[60]

***B-to-B Success Tip #3:***
***Give customers the ammunition and tools they need to make purchasing decisions.***

Cisco Systems discovered that customers were having trouble configuring and purchasing systems on its Web site because the products were so complex. For example, what interface boards and software could be combined with what routers? So the company added new and more sophisticated software to its site to assist customers with mixing and matching configuration options. Configuration constraints could be entered into the new software to ensure that customers could experiment with different configurations but always end up with a configuration that would work.

***B-to-B Success Tip #4: Prepare bills the way your customers need them.***

Seybold notes that, while most consumers are satisfied with a few simple billing options—check or credit card—business customers can be quite demanding. They may want their bills customized by geography, division, product line, department, or dozens of other ways in order to allocate costs correctly. If your systems can't prepare bills the way the customers need them, many companies will just decide to take their business elsewhere.

***B-to-B Success Tip #5: Make it easy for your customers to satisfy their customers.*** Ultimately, says Seybold, the best help you can provide your business customers is to help them help *their* customers. She cites Johnson & Higgins/Marsh & McLennan, the world's largest insurance brokerage for businesses, as an example of a company that made innovative use of its systems to help its business customers:

> Johnson & Higgins/Marsh & McLennan . . . linked its customers electronically to all the relevant insurance underwriters, who now receive the clients' request for proposals electronically and can respond electronically, dramatically shortening the time it takes to negotiate these large and complex insurance contracts. By making it easier for its corporate customers to do their jobs, J&H has ensured its role as the valued middleman in the process.[61]

### *Critical Success Factor #6: Deliver Personalized Service*

"Customers don't relate to anonymity on your part or theirs," writes Seybold. "If you want to differentiate yourself, . . . you need to be prepared to interact with customers—even millions of them—as individuals. That means greeting them by name and giving them yours."[62] Ultimately, it means personalizing the service you provide. Of course, you can't personalize your service unless you know something about the customer. That's where profiling comes in. A customer's profile is a repository of information about an individual customer's identity, address, preferences, needs, and expectations. Some companies survey customers directly to collect such information. For example, a rental-car firm might ask you to fill out an on-line or off-line form giving such information as your driver's license number, credit-card number, size of car you prefer, smoking or nonsmoking, and so on. Other companies build customer profiles incrementally. That's the approach Microsoft takes, as Seybold explains:

> The first time you visit Microsoft's Web site with a specific browser and Internet address, a profile is automatically created for you. Each time you return to the site from the same Internet address, using the same browser, any information you volunteer will be captured in your profile. If you download some software and supply an e-mail address in the process, it will be added to your profile. If you supply your name, title, and company in a feedback form, that information will flow directly into your profile. At any time, you can ask to see your profile, add to it, or modify it. Microsoft has been pleasantly surprised by both the type and quality of information its customers volunteer. What's surprising to me is how many Web sites don't

> automatically capture the information provided by customers' transacting business with them and place that information directly into a customer profile. Microsoft's approach is the exception, not the rule.[63]

(See Chapter 4 for more details on customer profiles.)

Once you have a customer's profile, you should put it to good use. One obvious use, says Seybold, is to use the information you have obtained to make it easier for the customer to do business with you. Don't ask for information that is in your customer's profile. For example, Amazon.com maintains customers' credit-card numbers, shipping information, and so on and uses this profile information to offer simplified "One-Click" shopping. Another way you can use the information you have collected is to identify and alert customers via e-mail or on your sign-on page about special offers in which they might be interested. For example, Amazon.com uses profiles to notify customers of new books or CDs they might find of interest.

Personalization, writes Seybold, can cement and deepen the relationship you have with customers. But, she warns, proceed carefully. There are obvious privacy issues—you have to protect the data you are storing in customer profiles—and you can actually damage your relationship with customers if they become disaffected or distracted or if the information you have becomes outdated.

> Personalization can backfire. It can seem too intrusive (How did you know that my wife likes Italian food?) or unresponsive (I don't care about the Internet anymore; that's passe; why do I keep seeing this stuff?). Your goal, therefore, is first to ensure that there's enough value in your basic offering to keep the customer satisfied and coming back for more. Next, you want to make it as easy as possible for the customer to see and change his profile at any time. And you want him to be aware that the quality of the personalized services you can provide him as an option is dependent on the quality of the information he's willing to give you about his preferences and interests.[64]

(See Chapter 4 for a discussion of privacy issues.)

### *Critical Success Factor #7: Foster Community*

"If you have a customer base that shares a common interest or practice," says Seybold, "then you have it made. You can create a community to keep customers coming back for more. And by eavesdropping electronically on customers' public communications with one another, you'll learn what's on their mind, what they value, and what they care about."[65] How do you go about building communities? Seybold offers the following four suggestions:

1. **Try subdividing your site into separate areas that will appeal to people with common interests.** For your business customers, for example, set up an

area where customers can share tips and techniques for using your products or solving problems.

2. **Examine your customer profiles and try to identify topics or interest areas.** Then create areas on your Web site where people with similar interests can interact.
3. **Introduce and reinforce common terminology and values.** Participants in communities of interest need to feel that they are in a "safe space." As the moderator of the communities you establish, it is your responsibility to set the rules and remind members that, among other things, they can't violate other members' privacy or say things that members of the community might find offensive.
4. **Encourage community members to take ownership of the community by voicing their opinions about community policies and practices.** Consider inviting some members to become "premium members" by participating in surveys and taking a more active role in setting the direction the community will take.

Seybold notes that the notion of fostering community isn't new to business. Most industries have associations, trade groups, and other special-interest groups. Most companies have long recognized that customers like to "join up," become "frequent buyers," get their gold or platinum card, and generally become part of the "in crowd." The Internet provides another opportunity to foster this sense of membership among your customers.

## The Ultimate Critical Success Factor: Be Paranoid

We conclude this chapter with one more piece of advice about the things you have to do to succeed in e-commerce. Bruce Judson offers this advice in his book *Hyper Wars,* and it may well be the ultimate critical success factor of all. If you want to succeed in e-commerce, never stop looking over your shoulder. Of course, that's good advice in any highly competitive environment, but it is especially important advice in the world of e-commerce. Why? Speed, says Judson. The Internet speeds everything up:

> In the past, products were launched and improved in fixed cycles. Every aspect involved in creating and distributing a product was allotted a certain amount of time, and time was also allotted for successfully communicating product information to prospective buyers.
>
> Today the Internet has turned the "fixed cycle" process upside down. Using a Web site, it's possible to distribute detailed information about a product, or even the product itself (such as the latest release of the Netscape browser), to millions of people in one day. For the first time, it is

> also possible to receive instant feedback from customers on specific aspects of products or services. Companies are now able to watch the activity at their Web sites and glean far more information than ever before about how a product is being received and what kinds of improvements might be valuable.
>
> Moreover, a Web site makes it possible to test out new ideas instantly. I can decide today to change some attribute of a service I might be offering or to alter my marketing campaign. These changes might be permanent or an experimental effort where I'm testing the response of customers and prospects. This type of real-customer real-time experimentation was simply not possible before the Web. Previously, I would have had to spend time and money on focus groups to get this type of feedback. Why is this significant? Because it is an indication of how companies that succeed now approach the market. We have entered an era of almost-constant experimentation and refinement.[66]

In short, say Judson, no matter how good your Web site is, someone right now is about to launch a better one. No matter how good a job you have done in streamlining your business processes, someone right now is wringing more waste out of theirs. No matter how smoothly you have linked your databases and applications, someone right now is developing a better e-business applications architecture. No matter how good a job you are doing in fostering communities to build customer loyalty, someone right now is setting up a more-attractive community designed to steal away your customers. Look over your shoulder; someone is gaining on you. So, get e-busy getting e-better. Your time just may be running out. As Judson puts it, "Paranoid? Maybe. Smart? Absolutely."[67]

## KEY POINTS

- E-commerce isn't limited to shopping over the Internet or supply-chain transactions between businesses. It embodies all aspects of doing business electronically, from advertising and marketing through to sales, ordering, manufacturing, distribution, customer service, after-sales support, and replenishment of inventory.

- E-commerce is to the information revolution what the railroad was to the industrial revolution—a totally new, totally unexpected, and totally unprecedented development that will rapidly change the economy, society, and politics.

- E-commerce is a threat to all traditional businesses for three reasons:

  1. It offers distinct advantages to consumers that traditional businesses cannot easily match.

2. It makes both supply and demand more apparent and thereby changes pricing models.

3. It negates the value of conventional branding.

- The biggest mistake most companies make with their e-commerce efforts is launching a Web site before they first develop a strategy for integrating the Internet into their overall business objectives.

- Prior to undertaking e-commerce, companies should thoroughly reexamine their business models and assumptions in light of the unique capabilities that the Internet offers.

- The most-successful e-commerce strategy is one that offers a more complete, convenient, and timely solution to a customer than the one offered by traditional business.

- Companies should rethink the core competencies they will need in light of the new Internet customer and their e-commerce strategy.

- The needs and expectations of on-line customers differ from those of traditional customers. Among other things, on-line customers demand convenience, simplicity, guaranteed fulfillment, security, personalization, and wide choice.

- Web-site design should be taken seriously. Among other things, Web-site designers should remember that content is king and that fast downloads and simple interfaces are critical.

- The most important thing to keep in mind in designing a Web site is that the site exists to serve the customer.

- The ultimate critical success factor is paranoia.

## KNOWLEDGE MANAGEMENT—The Gurus

**Verna Allee,** founder and president of Integral Performance Group and author of *The Knowledge Evolution*

**Annie Brooking,** managing director and founder of The Technology Broker and author of *Corporate Memory*

**Thomas H. Davenport,** professor of business at the University of Texas at Austin and coauthor of *Working Knowledge*

**Leif Edvinsson,** coauthor of *Intellectual Capital*

**C. Jackson Grayson Jr.,** founder and chairman of the American Productivity & Quality Center and coauthor of *If Only We Knew What We Know*

**Frances Horibe,** president of VisionArts, Inc., and author of *Managing Knowledge Workers*

**Dorothy Leonard,** professor of business administration at the Harvard Business School and author of *Wellsprings of Knowledge*

**Michael S. Malone,** coauthor of *Intellectual Capital*

**Ikujiro Nonaka,** professor at Hitotsubashi University and coauthor of *The Knowledge-Creating Company*

**Carla O'Dell,** president of the American Productivity & Quality Center and coauthor of *If Only We Knew What We Know*

**Jeffrey Pfeffer,** professor of organizational behavior in the Graduate School of Business, Stanford University, and coauthor of *The Knowing-Doing Gap*

**Laurence Prusak,** coauthor of *Working Knowledge*

**James Brian Quinn,** professor emeritus at the Amos Tuck School at Dartmouth College

**Thomas A. Stewart,** member of the board of directors of *Fortune Magazine* and author of *Intellectual Capital*

**Robert I. Sutton,** professor of organizational behavior in the Stanford Engineering School and coauthor of *The Knowing-Doing Gap*

**Karl Erik Sveiby,** independent advisor to knowledge organizations and author of *The New Organizational Wealth*

**Hirotaka Takeuchi,** professor at Hitotsubashi University and coauthor of *The Knowledge-Creating Company*

**Scott I. Tannenbaum,** president of the Executive Consulting Group, Inc.

**Amrit Tiwana,** professor of information technology at Georgia State University and author of *The Knowledge Management Toolkit*

# 3

# Knowledge Management

In *The Guru Guide: The Best Ideas of the Top Management Thinkers,* we wrote that the discipline of organizational learning was "murky, confusing, and filled with obtuse jargon, . . . a 'big conceptual catchall' whose tentacles reached into everything from customer service to quality to corporate strategy and change."[1] Knowledge management is an erstwhile descendent of organizational learning with tacked-on subtleties of everything from reengineering to change management to technobabble. It has the same problems and possibilities as organizational learning. Knowledge management is a discipline buried in jargon and perpetually in search of itself. In other words, knowledge management is a consultant's dream—promises without end, certainties that are impregnable, definition that is impossible—a wonderful, spectacular, multimillion-dollar blur. Knowledge management's tentacles are so far reaching that it's impossible to cover the topic adequately in any single chapter, so we will not try. What we will do here is introduce you to some of the key issues addressed by knowledge-management gurus—such things as the difference between data, information, and knowledge; the difficulties organizations have in measuring their intellectual capital; the process of knowledge creation; the concept of knowledge markets; strategies for implementing knowledge management; and the human aspects of knowledge creation and transfer. We begin with the most basic of questions: What is knowledge management?

## WHAT IS KNOWLEDGE MANAGEMENT?

Scott I. Tannenbaum, president of the Executive Consulting Group, Inc., notes that, if you listen to an accountant, an information-technology expert, and a human-resource management professional discussing knowledge management, the experience will be similar to that of listening to three blind men describing an elephant.

One feels the trunk, one the leg, and another the tail. None of their descriptions match. When asked about knowledge management, for example, an accountant is likely to say that it is largely concerned with measuring the intellectual capital of a firm. The human-resource professional is likely to emphasize attracting and retaining talent and issues surrounding the creation of a "learning organization." On the other hand, the information-technology expert will likely stress that knowledge management is primarily about computer systems, "networks," "data warehousing," "systems integration," and so on. None of these descriptions is wrong, given the perspective of the individual, but they are very different. What then is knowledge management? Tannenbaum offers the following "consensus" definition:

- Knowledge management involves gathering, structuring, storing and accessing information to build knowledge. When utilized appropriately, information and computer technology can serve as powerful enablers of knowledge management, but technology in and of itself is not knowledge management.
- Knowledge management involves knowledge sharing. Without knowledge sharing, knowledge management efforts will fail. An organization's culture, dynamics and practices (e.g., reward systems) can greatly influence knowledge sharing. The cultural and social aspects of knowledge management can pose significant challenges.
- Knowledge management relies on knowledgeable people. At the moment of truth (job performance), we need competent people to interpret and utilize information effectively. We rely on key individuals to innovate and guide us. We also rely on subject matter experts to provide input into knowledge management applications. Therefore, we must consider how to attract, develop, track, and retain knowledgeable people as part of the KM [knowledge management] domain.
- Knowledge management is about enhancing organizational effectiveness. We are concerned with knowledge management because we believe it can contribute to our company's vitality and success. Efforts to measure intellectual capital and to assess the effectiveness of KM applications should help us understand the extent to which we are managing knowledge effectively.[2]

According to Tannenbaum, knowledge management may involve any or all of the following activities:

- developing shared databases about customers, common problems and prior solutions,
- identifying internal experts, clarifying what they know, and developing a yellow pages that describes these key internal resources and identifies how to find them,
- eliciting and capturing knowledge from these experts to disseminate to others,
- designing knowledge structures that help organize information in a way that is accessible and readily applicable,

- creating forums for people to share their experiences and ideas (face-to-face or at a distance via intranets, Web sites, chat rooms, e-mail, listserves, etc.),
- utilizing groupware to allow multiple people, in different locations, to work on problems together, serving as knowledge managers—soliciting, capturing, screening, and posting information within a selected knowledge domain,
- taking action to identify, track and retain talented people who possess knowledge required in key core business areas,
- designing training and other developmental activities to assess and build internal knowledge,
- implementing reward, recognition, and promotional practices that encourage information sharing (and discourage information hoarding),
- building job aids and performance support tools that allow people to access and apply knowledge when needed,
- mining large databases about customers, products, transactions, or results to identify trends and extract information nuggets,
- measuring intellectual capital in an attempt to better manage knowledge, and
- capturing and analyzing information about customer concerns, preferences, and needs from field, front line or service personnel to better understand customer trends.[3]

As we noted at the beginning of this chapter, knowledge management is about a little bit of everything. Consequently, it has been spectacularly noticed by marketers and consultants. By the late 1990s, practically every consulting firm, document-management company, and computer vendor pretended to offer some type of knowledge-management solution. Academics weighed in with their own sometimes heavy-handed approach to the subject matter. For example, two professors at Southern Illinois University offered their opinion that the goal of knowledge management is to maximize the increase in knowledge of the receiver, expressed as DK = K1−K0 where the knowledge transfer function could be written as follows:

$$K1 = [(I \times Wsystem \times BWsource) + (K0 \times Wreceiver)] \text{ where:}$$

K1 is the amount of knowledge held by the receiver.
K0 is the amount of original knowledge held by the receiver.
Wsystem is the warrant of the knowledge-management system itself.
B is a number between zero and 1 that modifies the value of warrant assigned to the provider.
Wsource is the warrant of the knowledge provider.
Wreceiver is the warrant of the receiver.
I is the target information to be transferred.[4]

Such excesses have led some of our knowledge-management gurus, such as Verna Allee, author of *The Knowledge Evolution,* to lament: "If managing knowledge is the solution, what is the question? Just exactly what are we trying to 'solve' when we attempt to manage, create, or build knowledge?"[5] Indeed, what is the question knowledge management seeks to answer? More important, why should we care? To answer those questions, we turn to the wisdom of a master chronicler of the knowledge-management field, Thomas A. Stewart.

## KNOWLEDGE: THE NEW WEALTH OF ORGANIZATIONS

Thomas A. Stewart is a member of the board of directors of *Fortune Magazine*. He has been called a leading proponent of knowledge management in the business press, primarily for a series of articles he wrote for *Fortune* in the early 1990s and for *Intellectual Capital: The New Wealth of Organizations,* the highly entertaining book on the subject he wrote in 1997. The problem we are trying to solve with knowledge management, writes Stewart, is how businesses should care for their corporate brainpower. And we should care about that, he continues, because "information and knowledge [the intellectual capital of businesses] are the thermonuclear competitive weapons of our time."[6] Welcome to the revolution, says Stewart. The knowledge economy (see Chapter 1 of this book) is an economy of the intangible. "Knowledge has become the preeminent economic resource—more important than raw material; more important often, than money. Considered as an economic output, information and knowledge are more important [today] than automobiles, oil, steel, or any of the products of the Industrial Age."[7] Want proof? Look around you, says Stewart; there is plenty of proof of the ascendance of knowledge and information. "Knowledge has become the primary ingredient of what we buy and sell."[8] For example:

- The Boeing 777 aircraft has three computers but only two engines.
- More than half the cost of finding and extracting the petroleum needed for the fuel to fly the 777 is for information.
- Today's automobile has more microchips than spark plugs, and the car's electronics are more valuable than its steel.
- Today, the value of all microchips produced exceeds the value of all steel produced, yet the chips themselves are basically nothing more than a small amount of sand. Their value lies not in their physical content but in their intellectual content, their design.

"You would be hard-pressed," writes Stewart, "to find a single industry, a single company, a single organization of any kind, that has not become more 'information intensive'—dependent on knowledge as a source of what attracts customers and clients and on information technology as a means of running the place."[9] In fact, according to the U.S. Department of Commerce, U.S. companies now spend more on information technology (computers and telecommunications) each year than they spend on industrial-age capital goods (engines and turbines, electrical distribution and control apparatus, metal-working machinery, materials handling and general industrial equipment, machinery for services, and equipment for mining and oil fields, agriculture, and construction).

Stewart cites one final piece of evidence for the ascendance of information and knowledge. Increasingly, the value of a company has less to do with its physical assets than its intellectual assets. Consider, for example, the difference between IBM, a computer company built on the industrial-age model, and Microsoft, clearly a knowledge-economy company. In 1996 IBM's total market capitalization was $70.7 billion. Microsoft's was $85.5 billion. In the same year, IBM's fixed assets (property, plant, and equipment) were worth $16.6 billion. Microsoft's were worth just $930 million. "Put another way," writes Stewart, "every $100 socked into IBM buys $23 worth of fixed assets, while the same $100 investment in Microsoft buys fixed assets worth just over a dollar. Clearly, an investor who acquires shares of Microsoft is not buying assets in any traditional sense; for that matter, he is not purchasing much in the way of assets if he buys IBM or Merck or General Electric. A dollar invested in a corporation buys something different from the same dollar invested in the same corporation a few years ago."[10] Which means, of course, that the value of the intellectual property of the company and the faith investors have in the company leaders' stewardship of that intellectual property is paramount. Value today lies in brains, not in tools, machines, and buildings. Stewart quotes the economist Brian Arthur:

> In the old economy, people bought and sold "congealed resources"—a lot of material held together by a little bit of knowledge. (Think of an ingot of aluminum, for example, made of bauxite and huge amounts of electricity according to a 100-year-old smelting process.) In the new economy, we buy and sell "congealed knowledge"—a lot of intellectual content in a physical slipcase. (Think of a piece of computer software, or a new aircraft, most of whose cost is R&D.)[11]

Value and competitive advantage come from the knowledge people hold in their heads and how they apply it. Knowledge, or intellectual capital, is the most-important corporate asset. That recognition, say our gurus, sparks the interest in knowledge management. The question then becomes, "What is this knowledge that must be managed?" or stated differently, "What is this intellectual capital that must be harnessed?"

## IN SEARCH OF INTELLECTUAL CAPITAL

Thomas Stewart defines intellectual capital as follows:

> Intellectual capital is intellectual material—knowledge, information, intellectual property, experience—that can be put to use to create wealth.[12]

He notes that the distinction between "intellectual material" and "intellectual capital" is an important one:

> An address on a Post-it note, a report fallen behind a credenza, a brainstorm while commuting to work, a piece of urgent news learned by a sales representative who can't get to a phone—all of these are intellectual material, but none is capital. An untethered idea or a mere piece of information—John Doe's address, say—isn't an asset, any more than a pile of bricks is a factory.
>
> *Intelligence becomes an asset when some useful order is created out of free-floating brainpower—that is, when it is given coherent form (a mailing list, a database, an agenda for a meeting, a description of a process); when it is captured in a way that allows it to be described, shared, and exploited; and when it can be deployed to do something that could not be done if it remained scattered around like so many coins in a gutter. Intellectual capital is packaged useful knowledge.*[13]

Fine, you say. Intellectual capital is packaged useful knowledge, but exactly what is "packaged useful knowledge," and equally important, where do you find it? Where does someone look for a company's intellectual capital? Two knowledge-management gurus who have sought answers to such questions are Leif Edvinsson and Michael S. Malone, the coauthors of *Intellectual Capital: Realizing Your Company's True Value by Finding Its Hidden Roots.*[14]

Edvinsson and Malone identify two forms of intellectual capital that they say form the roots of every company's value:

> 1. **Human capital.** The combined knowledge, skill, innovativeness, and ability of the company's individual employees to meet the task at hand. It also includes the company's values, culture, and philosophy. Human capital cannot be owned by the company.
> 2. **Structural capital.** The hardware, software, databases, organizational structure, patents, trademarks, and everything else of organizational capability that support those employees' productivity—in a word, everything left at the office when the employees go home. Structural capital also includes customer capital, the relationships developed with key customers. Unlike human capital, structural capital can be owned and thereby traded.[15]

Knowledge management, say our gurus, is at least about nurturing human capital and then turning human capital into structural capital (see Exhibit 3.1).

(See Exhibit 3.2 for types of intellectual capital identified by other gurus.)

> Trying to identify and manage knowledge assets is like trying to fish barehanded. It can be done, . . . but the object of the effort is damnably elusive.
>
> *Thomas A. Stewart*[16]

EXHIBIT 3.1. **Edvinsson and Malone: Two Types of Intellectual Capital**

EXHIBIT 3.2. **Types of Intellectual Capital**

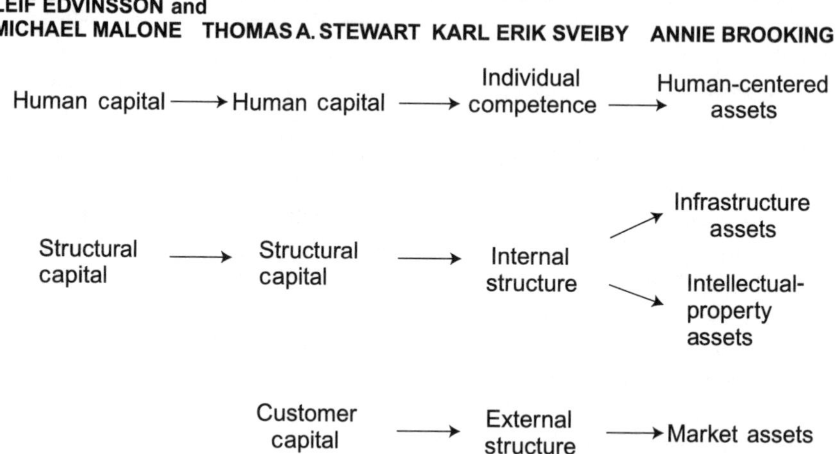


### Leif Edvinsson and Michael Malone

**Human capital.** The combined knowledge, skill, innovativeness, and ability of the company's individual employees to meet the task at hand. It also includes the company's values, culture, and philosophy. Human capital cannot be owned by the company.

**Structural capital.** The hardware, software, databases, organizational structure, patents, trademarks, and everything else of organizational capability that supports those employees' productivity. Structural capital also includes customer capital, the relationships developed with key customers. Unlike human capital, structural capital can be owned and thereby traded.

(continued)

**Thomas A. Stewart**

**Human capital.** The capabilities of the individuals required to provide solutions to customers . . . *Human Capital* . . . is the source of innovation and renewal, whether from brainstorms in a lab or new leads in a sales rep's little black book.

**Structural capital.** The organizational capabilities of the organization to meet market requirements. It includes such things as information systems, laboratories, competitive and market intelligence, knowledge of market channels, and management focus.

**Customer capital.** The value of an organization's relationships with the people with whom it does business. Brand equity is one form of customer capital.

**Karl Erik Sveiby**

**Individual competence.** Education, experience.

**Internal structure.** The organization's management, legal structure, manual systems, attitudes, R&D, software.

**External structure.** Brands, customer and supplier relationships.

**Annie Brooking**

**Human-centered assets.** The collective expertise, creative and problem-solving capability, leadership, entrepreneurial and managerial skills embodied by the employees of the organization.

**Infrastructure assets.** The managerial philosophy, corporate culture, management and business processes, financial relations, methodologies, and IT (information technology) systems that enable the organization to function.

**Intellectual-property assets.** Patents, copyright, design rights, trade secrets, trademarks, and other properties of the mind that belong to the company.

**Market assets.** Brands, positioning, customer base, company name, backlog, distribution channels, collaborations, franchise agreements, licensing agreements, favorable contracts, and so on that belong to the company and give it power in the marketplace.

*Sources:* Leif Edvinsson and Michael S. Malone, *Intellectual Capital: Realizing Your Company's True Value by Finding Its Hidden Roots* (New York: HarperBusiness, 1997), p. 11; Thomas A. Stewart, *Intellectual Capital: The New Wealth of Organizations* (New York: Doubleday, 1998), pp. 76–77; Karl Erik Sveiby, *The New Organizational Wealth: Managing and Measuring Knowledge-Based Assets* (San Francisco: Berrett-Koehler, 1997), p. 12; and Annie Brooking, *Corporate Memory: Strategies for Knowledge Management* (New York: International Thomson Business Press, 1999), pp. 16–22.

# THE HARSH REALITIES OF KNOWLEDGE MANAGEMENT

Knowledge management sounds like a straightforward concept. Nurture human capital. Then turn your human capital into structural capital. However, it is rarely so simple. Our knowledge-management gurus are bedeviled by three unsettling realities that make the implementation of knowledge management difficult, to say the least:

1. Knowledge is easy to talk about but hard to define.
2. The most-important knowledge is hard to share.
3. It is incredibly difficult to measure the true value of your knowledge assets.

Let's look at each of these realities.

## Reality #1: Knowledge Is Hard to Define

Quick. What is the difference between data, information, and knowledge? Here is how Thomas H. Davenport and Laurence Prusak, coauthors of *Working Knowledge,* define these terms. (Also see Exhibit 3.3 for a complete "Knowledge Archetype" offered by Vera Allee.)

- **Data.** "Data is a set of discrete, objective facts about events. In an organizational context, data is most usefully described as structured records of transactions. When a customer goes to a gas station and fills the tank of his car, that transaction can be partly described by data: when he made the purchase; how many gallons he bought; how much he paid."[17]
- **Information.** Information is "a *message,* usually in the form of a document or an audible or visible communication. As with any message, it has a sender and a receiver. Information is meant to change the way the receiver perceives something, to have an impact on his judgment and behavior. It must inform; it's data that makes a difference. . . . Unlike data, information has meaning. . . . Not only does it potentially shape the receiver, it *has* shape: it is organized to some purpose. Data becomes information when its creator adds meaning. We transform data into information by adding value in various ways, . . . all beginning with the letter C:

  *Contexturalized:* we know for what purpose the data was gathered.
  *Categorized:* we know the units of analysis or key components of the data.
  *Calculated:* the data have been analyzed mathematically or statistically.
  *Corrected:* errors have been removed from the data.
  *Condensed:* the data have been summarized in a more concise form."[18]

- **Knowledge.** "Knowledge is a fluid mix of framed experience, values, contextual information, and expert insight that provides a framework for evaluating and incorporating new experiences and information. It originates and is applied in the minds of knowers. In organizations, it often becomes embedded not only in documents or repositories but also in organizational routines, processes, practices, and norms. . . .

Knowledge derives from information as information derives from data. If information is to become knowledge, humans must do virtually all the work. This transformation happens through such C words as:

*Comparison:* how does information about this situation compare to other situations we have known?
*Consequences:* what implications does the information have for decisions and actions?
*Connections:* how does this bit of knowledge relate to others?
*Conversation:* what do other people think about this information?

Clearly, these knowledge-creating activities take place within and between humans. While we find data in records or transactions, and information in messages, we obtain knowledge from individuals or groups of knowers, or sometimes in organizational routines. It is delivered through structured media such as books and documents, and person-to-person contacts ranging from conversations to apprenticeships."[19]

## EXHIBIT 3.3. Vera Allee's Knowledge Archetypes

Verna Allee, author of *The Knowledge Evolution,* notes that there are different levels or complexities of learning and knowing. She proposes a "Knowledge Archetype" composed of seven levels as follows. Beginning with "Data," the lowest level, each level builds on the previous one.

**Data.** Data floats like so many whitecaps in a larger sea of Information. Data becomes Information through linking and organizing with other data.

**Information.** Information becomes Knowledge when it is analyzed, linked to other information, and compared to what is already known.

**Knowledge.** Knowledge operates in the larger social context of Meaning, which encompasses archetypal patterns and forces, as well as our social and cultural biases and interpretations.

**Meaning.** Meaning, in turn, is embedded in the larger and more abstract realm of Philosophy, which is the broad territory of assumptions, beliefs, and theories about how things work.

**Philosophy.** Philosophy and the systemic thinking that typifies this level are embedded in the yet more inclusive Wisdom perspective of values.

**Wisdom.** Wisdom enfolds our values and purpose. It encompasses the totality of our worldview.

**Union.** Union is an open, all inclusive, expansive feeling state of oneness enabled by the intellect that allows us to understand and change our values in relation to the ultimate good.

*Source:* Verna Allee, *The Knowledge Evolution: Expanding Organizational Intelligence* (Boston: Butterworth-Heinemann, 1997), p. 62.

Davenport and Prusak say that knowledge is such a slippery concept that it helps to understand some of its key components, including experience, truth, complexity, judgment, rules of thumb, and values and beliefs.

- **Experience.** People develop knowledge over time through experience, including the experience of reading books and taking courses. Because these "experts" have "been there and done it," they can recognize patterns and make connections between what is happening in the present and similar situations that happened in the past. In short, write Davenport and Prusak, experience is integral to true knowledge. (Note that James Brian Quinn defines four levels of knowledge that professionals might have about a subject matter depending on the amount and type of experience they have. See Exhibit 3.4.)
- **Truth.** Knowledge has what the U.S. Army's Center for Army Lessons terms "ground truth," or truth born of real world situations and not just theory or conjecture. People who have knowledge tell "war stories" and talk of "life in the trenches." "In other words," write Davenport and Prusak, "they share the detail and meaning of real experiences because they understand that knowledge of the everyday, complex, often messy reality of work is generally more valuable than theories about it."[20]

EXHIBIT 3.4. **James Brian Quinn's Levels of Knowledge**

| | |
|---|---|
| Level 1: Know-what | Cognitive knowledge, the kind a student might have when she graduates from college. |
| Level 2: Know-how | Ability to translate book knowledge into real-world results. This is the kind of knowledge the college graduate might develop after several years of being exposed to real-world, complex problems. |
| Level 3: Know-why | A deep understanding of the complex cause-and-effect relationships that underlie events and situations. This is the kind of knowledge one might develop on the basis of extensive problem-solving experience and discussions about this experience with others. |
| Level 4: Care-why | Self-motivated creativity. People with this level of knowledge have the will, motivation, and adaptability for success.<br>(Note: Amrit Tiwana says this is the only level of knowledge that cannot be supported by a knowledge management system.) |

*Source:* Adapted from Amrit Tiwana, *The Knowledge Management Toolkit: Practical Techniques for Building a Knowledge Management System* (Upper Saddle River, NJ: Prentice Hall PTR, 2000) p. 74; and David A. Klein, The Strategic Management of Intellectual Capital (Boston: Butterworth-Heinemann, 1997), p. 88.

- **Complexity.** Knowledge is valuable because people with knowledge can deal with complex problems in a complex way. That's a key part of the value of knowledge. People without knowledge are apt to look for clear, certain, and simple answers to complex problems. Consequently, they often get the answer wrong or only partially right.
- **Judgment.** People with knowledge use that knowledge to judge new situations in light of what they already know. They can also judge the adequacy of what they know and adapt and refine their knowledge in the light of new information and situations.
- **Rules of Thumb.** People with knowledge develop rules of thumb: shortcuts to solutions to problems that are drawn from trial and error and long experience. They apply these rules of thumb to respond appropriately to new situations.
- **Values and Beliefs.** Finally, say Davenport and Prusak, "values and beliefs are integral to knowledge, determining in large part what the knower sees, absorbs, and concludes from his observations. People with different values 'see' different things in the same situation and organize their knowledge by their values."[21]

See Exhibit 3.5 for some examples of data, information, and knowledge provided by Thomas A. Stewart, Annie Brooking, Amrit Tiwana, author of *The Knowledge Management Toolkit,* and Verna Allee.

If Davenport and Prusak's classification scheme sounds simple and logical to you, that's because it is simple and logical. The problem is that in the real world things are rarely simple and sometimes not even logical. As soon as a company's techies actually try to use the simple, logical data-information-knowledge classification scheme to do some "data warehousing" or "knowledge management," problems immediately arise. Knowledge is a slippery concept, as Stewart explains:

> The idea that knowledge can be slotted into a . . . hierarchy is bogus, for the simple reason that one man's knowledge is another man's data. For example, a lifetime of newspapers, magazines, conversations, and experience may give a voter political beliefs that she considers to be knowledge even wisdom. But what's knowledge to her is mere data to the poll taker hired by a politician running for reelection. Conversely, that politician's long-incubated and hard-won expertise in, say, environmental policy is just one bit of data in the voter's evaluation of his performance in office.
>
> Like beauty, knowledge exists in the eye of the beholder. Knowing the probably minuscule changes in the price of a company's stock just before or after it posts a quarterly dividend is of such trivial import to most investors that they consider it no better than data, and probably noise; but it's cornerstone knowledge to the "quants" at Fletcher Capital Management and a few other companies, who bet and make their fortunes by trying to exploit just such tiny changes.[22]

EXHIBIT 3.5. **Examples of Data, Information, and Knowledge**

| | Thomas Stewart | Annie Brooking | Amrit Tiwana | Verna Allee |
|---|---|---|---|---|
| **Data** | The temperature is 77 degrees. | Sequences of numbers, letters, pictures, etc. presented without a context. | I look up information about a flight from Atlanta, Georgia, to Shanghai, China, on a travel agent's Web site. The departure times are data. | I admire a painting and learn the name of the artist (a piece of data). |
| **Information** | That's hot for this time of the year. | Organized data, tables, sales statistics, a well-presented talk when presented in context. | I know that the flight will stop in London and that a flight that leaves in one hour will stop at Heathrow Airport while one that leaves in two hours will stop at Gatwick Airport. I have information. | I learn that the artist is one of several French Impressionists. (Now I have some *Information*.) |

(continued)

EXHIBIT 3.5. **(continued)**

| | Thomas Stewart | Annie Brooking | Amrit Tiwana | Verna Allee |
|---|---|---|---|---|
| **Knowledge** | We should postpone the ski trip. | Organized information, together with an understanding of what it means. | I know from a previous flight that flights originating in North America and stopping at Heathrow have to transfer passengers to Gatwick Airport for their connecting flights to the Asian continent. And I know that the bus ride from Heathrow to Gatwick takes over an hour. I realize that because of the transfer the plane that leaves in one hour will not get me to Asia any quicker than the plane that leaves in two hours. I use my judgment, based upon my past experience and take the later flight. I have knowledge. | I decide I like this style of painting and begin to learn about other French Impressionists and some of the particulars about their lives and work. (I now have *Knowledge* of French Impressionists.) |

*Source:* Thomas A. Stewart, *Intellectual Capital: The New Wealth of Organizations* (New York: Doubleday, 1998), p. 69; Annie Brooking, *Corporate Memory: Strategies for Knowledge Management* (New York: International Thomson Business Press, 1999), pp. 4–5; Amrit Tiwana, *The Knowledge Management Toolkit: Practical Techniques for Building a Knowledge Management System* (Upper Saddle River, NJ: Prentice Hall PTR, 2000), p. 59; and Verna Allee, *The Knowledge Evolution: Expanding Organizational Intelligence* (Boston: Butterworth-Heinemann, 1997), pp. 63–64.

Stewart asserts that there is a vital lesson about knowledge management to be learned from the unfortunate reality that knowledge is a messy concept. "Knowledge assets, like money or equipment, exist and are worth cultivating only in the context of strategy. You cannot define and manage intellectual assets unless you know what you are trying to do with them."[23]

## Reality #2: Much of the Really Useful Knowledge Is Hard to Share

In their 1995 book *The Knowledge-Creating Company,* Ikujiro Nonaka and Hirotaka Takeuchi draw an important distinction between the way Western and Japanese managers view knowledge.

> [Western managers] take for granted a view of the organization as a machine for "information processing." This view is deeply ingrained in the traditions of Western management, from Frederick Taylor to Herbert Simon. And it is a view of knowledge as necessarily "explicit"—something formal and systematic. Explicit knowledge can be expressed in words and numbers, and easily communicated and shared in the form of hard data, scientific formulae, codified procedures, or universal principles. Thus knowledge is viewed synonymously with a computer code, a chemical formula, or a set of general rules. . . .
>
> Japanese companies, however, have a very different understanding of knowledge. They recognize that the knowledge expressed in words and numbers represents only the tip of the iceberg. They view knowledge as being primarily "tacit"—something not easily visible and expressible. Tacit knowledge is highly personal and hard to formalize, making it difficult to communicate or to share with others. Subjective insights, intuitions, and hunches fall into this category of knowledge. Furthermore, tacit knowledge is deeply rooted in an individual's action and experience, as well as in the ideals, values, or emotions he or she embraces.[24]

Nonaka and Takeuchi say that there are two dimensions to tacit knowledge—technical and cognitive. The technical dimension "encompasses the kind of informal and hard-to-pin-down skills or crafts captured in the term 'know-how.'"[25] It is the expertise at their fingertips that master craftspeople compile after years of experience. The cognitive dimension consists of schemata, mental models, beliefs, and perceptions that provide a image of reality (what is) and a vision of the future (what ought to be) that shape how we perceive the world around us.

Tacit knowledge, write Nonaka and Takeuchi, is the kind of knowledge that is highly personal and hard to formalize and thus difficult for people to share with others. Yet tacit knowledge is very likely the most-important knowledge in the organization because it is critical to the creation of new knowledge. (For a slightly different view of the value of tacit knowledge, see Exhibit 3. 6.)

## EXHIBIT 3.6. **Tacit Knowledge and Innovation**

In a 1998 *California Management Review* article on the role of tacit knowledge in innovation, Dorothy Leonard and Sylvia Sensiper argue that tacit knowledge is extremely valuable to organizations in three ways.

1. Problem solving. Experts with tacit knowledge can usually solve a problem quicker and easier than novices because they can bring to bare a pattern that is born of experience. They quickly recognize the situation they are in and know instinctively what solutions might work.
2. Problem framing. Experts can employ tacit knowledge to reframe or restate the problem under consideration and thereby avoid the "obvious" or usual answers. For example, consultants sometimes find themselves uneasy with the way a client identifies a problem and the specifications they are given for a solution. They "know" that the real problem they should be addressing is different from the one the client is proposing although they may find it difficult to explain their unease logically and rationally.
3. Prediction and anticipation. Experts who have studied a phenomenon deeply often develop a semiconscious understanding that allows them to anticipate or predict events or have hunches or sudden flashes of insight.

*Source:* Dorothy Leonard and Sylvia Sensiper, "The Role of Tacit Knowledge in Group Innovation," *California Management Review,* Spring 1998, pp. 113–114.

Nonaka and Takeuchi argue that new organizational knowledge emerges from the interaction of tacit and explicit knowledge in a spiraling conversion process that consists of the following four steps, as illustrated in Exhibit 3.7.

## EXHIBIT 3.7. **Interaction of Tacit and Explicit Knowledge**

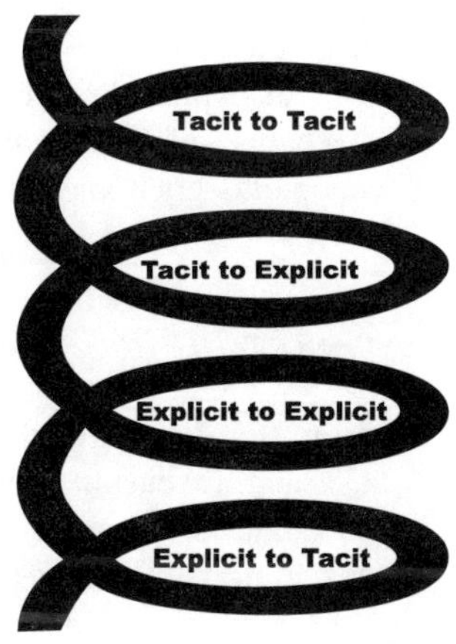

### Step #1: Socialization—Tacit to Tacit

In this stage, individuals share their tacit knowledge by being together, observing each other, and living in the same environment. (See our discussion of what are called "Communities of Practice" later in this chapter for more information on how this tacit-to-tacit knowledge exchange occurs.)

The key to this step, say our gurus, is experience. "Apprentices work with their masters and learn craftsmanship not through language but through observation, imitation, and practice."[26] New employees learn from experienced workers through on-the-job training. In Japan, Honda has used informal, off-site "brainstorming camps," called *tama dashi kai,* to accomplish this kind of tacit-to-tacit knowledge exchange in order to solve difficult problems in product development:

> The meetings are held outside the workplace, often at a resort inn where participants discuss difficult problems while drinking sake, sharing meals, and taking a bath together in a hot spring. The meetings are not limited to project team members but are open to any employees who are interested in the development project under way. In these discussions, the qualifications or status of the discussants are never questioned, but there is one taboo: criticism without constructive suggestions. Discussions are held with the understanding that "making criticism is ten times easier than coming up with a constructive alternative."[27]

### Step #2: Externalization—Tacit to Explicit

During this stage, the tacit knowledge acquired in step one is expressed in comprehensible forms. This stage, say our gurus, is the quintessential stage of the knowledge-creation process because it is the stage in which tacit knowledge is made explicit through the use of metaphors, analogies, and models.

### Step #3: Combination—Explicit to Explicit

During this stage, different bodies of explicit knowledge are combined through telephone conversations, the exchange of documents, meetings, the sorting, adding, combining, and categorizing of explicit knowledge in computer databases, and so on.

### Step #4: Internalization—Explicit to Tacit

Finally, the explicit knowledge from step 3 is converted once more to tacit knowledge. This process, write Nonaka and Takeuchi, is helped along if the explicit knowledge is incorporated into documents, manuals, or oral stories "Documentation," they write, "helps individuals internalize what they have experienced, thus enriching their tacit knowledge. In addition, documents or manuals facilitate the transfer of explicit knowledge to other people, thereby helping them experience the experiences of others indirectly. . . . If reading or listening to a success story makes some members of the organization feel the realism and essence of the story, the experience that took place in the past may change into a tacit mental model."[28] That new tacit knowledge can then be shared through socialization, made explicit through externalization, and so on. The knowledge-creation cycle continues, at least in theory. (See Exhibit 3.8 for an example of how Nonaka and Takeuchi's knowledge-creation cycle works in practice.)

## EXHIBIT 3.8. Knowledge Creation in Practice: The Matsushita Home Bakery Story

In the mid-1980s, Matsushita Electric Industrial Co., Ltd., set out to develop the first fully automatic bread-making machine for home use. In January 1985, the company created an 11-member cross-disciplinary team to design the product. The team was given the following product specifications:

The machine should knead, ferment, and bake bread automatically once the ingredients are put into the machine. Additional requirements included the following:

1. The machine should not need a special mix of ingredients.
2. A built-in timer must be provided to allow the user to prepare the ingredients at night and have bread ready to serve in the morning.
3. The bread making process must not be affected by room temperature.
4. The bread should be square to resemble English bread.
5. The bread produced by the machine should taste better than mass-produced and mass-marketed bread.
6. The retail price should be between 30,000 and 40,000 yen.

After a first abortive attempt that produced a prototype machine that yielded bread with an overcooked crust and raw dough inside, the design team decide to start over. The knowledge creating cycle began. [In their description of this process, Nonaka and Takeuchi take the reader through three complete cycles to show how the knowledge-creating spiral works. For simplicity, we show only one of the three cycles here.]

### Step #1: Socialization—Tacit to Tacit

One of the problems that the designed team faced was how to mechanize the dough-kneading process. In an effort to understand the tacit dough-kneading knowledge that master bread makers possessed, the team decided to send the head of software development, Ikuko Tanaka, to apprentice with the head baker at the Osaka International Hotel. There she learned kneading skills through observation, imitation, and practice.

(continued)

EXHIBIT 3.8. **(continued)**

**Step #2: Externalization—Tacit to Explicit**

One of the things that Tanaka learned from her apprenticeship was that in addition to stretching the dough during kneading, the master baker was also twisting the dough. The stretching and twisting motion seemed to be a secret of tasty bread, but neither Tanaka nor the master baker could explain to Matsushita's engineers how or why the process worked. Finally, Tanaka came up with the phrase "twisting stretch" to provide a rough image to the engineers of what the master baker was doing. The engineers *externalized* this tacit knowledge by designing special ribs inside the dough case to provide the "twisting stretch" motion.

**Step #3: Combination—Explicit to Explicit**

The "twisting stretch" concept and technological knowledge of the engineers was *combined* to produce a prototype.

**Step #4: Internalization—Explicit to Tacit**

Prior to the development of the Home Bakery, Matsushita had the reputation of being a conservative, status-quo oriented, price-based competitor. The success of the Home Bakery changed attitudes inside the company about the possibilities of new products and processes. Engineers *internalized* the technical and cultural lessons from the Home Bakery project. Later they were able to use this tacit knowledge to produce a string of new consumer products including a coffee maker that ground beans and brewed coffee automatically.

*Source:* Ikujiro Nonaka and Hirotaka Takeuchi, *The Knowledge-Creating Company* (New York: Oxford University Press, 1995), pp. 95–123.

Although the Nonaka-Takeuchi model sounds simple, in reality the sharing of tacit knowledge through socialization, and particularly the conversion of tacit knowledge to explicit knowledge during the externalization stage, is not easy. Dorothy Leonard, author of *Wellsprings of Knowledge,* writes in a 1998 article entitled "The Role of Tacit Knowledge in Group Innovation" that many barriers to generating and sharing tacit knowledge exist in organizations, including the following:

- Organizational reward systems may discourage people from sharing what they know. Why should I share the expertise that makes me valuable?
- Inequality in status may inhibit people from sharing. For example, nurses are often hesitant to suggest patient treatments to doctors.
- Both physical distance and distance in time may make it difficult for people to share the tacit dimensions of what they know. While modern communication technology can help, Leonard says, some preliminary research suggests that at least a certain level of face-to-face encounters and level of personal intimacy may be necessary before tacit knowledge can be shared.

- Business working groups often have a strong preference for communication styles that are logical, rational, and based on hard data. "Even if an individual could make some of the tacit dimensions of his or her knowledge explicit in the form of a physical demonstration or a drawing, such information would rarely be given a hearing because such evidence is not regarded in most business settings as relevant or useful unless backed up with analysis."[29]
- Finally, says Leonard, individuals possessing deep tacit knowledge may resist sharing it simply because they are afraid that their efforts to do so will fail. How do you express the inexpressible?

And there may be still another reason why knowledge isn't shared. Thomas Davenport and Laurence Prusak believe that there is a genuine market for knowledge in organizations and that how rapidly or slowly, usefully or unproductively knowledge flows though an organization depends on the efficiency of its knowledge market.

> Like markets for goods and services, the knowledge market has buyers and sellers who negotiate to reach a mutually satisfactory price for the goods exchanged. It has brokers who bring buyers and sellers together and even entrepreneurs who use their market knowledge to create internal power bases. Knowledge market transactions occur because all of the participants in them believe that they will benefit from them in some particular way. In economists' jargon, they expect the transactions to provide "utility."[30]

When knowledge markets work reasonably efficiently, write Davenport and Prusak, then knowledge is shared. "Knowledge buyers and sellers find each other and exchange their goods readily. A clear pricing system enables them to agree on the value of the goods being sold with the least possible friction. They have identical or similar ideas of the value of the currency used to buy the goods."[31] All goes well. However, in most organizations, argue our gurus, things don't go well. The knowledge market isn't efficient. In fact, it may be truly dysfunctional, as the following list demonstrates:

- Knowledge buyers and sellers can't find each other because there are no Yellow Pages or road maps to tell the buyers where the knowledge sellers are.
- There may be knowledge feasts and famines. For example, the marketing department may have a vast amount of information about customers that the sales department needs, but no mechanism exists by which the information can be shared.
- There may be knowledge monopolies. One person or group has exclusive or near-exclusive control over key knowledge and uses that knowledge to establish a position of power. The knowledge might be shared occasionally or rented but only at a high price.
- Knowledge hoarding may occur, resulting in an artificial scarcity of knowledge.

- Actual knowledge scarcity may occur due to downsizing and a resultant "brain drain."
- There even may be a "not-invented-here" mentality in the organization that effectively creates trade barriers that hamper the smooth functioning of the knowledge market.

Any and all of these conditions may make the knowledge market dysfunctional. Neither tacit nor explicit knowledge may be shared. Carla O'Dell and C. Jackson Grayson Jr. argue that there are even organizational personalities that inhibit knowledge transfer. (See Exhibit 3.9 for a discussion of these personalities.)

Later in this chapter, we will discuss some of our gurus' recommendations for overcoming these and other barriers to knowledge sharing and opening up knowledge markets. Suffice it to say at this point that the sharing of tacit, and sometimes even explicit, knowledge is much easier to describe than it is to accomplish.

### EXHIBIT 3.9. Organizational Personalities That Inhibit Knowledge Sharing

Carla O'Dell and C. Jackson Grayson Jr. state that the following five organizational personalities (sets of organizational structures, management practices, and measurement systems) discourage rather than encourage knowledge sharing. They warn that it is naive to ignore these ingrained personalities when designing knowledge-management systems.

- **The Silo Company, Inc.** This multinational company has structures that clearly promote "silo" thinking and behavior on the part of managers and employees. Silos can be as small as a function or department and as large as a division or business unit. Each, however, is focused on maximizing its own accomplishments and rewards. Groups tend to hoard information to prevent others from excelling while improving their own relative performance. As a result, they substantially suboptimize the performance of the organization as a whole. . . .
- **The NIH Company, Inc.** At the world-famous NIH Company, the prevailing culture values personal technical expertise and knowledge creation over knowledge sharing, on either the micro (interdepartmental) or macro (intercompany) level. Otherwise known as the Not Invented Here (NIH) syndrome, this sort of attitude is rampant in engineering-based organizations as well as knowledge-based organizations, such as consulting and research firms. The reason is simple enough: For these companies, the ability to provide unique products and services is the key value proposition and business driver. The emphasis is therefore on invention rather than adaptation of existing ideas/technologies. Whether on a corporate ("we don't use what others have invented") or intracompany basis (an employee's value is determined by original thought, not necessarily clever commercialization), the resulting culture makes individuals feel "bad" if they "borrow" someone else's idea. . . . [See a discussion of how to fight NIH syndrome later in this chapter.]

(continued)

EXHIBIT 3.9. **(continued)**

- **The Babel Company, Inc.** This company suffers from an acute case of "Babelitis." Far-flung employees and sometimes even co-workers lack a set of common perspectives and terms that can serve as the basis for effective communications and transfer of knowledge. In many cases, the left hand does not fully know or understand what the right hand is doing; it may not even know there is a right hand. Different departments use different words to describe, catalogue, and record their processes and practices. Such departmental dialect impedes cross-functional discourse. There is no single, coherent vocabulary to express processes and performance. Employees may be willing to share and absorb, but without a common "book of reference" this company cannot begin to record its collective know-how and best practices. No one would understand them.
- **The By-the-Book Company, Inc.** The By-the-Book Company is not averse to sharing. In fact, however, it considers documented knowledge the end-all and be-all of knowledge transfer. By-the-Book exhibits a serious tendency to rely solely on transmitting "explicit" rather than "tacit" knowledge. It builds elaborate databases and implements distributed computing platforms that allow one and all to record and access documented knowledge. That's valuable stuff. The problem is that most of the important information people need in order to implement a practice cannot be codified or written down.
- **The Bolt-It-On Company.** This enterprising firm believes you can add transfer and sharing responsibilities on top of everyone's regular work process and expect to get results. With lots of fanfare and high hopes, Bolt-It-On starts "sharing" programs, on-line chat groups, and the like. Then waits . . . and waits . . . and not much happens.

O'Dell and Grayson say that recognizing, understanding, and changing these organizational personalities are some of the highest hurdles managers face in managing knowledge. But they are hurdles that must be faced and surmounted.

*Source:* Carla O'Dell and C. Jackson Grayson Jr., *If Only We Knew What We Know* (New York: Free Press, 1998), pp. 18–19.

## Reality #3: Knowledge Is Difficult to Measure

Thomas A. Stewart writes that "one of the reasons organizations don't manage knowledge is that it almost always comes wrapped in some tangible form—in the paper of a book, in the magnetic tape of an audiocassette, in the body of a speaker, in the stones of a historical monument."[32] Companies manage the forms rather than the substance, which, says Thomas, is like a viticulturist paying more attention to the bottle than the wine inside it. But what are managers to do? They can see and count their knowledge "bottles." They can't see, much less count, the knowledge "wine," making knowledge difficult to measure.

The knowledge-measurement issue isn't about demonstrating return on investment for a single knowledge-management project or limited consultant engagement. Consultants are masters at doing that, as the examples at Exhibit 3.10 substantiate. The measurement problem is more fundamental. It has to do with establishing and accounting for value. Perhaps more important from a management and investor perspective, it is about predicting value. How, why, and approximately when will value be generated from an investment in and accumulation of knowledge resources and intellectual assets? Our gurus say that most companies cannot answer those questions.

### EXHIBIT 3.10. **Results from Knowledge-Management Projects**

Here are some documented results of knowledge-management-projects as reported by Carla O'Dell and C. Jackson Grayson Jr.

- At Buckman Laboratories, their transfer of knowledge and best practices system helped push new product-related revenues up 10 percentage points and sales of new products up about 50 percent (from 22 percent to almost 35 percent in 1996). Responding to customer inquiries about products now takes hours instead of weeks.
- Texas Instruments generated $1.5 billion in annual increased fabrication capacity (in effect, a "free" plant) by comparing and transferring best practices among its existing thirteen fabrication plants. Plant managers and teams from Texas Instruments' Semiconductor Group, led by that group's president, created the equivalent capacity of an additional semiconductor wafer fabrication plant, thereby avoiding a $500 million investment and providing needed capacity to customers. They called it a "free fab," and have repeated this triumph two more times, for a total of more than $1.5 billion in cost avoidance, in addition to going from last (1992) to first (1994) in on-time delivery satisfaction in customer rankings.
- At Dow Chemical, early efforts to manage intellectual capital brought an immediate kickback in the form of $40 million in savings. Analysis of existing patents to determine which technology streams were the strongest and which were weakest allowed more effective negotiations with joint venture partners.
- At Kaiser Permanente, benchmarking of their internal best practices helped drastically cut the time it took to open a new Woman's Health Clinic. And it opened smoothly, with no costly start-up problems.
- At CIGNA Property & Casualty, knowledge-sharing efforts, combined with a reengineering campaign, lifted profits back into the black. In 1993, CIGNA lost more than a quarter of a billion dollars. By 1995, it sported a $90 million profit and has continued with healthy profits since then.
- Skandia has leveraged internal know-how to dramatically reduce start-up time for new ventures to seven months, compared to an industry average of seven years.

*Source:* Carla O'Dell and C. Jackson Grayson Jr., *If Only We Knew What We Know* (New York: Free Press, 1998), pp. 8–9.

The problem, writes Stewart, is that most companies are still stuck with accounting practices that assume that labor and materials account for most of the value of a business, and therefore they only measure those assets.

> People who allocate resources—managers, the board, investors—get plenty of information about physical and financial assets. They can tell you how much money a company has in the bank, how large a credit line it has, the price of its stock, the value of its land and buildings; they can and do measure its use of working capital, inventories, and the like.[33]

While such measurement may have been appropriate for an economy of "congealed resources," says Stewart, they are totally inadequate for an economy of "congealed knowledge." Yet such measures are the only ones most companies and investors have. Consequently, the value of knowledge assets is frequently unaccounted for or is tremendously undervalued. Stewart cites the valuation of Andrew Lloyd Webber's company as a case in point:

> In 1976, Andrew Lloyd Webber, the composer/creator of the musicals *Cats, Evita, Phantom of the Opera,* and *Sunset Boulevard,* among others, formed The Really Useful Company, which held the rights to all his work. Whatever you think of Webber's music, The Really Useful Company's leader has written Really Successful Stuff. In 1986, Webber took the company public. Its assets: the Palace Theatre in London, worth about £2 million, the rights to Webber's musicals and songs (chiefly *Cats*), a seven-year contract with Webber, and an insurance policy on his life (he was thirty-seven). The deal was done; the total value of all the shares, including a sizable chunk Webber retained, was £35.2 million. Four years later, Webber bought it back. Based on what he paid for the shares he didn't already own, the value of the company was now £77.4 million—a figure derived chiefly from calculations by investment bankers who used established ways to evaluate intellectual property like copyrights and patents. A year later, Webber sold 30 percent of the company to the record company PolyGram. The price: £78 million, more than the entire operation was supposedly worth a year before. Webber's *Sunset Boulevard* had opened in the meantime, but that did not turn out to be the main reason the company more than tripled in value. Rather, the City's best analysts had grievously underestimated the revenue and hence the worth of the old copyrights.[34]

Of course, bean counters don't totally ignore intellectual assets. When a company is sold for more than its book value, the difference has to be taken into account because accounting rules don't allow you to pay something for nothing. The traditional solution is simply to subtract the book value from the purchase price and assign the difference to "good will." That worked reasonably well in the old economy, but it doesn't any more. Frances Horibe, author of *Managing Knowledge*

*Workers,* cites research that shows that the "goodwill" fudge factor has grown steadily over the last 20 years. For example, one study of manufacturers found that the portion of a typical company's worth attributed to its book value had declined from 62 percent in 1982 to 38 percent in 1992. For high-tech companies, the situation was even more extreme. For example, Microsoft has traded at 10 times its book value. In other words, only 10 percent of Microsoft's worth was in hard assets, while the rest was in essentially unmeasured intellectual capital—knowledge.[35]

Our gurus have tried to address this problem with a wide range of measures of intellectual asset, some of which we discuss later in this chapter. In reality, none have really caught on. Some financial officers and economists resist the idea of cluttering corporate financial statements with what they consider "untried, possibly subjective, non-financial measures."[36] Consequently, the harsh reality remains. A company's knowledge assets are difficult, some would even argue impossible, to measure.

## IMPLEMENTING KNOWLEDGE MANAGEMENT

Despite the harsh realities we have just discussed, our gurus argue that there are compelling reasons for you and your company to undertake the difficult task of managing knowledge. Knowledge, Thomas A. Stewart asserts, is the new wealth of organizations, and you had better manage that wealth judiciously. The question then becomes, How? Where do you begin? What exactly do you do first, second, and third? What steps should you follow to effectively manage your most-valuable resource? Here, most of our gurus are long on theory—as we have seen—and extremely short on practical steps. An exception is Amrit Tiwana. In his book *The Knowledge Management Toolkit,* he offers one of the first genuine how-to guides for knowledge management. His 10-step road map may not be perfect—in fact, we believe he places far too much emphasis on the technical issues—but it is one of the most specific implementation plans published to date. Here are Tiwana's 10 steps:

1. Analyze the existing infrastructure.
2. Align knowledge management and business strategy.
3. Design the knowledge-management infrastructure.
4. Audit existing knowledge assets and systems.
5. Design the knowledge-management team.
6. Create the knowledge-management blueprint.
7. Develop the knowledge-management system.
8. Prototype and deploy.
9. Manage the change, culture, and reward structures.
10. Evaluate performance, measure ROI (return on investment), and incrementally refine the knowledge-management system.

In the following sections, we discuss each of these steps in detail.

## Step #1: Analyze the Existing Infrastructure

Tiwana's first step is an audit of your existing technological infrastructure to determine what technology you currently have that could be used as is or enhanced to support knowledge management. He writes, "By analyzing and accounting for what is already in place in your company, you can identify critical gaps in the existing infrastructure. Consequently, you will be able to build upon what already exists. The key lies in accurately identifying *and fixing* what will work as part of the knowledge management system."[37] Tiwana notes that many of the technologies that support knowledge management have been around for some time and that you should be seeking to leverage these. Among others you should look for and evaluate, says Tiwana, are the following existing technologies.

### *Knowledge-Flow Technologies*

Knowledge-flow technologies are technologies that facilitate the flow of knowledge in your organization. Examples include the following:

- Collaborative environments and GroupWare tools such as Lotus Notes, Netscape Collabra, Microsoft's NetMeeting, and so on.
- Intranets (internal company Internet) and extranets (intranet extended to include the company's allies, partners, suppliers, and major customers).
- Pointers to expertise or electronic yellow pages that provide searchable directories of persons inside and outside the company with specific skill sets or expertise.

### *Information- or Document-Mapping Technologies*

Information- or document-mapping technologies are technologies that support versioning control, scanning/electronic formatting, indexing and retrieval, and automatic database creation.

### *Information Source Technologies*

Information source technologies feed information into the knowledge-management system. Examples include project-management tools and multimedia technology. Tiwana notes that, although the role of project-management tools in the actual creation of knowledge is limited, "these tools can provide a good basis for organizing and storing documents, records, notes, etc., coming out of a single project engagement."[38] Multimedia is valuable because, among other things, it bypasses the limitations of language, which can be a barrier to knowledge sharing among transnational teams.

### *Information- and Knowledge-Exchange Technologies*

Information- and knowledge-exchange technologies assist people in sharing and exchanging knowledge. Examples include such low-tech tools as the telephone and fax machine all the way to Internet-conferencing systems, video-conferencing tools, and electronic chat rooms.

### *Intelligent Agent/Network-Mining Technologies*

Network-mining technologies help people locate and extract information. They include search engines, intelligent-decision support systems, case-based reasoning (CBR) systems, and contextual information retrieval systems that support filtering, editing, searching, and organizing knowledge.

## Step #2: Align Knowledge Management and Business Strategy

"If knowledge creation is to be successfully directed," writes Tiwana, "there must be an indisputable link between your company's business strategy and its knowledge management strategy. . . . An effective knowledge management strategy is not simply a technology strategy but a well-balanced mix of technology, cultural change, new reward systems, and business focus that is perfectly in step with the company's business strategy."[39]

Tiwana cites research by Morten Hansen, Nitin Nohria, and Thomas Tierney reported in the March–April 1999 *Harvard Business Review* in which the authors identify two basic approaches companies have taken to knowledge management: codification or personalization. Your choice of approach, writes Tiwana, should be consistent with your business strategy. Here is how Hansen and coauthors define the two approaches.

- **Codification.** Companies that pursue a codification strategy invest heavily in information technology in order to develop an electronic document system that codifies, stores, disseminates, and allows reuse of knowledge with the goal of connecting people to reusable knowledge.
- **Personalization.** Companies that adopt a personalization strategy invest moderately in information technology in order to develop networks that link people so that knowledge can be shared. Their goal is to facilitate conversations and the exchange of tacit knowledge.

Hansen, Nohria, and Tierney emphasize that there is no single right strategy and that most companies do some of both. However, they write, "companies that use knowledge effectively pursue one strategy predominantly and use the second strategy to support the first [in a kind of] 80–20 split: 80% of their knowledge sharing

EXHIBIT 3.11. **Choosing a Knowledge-Management Strategy**

| | **Codification** | **Personalization** |
|---|---|---|
| What is your competitive strategy? | Your strategy is to quickly provide high-quality, reliable, and cost-effective products and/or services. | Your strategy is to provide creative, rigorous, and highly customized products and services. |
| How much old material do you reuse in producing new products/services? | You frequently reuse large portions of old documents and products to create new ones. | Almost every problem is unique. You rely on cumulative learning to find highly creative solutions. Old documents/ products cannot generally be recycled or reused. |
| Do you offer standard or customized products/ services? | Standard | Customized |
| Do you have a mature or innovative product? | Mature | Innovative |
| Do your people rely largely on explicit or tacit knowledge to do their work and solve problems? | Explicit | Tacit |
| What is your costing model? | Price-based | Expertise-based |
| What is your profit margin? | Low | High |

*Source:* This discussion and list of questions is based on Morten T. Hansen, Nitin Nohria and Thomas Tierney, "What's Your Strategy for Managing Knowledge?" *Harvard Business Review,* March–April 1999, p. 115; and Amrit Tiwana, *The Knowledge Management Toolkit: Practical Techniques for Building a Knowledge Management System* (Upper Saddle River, NJ: Prentice Hall PTR, 2000), pp. 151–152.

follows one strategy, 20% the other."[40] They caution that companies that try to excel at both strategies risk failing at both. Therefore, the choice of strategy to pursue is important. How do you choose? Tiwana, Hansen, Nohria, and Tierney believe that your choice should be based on how you answer the questions in Exhibit 3.11.

## Step #3: Design the Knowledge-Management Infrastructure

In this step, you make an initial determination of the kinds of technologies and tools that you need for your knowledge-management system. Among other things you must answer the following questions.

### What Are Your Must-Have Technologies?

Given your business strategy and approach to knowledge management (see step 2), what technologies do your people need in order to find, create, assemble, and apply knowledge in a timely and cost-effective manner? These technologies include those designed to do the following:

- Assist your people in creating and acquiring knowledge by interacting, recording failures, and documenting successes.
- Support your efforts to convert tacit knowledge into explicit knowledge.
- Identify and remove hurdles to best practice and skills transfer.
- Support the rapid delivery of the right knowledge to the right person at the right time.
- Assist with the indexing, screening, classifying, aggregating, synthesizing, cataloging, and otherwise organizing of knowledge.
- Enable the package, delivery, and storage of knowledge.
- Support the importation of knowledge from outside the firm.
- Support communication and networking among employees.
- Assist with what-if analysis.

### Will Your Knowledge-Sharing User Interface Be Web-Based or Lotus Notes–Based?

Tiwana argues that the Web is a better alternative as an interface for knowledge sharing than the Notes system developed by Lotus Development Corporation, a subsidiary of IBM.

> Although solutions like Notes require less up-front development time because of their more comprehensive out-of-the-box attributes and have capabilities like replication, security controls and development tools tightly integrated with them, . . . the Web provides a universal platform for the integration of structured knowledge across any existing platform or a combination of platforms. . . .
>
> Increasingly high levels of integration of multimedia capabilities into Web browsers along with guaranteed backward compatibility allow easier representation of informal content than is possible using proprietary technology such as Notes. Since tens of thousands of companies are developing Web-based applications as compared to essentially one company (and associated developers) developing for Notes, it is more likely that cost-effective, innovative tools will first emerge for Web-based knowledge management systems. There is also a significant level of competition in the market for Web-based tools, which favorably shifts the balance toward this base in terms of price competitiveness.[41]

### To What Extent Will the Knowledge-Management System Require Tools and Technologies to Assist People in Finding, Summarizing, Interpreting, and Analyzing Large Volumes of Data?

Examples of tools and technologies that will help people find and use large volumes of data include the following:

- **Artificial intelligence,** which is "the use of human models for cognition and perception to create computer systems to solve human-like problems."[42]
- **Data mining,** "a technique to analyze data in very large databases with the goal of revealing trends and patterns."[43] (For more information about data mining see Chapter 4.)
- **Data warehouses.** Data warehouses aggregate data from multiple databases, combine their content, and make it possible to run queries across several different databases simultaneously.
- **Genetic algorithm tools.** Developed by John Holland in the 1970s, genetic algorithm tools "apply Darwin's survival of the fittest theory to computer programs and data. The programs and data that solve a problem survive and those that do not, die. . . . A genetic algorithm experiments with new and novel solutions to problems. If an experimental solution is not successful, it is assigned a low rank and discarded. If it solves a problem, such as an optimization problem, it is ranked high and retained for *genetic refinement.* The good parts of this solution are kept, and the less useful parts are simply discarded. Genetic algorithms can be used very effectively in making decisions where the amount of data to be taken into account is very large and there are discontinuities in available data."[44]
- **Neural networks.** A neural network is "a networked computing architecture in which a number of [computer] processors are interconnected in a manner suggestive of the connections between neurons in a human brain and that can learn by a process of trial and error. . . . A neural network becomes immensely promising when you have the data but lack experts to make judgments about it. A neural network can identify patterns with such data without the need for a specialist or expert."[45]
- **Expert reasoning and rule-based systems.** Rule-based systems embed the logic of experts into computer programs. For example, if {condition A is true} then {do this} otherwise {do this}.
- **Case-based reasoning.** "Case-based reasoning . . . allows companies to take advantage of previous problems or cases and related attempts to solve them. When faced with a problem, a case-based reasoning system searches its case base (i.e., a collection of previous cases) for past cases with attributes that match the current case in hand. . . . Cases that are closest matches are retrieved."[46]

### *What Level of Detail Will Your Knowledge-Management System Capture?*

Knowledge in a knowledge-management system can be captured in different levels of detail. For example, tasks in previous projects can be recorded at the level of individual steps or as broad categories of activities. Tiwana writes:

> A key failure point in the design of a knowledge management system is not deciding at the start the right level of detail. . . . Too high a level of granularity will result in loss of knowledge richness and context; too low a level will cause unnecessary drain on network, storage, and human resources, raise the cost, and reduce the value of the [knowledge] object. . . . The key lies in selecting the right level of molecularity of knowledge that will be stored in your knowledge management system: the level that strikes the optimum balance between the two opposite extremes of too much detail and too little detail, both of which can render knowledge only marginally useful.[47]

### *What Mix of Searching, Indexing, and Retrieval Components Will You Include in Your Knowledge-Management System?*

Indexing and retrieval systems assist users in finding relevant knowledge in the knowledge-management system. The following types of search facilities exist:

- **Meta searching.** Users input a key word such as *programming*. The system returns subcategories such as "Assembly Language Programming," "C&C++," "Software Design," and so on. Users then select from these subcategories to narrow their search.
- **Hierarchical searching.** "A hierarchical search strategy organizes knowledge in a fixed hierarchy. User can follow or traverse links within such a structure to efficiently locate the right knowledge element in a timely manner."[48] The concept is similar to hyperlinks on a Web page.
- **Content Search.** Users enter a keyword or text string and the system returns all documents containing matches.

### *What Knowledge Attributes Will You Use to Identify Knowledge Objects?*

Examples of attributes that can be assigned to knowledge objects include the following:

- **Activities attributes** identify the activities in the company to which the knowledge object relates. For example, a knowledge object related to the testing of computers in a computer-manufacturing company might be tagged with the activities attribute of "testing" or "quality control."

- **Form attributes** identify the physical form of the knowledge object—for example, paper, electronic, pointer—to a person with expertise in the subject matter.
- **Type attributes** refer to procedures, guidelines, manuals, best-practice reports, failure reports, success reports, press releases, and so on.
- **Product or service attributes** specify the product or service to which the knowledge object relates.

## Step #4: Audit Existing Knowledge Assets and Systems

The purpose of the knowledge audit is to assess what knowledge currently exists in the company and determine the focus for knowledge-management activities. To accomplish the audit, Tiwana suggests that you assemble an audit team composed of a corporate strategist, a senior manager, a financial officer, your human-resources manager, a marketer, an information-technology expert, and your knowledge manager, or chief knowledge officer. Among other things, the audit team should identify a minimum of five key knowledge resources they feel the company must have. (For example, knowledge of coffee making would be a key resource for a company such as Starbucks.)[49] The team should then ask the following types of questions about each of the knowledge resources:

- How is the stock of this knowledge resource increasing or decreasing?
- How can we ensure that the stock of this knowledge continues to increase?
- Are we making the best use of this knowledge resource?
- How durable is this knowledge asset?
- Can the competition easily nurture and grow this knowledge without copying it?
- Is there any aspect of this knowledge that the competition has leveraged which we have not?
- Can this knowledge "walk out the door?"
- What level of knowledge do we currently have about this product, service, or process?

In respect to the last question, Tiwana identifies nine levels (numbered from zero to 8) of knowledge a firm may possess about a product, service, or business process. He notes that most companies are at levels 2 or 3 but need to move to levels 5, 6, or 7 in order to effectively manage knowledge. The nine levels of knowledge are explained in Exhibit 3.12.

## EXHIBIT 3.12. **Nine Levels of Knowledge**

| Level | Description | Example: Knowledge of Coffee Making |
|---|---|---|
| 0 | Total ignorance | You don't know the difference between good and bad coffee. |
| 1 | Pure art | You know it when you taste good coffee. |
| 2 | Awareness | You begin to figure out that the "goodness" of coffee is related to some attributes such as strength, temperature, viscosity, etc. and that the amount of coffee beans, brewing temperature, etc. affect the "goodness" of the resulting coffee. |
| 3 | Measure | You can tell which attributes you identified at level 2 are important and unimportant. E.g., Hot coffee= 100 degrees < serving temperature > 80 degrees; Coffee made > 15 minutes ago = bad. |
| 4 | Control of the mean | You develop measures to help you make "good" coffee repeatedly.<br>• Weight of coffee beans<br>• Volume of water<br>• Brewing temperature<br>• Brewing time, etc. |
| 5 | Process capability | Your develop a formal recipe for making what is *typically* considered to be a "good" cup of coffee. This recipe or formal methodology covers all the key steps in coffee making: temperature settings, timing, amount of coffee to serve per cup, etc. |
| 6 | Process characterization | You are able to adapt the recipe for different types and flavors of coffee. For example, you know how to adjust the standard recipe to make it work for Colombian coffee versus Italian Supreme versus Starbucks house brand. |
| 7 | Know why | You have a fully blown formal model or formula. Good Coffee = (0.56 × weight of coffee beans) + (0.12 × volume of water). The formula or model specifies the exact relationship that exists between all of the important elements that go into making "good" coffee. |
| 8 | Complete knowledge | You have complete knowledge of "perfect" coffee. Rarely is the level ever reached. |

*Source:* Amrit Tiwana, *The Knowledge Management Toolkit: Practical Techniques for Building a Knowledge Management System* (Upper Saddle River, NJ: Prentice Hall PTR, 2000), pp. 245–252.

Based on the knowledge audit, the audit team determines the strategic and competitive position of the company in respect to management of its key knowledge resources and identifies the critical areas of focus for the knowledge management effort. The results of the knowledge audit become a guide for the knowledge-management design team picked in Step 5.

## Step #5: Design the Knowledge-Management Team

Tiwana recommends that you create a knowledge-management design team composed of the following:

- **Local experts and interdepartmental gurus.** These are early adopters of technology who work in the various functional areas of your company. They have knowledge of their particular subject area (e.g., marketing, finance, etc.) plus knowledge of existing technology.
- **Internal information-technology experts.**
- **Nonlocal experts and extradepartmental gurus.** These people have expertise that crosses organizational and functional boundaries. They can relate to people from different functional areas and serve as interpreters between people with different backgrounds, skills, and specialization.
- **Consultants.** These are people from outside the company with special expertise. Tiwana recommends keeping the use of external consultants to a minimum because of concerns about the possible disclosure of confidential material.
- **Senior managers.** Tiwana argues that senior managers should actively participate because their support is necessary to legitimize and champion knowledge-management efforts. Additionally, they bring a strategic perspective to the effort.

## Step #6: Create the Knowledge-Management Blueprint

In this step, the knowledge-management team designs the new knowledge-management system. The system design, says Tiwana, should contain specifications for the following key subcomponents:

- **Knowledge repositories.** These are the databases in which knowledge will be stored. There may be one or more databases, but they are all logically linked in a way that is transparent to the user.
- **Collaborative platform.** This provides users access to the knowledge databases and supports the flow of knowledge throughout the organization. Among other things, the collaborative platform makes it possible for users to search for content or subscribe to content from the databases.

- **Networks.** "Networks support communications and conversation. These might include hard networks such as your company's leased lines, your intranet, your extranets, and soft networks such as shared spaces, industry-wide firm collaborations, trade nets, industry forums, and exchanges (both live and teleconferenced)."[50]
- **Culture.** This refers to methods to encourage people to use the knowledge-management system and to share their knowledge. (See our discussion of the human aspects of knowledge management later in this chapter for more information on this subcomponent.)

## Step #7: Develop the Knowledge-Management System

This is the stage in which you put together a working version of the knowledge-management system you designed in step 6. Construction of the system, says Tiwana, involves building seven layers:

1. **Interface layer.** This top layer connects people to the knowledge-management system to create, explicate, use, retrieve, and share knowledge. It is the part of the system that the user sees and works with. For many companies, this interface layer is the home page the user accesses over the company's intranet.
2. **Access and authentication layer.** This is the layer that authenticates valid users (Who has access to which databases?), provides for security—so-called firewalls—to prevent unauthorized access, and provides for backups and disaster recovery (How will the system be restored in case of a hardware failure, security violation, breach by an undetected virus, etc.?).
3. **Collaborative filtering and intelligence layer.** This layer contains the tools for content personalization, searching, indexing, and so on. See our discussion of search facilities and knowledge attributes in step 3.
4. **Application layer.** This layer contains skills directories, yellow pages, collaborative work tools, video conferencing hardware and software, digital whiteboards, electronic forums, and so on.
5. **Transport Layer.** This layer includes the technology for TCP/IP connectivity, Web servers, POP3/SMTP or MAIL servers, support for streaming audio and video, and so on.
6. **Middleware and legacy-integration layer.** Legacy systems are mainframe and other customized and/or retired computer systems. Middleware provides connectivity between old and new data formats.
7. **Repositories.** This layer consists of the operational databases, discussion databases, Web-forum archives, legacy data, document archives, and other databases that represent the foundation of the knowledge-management system.

## Step #8: Prototype and Deploy

Tiwana suggests that you build a number of prototypes to test and incrementally refine your knowledge-management system design. He writes, "Prototypes are perhaps the most underused form of rejection insurance that a development team can ever purchase."[51] He also suggests what he calls "results-driven incrementalism" (RDI) as the best deployment strategy. (Note that RDI is similar to the phased approach to e-commerce that Gascoyne suggested in Chapter 2.)

> The RDI methodology specifies that the project be broken up into a series of short, fast-paced development cycles coupled with intensive implementation cycles, each of which delivers a measurable business benefit. . . . Benefits are realized as each discrete stage is completed . . . as opposed to cumulatively at the end of several stages.
>
> The most obvious benefit of the RDI approach is that business benefits of the knowledge management system can be realized much sooner compared to a more traditional big-bang approach. Implementers using this methodology report that the method increases not only the speed of the achievement of some tangible business benefit, it also increases the over-all level of benefits. In addition, it dramatically reduces the overall time required to implement the project. Since every step taken is a concrete one and points of failure are rectified right after that step, it is more likely that the project will actually get completed.[52]

Tiwana cites five keys to making the RDI methodology work:

1. **Objective-driven decision support.** Use targeted business results and end objectives to drive decision making at each point throughout the deployment process. For example, each phase of knowledge-management system implementation has its desired results (the whys) and projected outcomes (the so whats) clearly answered before it is initiated.

2. **Incremental but independent results.** "Divide the implementation into a series of nonoverlapping increments, each of which enables measurable business benefits and improvements, even if no further increments are implemented."[53]

3. **Software and organizational measures clearly laid out at each stage.** Each increment must implement everything required to produce the desired subset of results. This means that software functionality must be accompanied by the necessary changes in policies, processes, and measures that are needed to make it work. For example, if one step includes the deployment of a discussions database, it must be accompanied by changes that motivate employees to use it, look for information on it, and contribute to it.

The deployment plan should also include appropriate rewards that encourage employees to integrate it into existing work processes. In a collaborative environment such as a university, this would mean that participation in such discussions should or could count toward participation measures for student grades. In a software company, it might be counted toward peer-peer assistance. In a consulting company, it might count toward aggregated measures of overall participative problem solving by individual consultants.

4. **Intensive implementation schedules.** Each increment must be planned in a way that it can be implemented within a short time frame. Depending on the overall complexity of the knowledge-management project, the time for completion of each incremental feature should range from two weeks to three months.

5. **Results-driven follow-ups.** The results of each increment must be the basis for adjusting and fine-tuning potential flaws in subsequent increments.

## Step #9: Manage Change, Culture, and Reward Structures

In his introduction to this step, Tiwana writes: "Successful knowledge management takes more than just technology; it takes cultural change and a change in the reward structures that drive work in most companies. *You have to gain the hearts and the minds of the workers. They are not like troops; they are more like volunteers.*"[54]

### OUR VIEW

Tiwana is right. Knowledge management is at least as much about culture as technology. Unfortunately, for all the time he spends talking about technology in his 10-step plan, he offers very little advice on the subject of getting the culture right. He says only that you need to appoint a chief knowledge officer (CKO) or someone to champion the knowledge-management cause (see the discussion of the roles and responsibilities of the CKO in Exhibit 3.13) and that you need to revise your reward systems to encourage knowledge sharing. Dorothy Leonard offers a much better treatment of the human aspects of implementing knowledge management. We will summarize some of her key recommendations in the next section. For now, let's complete the discussion of Tiwana's 10 steps.

EXHIBIT 3.13. **Roles and Responsibilities of the Chief Knowledge Officer (CKO)**

- **Championing.** Actively promoting the KM [knowledge-management] project, its adoption, and use.
- **Educating users.** Users not only need to know about the use and value of knowledge management; they also need to be shown what's in it for them. That is, corporate knowledge objectives should be tied to personal rewards such as compensation and promotion.
- **Educating the management team.** Management support is critical for the long-term success of any strategic KM system, and showing managers the value of KM is a necessary precursor to successful management of knowledge.
- **Measuring the impact of knowledge management.** Metrics, the hardest part of KM, are also the most convincing of all talking points. . . . [See the discussion of measurement in step 10.]
- **Mapping existing knowledge.** Knowledge management must begin with what already exists. Don't try to build new knowledge repositories before you've inventoried the critical parts of explicit and tacit knowledge that already exist.
- **Defragmenting scattered knowledge.** Knowledge might be scattered. Linking this extant knowledge is, for the most part, a technology-based problem.
- **Creating the technology channels.** Technology channels are the sociotechnical networks that help move knowledge around the organization in an efficient manner. Technology channels and their choice are largely determined by the CKO's understanding of what would work, user perceptions of what they need, and organizational work culture.
- **Integrating business processes with the technology enablers.** Knowledge management systems must be built to support business processes. A high-level manager (CKO or equivalent) is usually in the best position to identify business processes that most affect the bottom line.

*Source:* Amrit Tiwana, *The Knowledge Management Toolkit: Practical Techniques for Building a Knowledge Management System* (Upper Saddle River, NJ: Prentice Hall PTR, 2000), p. 396.

## Step #10: Evaluate Performance, Measure ROI, and Incrementally Refine the Knowledge-Management System

Tiwana closes out his 10-step implementation plan with a call for measurement of knowledge management results while simultaneously recognizing the harsh realities of the measurement problems we mentioned earlier. "I have researched several companies that have been successful in implementing knowledge management," he writes, " but have yet to come across one that has a strong measurement program in place."[55] As a remedy for the measurement problem, Tiwana proposes a modified version of Robert Kaplan and David Norton's balanced scorecard.[56] Here's how Tiwana describes his modified balanced scorecard, followed by some additional measurement recommendations from other gurus.

### The Modified Balanced Scorecard for Knowledge Management

Kaplan and Norton's original scorecard presents performance metrics from four perspectives, as follow:

- **Financial.** How is our strategy, implementation, and execution contributing to bottom-line improvement?
- **Customer.** How do our customers perceive us? Are they happy and satisfied?
- **Internal business process.** Are our internal processes effective, efficient, and at their best?
- **Learning and growth.** How well are we doing the things we need to do to sustain our competitive advantage over time, such as retaining key employees, enhancing our systems and technology, and developing capabilities in our people?

For the purposes of measuring knowledge-management outcomes, Tiwana proposes substituting the following for Kaplan and Norton's perspectives:

- **Financial perspective.** Is our investment in knowledge management yielding any financial gains on the balance sheet?
- **Human-capital perspective.** Are our employees performing better and sharing more?
- **Customer-capital perspective.** Have we improved customer relations, increased prospects, and brought in new customers through better knowledge management?
- **Organizational-capital perspective.** Do we now have superior process knowledge, more distinct capabilities, a stronger ability to innovate faster than our competition through better knowledge management?

**OUR VIEW**

While all of this sounds plausible, Tiwana offers few specifics. For example, what measures are we to use for his various perspectives? He provides no examples and little guidance. Divorced from technology, Tiwana has little to say. We prefer the measurement advice of three other gurus for their specifics if nothing else. They are Leif Edvinsson, Michael S. Malone, and Karl Erik Sveiby. We will look first at Edvinsson and Malone's ideas, the Skandia method, and then summarize those of Karl Eric Sveiby.

## *Edvinsson and Malone: The Skandia Method of Knowledge Measurement*

You will recall Leif Edvinsson and Michael S. Malone from our earlier discussion of types of intellectual capital. In their 1997 book *Intellectual Capital,* Edvinsson and Malone report on the efforts of Skandia AFS, a Swedish financial-services company, to develop measures of intellectual capital to supplement financial measures in their annual report.

Skandia's efforts began in the 1980s when then chief executive officer (CEO) Bjorn Wolrath and first executive vice president Jan Carendi became convinced that Skandia's competitive strength rested less in its traditional accounting assets, such as buildings, equipment, and inventories, and more in its intangible assets, such as employee knowledge, customer relations, ability to manage the flow of competence in the organization, and so on. They reasoned that, if they could find a way to nurture these intangible assets, they might have "a new, holistic and more balanced set of tools for growing Skandia."[57]

In 1991 Wolrath and Carendi created an intellectual-capital function within Skandia to tackle the intangible asset issue. They established the new function on an organizational level equivalent to the existing functions of marketing and finance and charged it with three responsibilities: (1) forge a link with business development, human resources, and information technology; (2) develop new tools for measuring the company's intellectual assets; and (3) implement programs to speed up knowledge sharing within the company. They recruited Edvinsson to oversee the new function.

Between 1991 and 1994, Edvinsson assembled an intellectual-capital (IC) team to work on the issues of defining Skandia's intellectual capital and developing a measurement system. By mid-1992 the IC team had arrived at the following simple definition:[58]

Intellectual Capital = Human Capital + Structural Capital

where

**Human Capital** = the combined knowledge, skill, innovativeness, and ability of the company's individual employees to meet the task at hand plus the company's values, culture, and philosophy.

**Structural Capital** = the hardware, software, databases, organizational structure, patents, trademarks, and everything else of organizational capability that supports those employee's productivity—in a word, everything left at the office when the employees go home plus customer capital, the relationships developed with key customers.

The team later expanded this initial definition into a full-blown scheme for incorporating intellectual capital into the market valuation of the company, as illustrated in Exhibit 3.14.

EXHIBIT 3.14. **Skandia Market-Value Scheme**

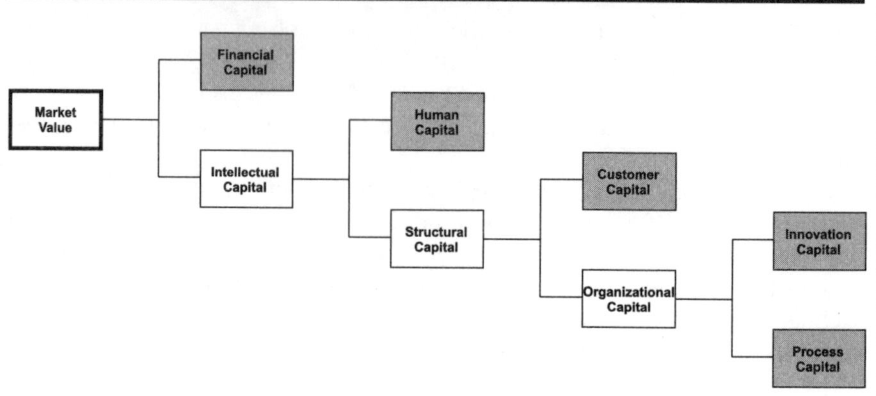


In 1994 Skandia issued its first annual IC report as a supplement to the 1994 Skandia annual report to stockholders. It based the IC report on the market-value scheme Edvinsson's IC team had devised. The report contained measures in five focus areas (corresponding to the shaded boxes in Exhibit 3.15): financial focus, customer focus, process focus, renewal and development focus, and human focus. Skandia's original report contained 164 measures cobbled together from some half-dozen different division reports. Consequently, the measures contained some overlap and duplication. In preparing their book, Edvinsson and Malone reviewed the original list of measures, removed redundant and less-important measures, and presented what they call their universal IC report. It contains 110 measures covering everything from market value to customer ratings to information-technology capacity to R&D expenses to employee training (see Exhibit 3.15).

EXHIBIT 3.15 **Skandia's Intellectual-Capital Measures**

**Financial Focus (Financial Capital)**

1. Total assets ($).
2. Total assets/employee ($).
3. Revenues/total assets (%).
4. Profits/total assets ($).
5. Revenues resulting from new business operations ($).
6. Profits resulting from new business operations ($).
7. Revenues/employee ($).
8. Customer time/employee attendance (%).
9. Profits/employee ($).
10. Lost business revenues compared to market average (%).

(continued)

EXHIBIT 3.15. **(continued)**

11. Revenues from new customers/total revenues (%).
12. Market value ($).
13. Return on net asset value (%).
14. Return on net asset resulting from new business operations ($).
15. Value added/employee ($).
16. Value added/IT employees ($).
17. Investments in IT ($).
18. Value added/customer ($).

**Customer Focus (Customer Capital)**

1. Market share (%).
2. Number of customers (#).
3. Annual sales/customer ($).
4. Customers lost (#).
5. Average duration of customer relationship (#).
6. Average customer size ($).
7. Customer rating (%).
8. Customer visits to the company (#).
9. Days spent visiting customers (#).
10. Customers/employees ($).
11. Revenue generating staff (#).
12. Average time from customer contact to sales response (#).
13. Ratio of sales contacts to sales closed (%).
14. Satisfied Customer Index (%).
15. IT investment/salesperson ($).
16. IT investment/service and support employee ($).
17. IT literacy of customers (%).
18. Support expense/customer ($).
19. Service expense/customer/year ($).
20. Service expense/customer/contact ($).

**Process Focus (Process Capital)**

1. Administrative expense/total revenues (#).
2. Cost for administrative error/management revenues (%).
3. Processing time, outpayments (#).
4. Contracts filed without error (#).
5. Function points/employee-month (#).
6. PCs and laptops/employee (#).
7. Network capability/employee (#).
8. Administrative expense/employee ($).

(continued)

EXHIBIT 3.15. **(continued)**

9. IT expense/employee ($).
10. IT expense/administrative expense (%).
11. Administrative expense/gross premium (%).
12. IT capacity (CPU and DASD) (#).
13. Change in IT inventory ($).
14. Corporate quality performance (e.g., ISO 9000) (#).
15. Corporate performance/quality goal (%).
16. Discontinued IT inventory/IT inventory (%).
17. Orphan IT inventory/IT inventory (%).
18. IT capacity/employee (#).
19. IT performance/employee (#).

**Renewal and Development Focus (Innovation Capital)**

1. Competence development expense/employee ($).
2. Satisfied Employee Index (#).
3. Relationship investment/customer ($).
4. Share of training hours (%).
5. Share of development hours (%).
6. Opportunity share (%).
7. R&D expense/administrative expense (%).
8. Training expense/employee ($).
9. Training expense/administrative expense (%).
10. Business development expense/administrative expense (%).
11. Share of employees under age 40 (%).
12. IT development expense/IT expense (%).
13. IT expenses on training/IT expense (%).
14. R&D resources/total resources (%).
15. Customer opportunity base captured (#).
16. Average customer age (#); education (#); income (#).
17. Average customer duration with company in months (#).
18. Educational investment/customer ($).
19. Direct communications to customer/year (#).
20. Non-product-related expense/customer/year ($).
21. New markets development investment ($).
22. Structural capital development investment ($).
23. Value of EDI system ($).
24. Upgrades to EDI system ($).
25. Capacity of EDI system (#).
26. Ratio of new products (less than two years) to full company product family (%).

(continued)

EXHIBIT 3.15. **(continued)**

27. R&D invested in basic research (%).
28. R&D invested in product design (%).
29. R&D invested in applications (%).
30. Investment in new product support and training ($).
31. Average age of company patents (#).
32. Patents pending (#).

**Human Focus (Human Capital)**

1. Leadership Index (%).
2. Motivation Index (%).
3. Empowerment Index (#).
4. Number of employees (#).
5. Employee turnover (%).
6. Average years of service with company (#).
7. Number of managers (#).
8. Number of women managers (#).
9. Average age of employees (#).
10. Time in training (days/year) (#).
11. IT-literacy of staff (#).
12. Number of full-time/permanent employees (#).
13. Average age of full-time/permanent employees (#).
14. Average years with company of full-time permanent employees (#).
15. Annual turnover of full-time permanent employees (#).
16. Per capita annual cost of training, communication, and support programs for full-time permanent employees ($).
17. Full-time permanent employees who spend less than 50 percent of work hours at a corporate facility; percentage of full-time permanent employees; per capita annual cost of training, communication, and support programs.
18. Number of full-time temporary employees; average years with company of full-time temporary employees.
19. Per capita annual cost of training and support programs for full-time temporary employees ($).
20. Number of part-time employees/non-full-time contractors (#).
21. Average duration of contract (#).
22. Percentage of company managers with advanced degrees:
    - •Business (%).
    - •Advanced science and engineering degrees (%).
    - •Advanced liberal arts degrees (%).

*Source:* Leif Edvinsson and Michael S. Malone, *Intellectual Capital: Realizing Your Company's True Value by Finding Its Hidden Roots* (New York: HarperBusiness, 1997), pp. 151–155.

### Karl Erik Sveiby: The Intangible Assets Monitor™

In the mid-1980s, Sveiby, a Swedish-born consultant and author of the 1997 book *The New Organizational Wealth,* developed a method for measuring intangible assets—dubbed the Intangible Assets Monitor™—which has been widely used in Sweden. It is a potentially useful alternative to Tiwana's modified balanced scorecard and Edvinsson and Malone's intellectual-capital measures.

Sveiby identifies three types of intangible assets and suggests three types of measures, involving growth, efficiency, and stability, for each type of asset:

1. **External structure.** Brands and customer and supplier relations.
   - Indicators of growth, such as profitability per customer.
   - Indicators of efficiency, such as customer satisfaction.
   - Indicators of stability, such as customer longevity.
2. **Internal structure.** The organization: management, legal structure, manual system, attitudes, R&D, and software.
   - Indicators of growth, such as investment in information technology.
   - Indicators of efficiency, such as sales per support staff.
   - Indicators of stability, such as support staff turnover.
3. **Individual competence.** Employee education and experience.
   - Indicators of growth, such as education level of professionals.
   - Indicators of efficiency, such as profit per professional.
   - Indicators of stability, such as professional turnover.[59]

See Exhibit 3.16 for an example of an Intangible Assets Monitor™ for a company, with some suggested measures.

EXHIBIT 3.16. **Karl Eric Sveiby's Intangible Assets Monitor™ with Suggested Measures**

| EXTERNAL-STRUCTURE ASSETS | INTERNAL-STRUCTURE ASSETS | PEOPLE-COMPETENCE ASSETS |
|---|---|---|
| **Growth/Renewal** | **Growth/Renewal** | **Growth/Renewal** |
| • Profitability per customer.<br>• Organic growth (increase in billings with income from acquisitions deducted). | • Investment in internal structure (e.g., Invest in information technology).<br>• Proportion of assignments that are competence enhancing.<br>• Time devoted to R&D. | • Total number of years company professionals have worked in their professions.<br>• Education level of professionals.<br>• Training costs as percentage of turnover. |

(continued)

EXHIBIT 3.16. **(continued)**

| | | |
|---|---|---|
| **Growth/Renewal** | **Growth/Renewal** | **Growth/Renewal**<br>• Number of days devoted to education per professional.<br>• Personnel turnover.<br>• Competence enhancing customers—% of projects professionals considered educational. |
| **Efficiency**<br>• Customer satisfaction.<br>• Bid Win/Loss Index.<br>• Sales per customer. | **Efficiency**<br>• Support staff/total employees.<br>• Sales per support staff.<br>• Employee attitudes—survey results. | **Efficiency**<br>• Proportion of professionals in company.<br>• Profit per professional.<br>• Value added per professional. |
| **Stability**<br>• Percentage of billings attributable to five biggest customers.<br>• Number of customers accounting for 50 percent of billings.<br>• Customer longevity.<br>• Frequency of repeat orders. | **Stability**<br>• Age of organization.<br>• Support staff turnover.<br>• Rookie ration—number of employees with less than two years employment.<br>• Administrative staff seniority in years. | **Stability**<br>• Average age of employees.<br>• Seniority of professionals.<br>• Seniority of managers.<br>• Relative pay levels compared with other companies.<br>• Professional turnover rate. |

•*Source:* Based on Karl Erik Sveiby, *The New Organizational Wealth: Managing and Measuring Knowledge-Based Assets* (San Francisco: Berrett-Koehler, 1997), pp. 163–202; Karl Erik Sveiby, "The Intangible Assets Monitor," http://203.147.220.66/IntangAss/CompanyMonitor.html, (March 13, 2000); and Karl Erik Sveiby, "The Balanced Score Card (BSC) and the Intangible Assets Monitor," http://203.147.220.66/BSCandIAM.html, (March 13, 2000).

Of the three measurement systems presented here, we prefer Sveiby's for its comprehensiveness and simplicity. Tiwana's offering lacks specifics. Edvinsson and Malone's is overly specific, if anything, and is loaded with too many measures. Can anyone, investor or manager, really make sense of 110 indicators? Still, Sveiby's Intangible Assets Monitor™ is far from ideal. Some of his measures are subject to a variety of interpretations. For example, is the seniority of professionals in a company a sign of stability or stagnation? Does low professional turnover mean that the company is retaining tacit knowledge or failing to bring in new thinking? We aren't sure.

Anyway, do any of these measurement systems truly evaluate what almost all of our knowledge gurus say is really important—the ability of the organization to grow and nurture tacit knowledge and to convert it to explicit knowledge that can be shared? We have our doubts. Thus, the harsh reality of the difficulty of measuring success in knowledge management remains just that—an unpleasant, harsh reality.

For additional advice on implementing knowledge management in organizations, see Tiwana's 24 critical success factors for successfully managing knowledge (Exhibit 3.17).

## EXHIBIT 3.17. **Knowledge-Management Critical Success Factors**

In his book *The Knowledge Management Toolkit,* Amrit Tiwana offers the following 24 lessons or critical success factors for knowledge-management initiatives, based on a review of practices in two dozen companies that successfully manage their knowledge assets.

1. There is no silver bullet for knowledge management. In spite of what consultants eyeing your checkbook might say, all research suggests that there is no one right way to do it.
2. Successful knowledge management projects begin with a working definition of knowledge that is accepted equivocally throughout the company.
3. A process focus is required, not a technology focus.
4. Successful projects begin with the acceptance that there are no perfect measures or metrics for knowledge work. However, some metrics, even if vague, are needed to gauge the effectiveness of knowledge management.
5. Selling knowledge management to both managers and end users requires demonstration of at least some short-term impact.
6. Effective knowledge management must count in tacit knowledge right from the outset, even if the primary focus is on codification. Codification with no personalization is bound to fail.
7. Shared knowledge requires the creation of a shared context.
8. A successful knowledge management project must begin with knowledge that already exists, deliver initial results, and then continue to expand. Without such orientation, your knowledge management project risks being stifled in its early days.
9. Accommodation for reasoning and support for assumption surfacing must be an integral part of knowledge management.
10. KM projects that succeed have an eye on the future and not the past or present. In contrast, information management handles the present, and data archives document the past.
11. Knowledge management systems must minimize unnecessary routing retransmissions—a common source of noise and distortion.

(continued)

EXHIBIT 3.17. **(continued)**

12. What your employees need are incentives, not faster computers. Technology provides many enablers except the biggest one of all: an incentive to share knowledge.
13. A knowledge management system must allow everyone to both contribute and access knowledge. However, critical knowledge that represents confidential, competitive and innovative process knowledge or private records must be protected.
14. Effective systems for knowledge management respect confidentiality of users by allowing them to choose not to identify themselves. Although anonymity goes contrary to the idea of linking contributions to their originators, this balance is necessary.
15. Most successful knowledge management systems allow users to access, read and contribute from anywhere and at any time. Remote connectivity therefore becomes necessary.
16. If the system is used extensively, its technical design should be such that its users can see updates and additions in real time without having to manually refresh content. This is a trivial technical problem that is often overlooked with disastrous results.
17. As explicated content and tacit knowledge pointers within a knowledge management system grow, resource maps must be provided to help users navigate through them.
18. Best practice databases are essential, but they are not the primary component of an effective knowledge management system.
19. Ongoing management support is needed for both the knowledge strategy and the knowledge management system.
20. Effective knowledge management systems must support collaborative work and internal consulting. Knowledge management must also focus on product and service development processes.
21. Knowledge management systems need to be informal and communicatively rich. Effective knowledge management systems are easy to use. Extensive features that make the system cumbersome to use or less intuitive can discourage its use.
22. Packaging knowledge is a goal that must be supported by knowledge management systems right from the outset. Remember that less (volume) is more when it comes to knowledge and its effective management.
23. Knowledge management technology should provide a logical extension for business units, and its choice should create a win-win situation primarily for its users, not your company's technologists.
24. Different users prefer different delivery mechanisms. This distinction implies that users of a knowledge management system should be able to choose whether they will pull content or it will be pushed to them. Similarly, users must not be bombarded by all-inclusive content.

*Source:* Amrit Tiwana, *The Knowledge Management Toolkit: Practical Techniques for Building a Knowledge Management System* (Upper Saddle River, NJ: Prentice Hall PTR, 2000), pp. 160–162.

## THE HUMAN ASPECTS OF KNOWLEDGE MANAGEMENT

In our discussion of Tiwana's 10-step implementation plan, we noted that he had little to say about the process of creating a culture to support the growth of tacit knowledge within a firm and the sharing of that knowledge. We indicated that a much better treatment of this topic was provided by two other gurus, Dorothy Leonard and Frances Horibe. We examine Leonard's and Horibe's ideas in this section. We then conclude this chapter with some ideas by authors Jeffrey Pfeffer and Robert I. Sutton on the all-too-human problem of turning knowledge into action.

### Dorothy Leonard and the Wellsprings of Knowledge

In her highly regarded 1998 book *Wellsprings of Knowledge,* Dorothy Leonard identifies what she calls "four primary learning activities" that managers must manage in order to encourage knowledge creation and transfer in their companies. We look at each of these in more detail below, but before we do so, we want to point out an important distinction Leonard makes between "core capabilities" (intellectual assets critical to competitiveness) and "core rigidities" (a kind of intellectual stagnation that companies are prone to develop).

Leonard notes that many authors have argued that core capabilities, or firm-specific organizational competencies, bestow competitive advantages on firms when they are nurtured and deployed effectively. She identifies four interdependent dimensions of core capabilities:

1. Employee knowledge and skill.
2. Physical technical systems (knowledge embodied in databases, machinery, and software).
3. Managerial systems (systems of education, rewards, and incentives that support and reinforce the growth of knowledge).
4. Values and norms that serve to screen and encourage or discourage the accumulation of different types of knowledge.[60]

It is the unique combinations of these four dimensions, says Leonard, that provide a company with its strategic advantage. "The perplexing paradox involved in managing core capabilities," writes Leonard, "is that they are *core rigidities.*"[61] Core rigidities are the flip side or dark side of core capabilities; "That is, a firm's strengths are also—*simultaneously*—its weaknesses."[62] In short, the capabilities that give a company an advantage at one point in time can become handicaps when conditions change. Core capabilities can turn into core rigidities for two reasons, says Leonard. First, managers can become so internally focused and comfortable with the status quo that they fail to notice new competitors, new technologies, or political/social changes that are shifting the competitive environment and making old capabilities obsolete. Second, core capabilities can turn to core rigidities when they are so successful that they lead managers to overshoot the target by succumbing to the notion that more of a good thing is always better; for example, if giving our customers the choice of 20 options is good, giving them the choice of 200 options would be even better.

The flip side of nurturing the growth of core capabilities, explains Leonard, is avoiding having these capabilities turn into core rigidities. You do both when you effectively manage the four primary learning activities.

### *Learning Activity #1: Integrating Problem Solving across Cognitive and Functional Boundaries*

One of the limitations on learning and problem solving in organizations, writes Leonard, is the growth of *signature skills.*

> A signature skill is an ability by which a person prefers to identify himself or herself professionally. Signature evokes the idiosyncratic nature of the skill—a personally defining characteristic, as much a part of someone's identity as the way the individual signs his or her name. Signature skills may be acquired through schooling or by experience, but they are ones to which we bond our professional identity because we have chosen to do so. . . .
>
> A signature skill is an outgrowth, an interactive expression, of three interdependent preferences—preferred type of task [what types of problems we seek to solve], preferred cognitive approach to problems [how we set up a task/solution], and preferred technology [how we execute the task]."[63]

Leonard notes that one of the consequences of our technologically advanced society is that specialists are encouraged to develop and employ their signature skills. Consequently, we encourage the growth of enclaves of specialists who consider only a few similar ways of defining, framing, and solving problems. Managers in innovative organizations, writes Leonard, realize that one way to encourage both the growth and sharing of knowledge is to intentionally bring together people with widely different signature skills in the hope that, as different ideas, preferences, and approaches rub together, sparks will fly. The trick, of course, is to make the sparks creative rather than personal through something called "creative abrasion," in which managers bring together specialists with widely divergent signature skills in "an atmosphere that encourages people to respect each other's viewpoint without always agreeing with it."[64]

Leonard says creative abrasion is different from other more familiar sources of friction in organizations.

> First, creative abrasion is not equivalent to a celebration of diversity on the basis of gender, sexual preference, or ethnic background. Although diversity

on these bases surely introduces different perspectives and problem-framing approaches, managing creative abrasion requires both more and less than structuring an organization to attract and hold a group of people with mixed backgrounds. It requires more because merely introducing diversity in this general sense does not ensure that different kinds of creative problem solving occur.... And creative abrasion requires less because people of similar ethnic backgrounds or of the same gender can draw upon extremely different sources and types of creativity. In short, "diversity," as popularly conceived, is not essential to the presence of creative abrasion between contrasting cognitive styles....

Nor is creative abrasion identical to the "constructive confrontation" encouraged at Intel and other fast-paced companies where... corporate culture encourages employees to confront problems very openly and aggressively and not to allow politeness to mask important differences of opinion and lapses in needed action. Such confrontation does not necessarily arise from different perspectives on the world, and the norm applies to all interpersonal behavior. Thus, although creative abrasion is one form of constructive confrontation, its purpose is specifically to support innovation and encourage the integration of different problem-framing and problem-solving approaches—to create something that no single perspective could have.

Creative abrasion is also unlike personal confrontation and abuse.... Personally demeaning someone is antithetical to creative abrasion; managers expecting the abrasion thus engendered to result in creativity risk misdirecting much energy into nonproductive paths.[65]

What can you do to cause creative abrasion? Leonard offers 10 suggestions:

1. **Include people with T-shaped skills.** These are people who have depth of knowledge in one discipline (the stem) and more superficial knowledge about how the discipline interacts across one or more other disciplines. Consequently, they can speak two or more professional "languages."
2. **Include people with A-shaped skills.** These are people who have actually learned two disciplines in depth and so have acquired, in effect, two disciplinary legs to stand on. Leonard notes that it is rare for anyone to learn more than two disciplines.
3. **Use multilingual managers.** These are managers who are capable of operating in more than one specialized realm and who can use more than one cognitive style. For example, a manager who was formally trained as both an engineer and an artist would be multilingual.
4. **Acknowledge different cognitive styles.** Nissan Design had its employees take a "personalysis" test to determine their cognitive preferences. Results were color coded, and employees were invited to display a color chart of their cognitive style on their desktops.

5. **Hire and select for collaborative skills.** Chaparral Steel hires workers in part for their interpersonal communication skills, their interest in learning, and their ability to learn.
6. **Retain trained facilitators from the outside.** These people are trained in group facilitation and are available to staff members who experience difficulty communicating with each other.
7. **Introduce totally different methodologies.** Xerox's Palo Alto Research Center often includes philosophers and anthropologists on technical teams in order to introduce different methodologies to the team.
8. **Shift the terms of debate.** When wars irrupt over competing technical methodologies, some managers have found it useful to change the terms of debate. For example, when faced with a debate over a new technology, managers might shift the debate from technical-based criteria (What is the best technology?) to business strategy-based criteria (What technology best meets the business objectives?). By switching the terms of the debate, managers can often defuse tensions.
9. **Use physical prototypes as boundary-spanning objects.** Boundary objects are physical objects that "have different meanings in different social worlds but their structure is common enough to more than one world to make them recognizable, a means of translation."[66] Boundary objects can include everything from concept sketches and drawings to mock-ups and simulations to working prototypes to first production units.
10. **Construct a clear shared vision of the project outcome.** Finally, says Leonard, "a manager's most powerful ally in fostering creative energies is a very clear project destination."[67]

### *Learning Activity #2: The Implementation of New Methodologies and Process Tools*

The second learning activity managers must manage well, if they wish to encourage the creation and transfer of knowledge, advises Leonard, is the introduction of new process methodologies and technologies. Here, she says, two things are critical: (1) the level of user involvement in the design and delivery of the new system or methodology and (2) the extent to which both the technology and user environment are adapted to the new methodology.

Leonard says that advocates of user involvement usually cite two generic reasons for its importance: "(1) implementation implies some level of change in the user's work, and research on change suggests that people are more receptive when they have contributed to its design; and (2) involving users in the design of their tools results in superior designs since users have specialized knowledge about the environment in which the tools will be utilized, and that knowledge should be embodied in the design."[68]

While most people recognize the importance of user involvement, Leonard notes that the level of involvement users have in reality varies greatly. She identifies four levels of involvement practiced by companies:

1. **Delivery mode, or "over-the-wall,"** in which there is no user involvement and developers simply design the tool they want for themselves.
2. **Consultancy,** in which developers consult with users about features and functions periodically during the design and development process.
3. **Codevelopment,** in which users were actually part of the development team.
4. **Apprenticeship,** in which users travel to the developer site and apprentice themselves to the tool designer. Users assume total responsibility for becoming expert and implementing in the underlying technology. Developers play the role of tutors.

While Leonard admits that all four involvement methods can be successful, she argues that codevelopment was the most effective in encouraging knowledge creation and transfer in the companies she studied.

> Codevelopment projects *forced* the developer and user groups to share problem-solving activities, to create and integrate knowledge, and that shared responsibility educated both groups to a better understanding of each other's worlds. Integration occurs at a group rather than an individual level. The developers came to understand the demands of the production process, and the production personnel began to see the potential inherent in the technologies offered them. . . . Not only were advanced proprietary tools created, but some corporate barriers to knowledge integration had been considerably truncated. Codevelopment, in short, had much more effect on the organization" learning process than the other modes.[69]

Additionally, writes Leonard, codevelopment, to a greater extent than the other methods of employee involvement, typically resulted in mutual adaptation of both technology and the work environment. The technology was reconfigured and in some cases reinvented to conform to the demands of the work environment while simultaneously the organization was adapted to use the new technical system.

### *Learning Activity #3: Experimentation*

One important way knowledge is created and shared in organizations, says Leonard, is through experimentation. A key learning activity, therefore, is for managers to create an organizational climate that encourages experimentation and in which people learn from their experiments, particularly those that fail. They do so by (1) separating intelligent failure (e.g., failure resulting from creative experiments) from unnecessary failure (e.g., failure resulting from inherently doomed enterprises) and (2) recognizing the role of failure in building organizational knowledge.

Among other things, Leonard recommends the following to encourage increased experimentation and learning from failure:

- **Prototyping.** Prototypes can range from two-dimensional sketches to fully functioning products demonstrated in a real work environment. "Prototyping," writes Leonard, " is an essential exercise in both outbound communication and elicitation of information. Organizations conduct rapid prototyping cycles in order to learn quickly."[70] (You will recall that Tiwana also recommends prototyping, calling it "the most underused form of rejection insurance.)

  Despite the value of prototyping, Leonard notes that it is handicapped in many companies by two preconceptions—that a "quick-and-dirty" prototype will reflect poorly on the developer and that a prototype may be misinterpreted by managers as a product ready to launch.

> Both are real dangers. Product and process developers relate cautionary tales about two types of encounters with managers—times when managers could not extrapolate from the prototype to the finished product and times when they did so prematurely. Designers themselves are accustomed to developing ideas through "a kind of reflective conversation with the materials of a design situation." They are able to fill in the missing information—or use what is present to suggest what is possible. Many people, however, seem unable to tolerate incompleteness, to fill in missing details, to see the potential in the prototype—and they are the bane of designers' lives. They will take every presentation of line, shape, and color as absolute and final. Consequently, designers soon learn that some clients cannot be shown preliminary ideas at all. In companies where such people predominate, prototypes are treated as "an end product of thought, not as a vehicle for it." Unsurprisingly, interaction about the prototype in these situations is much less likely to stimulate new ideas or allow client and designer to explore, back and forth, the most creative matching of need and solution.
>
> Other developers describe the unfortunate experience of carefully warning managers that what they were about to see was a prototype, only to have the latter consider the product almost ready to launch. At Digital Equipment, a prototype of an expert system (software) productivity tool was shown to a vice president of marketing and sales in September 1982. Although proud of their accomplishments to date, members of the development team were keenly aware that at least a full year's work lay ahead of them before launch. Yet the vice president was so impressed with the demonstration that he insisted they should be able to have the software tool in the hands of every sales representative by Christmas. The team began to call the incident their "Christmas goose," believing the early demonstration had "cooked their goose."[71]

Managers must guard against both types of preconceptions to encourage creativity and learning.

- **Internal wrecking crews.** Another way to encourage learning, says Leonard, is to employ "internal wrecking crews." Internal wrecking crews are composed of employees who act like surrogate users and serve developers by prototyping the conditions a product will face when it is launched. For example, Gillette's male employees try out new razors and blades and provide feedback to designers, and Kodak provides free film to its employees on the condition that they will report back on their use of it.
- **Local expert users.** Employees of the organization targeted for a process or technology change can also be used to test out the product in advance of its general use. "These advance scouts serve two purposes," writes Leonard, "they anticipate organizational changes likely to be needed, and they become readily available, customized local resources to support implementation. When drawn from the ranks of those actually affected by the proposed new system or procedures, such representatives integrate expertise about their own tasks and work environments with acquired knowledge about the innovation—and understand the interaction of the two."[72]
- **Project audits.** Finally, says Leonard, managers can encourage learning by conducting project audits. These are formal reviews conducted by development teams at the end of projects for the purpose of determining what went right and wrong and what could be done better next time. The usefulness of a project audit depends on three things, writes Leonard. First, all team members must participate. If some of the team members have moved on to other projects and aren't available to participate in the audit, then the audit is incomplete. Second, all projects should be audited, even those that do not result in a marketable product or actual process change, because the most-valuable information and most-chronic problems often show up across projects. Finally, managers must systematically act on the information gathered from the audit. It shouldn't just languish in a discarded written report.

### *Learning Activity #4: Importing Know-How from the Outside*

All companies at one time or another need to import knowledge from outside the organization in order to build capabilities and competencies. Leonard refers to the ability of a company to recognize the value of new external information, assimilate it, and apply it to constructive ends as the company's "absorptive capacity." She says companies build absorptive capacity in five ways:

1. **Scanning broadly.** The most-innovative managers range far afield in the search for new knowledge.
2. **Providing for continuous interaction.** Companies that are most successful in importing new knowledge from the outside, writes Leonard, do so continuously. While such constant attention to outside sources is difficult because it consumes time and resources, these companies recognize that it is necessary

because competitors and information sources develop new knowledge or information between contacts.

3. **Nurturing technological gatekeepers.** There are some people in every business who expose themselves to more outside sources than do their colleagues. Innovative companies identify and reward these people for keeping others informed of the latest happening in their field.
4. **Nurturing boundary spanners.** These are people who understand the world of the source and the world of the receiver and translate as well as disseminate knowledge. For example, Leonard states that boundary spanners must have a certain degree of entrepreneurial spirit "since working at the interface between two organizations requires the skill and risk-taking aplomb of Odysseus sailing between the twin threats of Scylla and Charybdis."[73]
5. **Fighting not invented here.** Not invented here (NIH) can include everything from a general dislike for someone else's idea no matter how good it is to the firm conviction (sometimes right) that the idea or technology is flawed. Leonard notes that some companies have sought to fight NIH by rewarding employees for the best "stolen" idea, for example, the "Golden Thief Award." "However, the most successful NIH antidote," says Leonard, "is an organizational culture that embodies a sense of urgency for innovation, encourages interaction with outside sources of expertise, and helps employees understand the wellsprings of creativity—which are almost never filled in isolation."[74]

## Frances Horibe on Managing Knowledge Workers

Frances Horibe is a consultant and author of the 1999 book *Managing Knowledge Workers.* Her contribution to the knowledge-management literature is interesting for the specificity of her advice. While many knowledge-management gurus seem to be perpetually stuck in the rarefied air of theoretical discourse, Horibe is down-to-earth practical. Her book is filled with suggestions on what you should do to manage effectively and create an organization in which knowledge is created effortlessly and flows freely. She even scripts dialogue you should have with your employees. We won't go into that level of detail, but we consider here some of Horibe's better ideas.

### *Actions to Encourage Knowledge Creation*

In order to encourage employees to generate new ideas, Horibe suggests that you do the following:[75]

- **Help employees understand your company's strategic direction and how it applies to what they do.** Horibe says that, if employees understand how your strategy and their jobs connect, they are more likely to come up with ideas consistent with your strategy.

- **Provide employees with some time to work on their ideas, even if you don't agree with what they are working on.** 3M allows employees to spend up to 15 percent of their time working on ideas of interest to them.
- **Listen vigilantly.** Little ideas grow to big ideas only with encouragement, says Horibe. People need to hear things like, That's interesting, or, Why don't you give it a try?
- **When it becomes obvious that an idea isn't going to work, kill it.**
- **Don't punish failure.** Instead, reward employees for admitting mistakes.
- **Set an example.** Admit your own mistakes and failures.

### *Actions to Encourage Knowledge Sharing*

Horibe suggests that one of the most effective things you can do to encourage knowledge sharing is to encourage the growth of communities of practice. These are "groups of people informally bound together by shared expertise and passion for a joint enterprise—engineers engaged in deep-water drilling, for example, consultants who specialize in strategic marketing, or frontline managers in charge of check processing at a large commercial bank."[76]

Here is how Etienne Wenger describes a community of practice he encountered while doing research on the jobs of claims processors at a large insurance company:

> I found . . . that this supposedly routine job gives rise to a very complex social community. In order to work together, claim processors have established a versatile web of informal networks. Through exchanging questions, meeting in hallways, telling stories, negotiating the meaning of events, inventing and sharing new ways of doing things, conspiring, debating and recalling the past, they complement each other's information and together construct a shared understanding of their environment and work.
>
> In fact, the claim processors' ability to learn and perform their jobs depends on their community—its shared memories, routines, improvisations, innovations and connections to the world. The community functions within and without—and sometimes in spite of—the company's official organizational and procedural frameworks, etc.[77]

Note that communities of practice are not the same thing as work groups or project teams. See Exhibit 3.18 for a comparison.

Horibe says there is clear evidence that organizational learning occurs primarily through these informal groups. For example, they are vital to the socialization–tacit-to-tacit step in the spiraling knowledge conversion process that Nonaka and Takeuchi discuss. (See our previous discussion of knowledge-management reality #2.) The fortunate thing about communities of practice, says Horibe, is that they

**EXHIBIT 3.18. Communities of Practice versus Work Groups and Project Teams**

**Community of Practice**

Purpose: To build and exchange knowledge.
Membership: Self-selected.
Common Interest: Group's expertise.
Duration: Indefinite; as long as group members are interested.

**Work Group**

Purpose: To deliver product or service.
Membership: Employees reporting to same manager.
Common interest: Job requirements and work-team goals.
Duration: Until next reorganization or reassignment.

**Project Team**

Purpose: To accomplish a specific task.
Membership: Assigned by management.
Common interest: Project goals and milestones.
Duration: Length of project.

*Source:* Etienne C. Wenger and William M. Snyder, "Communities of Practice: The Organizational Frontier," *Harvard Business Review,* January–February 2000, p. 142.

occur on their own without management support and sometimes even in the face of management opposition. You can't direct communities of practice or dictate their membership, but you can encourage their formation and operation. Here are some of Horibe's suggestions:

- **Bring in experts from other organizations to address your group.** Knowledge workers are usually very keen to know how someone else in their field has tackled the problems they face. If you fund the travel and other expenses of these experts, they will often be willing to share their knowledge with your people.
- **Encourage people from outside the company to participate in your unit's bull sessions regularly.** Rather than assuming that all group sessions are for the team only, open some of the brain-storming sessions to other members of the community of practice. It will help to stimulate the thinking and possibly bring in a new perspective. Naturally, issues of confidentiality and proprietary information need to be attended to, but there are usually large areas of knowledge that can be discussed freely even given these constraints.

- **Pay for memberships in relevant associations.** Associations are usually ready-made communities of practice. By encouraging your employees to join, you increase the likelihood they can add to their store of knowledge.
- **Give employees a limited amount of time to work on association activities.** Having your employees actively involved in their community of practice will pay dividends. Allowing some work time to be devoted to association work (e.g., telephoning, conference organization) can have a useful payoff.
- **Fund/sponsor some association activities.** Funding doesn't always have to be in cash. You can loan a meeting room or arrange for them to buy meals for their conference under your company's umbrella agreement with a caterer. Sponsorship doesn't have to be costly.
- **Pay for the occasional lunch or coffee meeting.** When like-minded colleagues meet, even over lunch or coffee, work often gets discussed. While a blanket expense approval is probably inappropriate, allowing employees to claim the occasional meal when the conversation was primarily about work will encourage them to tap their community of practice for the knowledge your company needs.
- **Create a center of excellence in your own workplace.** A center of excellence is a workplace that considers itself to be the best in the company, country, or world class on some well-defined piece of knowledge. . . . Creating a center of excellence increases the chances that the elusive community of practice that you can neither control nor direct, will take up residence in your unit. If your unit becomes the focal point for the local community of practice, that usually means a number of the community members are on your team. This increases the likelihood that the issues the community of practice will work on will be those you actually want addressed simply because your guys want . . . a chance to toss around solutions to problems they're presently struggling with.[78]

## THE ULTIMATE HARSH REALITY: THE KNOWING-DOING GAP

Let's assume you undertake all that we have discussed so far. You struggle to identify your company's intellectual capital. You try, somehow, to distinguish between data, information, and knowledge. You adopt one of the knowledge-measurement schemes our gurus recommend or develop one of your own. You develop a phased approach to implementing knowledge management, just as Tiwana recommends. And you follow Dorothy Leonard's and Frances Horibe's advice for managing the human aspects of knowledge. What results can you expect? Will your people happily share their tacit knowledge, create databases filled to the brim with best practices, and most important, act on their new-found knowledge? Don't bet on it, say Stanford business professors Jeffrey Pfeffer and Robert I. Sutton. These gurus say that the last and harshest knowledge-management reality of all is the existence of a knowing-doing gap. Just because people have knowledge doesn't mean they will use it.

## The Evidence of a Knowing-Doing Gap

In their 1999 book *The Knowing-Doing Gap,* Pfeffer and Sutton point to the following as evidence that people don't act on what they know.

- Each year in the United States, thousands of business books are published. Many contain the same analyses and same advice found in similar books published the year before. The books find a ready audience, yet the advice in the books, although widely known and proven to be useful, goes largely unimplemented. (Readers of our *Guru Guides* are known to be exceptions to the "read—don't use" rule—we hope.)
- Each year $60 billion or more is spent on training, much of it on the same management subjects covered in the business books published each year. Regardless of the quality of training and the frequency with which it is repeated, little of the skills taught are actually used.
- Organizations spend billions of dollars on outside consultants each year. The consultants write volumes of reports suggesting changes and improvements, many of which are potentially valuable, but the advice is rarely implemented.
- Each year, over 80,000 people graduate with a masters in business administration (MBA) from U.S. business schools. Business education grows each year, although "there is little evidence that being staffed with people who have an advanced education in business is consistently related to outstanding organizational performance."[79] Many top-performing companies like Southwest Airlines and Wal-Mart don't even recruit at business schools, and 73 percent of MBA graduates say that the skills they learned in business school were only marginally helpful to them in their initial business assignments.
- Superior ways of managing people and organizing work within single industries are often widely known in the industry but not implemented. For example:
    - □ In the apparel industry, research has clearly established that modular production with an emphasis on team-based production is far superior to the traditional bundle system. Trade publications, industry associations, and unions have all taken this position since the early 1980s, yet in 1992 80 percent of apparel-manufacturing plants were still using the bundle system.
    - □ In the auto industry, flexible or lean production has been shown repeatedly to be the preferable method of auto assembly, but a five-year study of the industry showed that there had only been a modest increase in the use of flexible-manufacturing systems.

- Even within a single firm, knowledge of best practices often isn't transferred from department to department, plant to plant, or function to function. For example, a study of 42 plants in a single company found differences in performance between plants with the same manufacturing tasks and similar technologies to be as much 300 percent.
- In one study that Pfeffer and Sutton conducted of 120 units of a restaurant chain, managers and assistant managers were asked to evaluate the extent to which they felt 25 management practices listed on a survey form enhanced a restaurant's financial performance. The same managers were then asked the extent to which they employed the practices in their own restaurants. "For 17 of the 25 management practices, there was a statistically significant difference between what they thought was important and what they . . . reported using in [their] restaurant. In each instance, the direction of the difference indicated that they weren't doing what they knew to be important."[80]

## Turning Knowledge into Action: Some Guidelines

So, what causes the knowing-doing gap, and more important, what can you do to close it? Pfeffer and Sutton offer the following guidelines for action.

### *Guideline #1: Have People Learn by Doing, Not by Listening or Reading*

Pfeffer and Sutton write, "In a world of conceptual frameworks, fancy graphics presentations, and, in general, lots of *words,* there is much too little appreciation for the power, and indeed the necessity, of not just talking and thinking but of *doing*—and this includes explaining and teaching."[81] If you want people to apply what they learn, say our gurus, then have them learn by apprenticing and coaching and mentoring others. Pfeffer and Sutton admit that knowing by doing is a less-efficient way of transmitting knowledge. "There is less ability to leverage the Internet or to put lots of people in a large room with one instructor, which are, unfortunately, the modes of instruction at most business schools today. But both evidence and the logic seem clear: Knowing by doing develops a deeper and more profound level of knowledge and virtually by definition eliminates the knowing-doing gap."[82]

### *Guideline #2: Take a Ready-Fire-Aim Approach to Knowledge Acquisition*

In too many organizations, conclude our gurus, sounding smart has become a substitute for doing something smart. People let planning, decision making, meeting, and talking substitute for implementing. Managers assume that, if there is a discussion, plan, and decision to act, there will be action. Companies that learn by doing take action. They fire and then aim. Planning comes after doing. They establish a culture that says action is what is valuable; talk without action is unacceptable.

### *Guideline #3: Provide Soft Landings for Failure*

One of the most-critical elements to building a culture of action, say Pfeffer and Sutton, is accepting reasonable failure. When failure is treated harshly, then people are encouraged to plan, study, and analyze ideas to death.

### *Guideline #4: Drive Out Fear*

Firms that are able consistently to turn knowledge into action put people first and demonstrate that they care about their employees. Pfeffer and Sutton say this attitude must start at the top:

> It is unfortunate, but true, that a formal hierarchy gives people at the top the power to fire or harm the careers of people at lower levels. Fear of job loss reflects not only the reality of whether or not one can readily find another job, but also the personal embarrassment that any form of rebuke causes. Organizations that are successful in turning knowledge into action are frequently characterized by leaders who inspire respect, affection, or admiration, but not fear. Jim Goodnight, CEO of SAS Institute, has a modest and unassuming personal style that includes driving a station wagon to work, sitting in an office with the door open (he has a chair in front of the door, so it's not even clear it could be closed), dressing informally, and taking every opportunity to speak informally to people in the company. Herb Kelleher of Southwest Airlines is notorious for his antics such as dressing up as Elvis, Ethel Merman, or Corporal Klinger from M*A*S*H, attending parties with his people, and taking opportunities to talk to everyone in the company he sees. Dennis Bakke of AES likes to visit power plants and talk to operators in the middle of the night. George Zimmer of The Men's Wearhouse attends more than 50 Christmas parties and also seizes every opportunity to visit the stores, a norm that the company encourages for all of its leadership.
>
> Hierarchy and power differences are real. But firms can do things to make power differences less visible and, as a consequence, less fear-inducing. This is possibly one of the reasons why removing status markers and other symbols that reinforce the hierarchy can be so useful and important. Those symbols of hierarchy serve as reminders that those farther down have their jobs, their salaries, and their futures within the firm mostly at the sufferance of those in superior positions. Although to some extent this is always true, removing visible signs of hierarchy—things such as reserved parking spaces, private dining rooms, elaborate separate offices, differences in dress—removes physical reminders of a difference in hierarchical power that can easily inspire fear among those not in the highest-level positions.[83]

### Guideline #5: Promote Internal Cooperation, Not Competition

There is a mistaken idea prevalent in most businesses, write Pfeffer and Sutton, that, because competition is good between companies, it is also good within companies. Nothing, they say, could be further from the truth when it comes to closing the knowing-doing gap.

> Turning knowledge into action is easier in organizations that have driven fear and internal competition out of the culture. The idea that the stress of internal competition is necessary for high levels of performance confuses *motivation* with *competition*. It is a perspective that mistakes internal competition and conflict, accompanied by a focus on "winning" internal contests, for an interest in enhancing *organizational* performance and winning the battle in the marketplace.[84]

### Guideline #6: Measure the Knowing-Doing Gap

Pfeffer and Sutton note that, even when organizations attempt to measure knowledge, few make any effort to measure the knowing-doing gap.

> Typical knowledge management systems and processes focus instead on the stock of knowledge, the number of patents, the compilation of skills inventories, and knowledge captured on overheads or reports and made available over some form of groupware. Holding aside whether these systems even capture the tacit, experiential knowledge that is probably more important than what can be easily written down, such systems certainly don't capture whether or not this knowledge is actually being used. Organizations that are serious about turning knowledge into action should measure the knowing-doing gap itself and do something about it.[85]

### Guideline #7: Create a Culture That Values Knowledge

Finally, say Pfeffer and Sutton, organizations that turn knowledge into action don't do so simply because they have smart people. They do so because they have a culture that values creating, transferring, and most important, people acting on knowledge.

> Leaders of companies that experience smaller gaps between what they know and what they do understand that their most important task is not necessarily to make strategic decisions or, for that matter, many decisions at all. Their task is to help build systems of practice that produce a more reliable transformation of knowledge into action. . . . Leaders create environments, reinforce norms, and help set expectations through what they do, through their actions and not just their words.[86]

## KNOWLEDGE MANAGEMENT AND THE KNOWING-DOING GAP

Pfeffer and Sutton add that one final thing stands in the way of closing the knowing-doing gap. We think it is a fitting end to this chapter because it points out the frustrations and contradictions of the knowledge-management discipline. One of the major contributors to the knowing-doing problem, say our gurus, is knowledge management itself, or at least the way it is typically implemented.

Pfeffer and Sutton point to two ways in which knowledge management contributes to the knowing-doing problem. First, they say, many knowledge-management consultants and writers treat knowledge as "something to be acquired, measured, and distributed—something reasonably tangible, such as patents. . . . [This] conception of knowledge as something explicit and quantifiable draws a problematic distinction between knowledge as a tangible good and the use of that good in ongoing practice. The emphasis that has resulted has been to build the stock of knowledge, acquiring or developing intellectual property (note the use of the term *property*) under the presumption that knowledge, once possessed, will be used appropriately and efficiently."[87] Second, this conception of knowledge as something tangible treats knowledge as something distinct from philosophy and values when, in fact, knowledge is imbedded in philosophy and values. Consequently, companies overestimate the importance of learning what best-practice organizations do and underestimate the importance of learning why they do it. "Although specific practices are obviously important, such practices evolve and make sense only as part of some system that is often organized according to some philosophy or meta-theory of performance. As such, there is a knowing-doing gap in part because firms have misconstrued what they should be knowing or seeking to know in the first place."[88]

Are Pfeffer and Sutton saying that the very process of managing knowledge, at least as it is often done, may contribute to knowledge mismanagement and nonuse? Are they hinting that you might be better off not trying to manage knowledge at all rather than managing it the way many knowledge-management solution vendors want you to? Yep. Such is the irony of knowledge management, a discipline in search of itself.

### KEY POINTS

- Knowledge management involves gathering, structuring, storing, and accessing information to build knowledge. It also involves creating a culture that encourages and facilitates the creation and sharing of knowledge within an organization.
- Information and knowledge are the "thermonuclear competitive weapons" of the economy. Value and competitive advantage come from the knowledge people hold in their heads and how they apply it.

- There are two types of intellectual capital:

  - **Human capital,** which is the combined knowledge, skill, innovativeness, and ability of the company's individual employees.
  - **Structural capital,** which is the hardware, software, databases, organizational structure, patents, trademarks, and everything else of organizational capability that supports employee productivity.

- Knowledge is easy to talk about but hard to define.
- It is not always easy to distinguish knowledge from data and information.
- There are two types of knowledge:

  - **Explicit knowledge** that is codified.
  - **Tacit knowledge,** which is contained in people's heads, highly personal, and hard to codify.

- Tacit knowledge is the most-important knowledge for creativity and innovation.
- New organizational knowledge emerges from the interaction of tacit and explicit knowledge in a spiraling conversion process.
- There are many barriers in traditional organizations to the sharing of tacit knowledge, including reward systems that discourage sharing and the fear on the part of employees that they will be unable to express the inexpressible.
- There are genuine markets for knowledge in organizations with knowledge buyers and sellers. When these markets work efficiently, knowledge is shared. However, most knowledge markets are inefficient.
- The value of knowledge in organizations is difficult to measure. While several different measurement schemes have been developed, none has gained wide acceptance.
- Companies typically emphasize one of two approaches to knowledge management:

  - **Codification,** in which the focus is largely on investing heavily in technology to codify, store, and disseminate knowledge.
  - **Personalization,** in which the focus is on facilitating conversations and the sharing of tacit knowledge with a moderate investment in technology.

There is no single right strategy, and most companies do some of both.

- Successful knowledge management takes more than technology. It takes cultural change and changes in the reward structures that drive behavior in most companies.
- Managers should use "creative abrasion" to encourage creativity and the exchange of tacit knowledge. Creative abrasion involves bringing together specialists with widely divergent skills in an atmosphere that encourages people to respect each other's viewpoint.
- Experimentation is critical to the creation and sharing of knowledge. Experimentation is encouraged when intelligent failure is treated as different from unnecessary failure and failure is recognized as necessary in building organizational knowledge.
- Communities of practice—informal groups of people with common interests—are critical for knowledge creation and sharing. Managers cannot create or direct communities of practice, but they can encourage their growth.
- The ultimate harsh reality of knowledge management is that there is a knowing-doing gap. People often fail to act on the knowledge they have.

## CUSTOMER-RELATIONSHIP MANAGEMENT— The Gurus

**Michael Berry,** coauthor of *Data Mining Techniques: For Marketing, Sales, and Customer Support*

**Keki R. Bhote,** former senior corporate consultant on quality and productivity at Motorola and author of *Beyond Customer Satisfaction to Customer Loyalty*

**Stanley A. Brown,** author of *Strategic Customer Care: An Evolutionary Approach to Increasing Customer Value and Profitability*

**Jay Curry,** chairman of the Customer Marketing Institute and coauthor of *The Customer Marketing Method: How to Implement and Profit from Customer Relationship Management*

**Frank W. Davis Jr.,** coauthor of *Customer Responsive Management*

**George S. Day,** marketing professor, director of the Huntsman Center for Global Competition and Innovation at the Wharton School of Management of the University of Pennsylvania, and author of *The Market Driven Organization*

**James H. Gilmore,** cofounder of Strategic Horizons, LLP, member of The Institute for Organization Management for the U.S. Chamber of Commerce, and coauthor of *The Experience Economy: Work Is Theater and Every Business a Stage*

**Seth Godin,** vice-president of direct marketing at Yahoo! and coauthor of *Permission Marketing*

**Ian Gordon,** marketing consultant and author of *Relationship Marketing*

**Thomas O. Jones,** president of Elm Square Technologies and a former senior lecturer in the Harvard Business School's service management interest group

**Philip Kotler,** author or coauthor of 15 books on marketing, including *Marketing Management and Strategy* and *Kotler on Marketing*

**Gordon Linoff,** coauthor of *Data Mining Techniques: For Marketing, Sales, and Customer Support*

**Karl B. Manrodt,** coauthor of *Customer Responsive Management*

**Regis McKenna,** author of *Relationship Marketing and Real Time*

**Frederick Newell,** CEO of the consulting firm Seklemian/Newell and author of *Loyalty.com*

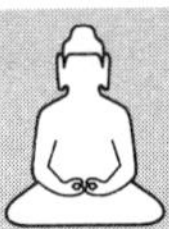

**Don Peppers,** cofounder of Peppers and Rogers Group and coauthor of *The One-to-One Future, Enterprise One-to-One, The One-to-One Manager,* and *The One-to-One Fieldbook.*

**B. Joseph Pine II,** cofounder of Strategic Horizons LLP, guest lecturer, award-winning author of *Mass Customization: The New Frontier in Business Competition,* and coauthor of *The Experience Economy: Work Is Theater and Every Business a Stage*

**Frederick Reichheld,** coauthor of *The Loyalty Effect*

**Martha Rogers,** co-founder of Peppers and Rogers Group and coauthor of *The One-to-One Future, Enterprise One-to-One,* and *The One-to-One Fieldbook.*

**W. Earl Sasser,** professor of management at the Harvard Business School and coauthor of *The Service Profit Chain*

# 4

# Customer-Relationship Management

In the summer of 1989, Don Peppers, a New York advertising-agency executive, received an urgent call from a member of the American Advertising Federation. One of the speakers at the federation's upcoming annual convention had canceled, and the caller was looking for someone who could fill in at the last minute on the topic of "the future of media." Peppers recognized the speaking opportunity as a chance to get someone from his firm, Lintas: USA, before an audience of important executives with large advertising budgets. He accepted the invitation immediately, certain that Lintas's media director could handle the presentation with little difficulty. A few hours later, Peppers regretted his hasty decision when he learned that Lintas's media director couldn't give the speech because of a scheduling conflict. Peppers was stuck. He couldn't back out of the commitment, so he would just have to give the speech himself. There were just three minor problems: (1) He was wasn't an "expert" on new media, (2) he had only a few days to prepare, and (3) according to the media director, there was little new to be said about the future of the media anyway. The topic had already been picked to death. Peppers's solution to these problems was simple. He changed the topic. Instead of speaking about the future of media, he spoke about the effect he felt the new media would have on mass marketing. The communications and information technologies expected in the decade of the 1990s would not improve the efficiency or effectiveness of mass marketing at all, said Peppers. To the contrary, they would mark its end.

> In the business world, what might be called the Era of Mass Marketing has now entered the twilight, and the sun is rising on a new age.
>
> *Don Peppers and Martha Rogers*[1]

When you think about it, Peppers's message predicting the death of mass marketing was either extraordinarily brave or downright loony. After all, Peppers worked for a company that developed advertising for mass marketers like GM and Coca-Cola, and he was speaking to an audience filled with people whose very livelihood depended on the continuing success of mass marketing. Surprisingly, given the audience, rather than being attacked as heresy, Peppers's prophecy was well received. It was covered by the *New York Times,* and soon Peppers was flooded with requests to speak to advertising groups across the country. A new marketing guru had been born.

By 1993 Peppers had formed his own consulting firm to preach the gospel of what he began calling "one-to-one" marketing. Together with Martha Rogers, an associate professor of marketing at Bowling State University, he wrote a business best-seller, *The One-to-One Future,* followed by four other best-sellers throughout the 1990s. Peppers and Rogers's books sparked one of the hottest topics in business—customer-relationship management.[2]

## WHAT IS CUSTOMER-RELATIONSHIP MANAGEMENT?

Peppers and Rogers call customer-relationship management "One-to-One Marketing" or "Marketing 1:1." Others refer to it as one or more of the following:

- Permission marketing.
- Customer intimacy.
- Real-time marketing.
- Continuous-relationship marketing.
- Technology-enabled relationship marketing.
- Enterprise-relationship management.

As Peppers notes, all of these labels represent nothing more than each consultant's branded version of "toasted oats," or in this case, the toasted oats of good old generic customer relationship management (CRM).[3] All of our gurus have their own individual explanations of what CRM is, but let's look at the way Peppers and Rogers describe it in their first book. As you read this, keep in mind that Peppers and Rogers were writing in the early 1990s, before the Internet and e-mail were widely available. Given the time frame, some of their predictions are extraordinary. (See Exhibit 4.1 for a complete list of their predictions.)

Peppers and Rogers begin with a brief description of how the new media differed from the mass media with which marketers were familiar at the time, using the term "1:1" for the new media:

> Using the new media of the 1:1 future you will be able to communicate directly with customers, individually, rather than shouting at them, in

groups. In fact, 1:1 media are different from today's [early 1990s] mass media in three important ways:

1. *1:1 media are individually addressable.* An addressable medium can deliver a single, separate message to a particular individual. Until very recently, virtually the only addressable medium of any significance was a slow, cumbersome, expensive postal system. Not anymore. New 1:1 media allow you to send information to individual consumers without using the mail at all.
2. *1:1 media are two-way, not one-way.* Today's mass media only convey one-way messages from the marketer to the customer. But new media are already available, and more are being invented literally every month, that allow your customers to talk to you. . . .
3. *1:1 media are inexpensive.* Imagine a business as small as a house painter, or an accountant, or a babysitter, reaching customers and prospective customers individually, in quantities small enough to be affordable. Businesses that today have little alternative but to send out printed flyers in the mail, or post three-by-five cards on supermarket bulletin boards, will be able to use individually addressable electronic media to reach new customers, and to keep the ones they have.[4]

The emergence of this inexpensive, two-way, and individually addressable media, write Peppers and Rogers, produces a totally new kind of business competition in which companies are forced to compete for customers one at a time. When that happens, mass marketing is dead, 1:1 marketing—or if you prefer, customer-relationship management—becomes the future, and the role of the marketer changes in fundamental ways.

The mass marketer visualizes his task in terms of selling a single product to as many consumers as possible. This process includes advertising, sales promotion, publicity, and frequently a brand management system for organizing the efforts of the company's marketing department. The marketer's task has always been to make the product unique in a way that would appeal to the largest possible number of consumers, and then to publicize that uniqueness with one-way mass-media messages that are interesting, informative, and persuasive to the "audience" for the product.

As a 1:1 marketer, however, you will not be trying to sell a single product to as many customers as possible. Instead, you'll be trying to sell a single customer as many products as possible—over a long period of time, and across different product lines.

To do this, you will need to concentrate on building unique relationships with individual customers, on a 1:1 basis. Some relationships will be more valuable than others. Your best relationships, and your most profitable business, will define your best customers. . . .

EXHIBIT 4.1. **Don Peppers and Martha Rogers's Technology for the 1:1 Future**

In addition to predicting that the new media would be individually addressable, two-way, and inexpensive, Peppers and Rogers predicted that the following 1:1 technological support structure would be in place by the year 2000.

- Major magazines would offer subscribers not only personalized advertising but personalized editorial content as well.
- Fax machines would be in 50 percent of U.S. households.
- Airplane seat backs would be equipped with interactive video screens that would be connected by satellite to program providers and catalog merchandisers.
- Microwave ovens and VCRs would respond to spoken instructions.
- Nintendo sets would be used for homework and would connect television sets by telephone to databases that would provide encyclopedias, textbooks, and news.
- Radios in cars would be able to receive customized programs delivered over cellular bandwidth.
- The average cable subscriber would have access to at least 150 channels and maybe as many as 500 channels.
- Many cable subscribers would have set-top boxes that would allow them to communicate back to the cable provider via cable, telephone, or satellite.
- Many homes would be connected to their cable or telephone service provider through fiber-optic cables that would allow anyone with a telephone and a television camera to go into the business of TV broadcasting.

*Source:* Adapted from Don Peppers and Martha Rogers, *The One-to-One Future: Building Relationships One Customer at a Time* (New York: Currency/Doubleday, 1993), pp. 12–14.

The most indispensable element of your relationship with each of your customers in the 1:1 future will be dialogue and feedback. . . . What does this customer really want? . . .

The nature of your relationship with each of your customers in this new environment will be collaborative. Instead of having to be "sold to," your customers increasingly will "sell themselves," stepping hand in hand with you through the complicated information exchanges that will, more and more, accompany individual product sales. . . .

As a 1:1 marketer, the more individualized this kind of collaborative interaction is with regard to a particular customer, the more you and that customer will develop a joint interest in the success of your own marketing effort—as it applies to that customer.

Instead of measuring the success of your marketing program by how many sales transactions occur across an entire market during a particular

> period, as a 1:1 marketer, you will gauge success by the projected increase or decrease in a customer's expected future value to your company. The true measure of your success, one customer at a time, will not be market share, but share of customer.[5]

See Exhibit 4.2 for a list of some additional ways our gurus explain that customer-relationship management differs from traditional marketing and Exhibit 4.3 for what Philip Kotler, author of *Marketing Management* and *Kotler on Marketing,* calls Neanderthal marketing practices.

### EXHIBIT 4.2. Customer-Relationship Management versus Traditional Marketing

In addition to the work of Don Peppers and Martha Rogers, the comparisons in this exhibit are based on the writings of the following gurus:

- Frank W. Davis Jr. and Karl B. Manrodt, coauthors of *Customer Responsive Management.*
- Ian Gordon, author of *Relationship Marketing.*
- Regis McKenna, author of *Relationship Marketing* and *Real Time.*
- Frederick Newell, author of *Loyalty.com.*

| Traditional Marketing | Customer-Relationship Management |
|---|---|
| Sells one product at a time to as many customers as possible through product managers. | Sell as many products as possible to one customer at a time through customer managers. |
| Uses information about what customers have in common to sell to the widest range of customers and find the next most logical customer for a product. | Uses information about individual customers to find the next most logical product for that customer. |
| Differentiates products. | Differentiates customers. |
| Tries to acquire a constant stream of new customers. | Tries to get a constant stream of new business from existing customers. |
| Competes for market share. | Competes for share of customer. |
| Makes customers and marketers adversaries. | Makes customers and marketers collaborators. |
| Manages products. | Manages customer relationships. |
| Talks to customers—tell and sell. | Engages in a dialogue with customers—listen and learn. |

(continued)

EXHIBIT 4.2. **(continued)**

| TRADITIONAL MARKETING | CUSTOMER-RELATIONSHIP MANAGEMENT |
|---|---|
| Disseminates the same information to everyone in predigested form. | Allows individual consumers access to the information they want, where and when they want it, and in the form they want it. |
| Takes customers to products. | Takes products to customers. |
| Focuses on satisfying customers. | Focuses on allowing customers to satisfy themselves through self-service. |
| Presents brand as a product differentiator created chiefly by advertisements broadcast by mass media. | Presents brand as an encapsulation of actual, experienced value, created through customer preferences expressed in dialogue with producers or service providers. |
| Bases the marketplace on impersonal, arm's-length transactions during which buyers examine products and make selections based on their individual needs. | Bases the marketplace on relationships in which customers seek not only products but advice and consistent care. |
| Views purchase events as independent of each other. Whether one customer buys a product is completely independent of whether another customer buys it. The rule of the marketer is to "line up" as many customers as possible who are satisfying a need the company can fill. If necessary, the company must cut its price to whatever level is required to attract the last, most-marginal, least-interested customer. | Views purchase events as conditional on previous purchase events. The customer is presumed to remember the company from one purchase event to another. Thus, the company must ensure that the purchase events undertaken by any single customer remain linked together by the enterprise so that each successive purchase event becomes more convenient for that customer. |
| Creates an environment in which product and service providers compete on price. | Creates an environment in which product and service providers compete not just on economic price but also on hassle. Providers compete to see how effortlessly and completely they can meet customers' needs. |
| Is internally focused. Companies unilaterally anticipate future customer needs, define the ideal offering for | Is externally focused. Companies plan and build infrastructures that enable them to organize a network of services, communications, and |

(continued)

EXHIBIT 4.2. **(continued)**

| Traditional Marketing | Customer-Relationship Management |
|---|---|
| the market, set up production, produce and distribute the offering, and try to sell the offering. | processes so they can interact with customers, diagnose needs, develop customized delivery plans, and track results. |
| Depicts products as bundles of tangible and intangible benefits the company assembles in anticipation that customers will want them. | Depicts products as aggregations of individual benefits customers have participated in selecting and/or designing. |
| Sells products and/or services. | Sells *prodices* (*products/services*), things that look like products but act like services, in recognition of the fact that the consumers want *communication* and not phones, *meals* and not foodstuffs, *entertainment* and not CDs, *clean clothes* and not laundry products, etc. |
| Emphasizes planning and stability to anticipate, define, produce, and distribute the optimum product in the optimum way for the marketplace. | Emphasizes flexibility to be responsive to customers and minimize wasted capacity. |
| Sets the price for a product and offers the product/price set in the marketplace, perhaps discounting the price in accordance with competitive and other marketplace considerations. | Sets the value of the product, and therefore its price varies with the preferences and dictates of the customer. The price needed to reflect the choices made and value created is established through a process of collaboration. |
| Sees distribution as the channel that takes the product from the producer to the consumer. | Sees distribution as a process that allows the customers to choose where and from whom they will obtain the value they want. |
| Believes that customers must be treated equally. | Believes that customers must be treated individually. |

*Source:* Based upon Don Peppers and Martha Rogers, *One-to-One Future: Building Relationships One Customer at a Time* (New York: Currency/Doubleday, 1993); Don Peppers and Martha Rogers, *Enterprise One-to-One: Tools for Competing in the Interactive Age* (New York: Currency/Doubleday, 1997); Don Peppers and Martha Rogers, eds., *The One-to-One Manager: Real-World Lessons in Customer Relationship Management* (New York: Doubleday, 1999); Frank W. Davis Jr. and Karl B. Mandrodt, *Customer Responsive Management: The Flexible Advantage* (Cambridge, MA: Blackwell Business, 1996); Ian Gordon, *Relationship Marketing: New Strategies, Techniques, and Technologies to Win Customers You Want and Keep Them Forever* (Etobicoke, Ontario: Wiley, Canada, 1998); Regis McKenna, *Real Time: Preparing for the Age of the Never Satisfied Customer* (Boston: Harvard Business School Press, 1997); Frederick Newell, *Loyalty.com: Customer Relationship Management in the New Era of Internet Marketing* (New York: McGraw-Hill, 2000).

### EXHIBIT 4.3. Philip Kotler's Neanderthal Marketing Practices

Philip Kotler is the author or coauthor of 15 books on marketing, including *Marketing Management* which has been called one of the 50 best business books ever written. In his 1999 book *Kotler on Marketing*, he lists the following as outdated, Neanderthal marketing practices:

- Equating marketing with selling.
- Emphasizing customer acquisition rather than customer care.
- Trying to make a profit on each transaction rather than trying to profit by managing customer lifetime value.
- Pricing based on marking up cost rather than target pricing.
- Planning each communication tool separately rather than integrating marketing communication tools.
- Selling the product rather than trying to understand and meet the customer's real needs.

*Source:* Philip Kotler, *Kotler on Marketing: How to Create, Win, and Dominate Markets* (New York: Free Press, 1999), p. 12.

## FOUR KEY CONCEPTS OF CUSTOMER-RELATIONSHIP MANAGEMENT

Since Peppers and Rogers pronounced the end of mass marketing in 1993, many other CRM gurus and would-be gurus have come forward to offer their wisdom on this radical new approach to marketing and customer relations. Four key concepts have emerged from these writings. Think of them as both the justification and intellectual underpinnings of CRM:

1. Customer retention is the key to long-term profits.
2. Customer satisfaction does not ensure customer loyalty.
3. Customers aren't created equal.
4. Customers must grant their permission to be marketed.

In the following sections, we look at each of these concepts in more detail.

### Key Concept #1: Customer Retention Is the Key to Long-Term Profits

All of our CRM gurus preach the gospel of customer loyalty. None does it better or more authoritatively than Frederick Reichheld, director of the strategy consulting firm Bain & Company and coauthor of *The Loyalty Effect*. Therefore, we will turn to Reichheld as the principal source of this key CRM concept.

Reichheld begins his argument with the following statistic from research: By raising customer retention rates by as little as five percentage points, companies can increase the lifetime value of their average customer by 25 to 100 percent, depending on the industry.[6]

In other words, if an advertising agency can retain just 5 percent more clients—for example, increase its retention rate from 90 percent to 95 percent—then it can be expected to increase its total lifetime profits from a typical client by an average of 95 percent. An insurance company would see a 90 percent increase from the same improvement in retention rates, and a branch bank could be expected to see an 85 percent increase. Similar gains have been found across industries. (See Exhibit 4.4 for examples.)

Reichheld states that two factors are at work here. First, customer loyalty has a substantial impact on the growth of customer inventory. Think of your customer base as water in a bucket, says Reichheld. If you have a hole in the bottom of your bucket, that is, losing customers, then you have to keep pouring water into the top of the bucket—keep adding new customers—just to keep your volume the same.

EXHIBIT 4.4. **Impact of a Five Percent Increase in Retention Rate on Total Lifetime Profits from a Typical Customer**

| Industry | Increase in Profits |
|---|---|
| Advertising agency | 95% |
| Life-insurance company | 90% |
| Branch bank deposits | 85% |
| Publishing | 85% |
| Auto service | 81% |
| Auto/home insurance | 80% |
| Credit card | 75% |
| Industrial brokerage | 50% |
| Industrial distribution | 45% |
| Industrial laundry | 45% |
| Office-building management | 40% |

*Source:* Frederick Reichheld and Thomas Teal, *The Loyalty Effect: The Hidden Force behind Growth, Profits, and Lasting Value* (Boston: Harvard Business School Press, 1996), p. 36

> Say you steadily add new customers to the top of your inventory, but old customers are steadily vanishing from the bottom. If you could slow the defection rate, the new customers you gained would increase the total at a much faster rate. It's like a leaky bucket. The bigger the leak in your bucket of customers, the harder you have to work to fill it up and keep it full.
>
> Imagine two companies, one with a customer retention rate of 95 percent, the other with a rate of 90 percent. The leak in the first firm's customer bucket is 5 percent per year, and the second firm's leak is twice as large, 10 percent per year. If both companies acquire new customers at the rate of 10 percent per year, the first will have a 5 percent net growth in customer inventory per year, while the other will have none. Over fourteen years, the first firm will double in size, but the second will have no real growth at all. Other things being equal, a 5-percentage-point advantage in customer retention translates into a growth advantage equal to a doubling of customer inventory every fourteen years. An advantage of ten percentage points accelerates the doubling to seven years.[7]

Second, explains Reichheld, customer retention is critical for profits in most industries because customers almost always become more profitable over time.

> This is harder to see than the customer volume effect, but it often makes an even bigger difference in profits. In most businesses, the profit earned from each individual customer grows as the customer stays with the company. . . . Clearly, the economic consequences of losing mature customers and replacing them with new ones are not neutral. In businesses like auto insurance, life insurance, or credit cards, firms actually lose money on first-year customers, so no number of new prospects can fill the void left by a seasoned customer who defects. In most other industries, new customers contribute to profits right away, but it still takes several newcomers to compensate for the loss of one veteran.
>
> In addition, the consequences of customer retention compound over time, and in ways that are sometimes surprising and nonintuitive. While a change in defection rates may have little effect on this year's profits, even a tiny change in customer retention can cascade through a business system and multiply over time. The resulting effect on long-term profit and growth can be enormous.[8]

It is clear from the research, writes Reichheld, that loyal customers are extremely valuable, and yet most companies don't know the cash value of their customers. Worse, they draw the wrong conclusions from data on their sales figures and average customer tenure. The fault, says Reichheld, lies in the basic language of business accounting.

Accountants have developed sophisticated techniques for appraising capital assets and their depreciation; they have learned how to monitor the constantly changing value of work-in-progress; but they have not yet devised a way to track the value of a company's customer inventory. They make no distinction between sales revenue from brand-new customers and sales revenue from long-term, loyal customers, because they do not know or care that it costs much more to serve a new customer than an old one. Worse, in most businesses, accountants treat investment in customer acquisition as one more current expense, instead of assigning it to specific customer accounts and amortizing it over the life of the customer relationship. The result is that generally accepted accounting principles actually hide the value of a loyal customer, an impressive feat of concealment given what loyalty can do for the great majority of companies.[9]

### The Key Components of Long-Term Customer Value

Reichheld says you shouldn't look to your accountants for help with figuring out the value of your long-term, loyal customers. If you want that information, you will have to calculate it yourself. Fortunately, he explains, you can do the calculations with the following six basic pieces of information.

**1. Acquisition cost**. This is what it costs you to acquire a new customer. It includes the cost of advertising aimed at new customers, commissions on sales to new customers, sales force overhead, and so on. Many of these cost are obvious; some are not so obvious. For example, the cost of acquiring a retail customer includes the cost of opening and operating new stores until they reach a break-even point and the cost of loss-leader promotions. Whatever your industry, writes Reichheld, your first task is to capture all of your customer-acquisition cost.

**2. Base profit.** This is the profit you make on basic purchases customers make with you, unaffected by time, loyalty, efficiency, or any other considerations. In other words, it is the difference in the price they pay and your company's cost.

**3. Per-customer revenue growth**. One of the nicest things about keeping customers long-term is that they tend to spend more over time. For example, the customer who initially comes into the auto service center for an oil change is likely to return for more-expensive services such as tune-ups. Reichheld cites research that shows that typical auto service-center customers triple their spending between the first and fifth year of doing business with the center. The same pattern of increased spending over time occurs in many other industries. Insurance is another good example:

In personal insurance, the average premiums of loyal customers grow at a rate of 8 percent a year. A typical family's increasing affluence accounts for part of this increase. Insurance on the new Lexus costs more than it

> did on the old Toyota. An addition to the house means more coverage, and so does the vacation home. Another part of the 8 percent average derives from the fact that long-term customers also tend to consolidate their insurance policies, so that a single long-term agent or company picks up auto, home, and life. At Northwestern Mutual, 55 percent of new sales come from existing policyholders.[10]

Reichheld cautions that per-customer revenue growth is much easier to describe than it is to calculate accurately.

> To get a precise reading, you have to track the annual revenues from each entering class, or cohort, of customers separately. Few companies today are equipped to do this. Instead, they take a snapshot of their present customer base, divide it into groups by tenure, and measure the year's revenues from each group. The resulting bar chart—a long row of progressively longer columns showing per-customer revenues for each successive customer class—can be deceptive. Statisticians have a term for this approach—they call it estimating a time series with cross-sectional data—and they caution against it.
>
> The problem is, the bar chart seems to imply a revenue growth pattern for the entering class, but each bar represents a different entering class. That fact can mislead the unwary in three ways. First, different customer classes often have slightly different characteristics. There can be age differences, demographic differences, and differences in the marketing promotions that attracted them, to name a few of many possibilities. Second, the older the class, the smaller it has become. This fact can be hugely deceptive if you're trying to project future revenues from a thousand new customers and forget how few of them will still be around in ten or twelve years.
>
> Third, there is always a danger that the defectors from any class are quite different from the customers who stay. For example, if customers who purchase less also happen to be less loyal, then the snapshot approach—based exclusively on customers who stick around—will suggest revenue growth that is far too optimistic, and mislead managers trying to project the consequences of higher customer retention. In this situation, every saved defector would drag down the average rate of revenue growth per customer.
>
> It is not enough to correlate customer tenure with annual purchases and then use the implied growth pattern for everyone. What you have to do is analyze the behavior of defectors as well as that of loyal customers, then estimate growth separately for each customer segment that demonstrates a different underlying behavior pattern. If you are using cross-sectional customer data, this warning applies equally to all the other economic components that drive lifecycle profits.[11]

In short, to accurately calculate per-customer revenue growth you are going to need some of the customer databases and data-analysis tools we describe later in this chapter. For now, let's just assume that you can arrive at a reasonably precise measure of this revenue growth.

**4. Operating costs.** Another nice thing about keeping customers long-term, writes Reichheld, is that they are usually easier to serve. Not only have these loyal customers learned about your business and what services they can and cannot expect from you but your business has learned about them.

> In financial planning, for instance, planners log about five times as many hours on a first-year client as they do on a repeat customer. Much of this is simply the time it takes to understand a new client's balance sheet, tax status, income profile, and risk preference. Meanwhile, the client is learning to communicate with the planner and the company. Over time, this collaborative learning between client and planner can create enormous productivity advantages that translate directly into lower costs.[12]

The trick to getting an accurate fix on operating cost savings from customer retention, says Reichheld, is to find productivity and expense efficiencies that you can tie directly to long-term customers. For example, if you run a customer-assistance call center you are likely to receive most of your calls from new customers. It makes sense, then, to allocate most of the cost of operating the center to new customers rather than allocating the cost based on total revenues, which would likely charge most of the cost against repeat customers who purchase more. Reichheld notes that some analysis of operating costs can yield striking and important information. He cites the case of a catalog sales operation that tracked the time and cost of processing several hundred new customer orders and then compared the results to those of several hundred orders from long-term customers.

> To managers' amazement, they found that processing orders for customers who'd been with the company less than two years cost twice as much as processing orders for older customers. There were three key differences. First, new customers didn't know which items were kept in stock, and so were much more likely to request nonstandard items. Second, credit evaluations and losses drove up the general overhead for new customers. Third, new customers were much more likely to order at peak-volume times of the day, which stressed the system and created more errors.[13]

**5. Referrals.** In addition to spending more over time and costing less to service, loyal customers are an excellent source of referrals. That's important because personal referrals are a major source of new customers for many businesses. For example, insurance agents and home builders get the majority of their new clients, by far, from personal referrals. And, notes Reichheld, personal referrals provide another benefit. Research shows that "customers who show up on the strength of a personal recommendation tend to be of higher quality—that is, to be more profitable and stay with the business longer—than customers who respond to conquest advertising, sales pitches, or price promotions."[14] Reichheld notes that there are good reasons referral customers are better customers:

> Veteran customers paint a more accurate picture of a business's strengths and weaknesses than advertisements or commissioned salespeople. In addition, since people tend to associate with people like themselves, chances are good that referred customers will fit well with the products and services the company offers. Though businesses are quick to give the credit for good growth to sexy advertising, brilliant marketing campaigns, or skilled salespeople, the chances are their profitable growth is driven by referrals.[15]

And, says Reichheld, the more customers you retain long-term, the more referrals you are likely to receive.

**6. Price Premium.** Finally, long-term customers generate more profits because they often pay more for the same products or services than new customers. Frequently, this is because established customers aren't eligible for special introductory offers. Also, established customers are usually less price sensitive. They are acquainted with the company's procedures, employees, and product line and therefore get greater value from the relationship. Unfortunately, writes Reichheld, few companies capture and give long-term customers credit for this price premium.

> Even companies that have customer profitability systems generally miss the full impact [of the price premium for long-term customers], because most such systems merely reshuffle information originally gathered to measure product-line profitability. That is, they tote up profits product by product, then calculate the profit from a particular customer or group of customers on the basis of the products customers buy. This approach ends up averaging coupons and other price discounts across all customers, irrespective of the price actually paid. As a result, firms overvalue transactions and undervalue relationships.[16]

### *Assembling the Life-Cycle Profit Pattern*

When you have assembled data on all of these components of customer value—acquisition costs, base profit, revenue growth, operating costs, referrals, and price premium—you have what Reichheld calls a life-cycle profit pattern for your customers. It will very likely look something like the one for the credit-card-industry shown in Exhibit 4.5.

EXHIBIT 4.5. **Life-Cycle Profit Pattern for the Credit-Card Industry**

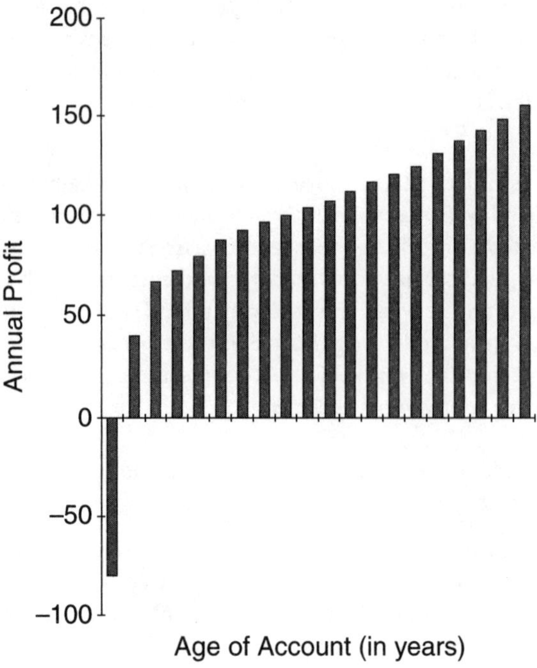


*Source:* Adapted from Frederick F. Reicheld and Thomas Teal, *The Loyalty Effect: The Hidden Force behind Growth, Profits, and Lasting Value* (Boston: Harvard Business School Press, 1996), p. 38.

The question becomes: What do you do with a customer life-cycle profit profile? How do you put the information to productive use? Reichheld suggest that you use the data to answer two important questions:

1. What is the actual value of a new customer in today's dollars?
2. How big an investment is an increase in customer loyalty actually worth?

***What is the actual value of a new customer in today's dollars?***

One of the things Richheld says you can do with your customer life-cycle profile is calculate the actual value of a new customer in today's dollars. Once you have that figure, then you can use it to determine how much you should invest in increasing your customer-retention rate. Here are the basic steps in arriving at the first figure, using the credit-card-company example in Exhibit 4.5.

**Step 1.** Determine the value of a new customer for different periods from your life-cycle profile. For example, a credit-card-company customer who stays with the company five years will generate $264 (−$80 + $40 + $66 + $72 + $79 + $87). See Exhibit 4.6.

EXHIBIT 4.6. **New Profit by Years of Customer Retention**

| YEAR | PROFIT (LOSS) | CUMULATIVE |
|---|---|---|
| 0 | −$80 | −$80 |
| 1 | $40 | −$40 |
| 2 | $66 | $26 |
| 3 | $72 | $98 |
| 4 | $79 | $177 |
| 5 | $87 | $264 |
| 10 | $106 | $760 |
| 20 | $161 | $2,104 |

**Step 2.** Discount the future earnings to bring them to present value. If you use a 15 percent discount rate, then the $760 in cumulative profits for a 10-year-credit-card customer would be worth a net present value of $304. See Exhibit 4.7.

EXHIBIT 4.7. **Net Present Value of Profit by Years of Customer Retention**

| YEAR | PROFIT (LOSS) | CUMULATIVE |
|---|---|---|
| 0 | −$80 | −$80 |
| 1 | $35 | −$5 |
| 2 | $50 | $52 |
| 3 | $47 | $97 |
| 4 | $45 | $140 |
| 5 | $40 | $480 |
| 10 | $26 | $304 |
| 20 | $10 | $463 |

*Note:* Assumes a standard discount rate of 15 percent and that the profit for each year comes on December 31. Net present value for first year is $40 divided by 1.15; for the second $66 divided by 1.15

***How much is an increase in customer loyalty really worth?***

Now that you know the value of your customers over time, you can calculate the value of increasing their retention rate. Here is a simplified version of how Reichheld suggests you do that.[17]

**1. First, determine the expected duration of a new customer.** The simplest way to do this, says Reichheld, is to count the number of customers who defect over a period of several months, annualize the figure, express it as a fraction of the total number of customers you had at the start, and invert the fraction. For example:

> 50 out of 2,000 customers defect in three months = 200 defections per year = 1/10th of customers.
>
> 1/10 inverted = 10, or 10 percent per year.

Your defect rate therefore is 10 percent per year, and your retention rate is 90 percent (100 percent – 10 percent). At that rate, you would lose 10 percent of your customers per year and your average customer tenure would be 10 years (see Exhibit 4.8).

EXHIBIT 4.8. **Average Customer Tenure and Different Retention Rates**

| RETENTION RATE (%) | AVERAGE CUSTOMER TENURE (YEARS) |
|---|---|
| 50 | 2 |
| 80 | 5 |
| 90 | 10 |
| 95 | 20 |

**2. Next, determine the impact of increasing your retention rate on your customers' net present value.** In our credit-card example, a 90 percent retention rate produced an average customer tenure of 10 years (see Exhibit 4.8), which translated into a average net present value of $304 (see Exhibit 4.7). However, if you could increase your retention rate to 95 percent (in other words, reduce your average customer defections per year from 10 percent to just 5 percent), you would increase your average customer tenure from 10 years to 20 years, and the average net present value of your customers would jump from $304 to $463, an increase of more than 50 percent.

What difference does all of this really make on the bottom-line profits of a firm? A lot, says Reichheld. In his hypothetical example, he examines what happens to the reported earnings of his mythical credit-card company over a 10-year period if it operates at a 95 percent retention rate versus a 90 percent retention rate. Reichheld assumes that the company has one million customers, acquires customers at the rate of a hundred thousand per year, has an unchanging customer-profit pattern, and earnings of $80 million per year. At a 90 percent retention rate, the company grows slowly over 10 years to reach earnings of $96 million. However, if it increases its retention rate to 95 percent, it grows almost 50 percent faster and reaches $141 million over the same period. In short, loyalty matters a great deal.

(For those of you who prefer a formula for calculating a customer's lifetime value, we offer one suggested by Don Peppers and Martha Rogers. See Exhibit 4.9.)

EXHIBIT 4.9. **Individual Customer's Lifetime Value (LTV) Formula**

$$LTV = \sum_{i=1}^{n} (1 + d)^{-i} \pi_i$$

Where:

$\pi_i$ = Sales profit from this customer in period **i,** plus any non-sales benefit (references, collaborative value, etc.) in period **i,** less cost of maintaining relationship with this customer in period **i.**

**d** = discount rate.

**n** = final period, estimated to be lifetime horizon for this customer.

*Source:* Don Peppers and Martha Rogers, *One-to-One Future: Building Relationships One Customer at a Time* (New York: Currency/Doubleday, 1993), p. 41.

## Key Concept #2: Customer Satisfaction Does Not Ensure Customer Loyalty.

Okay. Let's say you buy Reichheld's argument that loyal customers are your ticket to success. What should you do to retain your customers? What if you start a customer-satisfaction program? That should do it. Satisfied customers are happy customers, and happy customers don't go wandering off. Right? Wrong, say our gurus.

That's right—our gurus say that customer satisfaction isn't the same thing as customer loyalty. In fact, they caution, customer-satisfaction scores aren't even a very good predictor of customer loyalty. Satisfied customers still leave. Reichheld points to the experience of the U.S. automobile industry, which pioneered the use of customer-satisfaction surveys and spends more of its marketing budget on them than almost any other industry. Today, 90 percent of automobile industry customers report that they are satisfied or very satisfied, but only 30 percent to 40 percent of them purchase the same make the next time they buy an automobile. It is the same across most industries. In fact, says Reichheld, "in business after business 60% to 80% of lost customers reported on a survey just prior to defecting that they were satisfied or very satisfied."[18]

Keki R. Bhote, former senior corporate consultant on quality and productivity at Motorola and author of *Beyond Customer Satisfaction to Customer Loyalty,* says that almost all manufacturers in the appliance industry receive a respectably high customer-satisfaction rating from 90 percent of their customers, but customer-retention rates barely reach 50 percent. He notes that across industries the correlation between customer satisfaction and customer loyalty is very weak. In fact, Bhote goes on, "a high customer satisfaction rating is *no* predictor of customer loyalty."[19]

So, what's going on here? Our gurus note that there is a big difference between a customer being "satisfied" and being "completely satisfied." Anything short of total satisfaction results in a significant drop in loyalty, particularly in highly competitive industries. In short, say our gurus, the only truly loyal customers are totally satisfied customers. (Note that the satisfaction-loyalty relationship varies by industry and level of competition. See Exhibit 4.10.)

### EXHIBIT 4.10. **How the Competitive Environment Affects the Satisfaction-Loyalty Relationship**

In 1995 Thomas O. Jones and W. Earl Sasser reported on the results of a extensive study of the relationship between satisfaction and loyalty across five industries: local telephone, airlines, hospitals, personal computers, and automobiles. The results of their research showed that, while most managers assumed that there was a simple linear relationship between satisfaction and loyalty (i.e., loyalty increases proportionately as satisfaction increases), nothing could be further from the truth. The relationship between satisfaction and loyalty was neither linear nor simple. Instead, it varied by industry. In highly competitive industries where switching costs were low, any drop in satisfaction below the level of completely satisfied resulted in a precipitous drop in loyalty. In contrast, in industries where customers had limited choices, the cost of switching was high, or powerful loyalty programs, such as airline frequent-flyers programs, were in place, the drop-off in loyalty was much less drastic.

*Source:* Thomas O. Jones and W. Earl Sasser Jr. "Why Satisfied Customers Defect," *Harvard Business Review,* November–December 1995, pp. 88–99.

## Key Concept #3: Customers Aren't Created Equal

A third key concept underlying much of the writing about CRM is that customers vary greatly in their value to a company. While all of our CRM gurus preach this message, one of the best explanations of it can be found in *The Customer Marketing Method* by Jay Curry and Adam Curry. They say that the best way to start understanding how customers vary in their impact on your revenue and profits is to construct a "customer pyramid" like that shown in Exhibit 4.11.

EXHIBIT 4.11. **The Customer Pyramid**

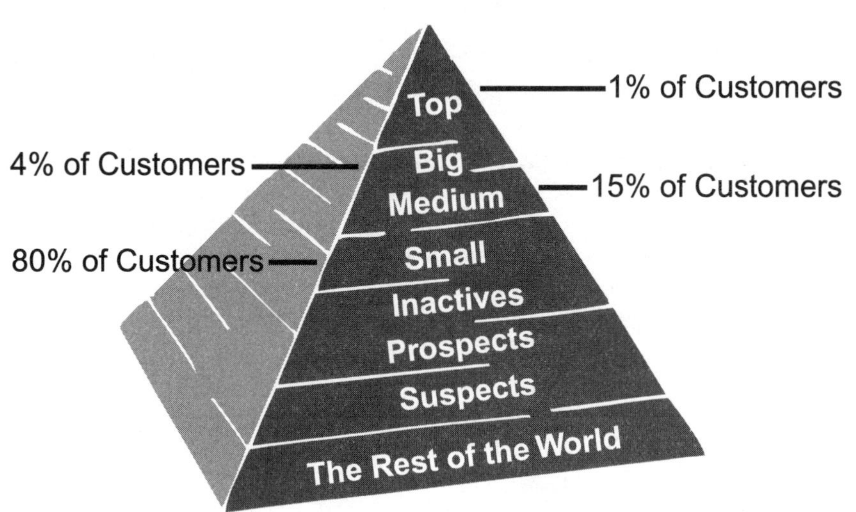


*Source:* Jay Curry and Adam Curry, *The Customer Marketing Method: How to Implement and Profit from Customer Relationship Management* (New York: Free Press, 2000), p. 9.

Here is how Jay Curry suggests you construct your customer pyramid.

1. Identify the top 1 percent of your customers in terms of sales. They go at the top of the pyramid—these are your "top" customers. (For example, if you have 1,000 active customers, the 10 customers who bought the most from you last year are your "top" customers.) (Note: Curry says that as an alternative you may find it more practical and useful to categorize your customers by something other than sales. Banks and insurance companies sometimes group customers by the number of products or product clusters each customer has purchased—one, two, three, or more accounts or types of policies, etc. Retail organizations might use number of visits per month or year cus-

tomers make to stores as the major factor. Automobile dealers might use consecutive purchases. For example, customers who had purchased four or more automobiles in the past would be "top" customers.)

2. Identify the next 4 percent of your customers, again in terms of sales revenues. These are your "big" customers. They go next on the pyramid.
3. Identify your "medium" customers. These are the next 15 percent of your active customers.
4. Identify the remaining 80 percent of your customers. These are your "small" customers.
5. Identify your inactive customers. These are customers who have done business with your company in the past but who haven't made a purchase recently, for example, in the last six months or year. They go next on the pyramid.
6. Identify your active prospects. These are people or companies with whom your sales department has established some kind of relationship but who have not purchased from you yet. They may be people who responded to a mailing, people who have requested information about your company, sales leads from trade shows, and so on. Ask your sales department for input.
7. Identify your suspects. These are people or companies that might need your products or services but with whom you have yet to establish a relationship. Check with your marketing department.
8. At the bottom of the pyramid, lump everyone else in the world. These are companies and people who have no need for your products or services. Curry says that, "while you will never make any money with this group, it is important to visualize them to dramatize how much marketing time and money you spend trying to communicate with people and companies with whom you will never do any business!"[20]

Now that you have your customers and prospects properly categorized, you are ready to do some analysis. Here are some of the questions Curry suggests that you ask about your customer pyramid and some of the lessons he says you might learn.

### *Question #1: Which Customers in Your Customer Pyramid Deliver Most of the Revenues?*

Find out what percentage of your total revenues come from your "top," "big," "medium," and "small" customers and how much revenue each of these categories of customers generate per customer. For example, see the percentages shown in Exhibit 4.12.

**A lesson you may learn.** If your company is like most, says Curry, you will probably be surprised to discover just how few of your customers are responsible for the bulk of your revenues. In the example shown in Exhibit 4.12, the top 20 percent of customers are responsible for over 75 percent of total revenues. Additionally,

EXHIBIT 4.12. **Revenues by Customer Category**

| Customer Category | Percentage of Customers | Percentage of Total Revenues | Revenue per Customer |
|---|---|---|---|
| Top | 1% | 22% | $129,774 |
| Big | 4% | 26% | $37,187 |
| Medium | 15% | 29% | $11,082 |
| Small | 70% | 16% | $1,201 |
| Inactives | 10% | 7% | $983 |

*Source:* Based on Jay Curry and Adam Curry, *The Customer Marketing Method: How to Implement and Profit from Customer Relationship Management* (New York: Free Press, 2000), pp. 18–27.

over 90 percent of revenues come from existing customers, which demonstrates how important an established base of customers is for the success of a business.

### *Question #2: Which Customers Generate the Most Profits?*

Now, determine the percentage of your company's profit and profit per customer for each of your customer groups—top, big, medium, and small. To do this, you will have to allocate direct, sales, marketing, and other costs to the various groups and then deduct those from revenues generated by each group. Curry notes that arriving at the proper allocations can involve some interesting discussions. For example, how should you allocate overhead—by revenues or by number of customers? Curry suggests 50 percent by revenues and 50 percent by number of customers. And how do you allocate marketing and sales costs? For example, where do your salespeople spend their time? Discuss the issues and reach a consensus with your top team concerning how these costs should be allocated. Curry says you shouldn't be concerned that the resulting numbers lack precision. You are not preparing a report for shareholders, the Securities Exchange Commission, or the IRS. You are just trying to get a good understanding of what kinds of customers are profitable and which are not. Once you have performed your calculations, you will probably come up with results that look something like that shown in Exhibit 4.13.

**Some lessons you may learn.** If your company is like most, says Curry, you will probably be surprised to discover that the top 20 percent of your customers not only deliver most of your revenues but actually over 100 percent of your profits. The costs associated with marketing, selling, invoicing, collecting revenues, and otherwise servicing your "small" customers and "inactives" eats up all of the margin for these customers. In other words, you are losing money on 80 percent of your customers!

EXHIBIT 4.13. **Profits by Customer Category**

| Customer Category | Percentage of Customers | Percentage of Total Profits (Losses) | Profit (Losses) per Customer |
|---|---|---|---|
| Top | 1% | 49% | $34,015 |
| Big | 4% | 23% | $8,620 |
| Medium | 15% | 40% | $2,649 |
| Small | 70% | (12)% | $(993) |
| Inactives | 10% | (8)% | $(489) |

*Source:* Based on Jay Curry and Adam Curry, *The Customer Marketing Method: How to Implement and Profit from Customer Relationship Management* (New York: Free Press, 2000), pp. 18–27.

### *Question #3: Where Do You Spend the Bulk of Your Marketing Budget?*

Next, examine how you are spending your marketing dollars. Your results may look something like that shown in Exhibit 4.14.

**Some lessons you may learn.** If your company is like most, says Curry, you will probably find that most of your marketing budget (60 to 80 percent) is spent on communicating with noncustomers. While that may not be too surprising—it takes time, effort, and money to turn noncustomers into customers—you may be surprised at how much you are spending to communicate with people who are not even suspects. A great deal of money is often spent, says Curry, on communicating with people in the "rest of the world" category—people who have no need for or interest in your products or services and who never will.

EXHIBIT 4.14. **Marketing Budget by Customer Category**

| Customer Category | Percentage of Marketing Budget | Percentage of Revenues | Percentage of Profits (Losses) |
|---|---|---|---|
| Top | 1% | 22% | 49% |
| Big | 3% | 26% | 23% |
| Medium | 8% | 29% | 40% |
| Small | 15% | 16% | (12)% |
| Inactives | 3% | 7% | (8)% |
| Prospects | 25% | not applicable | not applicable |
| Suspects | 35% | not applicable | not applicable |
| Rest of the World | 10% | not applicable | not applicable |

*Source:* Based on Jay Curry and Adam Curry, *The Customer Marketing Method: How to Implement and Profit from Customer Relationship Management* (New York: Free Press, 2000), pp. 18–27.

### *Question #4: What Would Be the Impact on Your Revenue and Profits of Moving a Small Number of Customers up the Pyramid?*

Curry suggests you perform some "what if" calculations, such as what would happen to your revenues and profits if you were able to move just a few small customers up the pyramid. See Exhibit 4.15 for an example.

**Some lessons you may learn.** You very likely will find that a small movement of customers up the pyramid can yield significant gains in revenues and substantial grains in profits. In the example in Exhibit 4.15, the movement of just six small customers—one to top, two to big, and three to medium—resulted in a 10 percent increase in revenues and an astounding 61 percent increase in profits. Curry notes that many small customers have the potential of becoming medium, big, or even top customers if given some attention. In fact, you may find that a small customer in your pyramid is actually a top customer in your competitor's. These customers are small in your pyramid because your "share of customer" is low. ("Share of customer" refers to the proportion of a customer's potential business you are getting. For example, if you are Office Depot and a customer buys her printer from you but buys her paper, toner, and ink cartridges from someone else, you are missing some share of customer.)

### *Question #5: What Would Be the Impact on Your Revenue and Profits of Losing a Small Number of Your Top or Big Customers?*

Now, says Curry, you should run some calculations to see what would happen if you lost a few of your top customers. See Exhibit 4.16 for an example.

**Some lessons you may learn.** You very likely will find that the loss of just a few key customers can do significant damage to your revenues and profits. In the example shown in Exhibit 4.16, just two customers defected—one top and one big. Their loss resulted in an 8 percent decline in revenues and a whopping 50 percent fall in profits. As Curry says, the lesson to be learned is that, "if you can't manage your relationship with your key customers, you are going to be in serious trouble."[21]

### *Question #6: Where Do You Want Your Customers to End Up in Your Customer Pyramid Next Year?*

Curry declares that your path to riches, power, and fame is simple. Get new customers into your pyramid, move your existing customers higher in your pyramid, and keep customers from leaving your pyramid. To accomplish these goals, you need to gather information about each and every customer and do some planning. Among other things, according to Curry, you need the following types of information:

EXHIBIT 4.15. **Effect on Revenues and Profits of Upward Migration of Six Customers**

| | Top | Big | Medium | Small | Inactive, Prospects, Suspects | Total |
|---|---|---|---|---|---|---|
| **1999** | | | | | | |
| Number of customers | 4 | 18 | 68 | 360 | N/A | 450 |
| Revenues | $566,115 | $462,561 | $550,633 | $447,674 | N/A | $2,026,983 |
| Profit | $161,586 | $95,322 | $76,605 | $ (96,113) | $ (145,900) | $91,499 |
| **2000** | | | | | | |
| Number of customers | 5 | 20 | 71 | 354 | N/A | 450 |
| Revenues | $707,643 | $513,957 | $574,926 | $440,213 | N/A | $2,236,739 |
| Profit | $201,982 | $105,913 | $79,985 | $ (94,511) | $ (145,900) | $147,469 |
| **Difference** | | | | | | |
| Number of customers | +1 | +2 | +3 | -6 | N/A | 0 |
| Revenues | $141,529 | $51,396 | $24,293 | $ (7,461) | N/A | $209,756 |
| Profit | $40,396 | $10,591 | $3,380 | $1,602 | N/A | $55,969 |
| Percentage Change in Revenues | 25% | 11% | 4% | (2)% | 0% | **10 %** |
| Percentage Change in Profits | 25% | 11% | 4% | (2)% | 0% | **61 %** |

*Source:* Based on Jay Curry and Adam Curry, *The Customer Marketing Method: How to Implement and Profit from Customer Relationship Management* (New York: Free Press, 2000), p. 122, fig. 11.16.

N/A = not applicable.

EXHIBIT 4.16. **Effect on Revenues and Profits of Losing Two Customers**

| | Top | Big | Medium | Small | Inactive, Prospects, Suspects | Total |
|---|---|---|---|---|---|---|
| **1999** | | | | | | |
| Number of customers | 4 | 18 | 68 | 360 | N/A | 450 |
| Revenues | $566,115 | $462,561 | $550,633 | $447,674 | N/A | $2,026,983 |
| Profit | $161,586 | $95,322 | $76,605 | $ (96,113) | $ (145,900) | $91,499 |
| **2000** | | | | | | |
| Number of customers | 3 | 17 | 68 | 360 | N/A | 448 |
| Revenues | $424,586 | $436,863 | $550,633 | $447,674 | N/A | $1,859,757 |
| Profit | $121,189 | $90,026 | $76,605 | $ (96,113) | $ (145,900) | $45,807 |
| **Difference** | | | | | | |
| Number of customers | −1 | −1 | 0 | 0 | N/A | −2 |
| Revenues | $(141,529) | $(25,698) | $0 | $0 | N/A | $(167,226) |
| Profit | $(40,396) | $(5,296) | $0 | $0 | N/A | $(45,692) |
| Percentage Change in Revenues | (25)% | (6)% | 0% | 0% | 0% | **(8)%** |
| Percentage Change in Profits | (25)% | (6)% | 0% | 0% | 0% | **(50) %** |

*Source:* Based on Jay Curry and Adam Curry, *The Customer Marketing Method: How to Implement and Profit from Customer Relationship Management* (New York: Free Press, 2000), p. 121, fig. 11.15.

N/A = not applicable.

### Customer/Prospect Data

**Basic information.** Name, address, phone, and so on.

**Total spend.** This is the total amount this customer will spend on your category of products/services in a year. For example, if you are a grocer, the total spend for the Smith family would be the total amount they would spend for food in a year. If you are a travel agent, the total spend for Company A would be the total amount that company would spend on business travel in a year. Curry suggests three possible sources for information about total spend. First is market research. For example, if you know the number of people in a family, their ages, and their zip code, you can obtain fairly reliable estimates on the amount of money the family will spend on food and clothing in a year. Second, you can interview the customer and ask them. Finally, if interviews are not possible or you don't have time to conduct them, you can ask your salespeople for their best "guesstimates."

**Revenues.** What did each customer spend with you last year? Curry suggests you break this down by type of product/service.

**Customer share.** This is the proportion of a customer's total spend that your company received last year. For example, if Customer A's total spend was $1,000,000 and you sold that customer $100,000 of products last year, your customer share for Customer A last year was 10 percent.

**Costs.** Marketing, sales, and other costs that can be allocated to this customer.

**Profit.** Revenues minus costs.

**Marketing and sales return on investment.** Profit as percentage of marketing and sales costs.

**Location in pyramid.** Top, big, medium, small, inactive, or prospect.

Once you have assembled this data, you then construct a table that looks something like the one shown in Exhibit 4.17.

Like us, you may be looking a little askance at these tables. It looks like a lot of work, and you may be somewhat skeptical about mixing "guesstimates" with hard numbers. Still, as Curry argues, this approach is intended to help you visualize the movement of customers in, up, down, and out of your pyramid and plan for your relationships with customers and prospects. The numbers are working tools and need only to be as precise and accurate as your comfort level dictates. The real test is whether they help you get new customers into your pyramid, get a larger share of the business of your existing customers, and avoid losing those who are most profitable. In other words, will the analysis Curry recommends help you manage your customer relationships? Curry at least thinks it will.

EXHIBIT 4.17. **Customer Goals**

| | Struckman | Green | Sentinel | Bates | Bristol | Bowdoin |
|---|---|---|---|---|---|---|
| **Last Year** | | | | | | |
| Total spend | $592.700 | $34,800 | $151,800 | $18,900 | $58,000 | $3,900 |
| Revenues | $296.337 | $31,010 | $13,659 | $1,717 | $0 | $0 |
| Customer share | 50% | 89% | 9% | 9% | 0% | 0% |
| Costs | $16.251 | $5,066 | $2,232 | $828 | $375 | $1,722 |
| Profit | $102.285 | $7,337 | $3,368 | $ (55) | $ (375) | $ (1,722) |
| Marketing and sales return on investment | 2,170% | 348% | 241% | (13)% | (192)% | (139)% |
| Pyramid | Top | Big | Medium | Small | Inactive | Prospect |
| **Plan** | | | | | | |
| Total spend | $616.408 | $36,192 | $156,354 | $19,467 | $59,740 | $4,017 |
| Revenue target | $354.419 | $32,250 | $28,138 | $3,537 | $8,961 | $0 |
| Percentage change | 20% | 4% | 106% | 106% | | |
| Customer share goal | 57% | 89% | 18% | 18% | 15% | |
| Customer goal | Keep | Keep | Upgrade | Keep | Reactivate | Keep |
| Target pyramid | Top | Big | Big | Small | Medium | Prospect |

*Source:* Jay Curry and Adam Curry, *The Customer Marketing Method: How to Implement and Profit from Customer Relationship Management* (New York: Free Press, 2000), pp. 120, 163, figs. II.14, II.42.

In terms of managing customer relationships, most of our gurus preach one final key concept. Especially today, your customers' relationships with you are strictly voluntary. In short, if you want to market to them, you have to get their permission.

## Key Concept #4: Customers Must Grant Their Permission to Be Marketed

The idea that marketers should first get permission from customers or prospects before marketing to them was first presented by Seth Godin, vice president for direct marketing at Yahoo! in the 1999 book *Permission Marketing.* Godin calls traditional mass marketing "interruption marketing." The marketer *interrupted* what the consumers were doing—"Now a word from our sponsor"—and asked them to take some action, for example, "Buy Super-Duper Pet Food Now!" Interruption marketing, says Godin, has long been the darling of brand managers and marketers for a number of good reasons:

- **It was easy.** All you had to do was develop a few ads and run them.
- **It was scalable.** If you needed more sales, you just bought more ads and interrupted people more often.
- **It was predictable.** Experienced marketers could predict with a fair degree of accuracy how many more dollars in revenue one more dollar in spending on advertisements would generate.
- **It fit the command-and-control mentality of big companies.** The advertiser was in control.
- **Most important, it was profitable.**[22]

The problem with interruption marketing, says Godin, is that it no longer works. Today, there are just too many products, too many services, too many options, and way, way too many ads. There is too much clutter. The only thing of which there is not too much is the consumer's time and attention. That fact, says Godin, poses a real Catch-22 situation for mass "interruption" marketers that goes like this:

1. **Human beings have a finite amount of attention.** You can't watch everything, remember everything, or do everything. As the amount of noise in your life increases, the percentage of messages that get through inevitably decreases.

2. **Human beings have a finite amount of money.** You also can't buy everything. You have to choose. But because your attention is limited, you'll be able to choose only from those things you notice.

3. **The more products offered, the less money there is to go around.** It's a zero sum game. Every time you buy a Coke, you don't buy a Pepsi. As the number of companies offering products increases, and as the number of products each company offers multiplies, it's inevitable that there will be more losers than winners.

4. **In order to capture more attention and more money, interruption marketers must increase spending.** Spending less money than your competitors on advertising in a cluttered environment inevitably leads to decreased sales.

5. **But this increase in marketing exposure costs big money.** Interruption marketers have no choice but to spend a bigger and bigger portion of their company's budgets on breaking through the clutter.

6. **But, as you've seen, spending more and more money in order to get bigger returns leads to ever more clutter.**

7. **Catch-22: The more they spend, the less it works. The less it works, the more they spend.**[23]

The answer to this Catch-22, argues Godin, is to quit interrupting and instead seek permission from the consumer. Godin uses an analogy about getting married to explain the difference between an interruption marketer and a permission marketer.

> The Interruption Marketer buys an extremely expensive suit. New shoes. Fashionable accessories. Then, working with the best database and marketing strategists, selects the demographically ideal singles bar.
>
> Walking into the singles bar, the Interruption Marketer marches up to the nearest person and proposes marriage. If turned down, the Interruption Marketer repeats this process on every person in the bar.
>
> If the Interruption Marketer comes up empty-handed after spending the entire evening proposing, it is obvious that the blame should be placed on the suit and the shoes. The tailor is fired. The strategy expert who picked the bar is fired. And the Interruption Marketer tries again at a different singles bar.
>
> If this sounds familiar, it should. It's the way most large marketers look at the world. They hire an agency. They build fancy ads. They "research" the ideal place to run the ads. They interrupt people and hope that one in a hundred will go ahead and buy something. Then, when they fail, they fire their agency! The other way to get married is a lot more fun, a lot more rational, and a lot more successful. It's called dating.
>
> A Permission Marketer goes on a date. If it goes well, the two of them go on another date. And then another. Until, after ten or twelve dates, both sides can really communicate with each other about their needs and desires. After twenty dates they meet each other's families. Finally, after three or four months of dating, the Permission Marketer proposes marriage.
>
> Permission Marketing is just like dating. It turns strangers into friends and friends into lifetime customers. Many of the rules of dating apply, and so do many of the benefits.[24]

Godin lists five steps to the permission marketing/dating process.

### Step #1: Offer the Prospect an Incentive to Volunteer

Godin states that the incentive for volunteering can range from information to entertainment to a sweepstakes to outright payment for the prospect's attention. "But," he notes, "the incentive must be overt, obvious, and clearly delivered."[25] You are going on a "first date" with the prospect, so you have to offer something interesting enough to be worth the prospect's investment of time, money, and ego. What happens at this stage of the permission-marketing process, according to Godin, is one of the most obvious differences between interruption marketing and permission marketing. "Interruption marketers spend all their time interrupting strangers, in an almost pitiful attempt to bolster popularity and capture attention. Permission marketers spend as little time and money talking to strangers as they can. Instead they move as quickly as they can to turn strangers into prospects who choose to 'opt in' to a series of communications."[26]

### Step #2: Using the Attention Offered by the Prospect, Offer a Curriculum Over Time, Teaching the Consumer about Your Product or Service

Once the prospects have granted you permission to market to them, it is easier to educate them about your product. "Instead of filling each ensuing message with entertainment designed to attract attention or with sizzle designed to attract the attention of strangers," writes Godin, "the Permission Marketer is able to focus on product benefits—on specific, focused ways this product will help that prospect."[27]

### Step #3: Reinforce the Incentive to Guarantee That the Prospect Maintains the Permission

Godin notes that even the best incentive will lose its affect over time. Fortunately, since the permission marketer is now engaged in a true dialogue with the prospect, the marketer has more precise information about the prospect's desires and can adjust the incentive, tailoring it specifically to the prospect's needs and interests.

### Step #4: Offer Additional Incentives to Get Even More Permission from the Consumer

Additional permission could be you gathering more information about the customer, providing product samples, or offering a new category of products or services for the prospect's consideration. See Exhibit 4.18 for six levels of permission Godin identifies, ranging from limited situational permission (for example, a customer orders a hamburger at McDonald's, and the employee takes advantage of the situation to ask, "Do you want fries with that?") to intravenous permission (the level of trust is so high between the department-store clerk and customer that the customer allows the clerk to select and send her apparel without prior approval). Exhibit 4.19 provides a slightly different way of looking at the levels of relationships customers may have with a company, as offered by Ian Gordon.

## EXHIBIT 4.18. The Levels of Permission

Godin lists six levels of permission, plus one level he describes as "below the baseline" of true permission marketing.

| Level | Description | Example |
|---|---|---|
| **Intravenous** (the highest level of permission) | The company has permission to select, bill, and ship an item without the customer's prior approval. | Poland Springs automatically replenishes the water cooler in your office and sends you a monthly bill. |
| **"Purchase on approval"** | The company has permission to select an item but needs prior approval before shipment. | Columbia Record Club chooses a record for you and sends you a notice a month in advance. You can reject the record, and they won't ship it. |
| **Points** | Customers receive "points" in return for their attention or repeat purchases. Some "points" have actual value since they can be exchanged for products or services. Others merely entitle customers to enter a lottery for a chance at winning an award. | Airline frequent-flyer programs. |
| **Personal relationship** | The attention and repeat business the customer grants the company stems from a personal relationship that has been established over time. | Your corner dry cleaner has permission to recommend a new treatment for a stained coat because you have known him for some time and trust his judgment. |
| **Brand trust** | Godin describes this as "the tried and true branding that is the mantra of most Interruption Marketers. It is the virtually unmeasurable but oh-so-fun way to be in the marketing business. (p. 123). | You buy Ivory soap because your mother bought Ivory soap. By extension, you'll also buy Ivory dishwashing liquid. |
| **Situational** | The consumer and salesperson/marketer are in close physical and social proximity, and the consumer has initiated the interaction. | You order a hamburger at McDonald's, and the order taker suggests, "Would you like fries with that?" |

(continued)

EXHIBIT 4.18. **(continued)**

| Level | Description | Example |
|---|---|---|
| **Spam** (below the baseline level) | There's no permission. The marketer just sends you the message on a one-in-a-million chance you might be interested. | Junk e-mail is the classic example. |

*Source:* Adapted from Seth Godin and Don Peppers, *Permission Marketing: Turning Strangers into Friends, and Friends into Customers* (New York: Simon & Schuster, 1999), pp. 97–130.

*Note:* Godin combines the intravenous and "purchase on approval" levels, but we believe the two are sufficiently different to be considered separate levels.

EXHIBIT 4.19. **Levels of Customer Bonding**

Ian Gordon describes six levels of customer bonding based on the share of business and "share of mind" a company derives from these customers. Share of business is basically the same thing as share of customer—how much of their total business a company receives. "Share of mind" has to do with the customer's favorable repeat-purchase intention and perception of the firm. From lowest to highest, the levels of customer bonding are as follows:

| | |
|---|---|
| **Prospects** | Customers drawn from the general population who fit the profile of your desired customer. |
| **Testers** | Prospects who have become aware of the company and have made an initial purchase. |
| **Shoppers** | Testers who were satisfied with their initial experience and have begun doing business with your firm on a regular basis. |
| **Accounts** | Shoppers who view your firm as a major supplier. |
| **Patrons** | Long-term accounts who trust your firm and over time give you an increasing share of their total business. |
| **Advocates** | These are patrons who have become so committed to your firm that they will stand up for your firm and tell us about it. They are a major source of business referrals. |

*Source:* Ian Gordon, *Relationship Marketing: New Strategies, Techniques, and Technologies to Win the Customers You Want and Keep Them Forever* (Etobicoke, Ontario: Wiley, Canada, 1998), pp. 100–101.

### Step #5: Over Time, Leverage the Permission to Change Consumer Behavior toward Profits

You take advantage of the consumers' permission to change their response from "no" to "yes," from "I don't" to "I do." You sell more and more products, in short, as Jay Curry puts it, increasing your customer share.

## The Rules of Permission Marketing

Godin maintains that permission brings significant advantages to the marketer. Even at the lowest level of permission, you have won the attention of strangers who have self-selected your company as one that could offer them value. As you interact with these strangers and gain increasing levels of permission, you gradually turn them into prospects, then customers, then loyal customers. You gain customer share through what Godin thinks is the perfect alternative to the nasty old ineffective mass interruption marketing. However, he warns, permission is worthless unless you can keep it and enhance it. To do that, you must be mindful of four simple rules of permission.

#### Permission rule #1: Permission is nontransferable.

"It doesn't matter how long you have been dating," writes Godin, "you're not allowed to send a stand-in on a date. You're not allowed to date your best friend's girlfriend or boyfriend."[28] Godin notes that traditional marketers have a problem with this rule. In traditional mass interruption marketing, it is not only okay but common practice to rent, sell, or transfer data you have about prospects or customers. In permission marketing, such clandestine transfers of data are forbidden. As Godin puts it, *permission rented is permission lost.* Just don't do it.

#### Permission rule #2: Permission is selfish.

Interruption marketers, writes Godin, like their approach because it allows them to be in control. You don't decide whether or when to watch a Tide commercial; they do. Permission marketers forfeit control. With permission marketing, the consumer is in charge, and, notes Godin, the consumer is very selfish. "Consumers care very little about you, your company, your products, your career, or your family. They're not likely to spend time trying to discover how you can help them solve their problems."[29] Instead, you have to give them a reason to pay attention. You have to answer the consumer's number-one question—What's in it for me?—constantly and correctly. If you can't keep answering that question to your customer's satisfaction, you lose permission.

***Permission rule #3: Permission is a process, not a moment.***

Permission marketing may begin with an interruption—after all, you have to get their attention somehow—but it rapidly becomes a dialogue. Permission marketing is a long-term relationship. It's a process of getting to know each other, akin to dating. Godin warns that you should expect it to take time, patience, and confidence. It won't work overnight.

***Permission rule #4: Permission can be canceled at any time.***

Godin notes that, because the consumer can cancel permission at any time, the permission marketer must craft every message so the consumer will be receptive to future messages. He illustrates this rule with the story of Scheherazade, who, in the Arabian tale, lived in a land ruled by a cruel dictator:

> Every day the dictator married another beautiful woman. He enjoyed their honeymoon and the next day had her beheaded.
>
> When it came Scheherazade's turn, she had the natural insecurity of a Permission Marketer—she knew that she might be canceled the next day. Her strategy was brilliant. That night, before she and the king went to bed, she told him a story. It was personal and relevant, and the king was eager to hear what happened next.
>
> A few paragraphs before the end Scheherazade decided that she was too tired to continue and promised to finish the story later. The next morning she turned to the king and said, "I guess it's time for my beheading." The king, eager to hear how the story turned out, demurred. "No, my dear. We can wait until tomorrow. Tonight you will complete the story for me."
>
> You can probably guess the ending. Each night for 1,001 nights, Scheherazade finished a story and then told a new story, promising the ending tomorrow. After more than three years, the king forgot all about beheading her, and she had a customer for life.[30]

## ARE YOU RIGHT FOR CRM? IS CRM RIGHT FOR YOU?

From the way our gurus describe CRM, it sounds like the be-all and end-all of marketing. If so, everyone should be doing it, right? Not necessarily. Despite their enthusiasm—and they are enthusiastic—our gurus admit that sometimes CRM just isn't worth the effort. So, how do you tell if it is worth your effort? Let's see what Don Peppers and Martha Rogers have to say.

According to Peppers and Rogers, the relevancy of CRM to your business depends on two things:[31]

1. How alike your customers are in terms of value to your company.
2. How alike your customers are in their needs.

They define four types of companies based on the customer's value and needs.

- Quadrant I companies. Those with customers of uniform value and uniform needs.
- Quadrant II companies. Those with customers with diverse needs but uniform value.
- Quadrant III companies. Those with customers with diverse value but uniform needs.
- Quadrant IV companies. Those with customers with diverse value and needs.

See Exhibit 4.20 for examples of each type of company.

EXHIBIT 4.20. **Types of Companies**

| Quadrant III | Quadrant IV |
|---|---|
| **Diverse Value:** 2% of your customers account for 50% of your revenues. | **Diverse Value:** 2% of your customers account for 50% of your revenues. |
| **Uniform Needs:** You provide commodity-like goods and services. Each customer's needs are similar to those of other customers. | **Diverse Needs:** Each customer's needs are complicated and unique; e.g., different from those of other customers. |
| **Examples:** | **Examples:** |
| Airlines | Computer systems |
| Car washes | Pharmacies |
| Packaged-goods manufacturers | Professional services |
| **Quadrant I** | **Quadrant II** |
| **Uniform Value:** Top 20% of customers account for 50% of revenues. | **Uniform Value:** Top 20% of customers account for 50% of revenues. |
| **Uniform Needs:** You provide commodity-like goods and services. Each customer's needs are similar to those of other customers. | **Diverse Needs:** Each customer's needs are complicated and unique; e.g., different from those of other customers. |
| **Examples:** | **Examples:** |
| Gas stations | Bookstores |
| Fast-food restaurant | Music stores |
| Commodity grain dealer | Florists |

*Source:* Adapted from Don Peppers and Martha Rogers, *Enterprise One-to-One: Tools for Competing in the Interactive Age* (New York: Currency/Doubleday, 1997), pp. 55–77.

Peppers and Rogers argue that if your customers fall primarily in quadrant IV, that is, they are highly differentiated both in needs and value to your business, then your business is a natural candidate for CRM. On the other hand, if your customers fall primarily in quadrant I, that is, they are highly uniform in terms of their needs and value, then CRM probably is not going to be a cost-effective strategy. Generally, say Peppers and Rogers, CRM is ideal for quadrant IV companies, possibly useful for quadrant II companies, somewhat problematic for quadrant III companies, and very problematic for quadrant I companies.

Does that mean you shouldn't consider CRM unless your customers are primarily in quadrant IV or II? No. What it means, say Peppers and Rogers, is that you have to try to change your customers' behavior to resemble quadrant IV customers more closely. They offer the following two strategies:

1. You can attempt to expand your customers' need set by offering additional services or benefits, like products, to your commodity. For example, a quadrant I commodity grain dealer could offer her customers tailored billing and/or delivery options in order to move her customer base more toward quadrant II. This strategy involves improving your production, logistics, and service-delivery functions—enhancing your ability to offer and deliver different products and services to different customers, even to the point of customizing your products and services for individual customers.
2. You can find more efficient ways to interact with your customers individually in order to better understand their value. For example, a quadrant II bookstore might increase its ability to interact with customers by establishing a Web site wherein it could capture information on individual customer preferences and interests and thereby move at least part of its customer base toward quadrant IV. This strategy focuses on the flexibility of your customer communications—making your communications more interactive so that you can better understand both customers' needs and their value.

## BASIC STEPS TO CRM

Let's assume that your customers fall primarily in quadrants II or IV or that you have a plan for migrating your customers toward quadrant IV behavior. That makes you a prime candidate for CRM. So, the questions become, How do I do it? What are the basic steps for implementing CRM? As you can imagine, each of our gurus has his or her own multistep process for taking your company from antiquated mass marketing to state-of-the-art customer-relationship management. Peppers and Rogers recommend one of the simplest processes. (Exhibit 4.21 shows a 12-step "route map" advocated by Stanley A. Brown, author of *Strategic Customer Care.*) The Peppers and Rogers process consists of just four steps:

1. Identify your customers.
2. Differentiate your customers.
3. Interact with your customers.
4. Customize some aspects of your enterprise's behavior.

In the following sections, we look at each of these steps in detail. Then we discuss how technology is making the execution of these steps both possible and practical for most businesses today.

## EXHIBIT 4.21. The Route Map to Customer Care

In his book *Strategic Customer Care,* Stanley A. Brown identifies three stages or levels of customer-management practices. Stage I companies focus primarily on customer acquisition and have low levels of customer loyalty and retention. Stage II companies recognize that customer retention is critical and make at least some effort to differentiate their customers. Stage III companies practice strategic account management. They recognize that some "crown jewel" customers require special attention, and they provide special benefits and highly differentiated service for these customers. Brown suggests the following 12 steps for moving to Stage III.

1. **Management alignment and mobilization.** Gain the buy-in, understanding, and consent of management to move to Stage III customer care.
2. **Change-readiness assessment.** Assess the potential constraints and relevant issues that could impact movement to Stage III, including management's ability to manage the change.
3. **Customer segmentation.** Segment your customers to identify the select few strategic customers for whom you can add value and with whom you can increase profitability.
4. **Customer profiling.** Assemble information to help you understand the characteristics of your strategic customers.
5. **Voice-of-the-customer (VOC) intervention.** Identify, from your customer's perspective, the areas in which you need to improve and where you should concentrate your efforts.
6. **Gap analysis.** Identify the gaps that exist in understanding customer requirements between your senior management, middle management, frontline support staff, and your customers.
7. **Strategic-account-team mobilization.** Establish a strategic account team for each of your strategic customers.
8. **Strategic action planning.** Plan and document specific actions you will take to address issues important to your customers.

(continued)

EXHIBIT 4.21. **(continued)**

9. **Customer alignment.** Obtain customer input and gain customer support for your strategic action plan.
10. **Team training.** Provide essential training to enable team members to address the customer's issues and manage the change process.
11. **Implementation mobilization.** Implement the actions and strategies you have identified.
12. **Performance monitoring and adjustment.** Track progress against your goals, evaluate your efforts, and make adjustments.

*Source:* Based on Stanley A. Brown, *Strategic Customer Care: An Evolutionary Approach to Increasing Customer Value and Profitability* (Toronto: Wiley, 1999), pp. 130–140, 152–154.

## Step #1: Identify Your Customers

Your first step, say Peppers and Rogers, is simply to identify as many of your customers as you can by asking yourself the following questions:

- How many customers does your firm actually *know,* individually?
- Do you have a customer database with identifying information on all your customers or any portion of them? ("Customer identifying information" is any information you can use to separate one particular customer from another, track your transactions and interactions with the customer over time, or get in touch with the customer individually: name, rank, and serial number. Other examples include postal address, phone number, e-mail address, position description or title, and account number.)[32]
- How current and accurate is that database?
- How much information about each customer does it contain?
- Does each different business unit within your company have its own database?
- Are there other sources of customer-identifying information?
- Are there any simple ways to increase the amount of customer data available to your firm?

Peppers and Rogers predict that one problem you will likely encounter as you attempt to answer these questions is arriving at a definition of "customer." "Is your customer simply the next step down in your distribution channel? Or is your customer better defined as the end user of your product?"[33] There is no correct answer, but, warn our gurus, the way you answer this question will significantly impact how you implement CRM. Take, for example, a manufacturer of building materials, such as Owens Corning. Is its customer the end user of the building materials, the chain retailer, or the wholesale distributor? If Owens Corning identifies the "first buyer" (the wholesale distributor) as its customer, it has a lot fewer customers than if it identifies its customer as one of the millions of end users of its products.

Once you have defined your customer, Peppers and Rogers instruct you to do three things:

1. Take an inventory of all customer data already available in an electronic format.
2. Locate customer-identifying information that is currently "on file" but not in an electronic format.
3. Devise strategies for collecting more information. This latter step may entail going to third-party database firms that sell individual customer information.[34]

Your goal at this stage, say our gurus, is to identify and bring together all of the information you can find for each and every customer, or at least for those customers who are most valuable to your firm. (See our previous discussion of the customer pyramid in this chapter.) For a list of the types of information one of our gurus thinks you should include in your customer database, see Exhibit 4.22 if your customers are individuals and Exhibit 4.23 if your customers are businesses.

EXHIBIT 4.22. **Customer Information: Individual**

The following is a partial list of types of information for an individual customer information file as suggested by Ian Gordon in his book *Relationship Marketing*.

### Identification

- Account or identification number.
- Name.
- Telephone number.

### Customer Rating

- Position in customer pyramid.
  Pyramid target.
- Permission level.
- Permission target.

### Background

- Household size.
- Family structure.
- Spouse.
- Children.

(continued)

EXHIBIT 4.22. **(continued)**

- Age.
- Date of birth.
- Home address.
- Business address.
- Shipping address.
- Salary income or range.
- Asset or wealth estimate or range.
- Highest level of education achieved.
- Educational institutions attended.
- Memberships of professional associations.
- Memberships of other organizations: leisure, community, religious or other.
- Height.
- Weight.
- Consumption habits or preferences.
- Color preferences evident in items of fashion, nonfashion.
- Purchase locations (where are purchases made).
- Timing of spending (e.g., any noticeable skews by time of day, day, week).
- Lifestyle categorization.
- Psychographic segment.
- Leisure pursuits.

## Presale Communication

Number of "touches" or contacts prior to purchases.

- Types of information sought.
- Channels of communication initiated by customer (telephone, Internet, etc.).
- Type of information sought.
- Offers and promotional material sent directly, by date.
- Sensitivity to different media.
- Medium that contributed to first purchase (telemarketing, Internet, etc.).

## Purchase Behavior

- Specific items by categorization code, such as SKU number.
- Date of customer's first purchase.
- Dates of all subsequent purchases.
- Date of last purchase.
- Frequency with which purchases are made (per day, week, month, year).
- Amount spent on customer's first purchase.
- Amount spent on all subsequent purchases.
- Amount spent on last purchase.
- Margin derived from customer's first purchase.
- Margin derived from all subsequent purchases.

(continued)

EXHIBIT 4.22. **(continued)**

- Margin derived from last purchase.
- Average expenditures.
- Average margin on expenditures
- For first purchase and all subsequent purchases, method of payment for goods or services bought: cash, credit card, store card.

### PostPurchase Behavior

- Items returned.
- Condition in which returned.
- Purchase amounts of returned product.
- Tone and manner of return, customer.
- Customer complaint frequency, recency.
- Customer satisfaction with issue resolution.
- Elapsed time between product purchase and return.

### Predicted Behavior

- Product or service expected to be bought next.
- Purchase location where product may be bought.
- Media of primary influence.
- Level of expenditure or price range of product.
- Ancillary services that customer may purchase together with the product.

### Creditworthiness

- Bad debt history.
- Balance on account.
- Default on minimum payments on account.
- Credit scoring and rating.

### Attitudes and Perceptions

- Key selection and patronage criteria, company overall.
- Key selection and patronage criteria, specific departments or product lines.
- Perceptions of the company in respect to criteria.
- Perceptions of competitors in respect to criteria.
- Opportunities to improve positioning, by major area of purchase.
- Opportunities to improve positioning, overall.

*Source:* Adapted from Ian Gordon, *Relationship Marketing: New Strategies, Techniques, and Technologies to Win the Customers You Want and Keep Them Forever* (New York: Wiley, 1999) pp. 206–209.

### EXHIBIT 4.23. **Customer Information: Business Customer**

The following is a partial list of types of information for a business customer information file as suggested by Ian Gordon in his book *Relationship Marketing*.

## Identification

- Account or identification number.
- Company name.
- Main telephone number.

## Customer Rating

- Position in customer pyramid.
- Pyramid target.
- Permission level.
- Permission target.

## Background

- Industry classification code (SIC).
- Employment levels.
- Date first incorporated.
- Date first started making relevant products.
- Corporate affiliations and interownerships.
- Head-office location.
- Regional offices.
- Manufacturing locations.
- Size, total sales.
- Growth rate, total.
- Size, relevant products.
- Growth rate, relevant products.
- Profitability, overall.
- Profitability, relevant products.
- Cash flow, overall.
- Financial position (relevant ratios, from financial statements). Could include the following:
  Return on investment.
  Operating profit on net sales.
  Asset turnover: sales/assets.
  Current ratio: current assets/current liabilities.
  Stability ratios, such as debt/assets.
  Overhead: general, selling, and administration/net sales.
  Coverage: times interest earned.
  Growth: sales growth/asset growth.
- Market size for customer's products.
- Market segment participation.
- Market share.

(continued)

EXHIBIT 4.23. **(continued)**

- Customer's major customers.
- Major suppliers to this company.
- Duration of relationships with major suppliers.

## Presale Communication

- Number of "touches" or contacts prior to purchases.
- Types of information sought.
- Channels of communication initiated by customer (telephone, Internet, etc.).
- Contact history, nonpersonal.
- Offers and promotional material sent directly, by date.
- Sensitivity to different media.
- Medium that contributed to first purchase (telemarketing, Internet, etc.).
- Call history: personal sales calls, by date, by audience.
- Call reports.

## Purchases

- Specific items or services bought by categorization code, such as SKU number.
- Date of customer's first purchase.
- Dates of all subsequent purchases.
- Date of last purchase.
- Frequency with which purchases are made (per day, week, month, year).
- Amount spent on customer's first purchase.
- Amount spent on all subsequent purchases.
- Amount spent on last purchase.
- Margin derived from customer's first purchase.
- Margin derived from all subsequent purchases.
- Margin derived from last purchase.
- Average expenditures.
- Average margin on expenditures.
- Financing: method of payment for first purchase and all subsequent purchases.

## Decision Makers

- Names.
- Titles.
- Our staff who have relationships with these people.
- Scoring of quality of relationships we enjoy.
- Relationship scoring we plan to achieve, by person.

## Decision Making

- Process.
- Decision initiators.
- Decision influencers.
- Decision makers.

(continued)

EXHIBIT 4.23. **(continued)**

- Decision confirmers.
- Executors of decision.
- Purchase cycle.
- Time required to make decision, by type of decision: new buy, rebuy.
- Month when decisions are initiated, by type of product.
- Month when decisions are final.
- Criteria and positioning.
- Vendor-selection criteria.
- Product-selection criteria.
- Key selection and patronage criteria, overall company.
- Key selection and patronage criteria, specific departments or product lines.
- Perceptions of our company in respect to criteria.
- Perceptions of competitors in respect to criteria.
- Opportunities to improve positioning, by major area of purchase.
- Opportunities to improve positioning, overall.

## Influences

- Factors influencing level of business contracted.
- Business cycle.
- Derived demand dependencies.

## Postpurchase Behavior

- Services required.
- Items returned.
- Condition in which returned.
- Purchase amounts of returned product.
- Tone and manner of return, customer.
- Customer complaint frequency, recency.
- Customer satisfaction with issue resolution.
- Elapsed time between product purchase and return.

## Channels

- Intermediaries used for product, type and name.
- Intermediaries used for service, type and name.
- Customer satisfaction with channel intermediaries.
- Opportunities to enhance aspects of intermediary performance.

## Pricing

- Pricing history.
- Pricing expectations.
- Win/loss assessments: prices of winning vendors.
- Pricing structures preferred.

(continued)

EXHIBIT 4.23. **(continued)**

**Predicted Behavior**
- Product or service expected to be bought next.
- Decision maker for next purchase.
- Value of purchase.
- Decision maker's expectations of supplier preceding purchase.
- Media of primary influence.
- Ancillary services which customer may purchase together with the product.
- Vendor preference, if any.
- Current incumbent, if any.

**Creditworthiness**
- Debt history.
- Receivables on account.
- Payment schedule.
- Credit scoring and rating.

**Selected Relevant Information**
- Customer's customers.
- Business strategies.
- Key initiatives.
- Account planning.

*Source:* Adapted from Ian Gordon, *Relationship Marketing: New Strategies, Techniques and Technologies to Win the Customers You Want and Keep Them Forever* (New York: Wiley, 1998), pp. 209–213.

As you peruse the lists in Exhibits 4.22 and 4.23, you may be struck, as we were, by the breadth and depth of information our gurus suggest you assemble about your customers. We can't help but believe that some of this is excessive. In addition, the exhaustive nature of the lists may raise some concerns about privacy. Peppers and Rogers recommend, and we agree, that you should develop and publish a policy on customer privacy before you start collecting customer data. At a minimum, they say, your privacy policy should include the following:

1. An itemized list of the kind of information collected about individual customers.
2. Specification of how personal information will be used by the company. If your policy is to use this kind of information only within the company on a need-to-know basis and not to make it accessible to unauthorized employees at any time, explain this policy explicitly.

3. A commitment not to use individual customer information in certain ways (e.g., personal information is never sold or rented to others or never used to change prices or insurance premiums, etc.).
4. A statement of the benefits individual customers can expect as a result of the enterprise's use of their information (faster or preferential service, reduced costs, etc).
5. A list of customers' options for directing the enterprise not to use or disclose certain kinds of information.
6. A statement of how customers can change or update personal information you've collected. For example, can consumers access their profile or account information on-line and modify it?
7. The identity of events that may precipitate notification to the customer by the enterprise. For instance, will you notify any customers whose information is subpoenaed by a court?
8. The name of the corporate executive assigned as the "data steward" and charged with overall responsibility for assuring the adherence to company information and privacy policies.
9. Specification of the situations in which your company accepts or denies liability for damages incurred through the collection and use of customer data, such as through credit card-fraud or misuse.
10. A provision for specific procedures allowing customers to order you to stop collecting data about them or to purge their information from your files.

For additional recommendations and assistance in drafting your privacy statement, see the Web site http://www.truste.com.

## Step #2: Differentiate Your Customers

Once you have identified your customers and the information that you have about them, your next step, say Peppers and Rogers, is to differentiate them by their value to your company and by their needs. We discussed how to rank your customers by their value earlier in this chapter, in our discussion of how to construct the customer pyramid. Therefore, we will focus here on how you differentiate your customers by needs. Peppers and Rogers explain that you will want to identify two types of needs:

1. **Community needs.** These are needs, preferences, or priorities that groups of customers have in common with each other. For example, if you run a bookstore, you may notice that some of your customers primarily purchase works of fiction while others prefer biographies. Thus, you have the fiction community and the biography community, each of whose customers have different needs. The value of understanding the communities to which each customer belongs and the needs of those communities, say Peppers and

Rogers, is that you can anticipate what your customers want. You may even be able to detect customers' wants before they do. Continuing with our example of the bookstore, if you know that a customer is in the biography community, then you may be able to suggest to them a new biography that has just come out. Like Amazon.com, you can say to your customer, "Here are examples of books that people with similar interest to yours are reading. I think you might like them too."

2. **Individual needs.** In addition to belonging to communities and sharing community needs with other customers, customers also have individual needs, or needs they don't share with any other customer. Suppose, say Peppers and Rogers, you are a florist and you track your customers' purchases. You know that John Smith bought a dozen roses for his mother on her birthday last year. Of course, celebrating John's mother's birthday isn't a need shared by a community, except perhaps the community of John's family. However, by knowing that John likes to send flowers to his mother on her birthday, you can help him fulfill that need. You can send him a reminder and simultaneously suggest an arrangement of roses. Like Hallmark, you might even develop the ability to offer a special service to John and your other customers. You'll keep track of their important dates (birthdays, anniversaries, etc.) and send them reminders, along with suggestions for flower arrangements that would fit the occasion. If your relationship with your customers is close enough, you may even move to the level of permission (recall our previous discussion of permission levels) so that you can pick and send flower arrangements without the customer having to do anything but pay the bill and take credit for being thoughtful.

Our gurus maintain that the best way to determine your customers' community and individual needs is to interview them, either in person, by phone, or through written questionnaires. Jay Curry argues that these "customer interviews—*ideally with each and every one of your customers (and prospects)*—are a critical element of [customer-relationship management]."[35] He identifies five important benefits you will obtain from conducting them:

1. **You will discover the real needs and problems of each customer.** Armed with this knowledge, you will be able to tailor precisely your offers and products and services to meet the customers' needs and solve their problems.
2. **You will find out what aspects of your business are not satisfying each customer and what things you are doing right.** You can then immediately act to fix the problem for the individual customer and, with the aggregated information, improve aspects that seem to be less than satisfactory for many customers. A customer interview can also prevent the defection of a customer. It is not impossible that you will hear something like this: "I am glad you are here so we could straighten out this problem. Because, believe me, I was about to stop buying from you."

3. **You will be able to determine the current and future potential of each customer.** Through the use of "funnel questioning," you can drill down to discover current budgets and future plans for purchasing your products and services. And if you do it correctly, you will also learn which of your competitors your customers are doing business with or are trying to eat your lunch. This information is essential in helping you set realistic targets for each customer and decide how much time to invest in reaching the targets.
4. **You will deepen your relationship with each customer.** "Let's talk about me!" is an unspoken wish of just about everyone. The most fascinating topic of conversation for people is themselves and their business. Aside from gaining critical information, the process of asking questions, listening carefully, and responding appropriately will inevitably strengthen your bond with every customer you interview. Normally, a face-to-face customer interview is scheduled to take 45 minutes. But quite often the customers find the experience so positive that they cancel other appointments to continue it for another 45 minutes of "face time" so valuable to you.
5. **You will generate additional sales revenues immediately and in the longer term.** The customer interview is not a sales call. You inform the customer in advance that you want to get his opinions about his industry, his needs, his plans. And you tell him that you will not bring your order book. But quite often, during the interview, the customer will say: "While you are here, let me tell you about a situation that your company may be able to solve." (It's tough to resist the temptation to suspend the interview but you should suggest that you will come back to the issue when the interview is completed!)[36]

Curry notes that financial and sales managers usually respond with considerable skepticism to his suggestion that they interview not just some but all of their customers. Financial managers are sure it will cost too much—"What? Do an interview with every customer? You're crazy. That'll cost too much money! A telephone interview costs $10 each, and we have 3,000 customers. That's $30,000. No way!" And sales managers are sure the effort will take up too much of their salespeoples' valuable time—"What? Spend an hour or two with each customer? That'll take too much time! We simply don't have the time to meet with each customer to find out what their needs are and how we can help them solve their problems with our products and services. *We have to go out and sell!*"

However, Curry says, when he points out that it normally costs a company as much as $30 a month just to invoice a customer, then the financial managers begin to understand that spending $10 to find out if a customer will stay a customer isn't so much. And, he says, sales managers begin to see the light once he explains that (1) face-to-face customer interviews can be conducted by salespeople during normal sales calls, (2) once they know more about a customer's needs, salespeople will be able to reduce the frequency of their sales calls, and (3) a number of the customer interviews will actually result in an unexpected sales.

Exhibit 4.24 summarizes the advantages and disadvantages of in-person and telephone interviews versus surveys or questionnaires. Our gurus maintain that, regardless of the method you choose, you should cover the following topics at a minimum:

- Satisfaction levels with your core products and services. (Remember that the only satisfaction level that correlates with customer retention is "completely satisfied.")
- Cross-selling and up-selling opportunities.
- Discrepancies, or "gaps," between importance of a value proposition and satisfaction.
- Loyalty indicators that ascertain if the customer:

  –Considers you the preferred supplier.
  –Is planning to buy from you next year.
  –Recommends you to colleagues, friends, and family.

- Budgets for your product/service category in the future (total spend data).
- Identification of competitive suppliers (customer share data).
- Customer preferences for contact methods and frequencies.
- Plus anything else you want to know from your customers but, until now, were afraid to ask![37]

EXHIBIT 4.24. **Personal, Telephone, and Questionnaire Interviews: Advantages and Disadvantages**

| Format | Advantages | Disadvantages |
|---|---|---|
| Telephone/In person | • The interviewer-customer dialogue allows opportunity to branch out into areas not covered in the interviewer's outline.<br>• The process permits more extensive and in-depth explorations of topics.<br>• Some executives may accord the interview more weight than | • Interviewers cannot target as many people—whether in person or by telephone—as can be reached by the mail survey.<br>• Studies have indicated that subjects may be more inhibited and less forthright in a personal interview than they are when |

(continued)

EXHIBIT 4.24. **(continued)**

| Format | Advantages | Disadvantages |
|---|---|---|
| | given to surveys and may therefore put more thought into their responses. | filling out a survey in the privacy of their offices.<br>• Busy executives tend to find the interview process time consuming, making scheduling and performing the actual interview more difficult.<br>• Because of the likelihood of a broader range of responses, summarizing, categorizing, or otherwise arranging the findings can be difficult. |
| Written-survey questionnaire | • The mailed form can reach a much larger number of customers than the personal interviews.<br>• The larger number of responses possible with the survey means greater statistical validity for the resulting data.<br>• Surveys enable you to evaluate a larger number of customer relationships.<br>• In some cases, a customer may be more forthright filling out a form than they would be in a face-to-face interview.<br>• Survey findings are easier to summarize and period-to-period comparisons to measure progress are easier to prepare. | • Executives may be more likely to dismiss a form as being unworthy of their time and attention.<br>• Feedback is confined to to the material and questions on the form. There is no opportunity to deviate into other areas. |

*Source:* Adapted from Stanley A. Brown, *Strategic Customer Care: An Evolutionary Approach to Increasing Customer Value and Profitability* (Toronto: Wiley, Canada, 1999), pp. 81–82.

## Step #3: Interact with Your Customers

Once you have differentiated your customers by their value to your company and their needs, your next step, say Peppers and Rogers, is to engage your customers in an ongoing dialogue so that you can learn more and more over time about their interests, needs, and priorities. Opportunities for customer interaction are endless and include the following:

- Direct sales calls.
- E-mail and electronic data interchange (EDI).
- Facsimile messages (inbound and outbound).
- Mail (postal).
- Point of purchase (information captured from customers at cash registers or checkout positions and/or during service delivery).
- Telephone (inbound and outbound).
- Web-site interaction.

Opportunities for interaction occur when a customer makes a payment, requests product specifications, makes an inquiry, or complains. Additional opportunities occur when your company fulfills orders, invoices the customer, conducts sales or promotions, or distributes information.

The possibilities for such interactions are endless, but don't abuse them, add Peppers and Rogers. Abuses include such practices as the following:

> The hotel that calls your room just to assure you that the concierge is "at your service."
>
> The credit-card company that mails an "important message" to *everyone* in its customer base to inform them about a new type of card that is actually of interest to fewer than 1 percent of the customers.
>
> The car company that calls you at home three different times, interrupting your day just to make sure that last week's service was acceptable.[38]

If your interaction is intended to build customer relationships, say Peppers and Rogers, then the following should apply:

- The interaction should minimize the customer's inconvenience.
- The outcome should be of some real benefit.
- The interaction should influence your specific behavior toward that customer.[39]

(See Exhibit 4.25 for some other "Rules of Engagement.")

EXHIBIT 4.25. **Rules of Engagement for Customer Interactions**

- Don't initiate an interaction with a customer without a clear objective.
- Don't ask a customer the same thing more than once.
- Interact in the medium of the customer's choice.
- When engaging in an interaction, start with the customer, not the product.
- Make the interaction personal and personalized.
- Ensure that your interactions with customers are always welcomed.
- Use mass-customization principles (and technology) to reduce the cost and increase the personalization of dialogue.
- Ensure that [your most valuable customers] are immediately identified and treated appropriately.
- Protect the customer's privacy.
- Invite dialogue by printing toll-free numbers and Web-site URLs on everything.
- Ensure that the customer can see the value from each interaction. Deliver information or value that reflects what has been learned.
- Be sensitive to the customer's time. Don't try to learn everything about a customer at once.

*Source:* Don Peppers, Martha Rogers, and Bob Dorf, *The One-to-One Fieldbook: The Complete Toolkit for Implementing a One-to-One Marketing Program* (New York: Bantam Doubleday Dell, 1999), p. 95.

## Step #4: Customize Some Aspects of Your Enterprise's Behavior

Your final step, according to Peppers and Rogers, is to take what you have learned from differentiating your customers and engaging them in a dialogue and customize at least some aspects of your enterprise's behavior toward your customers. Tailor your company's offerings to the specific needs, desires, and preferences of individual customers.

You can customize your products and services in a number of different ways. For example, James H. Gilmore and B. Joseph Pine II, who have written extensively on mass customization, identify four approaches.[40]

1. **Collaborative customization**. This is the approach that most people associate with the concept of mass customization. You conduct a dialogue with customers to discover their needs and preferences and then put together the precise goods and services that meet those needs. Gilmore and Pine provide the example of Paris Miki, a Japanese eyewear retailer. Paris Miki developed an eyeglasses design system called Eye Tailor that allows customers to pick

different lens and frame designs and sizes and virtually try them on a digitized picture of their face. When the consumer is satisfied with the proposed eyeglasses, a technician grinds the lenses and assembles the eyeglasses in the store in as little as one hour.

2. **Adaptive customization**. Instead of providing customized offerings, the company produces standard products and services that customers can tailor to their individual needs and preferences without any further intervention from the company. Gilmore and Pine cite electronic kiosks that allow customers to produce customer labels, greeting cards, and other printed material as examples of adaptive customization. Another example is America Online. It allows users to create customized stock portfolios that track just those stocks of interest to the individual user.
3. **Cosmetic customization**. The company offers a standard product but customizes some aspects of delivery of that product or service. For example, Hertz #1 Club Gold Program members receive standard rental cars but get customized treatment—they bypass the check-in counter, a large screen displays their name in lights and directions to their car, their name is displayed on a personalize agreement form hanging on the car mirror, and so on.
4. **Transparent customization**. The company changes the product or service in some indiscernible way to meet the requirements of individual customers. Gilmore and Pine cite the Ritz Carlton's practice of observing guest preferences for such things as radio stations, hypoallergenic pillows, and so on. The company then enters those preferences in a guest database so that services can be tailored for each guest on subsequent visits. The guest receives customized treatment but isn't bothered with the need to directly collaborate with the company.

## TECHNOLOGY AND CRM

The basic steps to CRM sound simple: Identify your customers, differentiate your customers, establish a dialogue with your customers, and customize some part of your product or service to meet your customers' individual needs. These steps may indeed be simple if you only have a few customers, but they are anything but simple if you have hundreds or thousands or hundreds of thousands of customers. That's where technology comes in. CRM is possible without sophisticated computing and communications technology, but technology makes it much easier. In fact, once your business reaches a certain size, say our gurus, technology is essential. You simply cannot do CRM efficiently without it.

A wide variety of technologies support CRM. To get an idea of just how extensive the offering is, go to the Internet and search for "customer relationship management." You'll be inundated with technology sites offering *the* CRM solution.

There is not enough space to cover all of the available technology here, and technology changes so rapidly that any specifics we would give here would surely be outdated by the time you read this. What we will do is cover one type of technology that most of our gurus deem critical for CRM: database technology that allows you not only to store large volumes of information about individual customers but more important, to analyze it. We are referring here to "data warehouses" and in particular, to tools for "data mining." (We discussed both of these briefly in Chapter 3 on knowledge management.)

As Frederick Newell, author of *Loyalty.com,* suggests, think of a data warehouse as the place where customer information is kept. Think of data mining as the process for turning that data into knowledge you can use to develop and maintain relationships with your customers.[41] Michael Berry and Gordon Linoff provide in their 1997 book *Data Mining Techniques* one of the best discussions of data warehouses, and particularly data-mining techniques.

Berry and Linoff note that, if you think about the way small-business owners build a relationship with their customers, you can break the process down into three primary activities: (1) they notice customers' needs, (2) they remember the customers' preferences, and (3) they learn from past interactions. Until recently, large businesses had difficulty doing these three things. They just had too many customers to notice, remember, and learn from each and every one of them. Thanks to some innovative applications of technology, that is no longer the case. When you do business with large enterprises, or even small ones today, a lot of noticing and remembering takes place due to on-line transaction processing. Consider, say Berry and Linoff, what happens when you place an order for a product:

> These days, we all go through life generating a constant stream of transaction records. When you pick up the phone to order a canoe paddle from L.L. Bean or a satin bra from Victoria's Secret, a transaction record is generated at the local phone company showing the time of your call, the number you dialed, and the long distance company to which you have been connected. At the long distance company, more records are generated recording the duration of your call and the exact routing it takes through the switching system. This data will be combined with other records that store your billing plan, name, and address in order to generate a bill. At the catalog company, your call is logged again along with information about the particular catalog from which you ordered and any special promotions you are responding to. When the customer service representative that answered your call asks for your credit card number and expiration date, the information is immediately relayed to a credit card verification system to approve the transaction. All too soon, the transaction reaches the bank that issued your credit card where it will appear on your next monthly statement. When your order, with its item number, size, and color, goes into the cataloger's order entry system, it will spawn still more records in the billing system and the inventory control system. Within hours, your order is also

generating transaction records in a computer system at UPS or FedEx where it may be scanned many times between the warehouse and your home, allowing you to call an 800 number or check the shipper's Web site to track its progress.[42]

Thanks to technology, most companies today can notice and remember hundreds of gigabytes of data. However, say Berry and Linoff, two things must happen for companies to learn from that data. First, the data that comes from many sources must be gathered together and organized in a consistent and useful way. Second, it must be analyzed, understood, and made actionable. Data warehouses take care of the first problem. Data mining is concerned with the second. In short, data warehouses provide memory. Data mining provides intelligence. It allows companies to automatically or semiautomatically explore and analyze large quantities of data in order to discover meaningful patterns and rules. According to Berry and Linoff, data mining is particular good at six tasks that are critical for CRM:[43]

1. **Classification.** For example, assigning customers to levels in the customer pyramid.
2. **Estimation.** Such as estimating the lifetime value of a customer.
3. **Prediction.** As in predicting which customers will leave in six months.
4. **Affinity grouping or "market-basket analysis."** Finding what things go together and thus might be candidates for cross-selling, as in people who buy cat food also buy cat litter.
5. **Clustering.** Finding "clusters" of people who have similar buying habits, such as book buyers in the "fiction" community versus those are in the "biography" community.
6. **Description.** Such as: Males between the ages of 17 and 21 like action films while females prefer romantic comedies.

Exhibit 4.26 provides some examples of specific data-mining tools, but here is a description of how data mining works in practice, courtesy of Berry and Linoff.

Bank of America [B of A] was anxious to expand its portfolio of home equity loans, but several direct mail campaigns had yielded disappointing results. The National Consumer Assets Group (NCAG) at B of A decided to use data mining to attack the problem. . . .

Before applying data mining to this task, the bank had developed two common sense models of likely prospects for the home equity loan product:

- People with college-age children wanting to borrow against their home equity in order to pay tuition bills
- People with high but variable incomes wanting a way to tap into their home equity to smooth out the peaks and valleys

Marketing literature for the home equity line product reflected this view of the likely customer, as did the lists drawn up for telemarketing. As it turns out, data mining led the bank to a new understanding of its home equity line customers.

## How Data Mining Was Applied

Since the mid-1980s, Bank of America had been storing data on its nine million retail customers in a relational database. . . . The corporate data warehouse is fed by 42 separate systems of record. Data from these feeder systems is cleaned, transformed, and aligned into consistent time frames, geographic codes, and customer codes. . . . In addition to fields collected directly by the bank, the database also contains demographic fields such as income, number of children, type of home, and so forth. These customer attributes were combined with transaction histories and analyzed. . . . Three different tools proved to be useful.

First, a decision tree tool was used to derive rules that could be used to classify customers as likely or unlikely to respond to a home equity loan offer. The decision tree software trained on thousands of examples of customers who had obtained the product and thousands who had not. Eventually, it learned to tell the difference. Once the rules were discovered, the resulting computer model was used to add yet another attribute to the record of each potential prospect. The new attribute was the "good prospect" flag generated by the data mining model.

Next, a sequential pattern-finding tool was used to determine when a customer was most likely to want a loan of this type. The goal of this analysis was to discover a sequence of events that had frequently preceded successful solicitations in the past.

Finally, a clustering tool was used to automatically segment the customers into groups with many similar attributes. The clustering tool came up with 14 different clusters of customers. As often happens, many of the clusters did not seem particularly interesting. One of them, however, was very interesting indeed. This cluster had two intriguing properties:

1. 39 percent of the people in the cluster had both business and personal accounts with the bank.
2. This cluster accounted for 27 percent of the 11 percent of the customers who had been classified by the decision tree as likely responders to a home equity loan offer.

This data immediately suggested that people might be using home equity loans to start up businesses. Upon further investigation, this hunch proved to be correct.

### The Resulting Actions

Upon obtaining this new understanding of the market, NCAG teamed with the Retail Banking Division and several district sales organizations to develop a campaign strategy. The teaming allowed field experience to be combined with the insights gained through data mining to produce new marketing materials. As a result of the new campaign, Bank of America saw the acceptance rate for home equity offers more than double.[44]

EXHIBIT 4.26. **Sample Data-Mining Tools**

**Market-Basket Analysis**

Used to find groups of items that tend to cluster together in a transaction. Frequently used in retail to identify products that are likely to be purchased together (in same market basket). Useful for cross-selling.

*Useful for:* prediction, affinity grouping, clustering and description.

**Memory-Based Reasoning**

Identifies similar cases from experience and then applies that information to current cases. For example, it can identify previous customers who have responded to an offer. Information about them is then used to identify prospects that might respond to the offer in the future because they have similar characteristics.

*Useful for:* classification, prediction, affinity grouping, and clustering.

**Automatic Cluster Detection**

Method used to search for groups of records in a data file that are similar to each other on a number of variables. Once these "clusters" are found, other data mining tools are used to determine what these clusters mean. Bank of America used this technique in our example (see the text) to identify 14 clusters of customers. Further analysis revealed that one of the clusters contained people who had personal and business accounts and were likely to respond to home equity loans. The bank came to the conclusion that people often used home equity loans to start businesses, which prompted it to develop a new marketing campaign.

*Useful for:* clustering.

**Link Analysis**

Link analysis traces links in relationships to uncover patterns. For example, a cell-phone company used link analysis to analyze the calling patterns of its customers and discovered that customers with similar minutes of usage had strikingly different calling patterns. Some customers made a few long calls to a few numbers, while others made many short calls to many numbers. They used this information to develop new and more targeted offers.

*Useful for:* classification, prediction, and affinity grouping.

(continued)

EXHIBIT 4.26. **(continued)**

### Decision Trees

Decisions trees are used to assign each record in a database to a few broad categories and to develop natural language rules for predicting customer behavior. For example, an automotive company used decision trees to uncover the characteristics of customers who responded favorably to a promotional mailing—i.e., what were the characteristics of prospects who responded to the mailing and bought the model and those who didn't? This information was then used to develop a mailing targeted more precisely to prospects who were most likely to respond.

*Useful for:* classification, prediction, clustering, and description.

### Neural Networks

These are general-purpose tools used for clustering, classification, and prediction. Neural networks are fed examples of previous transactions and learn from the experience much the way a human "expert" might learn. For example, a real estate company might feed a neural network examples of home sales to develop an automated system for calculating the appraised value of a home given its garage size, living space, number of bathrooms, etc. The neural network over time learns to recognize patterns or relationships between a large number of variables and to make predictions based on what has occurred in the past.

*Useful for:* classification, estimation, prediction, and clustering

*Source:* Adapted from Michael Berry and Gordon Linoff, *Data Mining Techniques: For Marketing, Sales, and Customer Support* (New York: Wiley, 1997), pp. 119–123.

## THE NECESSARY CULTURE AND ORGANIZATION FOR CRM

As we noted previously, most of our gurus agree that technologies such as the data mining tools we just discussed are critical to CRM in all but perhaps the smallest of companies, and they are useful even to them. Installing the technologies, getting them to work properly, and getting people to use them effectively is never easy. Many of the tools, while extremely useful, are frustratingly difficult for the less statistically and mathematically inclined to understand. For example, Berry and Linoff admit that, while the answers produced by neural networks are often correct, the actual workings of the networks themselves are "not readily understandable," so "neural networks are best approached as black boxes with mysterious internal workings."[45] We might draw from such comments the conclusion that getting the technologies right is the most difficult part of CRM, but we would be wrong. In fact, say our gurus, the technology piece is the easy part. Don Peppers and Martha

Rogers report that, in their experience, "the most difficult part of making this transition [to CRM] is usually not acquiring and installing the technologies required, but adapting the organization and people to use them. . . . The cultural and organizational obstacles posed are immense."[46] Among other things, Peppers and Rogers say that you can expect barriers to change such as the following:

1. People at or near the top [of your organization] who won't commit to change. ("Let's sit back and see what happens.")
2. Long-standing company policies that mandate identical treatment for all customers. ("I'm sorry, but that's our policy and I'm afraid we can't make any exceptions. If we treated you differently, we'd have to treat all our customers differently.")
3. Social climate that rewards and reinforces product-oriented [versus customer-oriented] behaviors. ("This car is a miracle of modern engineering. It's state-of-the-art technology!")
4. Paying more attention to competitors than to customers. ("That new Edsel has a push-button transmission! Why didn't we think of that?")[47]

If you are serious about CRM, declare our gurus, you will have to face and overcome these organizational and cultural barriers. How? Here is some advice from George S. Day, author of *The Market Driven Organization,* who examined the experiences of three firms—Owens Corning, Sears-Roebuck, and Eurotunnel—seeking to be more market driven. He identifies six necessary conditions for making the transition. They include the following:

1. The organization's leaders must demonstrate a commitment to change.
2. Employees and managers must understand the need to change.
3. An effective management team must be created to mobilize commitment to the change effort.
4. Managers and employees must understand how they should behave differently.
5. Organizational structures, systems, and incentives all must be aligned to focus on the customer.
6. The change will have to be sustained over time.

## Condition #1: The Organization's Leaders Must Demonstrate a Commitment to Change

Ask yourself if you have a leader who fits this profile:

- Sees the need to change the orientation.
- Is committed to making it happen.

- Makes market issues a priority.
- Is willing to invest time and resources.
- Sets aggressive goals for improvement.
- Has established a sense of urgency.

Among other things, says Day, the CEO should do the following:

- Demonstrate an enthusiastic emphasis on superior quality of service and customer relations even to the point of occasionally making direct interventions to help solve customer's problems.
- Personally spend time visiting with customers and listening for their point of view.
- Insist that all senior managers spend time with customers.
- Emphasize customer and market issues—trends, needs, requirements, and so on—during strategic reviews.
- Be willing to invest resources to gain a better understanding of customers and competitors.
- Insist that the firm's performance in serving target customers be compared against "best of breed."[48]

## Condition #2: Employees and Managers Must Understand the Need to Change

Ask yourself if the key implementers understand the following:

- What it means to be market-driven, and what changes are needed.
- The barriers to change.
- How the change program will benefit them and the business.

One of the best things you can do, says Day, is to make sure that all members of the management team hear directly from customers. "Until everyone has heard the complaints and frustrations," writes Day, "there will not be a pervasive sense of urgency."[49]

## Condition #3: An Effective Management Team Must Be Created to Mobilize Commitment to the Change Efforts

Ask yourself whether the people who are sponsoring the change effort have these characteristics:

- Have experience and credibility.
- Recognize who else needs to be committed to the change to make it happen.

- Know how to rally a coalition of supporters and overcome the expected resistance.
- Have the resources they need.

Days cautions that it is not enough to just create a council or steering committee and charge it with responsibility for elevating skills, sharing best practices, and understanding what it means to be market driven.

> These groups as they are implemented in many organizations have little chance of success. With as many as 30 to 40 people involved and shifting faces, the groups are too large for real work and have little continuity. Meetings are carefully orchestrated set pieces with outside speakers, but no mandate for serious follow-up actions. Resources are usually limited—perhaps a staff person and a modest budget—and time commitment of members is also too limited, usually less than 10 percent of their attention.[50]

A better approach, says Day, is the one taken by Monsanto:

> When Monsanto created a council to drive the company toward "best of class" market orientation, it established a small leadership team of ten VPs and general managers that was given a mandate to change basic behaviors, build market-driven capabilities, and transfer best practices. They were expected to spend at least 30 percent of their time on this effort, and they agreed to partially tie their compensation to the results. The council was given all the resources it needed, including a full-time Director of Marketing Core Capability. They met at least two times a week as a group, and focused their efforts on only a few big issues—such as relationship management—that they felt would have the greatest leverage in changing a culture that was very technology-driven.[51]

## Condition #4: Managers and Employees Must Understand How They Should Behave Differently

Ask yourself if all employees fit with the following behaviors:

- Understand how superior customer value will be created.
- See what they have to do differently.
- Get excited about the promised results.

All organization members, says Day, should have a "line-of-sight" understanding of how their individual contributions can add to or detract from superior customer value. If they don't, you have to teach them.

## Condition #5: Organizational Structures, Systems, and Incentives All Must Be Aligned to Focus on the Customer

Ask yourself whether there is a credible plan in place for the following:

- Modifying the organizational structure and systems.
- Recruiting, developing, and deploying people in the new structure.
- Developing the market-sensing and market-relating capabilities.
- Changing the systems.
- Encouraging and rewarding market-driven behavior.

### *Changing the Organizational Structure*

In respect to organizational design, Day recommends an organizational structure in which teams of employees focus on managing relations with distinct customer and consumer segment groups and creating superior value for those groups.

Jay Curry makes a similar argument. He points out that most companies that have not yet implemented CRM are typically organized around stand-alone functions. Their organization chart looks something like that shown in Exhibit 4.27. The problem, explains Curry, is that each of these stand-alone departments is talking to the customer, and inevitably, each is saying something different.

EXHIBIT 4.27. **Sample Organization Chart for Pre-CRM Company**

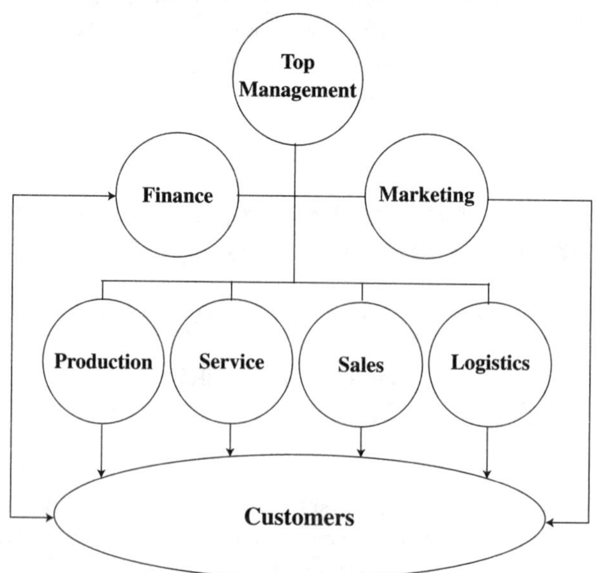

**Marketing:** "We love you. We love you."
**Sales:** "Buy this product."
**Production:** "It'll take three months to make."
**Logistics:** "What order for what machine?"
**Service:** "What? You bought this machine? I could have kept the old one going for another year."
**Finance:** "Pay or Die!" (This message arrives in the same batch of mail with marketing's latest "I love you" brochure.)

Curry says that, if you want to implement CRM and avoid these inconsistent messages to customers, you have to create customer teams, which he defines as groups of "people who have or are responsible for contacts with a specific group of customers, often represented in a customer pyramid."[52] Curry notes that, in a business-to-business situation, a customer team might consist of the following people:

The *Field Sales* person assigned to the customer.
The *Telesales* person who is "paired" to the Field Sales person or assigned to the customer.
The *Service Representative* whose route or territory includes the customer.
A *Marketing* person, who may have responsibility for marketing communications or a product manager who represents the marketing department in the team.[53]

In addition to these permanent members, customer teams receive support from other departments, such as finance, research and development, production, logistics, and so on, as needs arise. Additionally, there is a customer manager for each customer team. "The Customer Manager is responsible for detecting problems and selling opportunities while ensuring that the proper person takes proper action to achieve the goal."[54] Curry explains that the role of the customer manager should rotate among the members of the customer team depending on the customer relationship at the moment. For example:

The Field Sales person is manager of Customer X because there is a sales cycle in process for a major order.
The Telesales person is manager of Customer Y, who is a steady customer who normally orders by telephone.
The Service Representative is manager of Customer Z, who has just purchased a large machine and the service staff is on premises installing it.
The Marketing person is manager of Suspects, which he will, through telemarketing and direct mail, bring to Prospect status.[55]

Ultimately, say Peppers and Rogers, the customer team's goal is to satisfy each and every customer in its portfolio, whether the number of customers being managed by the team is a few, as in a business-to-business relationship, or millions, as in a packaged-goods organization. To do that, customer managers will have to assume additional management responsibilities:

> [The Customer Manager] must be able to assign tasks to your factory or your product managers so as to make products better, to make delivery faster, and to generate greater satisfaction overall for her own customers. . . .
>
> The production department, the product managers, and the marketing-services managers must provide the ammunition for a customer manager to leverage opportunities with her customers and work out collaborative solutions to their problems.
>
> The next area of interest for any good customer manager, of course, is new product development. . . . The customer manager should take responsibility for fashioning new products that meet the needs of the particular group of customers under her management.[56]

### *Changing the Rewards and Incentives*

In addition to changing your structure to organize around customers, Day and our other gurus say that you have to change your incentives and rewards. Day writes: "The best intentions of a market-driven change program will be thwarted if the compensation plan came from another era. . . . The research is unequivocal. If the change effort is to be taken seriously, the rewards and incentives have to be aligned."[57] (Peppers and Rogers say you should treat a customer team's portfolio of customers like a portfolio of stocks. Reward and evaluate the team based on one and only one criteria—the increase or decrease in the lifetime values of the customers in the portfolio.)[58]

### *Changing the Systems*

Finally, says Day, it is very likely that information systems will have to be completely redesigned because your existing systems may make it next to impossible for employees to get access to the information and analysis they need to focus on customers. (See our discussion of technology and CRM earlier in this chapter for information on the types of capabilities you may need.)

## Condition #6: The Change Will Have to Be Sustained Over Time

Ask yourself if the following describe those who are responsible for the change:

- Know how to get started and ensure an early success.
- Have benchmarks for measuring progress.
- Have a plan to keep attention focused on the change program.

Think of the process as painting a bridge, says Day. As soon as painters finally finish painting a large bridge, they find they just have to start all over and paint it again. You will, too. The process will be never ending.

Peppers and Rogers caution that the changes they, Day, and the other gurus encourage you to make won't happen quickly or be accomplished easily. In fact, they advise that you shouldn't try to undertake too much, too fast, or force the changes. Instead they recommend the following:[59]

1. Start small. (Maybe with just assigning customer teams to a few of your most valuable, top customers.)
2. Expand gradually. (Include just a few employees to begin with: then gradually take the culture of CRM to the rest of the company.)
3. Hold people accountable for the right things.
4. Reward those who jump on the bandwagon.

And, add Peppers and Rogers, don't be too concerned if CRM never reaches your entire organization. "Since you will always have some customers who are simply not worth the effort of setting up a 1 to 1 relationship, you will always need some employees to keep doing what they're doing now. In addition, even in an advanced stage, you're still going to need the tools of *mass marketing,* for general awareness, brand campaigns, and product introductions."[60]

Yes, you read that quote right. The gurus who proclaimed the death of mass marketing now say that maybe it isn't dead after all.

## MARKETING IN THE YEAR 2005

We began this chapter with some of the predictions Don Peppers made about the future of marketing back in 1989. Therefore, it seems fitting to close with another set of predictions. This time we will join Philip Kotler for what he calls a "look back into the future." Here is what Kotler thinks marketing will look like in the year 2005:

> Most companies have built proprietary customer databases containing rich information on individual customer preferences and requirements. They use this information to "mass-customize" their offerings to individuals. An increasing number of companies present online product platforms on which customers design their desired products. Many automobile, computer, appliance, and food companies invite customers to visit their web pages and design the market offering (product, service, systems, programs) by filling in choices on a form. The modified product is then visually displayed on the screen.

> Businesses are doing a better job of retaining their customers through finding imaginative ways to exceed customer expectations. As a result, competitors have found it increasingly difficult to acquire new customers. Consequently, most companies are spending time figuring out how to sell more products and services to their existing customers.
>
> Companies are focusing on building customer share rather than market share. Many have figured out new ways to increase cross-selling and up-selling. Companies are gaining segment and customer insight from their data warehouses by applying newer and more effective data mining techniques.
>
> Companies have finally managed to get their accounting departments to generate real numbers on profitability by segment, individual customer, product, channel, and geographical unit. Companies are now focusing attention on their most profitable customers, products, and channels. They are formulating reward packages for their more profitable customers.
>
> Companies have switched from a transaction perspective to a customer-loyalty-building perspective. Many have moved to customer lifetime supply thinking, whereby they offer to deliver a regularly consumed product (e.g., coffee, soft drinks) on a regular basis at a lower price per unit. They can afford to make less profit on each sale because of the long-term purchase contract.[61]

When you think about it, Kotler's "look back into the future" isn't a bad summary of this chapter.

## KEY POINTS

- The era of mass marketing is at an end.
- New marketing media are individually addressable, two-way, and inexpensive, making it possible for companies to compete for customers one at a time.
- Customer retention is the key to long-term profits. Raising customer-retention rates by as little as five percentage points can increase the lifetime value of the average customer by 25 to as much as 100 percent.
- It is possible to calculate a "lifetime profit pattern" for customers.
- Customers aren't created equal. In many companies, the top 20 percent of customers produce 80 percent of total revenues and over 100 percent of the total profits. The bottom 80 percent of customers actually cost more to service than they generate in revenues.
- In many companies, 60 to 80 percent of the marketing budget is spent communicating with noncustomers, a substantial number of which will never even become genuine prospects.

- The best way to build profits is to focus on increasing "share of customer"—the proportion of a customer's potential business you are getting.
- Customers today must grant their permission to be marketed. Permission is nontransferable, selfish, a process, and it can be canceled at any time.
- Customer-relationship marketing is most appropriate for companies with customers that have diverse value to the company (a few customers account for a large proportion of revenues) and diverse needs (each customer's needs are complicated and unique).
- The basic steps to implementing customer-relationship management are as follows:
  - Identify your customers.
  - Differentiate your customers.
  - Interact with your customers.
  - Customize some aspects of your enterprise's behavior.
- "Data warehouses," which store large volumes of customer information about individual customers, and data mining techniques, which are tools for analyzing large amounts of data and extracting knowledge, are critical for customer-relationship management in most companies.
- Six conditions are necessary for the implementation of customer-relationship management:
  - Organizational leaders must demonstrate a commitment to change.
  - Employees and managers must understand the need to change.
  - An effective management team must mobilize commitment to the change efforts.
  - Managers and employees must understand how they should behave differently.
  - Organizational structures, systems, and incentives must all be aligned to focus on the customer.
  - The change effort must be sustained over time.

## GLOBALIZATION—The Gurus

**Christopher A. Bartlett,** coauthor of *Managing across Borders*

**Lowell Bryan,** McKinsey consultant and coauthor of *Race for the World*

**Farid Elashmawi,** president of the consulting firm Global Success and coauthor of *Multicultural Management 2000*

**Jane Fraser,** McKinsey consultant and coauthor of *Race for the World*

**Cyrus F. Freidheim,** author of *The Trillion-Dollar Enterprise*

**Hilary F. French,** vice president for research at the Worldwatch Institute and author of *Vanishing Borders*

**Thomas L. Friedman,** Pulitzer Prize–winning journalist and author of *The Lexus and the Olive Tree*

**Sumantra Ghoshal,** coauthor of *Managing across Borders*

**Vijay Govindarajan,** professor of international business at Dartmouth College

**Anil K. Gupta,** professor of strategy and international business at the University of Maryland, College Park

**Philip R. Harris,** management and organizational psychologist and coauthor of *Multicultural Management 2000*

**Jean-Pierre Jeannet,** professor of global business at Babson College and author of *Managing with a Global Mindset*

**Rosabeth Moss Kanter,** professor of business administration at the Harvard Business School, former editor of *Harvard Business Review,* and author of *World Class: Thriving Locally in the Global Economy*

**Philip J. Kitchen,** professor of business strategy at the Queen's University School of Management, Belfast, and coauthor of *Communicating Globally*

**Edward Luttwak,** senior fellow at the Center for Strategic and International Studies in Washington, D.C., and author of *Turbo-Capitalism*

**John Micklethwait,** award-winning journalist and coauthor of *A Future Perfect: The Challenge and Hidden Promise of Globalization*

**Jeremy Oppenheim,** McKinsey consultant and coauthor of *Race for the World*

**Wilhelm Rall,** McKinsey consultant and coauthor of *Race for the World*

**Don E. Schultz,** president of the consulting firm Agora, Inc., and coauthor of *Communicating Globally*

**Ruth Stanat,** founder and president of SIS International Research and coauthor of *Global Jumpstart*

**Chris West,** managing director of Marketing Intelligence Services, Ltd., and coauthor of *Global Jumpstart*

**Adrian Woolridge,** journalist and coauthor of *A Future Perfect: The Challenge and Hidden Promise of Globalization*

# 5

# Globalization

Gurus who research and write about globalization tend to focus on one of two major issues:

1. The societal implications of the emerging global economy.
2. The implications of globalization for businesses.

We address each of these globalization issues in this chapter and highlight where our panel of gurus agree and disagree. You may choose, because of your personal perspective and interests, to proceed directly to the section of your choice. For example, if you are interested in the broader social, political, and economic issues surrounding globalization, you may want to read what our gurus have to say about globalization's impact on governments and societies first. If, instead, you are more interested in how globalization is likely to impact your business and the advice our gurus have about how to take your company global, then you may want first to check out the section on globalization's impact on business. However, we do encourage you to read the entire chapter. The topic of globalization is too important to dismiss any of its ramifications.

*Globalization* has been variously described as "a hollow word" with no generally accepted definition;[1] a "contentious, complicated subject" whose central elements inspire major debate among economists, environmentalists, left-wing radicals, political conservatives, religious leaders, cyberprophets, and just common businesspeople;[2] and an "emerging discipline" concerning which neither academics nor practitioners have yet defined a coherent body of knowledge or, for that matter, even any widely shared concepts.[3] Our gurus seem to agree only to disagree about the definition of globalization. As Hilary French, author of *Vanishing Borders,* says, "The term [globalization] means vastly different things to different people. To some globalization is synonymous with the growth of global corporations whose far-flung operations transcend national borders and allegiances. To others, it signals a broader cultural and social integration, spurred by mass communications and the Internet. The term can also refer to the growing permeability of international borders to pollution, microbes, refugees and other forces."[4] (See Exhibit 5.1 for other definitions.) French's definition of globalization may be considered as accurate as any: "Globalization is . . . a broad process of societal transformation that encompasses all of the above [definitions] including growth in trade, investment, travel, computer networking, and transboundary pollution."[5]

### EXHIBIT 5.1. **What Is Globalization**

In *The Complete MBA Companion in Global Business,* Vijay Govindarajan and Anil K. Gupta note that the term *globalization* can be defined in different ways, depending on whether one is speaking about the entire world, a single country, a specific industry, or a specific company. They write:

> **At a worldwide level** globalization refers to the growing economic interdependence among countries as reflected in increasing cross-border flows of goods, services, capital and know-how.
>
> **At the level of a specific country** globalization refers to the extent of inter-linkages between a country's economy and the rest of the world . . . [as measured by such things as] exports and imports as a ratio of GDP [Gross Domestic Product], inward and outward flows of foreign direct investment and portfolio investment, and inward and outward flows of royalty payments associated with technology transfer.
>
> **At the level of a specific industry** globalization refers to the degree to which a company's competitive position within that industry in one country is interdependent with that in another country. . . . Key indicators of the globalization of an industry are the extent of cross-border trade within the industry as a ratio of total worldwide production, the extent of cross-border investment as a ratio of total capital invested in the industry, and the proportion of industry revenue accounted for by companies that compete in major regions.
>
> **At the level of a specific company** globalization refers to the extent to which a company has expanded its revenue and asset base across countries and engages in cross-border flows of capital, goods, and know-how across subsidiaries. . . . Key indicators of the globalization of a company are international dispersion of sales revenues and asset base, intra-firm trade in intermediate and finished goods, and intra-firm flows of technology.

*Source: The Complete MBA Companion in Global Business* (London: Financial Times Pitman, 1999), pp. 5–7.

## THE EVIDENCE OF A GLOBAL ECONOMY

Regardless of the way you define globalization, our gurus agree that there is plenty of evidence that it exists and that it is irreversible. They produce reams of facts and statistics to prove their point, such as the following examples:

- In 1999 the world's largest companies spent \$440 billion to expand their overseas operations.[6]
- That same year, \$1.5 trillion in capital was being moved around the world everyday.[7]
- Between 1998 and 2005, world exports of goods and services are expected to double or reach 28 percent of world gross domestic product (GDP).[8]
- By 2030 it is estimated that 80 percent of the world's GDP will be produced and consumed in global markets. Worldwide, globally addressable GDP is expected to reach as much as \$73 trillion, which is 12 times what it is today.[9]
- World exports increased 17-fold between 1950 and 1998.[10] U.S. exports exceeded \$1 trillion (one thousand billion) in 1998, while U.S. imports were nearly \$1.2 trillion.[11]
- Between 1970 and 1998, foreign direct investments grew twice as fast as trade, and the number of transnational corporations grew from 7,000 to over 50,000.[12] U.S. investments abroad tripled between 1982 and 1996.[13]
- Americans had over \$320 billion invested in U.S.-based international or global mutual funds in 1996 versus \$16 billion 10 years earlier.[14]
- Between the 1950s and 1998, the tonnage of international shipping increased 6-fold while the number of international passenger-kilometers flown increased 100-fold and the number of international tourist arrivals increased 25-fold.[15]

On the surface at least, these are remarkable statistics, but some gurus warn that we should not read too much into them. See Exhibit 5.2 for some cautionary remarks about interpreting these statistics.

### EXHIBIT 5.2. **Globalization as Exaggeration**

In their book *A Future Perfect, Economist* correspondents John Micklethwait and Adrian Woolridge caution their readers to retain a healthy degree of skepticism when confronted with the "overwhelming" statistical proof of globalization. The "fact" of globalization so far, they argue, has been an exaggeration.

> Capital slips around the world ever more easily but not in the frictionless way that [some] fear. Most labor markets remain stubbornly national. Even in the richest countries, many markets for products still stop at national borders: A Canadian province trades twelve times as many goods and forty times as many services with

(continued)

EXHIBIT 5.2. **(continued)**

> another Canadian province than it does with an American state of similar size and proximity. In the supposedly open European Union, people are still six times more likely to trade with their fellow nationals. Industries have an irksome but entirely reasonable reason for sticking to certain areas: For example, there are plenty of cheaper places to locate a film industry than Hollywood, but none of them has the same people. And a surprising number of basic products come from local sources. Nearly all of America's lightbulbs are still made inside the country, largely because the transport costs are too high to justify moving the factories elsewhere.

On the other, hand Micklethwait and Wooldridge insist that something clearly has changed. Much of the fanfare about globalization may be what economist Paul Krugman terms just so much "globaloney," but undue skepticism may be as problematic as is exaggeration. The statistics the gurus cite to build their case for globalization are real, and they add:

> There is the danger of missing the wood for the trees. Globalization is not just about things such as the ratio of exports to gross domestic product. It has to do with the nonchalant way in which people under thirty make international calls, the reaction of General Motors workers in Flint, Michigan, when Chrysler was bought by Daimler-Benz, the new café in Shanghai where you can get a decent cappuccino (and sometimes surf the Internet), the more or less instantaneous availability all over the world of Viagra and Harry Potter, the clothes people wear, or even the fact that in the Himalayan hamlet of Lukla people setting off for Mount Everest are given French toast and Swiss muesli for breakfast, with soft toilet paper also on sale.

*Source:* John Micklethwait and Adrian Woolridge, *A Future Perfect: The Challenge and Hidden Promise of Globalization* (New York: Crown Business Books, 2000), pp. xix–xx.

In addition to statistics, our gurus cite a wealth of anecdotal evidence to bolster their case for globalization. Some of these anecdotes reflect the common experience of many, if not most of us, today. Other, often more intriguing anecdotes represent the uncommon experience of a few. Here are three examples, the first of which comes from the introduction to Micklethwait and Woolridge's *A Future Perfect.* The writer is struck by the irony of globalization while struggling to complete the author's introductory note to the book. He begins this way:

> This note is being written somewhere between Los Angeles and New York City—on an American computer in an American aircraft flown by an American airline—at the behest of an American publisher. But in fact, Random House [the publisher] is now owned by Germany's Bertelsmann; the IBM laptop was made in Mexico; the Boeing 757 includes parts from nearly forty countries; and the future of Delta Air Lines seems to lie in its code-sharing agreements with a dozen foreign-based carriers.

> On the back of the seat in front is an "airfone" that allows a passenger to telephone anywhere in the world for five dollars per minute, a price that, though extortionate, would have seemed impossibly cheap twenty years ago. Were the author more technologically competent, he could also connect his computer to the airfone's datapoint and reply to a colleague's e-mail from Thailand, which he had picked up this morning as . . . he used the computer to listen to Leicester City—a soccer team whose squad includes a French goalkeeper, a Jamaican full-back, a Greek midfielder, and an Icelandic striker—uncharacteristically beat Aston Villa 3–1 in the English Premier League.
>
> Look around you, wherever you are, and you will quickly find similar evidence that the world is becoming a smaller place.[16]

Indeed, the world is becoming a smaller place, as our second anecdote illustrates. In *The Lexus and the Olive Tree,* award-winning author Thomas L. Friedman tells us about Glenn Prickett, a senior vice president of the environmental group Conservation International, and his experience while visiting a Kayapo Indian village in a remote corner of the Brazilian Amazon rain forest in the late 1990s:

> Touching down on the grass landing strip we were met by the entire village in traditional dress—and undress—and painted faces, with a smattering of American baseball caps bearing random logos. . . . I was there with Conservation International to inspect the progress of a biological research station we were running upriver with the Kayapo. The Kayapo have defended a large chunk of intact Amazon for centuries through sheer force. Now they are learning to protect it through alliances with international scientists, conservationists and socially conscious businesspeople. Their village has a little main street with a Conservation International store and a branch of the Body Shop, the ecoconscious soap makers. So after a two-day stay at the biological research station, we came back to the village to do a final bit of business. We had arranged for an open-air market of Kayapo culture, artifacts, baskets, war clubs, spears and bows and arrows to be set up. Then our group proceeded to buy all of it for very steep prices in U.S. dollars. We then went and sat in the men's hut in the center of this Kayapo village, which could have come out of prehistory. While sitting in this hut with the leading men of the village, I noticed that they were all watching a single TV, connected to a large satellite dish. The men were flipping the channels back and forth between a Brazilian soccer match and a business channel that carded the running price of gold on world markets. The Kayapo men wanted to be sure that they were charging the small miners, whom they let dig on the edges of their rain-forest property, the going international rate for whatever gold they found. They then used these profits earned on the world gold market to protect their own unique lifestyle in the middle of the Amazon rain forest.[17]

This image of Amazon village leaders watching soccer matches via satellite television and monitoring international gold prices on the business channel is certainly extraordinary. We found another of Friedman's anecdotes about his own experience from the late 1990s while visiting NATO headquarters in Brussels equally extraordinary:

> I was sitting on a couch in the lobby waiting for an appointment. Nearby was a lady Russian journalist, speaking Russian into her cell phone. But what stuck me most was the fact that she was walking in circles next to the Coke machine, underneath a television tuned to CNN that was broadcasting the surprise entry of Russian troops into Pristina, Kosovo—ahead of NATO forces. A Russian journalist, circling the Coke machine, under the CNN screen, speaking Russian in a cell phone, in NATO headquarters, while Kosovo burned—my mind couldn't contain all the contradictions.[18]

While globalization may bring contradictions, say our gurus, it is reality—not just an economic fad or passing trend. It is a defining international system as important in shaping our destinies as the Cold War that shaped the destinies of individuals, businesses, and nations for fully 50 years after the end of World War II. (For Friedman's comparison of the Cold War and globalization as international systems, see Exhibit 5.3.)

EXHIBIT 5.3. **The Cold War and Globalization**

| | Cold War | Globalization |
|---|---|---|
| Overarching feature | Division, symbolized by the Berlin Wall and the "hotline." Two countries in charge—the United States and the Soviet Union. | Integration, symbolized by the Web and the Internet. No one truly in charge. |
| Economic rules | Less developed countries would nurture their national industries. Developing countries would seek export-led growth. Communist countries would focus on achieving economic self-sufficiency. Western economies would seek regulated trade. | All countries will open, deregulate, and privatized their economies in order to make them more competitive and attractive to foreign investment. |
| Dominant ideas | Clash between communism and capitalism; detente, nonalignment, perestroka. | Free-market capitalism; spread of Americanization (Big Macs, Mickey Mouse, etc.). |

(continued)

EXHIBIT 5.3. **(continued)**

| | COLD WAR | GLOBALIZATION |
|---|---|---|
| Demographic trends | East to west movement of people frozen by the Iron Curtain. Steady south to north flow. | Movement of people from rural areas and agricultural lifestyles to urban areas and urban lifestyles intimately tied to global fashion, food, and entertainment trends. |
| Most frequently asked question | Whose side are you on? | To what extent are you connected to everyone? |
| Second most frequently asked question | How big is your missile? | How fast is your modem? |
| Defining document | The Treaty. | The Deal. |
| Defining economists | Karl Marx and John Maynard Keynes. | Harvard professor, Joseph Schumpeter. (Key idea: The essence of capitalism is "creative destruction"—a perpetual cycle of destroying the old and less efficient products and services and replacing them with new and more efficient ones.) and Intel chairman Andy Grove. (Key idea: Only the paranoid survive. Innovation must constantly replace the past.) |
| Defining technologies | Nuclear weapons and second industrial revolution. | Computerization, miniaturization, digitization, satellite communications, fiber optics, and the Internet. |
| Defining measurements | Throw weight of nuclear missiles. Einstein's mass-energy equation, $e=mc^2$. | Speed of commerce, travel, communication, and innovation. Moore's Law that computing power will double every eighteen to twenty-four months, while the price will be cut in half. |
| Defining sport analogy | Sumo wrestling. | 100-meter dash. |

(continued)

EXHIBIT 5.3. **(continued)**

| | COLD WAR | GLOBALIZATION |
|---|---|---|
| Defining anxiety | Nuclear annihilation. | Fear of rapid change from an enemy you can't see, touch, or feel. |
| Defining defense system | Radar to expose the threats coming from the other side of the wall. | The X-ray machine to expose the threats coming from within. |
| Defining structure(s) | Nation-states. | Nation-states, global financial markets, and super-empowered individuals such as computer hackers or the Saudi millionaire Osama bin Laden who declared war on the U.S. in the late 1990s. |

*Source:* Thomas L. Friedman, *The Lexus and the Olive Tree: Understanding Globalization* (New York: Anchor Books, 2000), pp. 7–15.

## THE FORCES DRIVING GLOBALIZATION

If globalization is the defining international system, as our gurus maintain, the questions then become, Why has it emerged as such? What is driving this inevitable and irresistible trend to homogenize and interconnect the world? (Some of our gurus argue that the current drive to globalization is simply a return to pre–World War I conditions. See Exhibit 5.4 for an explanation.)

EXHIBIT 5.4. **Globalization Round II**

In *The Lexus and the Olive Tree*, Thomas L. Friedman argues that there are many similarities between the globalization of today and the economic conditions of the period roughly between the mid-1800s to World War I. He writes:

> If you compared the volumes of trade and capital flows across borders, relative to GNPs, and the flow of labor across borders, relative to populations, the period of globalization preceding World War I was quite similar to the one we are living through today. Great Britain, which was then the dominant global power, was a huge investor in

(continued)

## EXHIBIT 5.4. (continued)

emerging markets, and fat cats in England, Europe and America were often buffeted by financial crises, triggered by something that happened in Argentine railroad bonds, Latvian government bonds or German government bonds. There were no currency controls, so no sooner was the transatlantic cable connected in 1866 than banking and financial crises in New York were quickly being transmitted to London or Paris. . . . In those days, people also migrated more than we remember, and, other than in wartime, countries did not require passports for travel before 1914. All those immigrants who flooded America's shores came without visas. When you put all of these factors together, along with the inventions of the steamship, telegraph, railroad and eventually telephone, it is safe to say that this first era of globalization before World War I shrank the world from a size "large" to a size "medium."

Friedman notes that World War I, the Russian Revolution, the Great Depression, and finally, World War II dealt a series of hammer blows to the first era of globalization. By the end of World War II, the world had been divided and frozen in place. The Cold War became the international system that lasted from roughly 1945 until 1989, when the Berlin Wall came down and a new era—Globalization Round II—began.

Thus, says Friedman, globalization isn't new. What is new is that Globalization Round II differs from Globalization Round I in both degree and kind. First, this time many more people and countries are impacted, and trading is measured in billions rather than in millions of dollars. Second, the technology on which the new round of globalization is built is fundamentally different. Globalization Round I was made possible by the invention of the railroad, steamship, and automobile. The resulting drop in transportation costs made it possible for people to get to and trade with a lot more places faster and cheaper. Globalization Round II is made possible by microchips, satellites, fiber optics, the Internet, and the consequent falling telecommunications costs. Computers and cheap telecommunications tie people closer together and allow them to trade both products and services globally. Additionally, the new technologies not only empower corporations; they empower individuals also. Companies can reach markets farther away, faster and cheaper than ever before. So too can individuals. (See Chapter 2 of the present book for a discussion of the impact railroads had on the U.S. economy during the 1800s.)

*Source:* Thomas L. Friedman, *The Lexus and the Olive Tree: Understanding Globalization* (New York: Anchor Books, 2000), pp. xvi–xix.

Friedman offers one of the best explanations for why globalization has emerged. (See Exhibit 5.5 for other explanations.) He argues that the demise of the Cold War and the rise of globalization as the new, defining international system was driven by three fundamental changes: (1) the democratization of technology, (2) the democratization of finance, and (3) the democratization of information.

EXHIBIT 5.5. **The Drivers of Globalization**

| John Micklethwait and Adrian Woolridge | Lowel Bryan, Jane Fraser, Jeremy Oppenheim, and Wilhelm Rall | Don E. Schultz and Philip J. Kitchen | Jean-Pierre Jeannet | Vijay Govindarajan and Anil K. Gupta |
|---|---|---|---|---|
| • Technology that frees people from the tyranny of place.<br>• Free and rapid flow of massive amounts of capital around the world.<br>• Internalization of business best practices around the world. | • Digital technology and the concomitant drop in interaction costs.<br>• Wide availability and mobility of global capital.<br>• Removal of legal and regulatory barriers to international commerce. | • Information technology and the formalization of methods of data transfer that allows knowledge to be easily and quickly distributed around the world.<br>• Digitalization of knowledge and use of computing power for creative purposes.<br>• Increase in communication systems.<br>• Growing value of the intangible/knowledge. | • Availability of similar technological applications worldwide.<br>• Liberalization of trade, which opened access to markets worldwide.<br>• Deregulation of businesses worldwide.<br>• Expanded worldwide communication capabilities.<br>• Growing homogeneity of customer needs and expectations worldwide. | • Technological advances in worldwide communications.<br>• Opening of borders to trade, investment, and technological transfers.<br>• Shift from a "planning" mentality to a free-market mentality by economic policy makers worldwide.<br>• Shift of economic center from developed to developing countries. |

*Sources:* Keith H. Hammonds, "Good News: It's a Small World," *Fast Company,* May 2000, pp. 90–94; John Micklethwait and Adrian Woolridge, *A Future Perfect: The Challenge and Hidden Promise of Globalization* (New York: Crown Business Books, 2000), p. 29; Lowell Bryan, Jane Fraser, Jeremy Oppenheim, and Wilhelm Rall, *Race for the World: Strategies to Build a Great Global Firm* (Boston: Harvard Business School Press, 1999), pp. 14–28; Don E. Schultz and Philip J. Kitchen, *Communicating Globally: An Integrated Marketing Approach* (Lincolnwood, IL: NTC Business Books, 2000), pp. 3–5; Jean-Pierre Jeannet, *Managing with a Global Mindset* (London: Financial Times Prentice Hall, 2000), pp. 23–27; *The Complete MBA Companion in Global Business* (London: Financial Times Pitman, 1999), pp. 7–9.

## Globalization Driver #1: The Democratization of Technology

The first driver of globalization, says Friedman, is a fundamental change in the way we communicate. He calls this change "the democratization of technology" and says that it "is enabling more and more people, with more and more home computers, modems, cellular phones, cable systems and Internet connections, to reach farther and farther, into more and more countries, faster and faster, deeper and deeper, cheaper and cheaper than ever before in history."[19] Technology that was once the province of kings and would-be kings is now available to almost anyone worldwide. To illustrate the ubiquitous nature of modern technology, Friedman relates a story told to him by Deputy U.S. Treasury Secretary Larry Summers. While working on Michael Dukakis's presidential campaign in 1988, Summers was impressed that the car assigned to the campaign staff had a telephone in it. In fact, he found the cell phone so fascinating he called his wife just to tell her that he was actually riding around in a car that contained—Are you sitting down, honey?—a telephone. Nine years later, as Friedman says, that had all changed.

> In 1997, Summers, on Treasury business, was visiting [the] Ivory Coast, in West Africa. As part of his official visit he had to inaugurate an American-funded health project in a village upriver from the capital, Abidjan. The village, which was opening it first potable water well, could be reached only by dugout canoe. Summers, the big cheese from America, was made an honorary African chief by the villagers and decked out in African robes. But what he remembered most vividly was that on his way back from the village, as he stepped into the dugout canoe to go back downriver, an Ivory Coast official handed him a cell phone and said, "Washington has a question for you." In nine years Summers went from thinking it was neat to have a phone in his car in Chicago to expecting to have a phone in his dugout canoe in Abidjan.[20]

The democratization of technology, says Friedman, is driving globalization in at least three extraordinary ways: (1) connections in real time, (2) the globalization of production, and (3) the geographic dispersal of wealth creation.

### *Connections in Real Time*

The democratization of technology is making it possible for people anywhere and everywhere to connect with each other in real time. "Innovations in computerization, miniaturization, telecommunications and digitization . . . have made it possible for hundreds of millions of people around the world to get connected and exchange information, news, knowledge, money, family photos, financial trades, music or television shows in ways, and to a degree, never witnessed before."[21] Friedman cites NBC News president Lawrence Grossman: "Printing . . . made us all readers. Xeroxing made us all publishers. Television made us all viewers. Digitization [and the democratization of technology] makes us all broadcasters."[22]

### *The Globalization of Production*

According to Friedman, the democratization of technology makes it possible for everyone everywhere to be producers:

> Today's globalization isn't just about developing countries shipping raw materials to developed ones, letting them produce the finished goods and then shipping them back. No, today, thanks to the democratization of technology, all sorts of countries have the opportunity to assemble the technologies, raw materials and funding to be producers, or subcontractors, of highly complex finished products or services, and this becomes another subtle factor knitting the world more tightly together. . . . [T]his democratization of technology is how Thailand, in fifteen years, went from being primarily a low-wage rice-producing country to being the world's second-largest producer of pickup trucks, rivaling Detroit, and the fourth-largest maker of motorcycles.[23]

### *The Geographic Dispersal of Wealth Creation*

Finally, says Friedman, the democratization of technology doesn't just globalize the making of products like cars and motorcycles. Perhaps even more important, it globalizes knowledge-based services, which increasingly is the real source of wealth. He illustrates this geographic dispersal of wealth creation by repeating a story told to him by a friend in Hong Kong:

> [She] told me she once called the local Hong Kong number of Dell Computer's technical assistance and a customer-service specialist speaking perfect Cantonese, the dialect of Hong Kong, answered. My Hong Kong friend remarked to the Dell specialist how heavy it was raining in the central district of Hong Kong that day and she asked whether it was raining as heavily at the Dell office. The Dell specialist responded that it wasn't raining where she was at all, because she was thousands of miles away in Penang, Malaysia. That specialist was a Malaysian Chinese who was now able to get a good service job with Dell, while living in a relative backwater like Penang. The democratization of technology made that possible.[24]

The democratization of technology is turning India, Pakistan, the Philippines, South Africa, and communities all over the world with English-speaking high-school and college graduates into the back offices of the twenty-first century.

## Globalization Driver #2: The Democratization of Finance

The democratization of technology, writes Friedman, was helped by a change in investment, or "the democratization of finance," which he dates from the late 1960s.[25] Until that time, most companies looked to big commercial banks, investment banks, or insurance companies for the funds they needed to support operations and expansion. The banks and insurance companies were run by slow-moving, risk-averse executives who only wanted to lend to "creditworthy" companies with "investment-grade" ratings. Consequently, if your company was a start-up or had a less-than-sterling financial record, you found it difficult to raise the capital you needed. Then, says Friedman, several things happened that made capital much more available to start-ups and new players, such as the high-tech ventures that democratized technology.

1. In the late 1960s, corporations began to issue "commercial paper" directly to investors, thus by-passing banks and undermining their monopoly.

2. In the 1970s, investment banks began to purchase whole portfolios of home mortgages from banks and mortgage companies. They chopped the portfolios into $1,000 bonds and sold the bonds to individual investors. Investors got access to investments that offered slightly more interest than other investments, such as certificates of deposit, with only slightly more risk.

3. In the 1980s, Michael Milken, a graduate of the Wharton School of Business and Finance at the University of Pennsylvania, examined academic research on low-rated "junk bonds" (e.g., bonds that were considered risky because they were offered by blue-chip companies that had fallen on hard times or start-up companies with no track record). He discovered that these "high-risk" companies were only slightly more likely to go bankrupt than "top-rated" companies, while their "junk bonds" offered a substantially higher rate of return. Milken reasoned that, if he put a lot of different junk bonds in a single fund, he could minimize the impact of any single company going bankrupt. Thus he would be able to provide individual investors, as well as himself, the opportunity to make significant returns with very little additional risk. Traditional banks and investment houses doubted that Milken had really found what *Business Week* described as "the investment equivalent of a free lunch."[26] Others, however, watched, listened, and learned. When Milken branched out from trading existing junk bonds to financing a whole range of "risky" entrepreneurial ventures, people took note of his success. Soon a whole new "junk-bond" high-risk investment industry was born. Individual investors got the opportunity to engage in a type of investment that had been closed to them in the past. New companies, fallen companies, and entrepreneurs got a whole new source of investment capital.

4. In the late 1980s, U.S. Treasury Secretary Nicholas Brady changed the rules of international finance. When Latin America experienced a debt crisis, Brady tried a decidedly Milkenesque solution. He converted Latin American debts to major U.S. commercial banks into U.S. government-backed bonds. The bonds were then

sold to individuals or mutual and pension funds who were attracted to them by their higher-than-normal, junk-bond-like rates of interest. Banks were encouraged to make new loans to Latin American countries, knowing they could minimize the risk since (1) they had U.S. government guarantees and (2) the loans would be converted to government bonds that would be sold to the public. Brady's market-based solution changed the rules of finance for countries and investors. According to Joel Korn, who headed Bank of America Brazil at that time:

> [The "Brady bonds"] brought thousands of new players into the game. Instead of a country just dealing with a committee of twenty major commercial banks, it suddenly found itself dealing with thousands of individual investors and mutual funds. This expanded the market, and it made it more liquid, but it also put a whole new kind of pressure on the countries. People were buying and selling their bonds every day, depending on how well they performed. This meant they were being graded on their performance every day. And a lot of the people doing the buying and grading were foreigners over whom Brazil, Mexico or Argentina had no control.[27]

Friedman adds, "These bondholders were not like the banks, who, because they were already so exposed to these countries, felt they had to keep lending more money to protect their earlier loans. If a country didn't perform, the public bondholders would just sell that country's bonds, say goodbye and put their money into the bonds of a country that did perform."[28]

The Brady bonds changed the rules of the game of international finance, as Mexico learned in 1995 when it got in financial trouble again due to excessive spending. Prior to that time, the president of Mexico would have gone to the twenty or so banks holding Mexico's debts and asked for an extension. Under the new rules, as Friedman describes, "Mexico's debt had been democratized into too many hands,"[29] and its leaders had to go to the U.S. government for a bail out—this time one with conditions. Uncle Sam wasn't going to help unless Mexico (1) started running its economy better and (2) put up its oil reserves as collateral.

While Friedman admits that there is nothing new about governments issuing bonds to foreign holders, he maintains that there was now a difference. The players had changed. Once, only the wealthy could participate in international bond deals, but now the school janitor through his pension fund, Aunt Bev through her mutual fund, and just about everyone else can be part of the deal. Finance has been democratized and is global.

## Globalization Driver #3: The Democratization of Information

The third major change that is driving globalization, believes Friedman, is the democratization of information. "Thanks to satellite dishes, the Internet, and television we can now see through, hear through and look through almost every conceivable wall."[30] Friedman recalls that, in the 1980s, the Soviet Union ran a photograph in *Pravda* that purportedly showed Americans standing in breadlines, but as it turned out, the picture was actually of people waiting in line for a popular Manhattan bakery and delicatessen to open. No country could pull off such a trick today, according to Friedman, because of the democratization of information.

> Thanks to the information revolution and the falling costs of communicating by phone, fax, the Internet, radio, television and information appliances no wall in the world is secure anymore. And when we all increasingly know how each other lives, it creates a whole new dynamic to world politics. When it comes to atrocities happening in some dark corner of the world, leaders today no longer have the option not to know, only not to act. And when it comes to some opportunities being enjoyed in some bright corner of the world, leaders no longer have the option to deny them to their people, only not to deliver them. That's why the more we learn how each other lives, the more leaders all have to promise the same things. And when they can't deliver, they have a problem. And it's only going to become more acute. In a few years, every citizen of the world will be able to comparison shop between his own country and his own government and the one next door.[31]

And not only politics have been transformed and globalized by the democratization of information. Products have, as well. Friedman relates a story told to him by Laura Blumenfield, a feature writer for the *Washington Post,* who recalled that she and her mother had been traveling in the Middle East during the spring of 1998 to research a book. During a visit to Damascus, their Syrian guide, Walid, confided to them how he like to spend his evenings:

> He told us that he liked to sit at night, where he had a satellite dish, and watch Israel TV. As he described the scene, I pictured this man in this dark office, his eyes wide with fascination, watching this TV screen with people he hated but wanted to be like and was jealous of. He said, though, that of all the things that he watched on Israel TV, the thing that really bothered him was the yogurt commercials—the fact that the yogurt in Israel came in all these different fruit-colored containers—pink and orange, like in America—while in Syria they were just black or white. He even, dejectedly, pointed out to us the Syrian yogurt containers on the street one day. He also said to us, "Our cornflakes wilt right after you put them in the milk, but I can see [from the television commercials on Israel TV] that Israel's cornflakes are crunchy and don't wilt." Forget the Golan Heights, what really bothered him were the yogurt containers and Israel's corn-flakes. One day he said to us, "It's not fair that we are a hundred years behind the Israelis and they just got here."[32]

The democratization of information means that, wherever we are, we can all comparison shop for ideas, political solutions, products, or whatever else we desire. At least one guru thinks this may be the ultimate driver of globalization.

## Shopping: The Ultimate Driver of Globalization

Rosabeth Moss Kanter, professor at the Harvard Business School, author of numerous best-selling books, including *The Change Masters* and *When Giants Learn to Dance,* and former editor of *The Harvard Business Review,* has also been called one of the most important women in America. In a 1997 interview, she was asked what she believed was driving the growth of the global economy. Here is her reply:

> The best way to describe the changes that have created the global economy is to cite a story I heard at a dinner with a Hungarian economic minister and his wife. In explaining why Communism had failed in Eastern Europe and why markets are opening up all over the world, the Hungarian minister gave a long-winded, macroeconomic explanation about currency rates, oil prices, and trade flows. When he finished, his wife, who is an entrepreneur in Hungary, stood up and said, "I'm not sure I understand what my husband just told you, but I will tell you, my friends and I want to go shopping."[33]

Kanter admits that she wouldn't attribute every geopolitical change in the world to rampant consumerism, but she considers "shopping" what globalization is all about: "It's not about whether any one company does business internationally. It is about a fundamental shift as customers, particularly organizational customers, want to go shopping—to exercise choices, to have the best of the world's goods and services available wherever they are in the world."[34]

### OUR VIEW

We agree with Kanter. To a large degree, comparison shopping is what globalization is all about. The new technology, connectivity, networking, and so on are just making it possible for more and more people, for more and more of the time, and in more and more places, to go shopping for the best the world has to offer, whether it is for a new or replacement product, service, idea, political system, or whole new culture. The reality that globalization, at its core, is largely about the permeability of borders may be discomforting for some, but it is energizing for others. Consequently, it is at the heart of the first major globalization issue: the societal implications.

## THE SOCIETAL IMPLICATIONS OF GLOBALIZATION

In November 1999, the World Trade Organization (WTO) held a meeting in Seattle. Trade ministers from 135 countries came together to develop an agenda for the next round of world-trade negotiations.[35] The goal of the delegates was to find ways to increase international trade while simultaneously improving the well-being of the people of the world. The Seattle talks should have been routine, even somewhat drab. Instead, they turned violent as an estimated fifty thousand protesters fought with police, blocked the delegates' access to the meeting halls, and generally plunged downtown Seattle into a state of chaos. Ultimately, the WTO's opening ceremonies had to be canceled. Reflecting on what it called the "battle of Seattle," the *Washington Post* wrote: "If there is any clear message coming through the clouds of tear gas and broken glass in Seattle this week, it is that the terms of the debate about free trade have changed. . . . It is no longer a debate about trade at all, but rather a debate about globalization, a process that many now understand affects not only traditional economic factors such as jobs and incomes but also the food people eat, the air they breathe, . . . and the social and cultural milieu in which they live."[36]

As the protests in Seattle demonstrated, issues about the wisdom and consequences of globalization can generate heated, even violent, debate among supporters and detractors. And our gurus are no exception. Opponents of globalization make the following argument:

- It creates a rough-and-tumble, winner-take-all world in which enormous income inequalities allow the fortunate few to lavish themselves in luxuries while the wretched of the earth suffer in a continuous downward economic spiral.
- It forces countries throughout the world into a kind of "golden straitjacket" in which ancient cultures are destroyed and replaced by the American way of life.
- It unleashes rampant exploitation of the environment, destroying the world's forests, polluting its oceans, and endangering its species, including humans themselves.

Proponents and defenders of globalization counter as follows:

- For every evil cited by opponents to globalization, there is an offsetting benefit.
- While globalization can lead to economic inequalities, social safety nets can be built for those most endangered.
- Rather than exploiting people and the environment, globalization can lead to the spread of world-class standards for the treatment of workers and the harnessing of powerful forces to save the environment.

We discuss each of these arguments in more detail in the following sections.

## Globalization Can Lead to Rampant Income Inequalities

No one states the position that globalization can lead to enormous income inequalities more eloquently or with more passion than Edward Luttwak, a senior fellow at the Center for Strategic and International Studies. In his 1999 book *Turbo-Capitalism,* Luttwak argues that globalization is foisting onto the world a kind of capitalism that is quite different from the controlled capitalism that flourished from 1945 until the 1980s. Its advocates, writes Luttwak, refer to this new form of capitalism as *the* free market, but, he argues, they mean much more than just the freedom to buy and sell goods and services:

> What they celebrate, preach and demand is private enterprise liberated from government regulation, unchecked by effective trade unions, unfettered by sentimental concerns over the fate of employees or communities, unrestrained by customs barriers or investment restrictions, and molested as little as possible by taxation. What they insistently demand is the privatization of state-owned businesses of all kinds, and the conversion of public institutions, from universities and botanic gardens to prisons, from libraries and schools to old people's homes, into private enterprises run for profit. What they promise is a more dynamic economy that will generate new wealth, while saying nothing about the distribution of any wealth, old or new.[37]

Advocates of this turbo-capitalism hold tightly to three fundamental values:

1. **Free trade as ideology.** Turbo-capitalists don't just oppose barriers to international trade; they are offended by them. Remove the barriers, they argue, and the free interplay of supply and demand will tell producers what is the most efficient use of their scarce resources. Every producer will be free to exploit its own comparative advantages. Inefficiencies, waste, and contrived shortages will be eliminated. Planetary income and standards of living will quickly and significantly increase.[38]
2. **Money as religion.** Turbo-capitalists, says Luttwak, worship hard money. Inflation, even very moderate inflation, is seen as a deadly disease.[39]
3. **Shopping as therapy.** Finally, says Luttwak, turbo-capitalists view excessive consumption as something that is good even if funded by massive amounts of credit-card debt. After all, conspicuous consumption fuels the economy and simultaneously provides a kind of emotional fast-food release for the overworked and overstressed population. (Luttwak says that the United States is the most turbo-capitalist of all economies, and as a result, most Americans today are "emotional destitutes"[40] who go deeper and deeper into debt not to buy food or essentials but rather to purchase increasingly vast quantities of "expensive motor vehicles, designer clothing, signature watches, assorted recreational gadgets and all manner of other things that are scarcely necessities of life by anyone's definition.")[41]

So, what is wrong with this turbo-capitalism? According to Luttwak, it creates enormous inequities in income. As an example, he points to the income of households in the United States. In 1995, excluding income taxes, pensions, and welfare payments, the top-earning 20 percent of U.S. households received 52.9 percent of the total income of all households in the country. Put another way, of the approximate hundred million households in the United States that year, the highest-earning top 20 percent received over half of all of the income, while the remaining 80 percent were left to split up the other half (see Exhibit 5.6). The 20 million American households in the lowest quintile received less than 1 percent of the total income. Even when additional sources of income, such as government payments of Social Security and welfare, are added in and income and capital-gains taxes are subtracted, low-income households still suffer greatly, receiving only 5.2 percent of the total income versus over 44 percent for the top earners.

Luttwak maintains that the phenomenon of income inequality is not just an anomaly of the mid-1990s. Data on income distribution in the United States show a gradual but steady upward creep of the income of the top 5 percent of U.S. families and a steady downward drift for the bottom 40 percent for the last 20 years (see Exhibit 5.7). These years, argues Luttwak, correspond precisely to the ever-widening grasp of turbo-capitalism on the U.S. economy.

As additional evidence of income inequalities under turbo-capitalism, Luttwak points to changes in the average hourly earnings of nonsupervisory employees in the United States. During the post–World War II years of controlled capitalism, the average hourly wages of nonsupervisory employees grew slowly but steadily (see Exhibit 5.8). From 1980 to 1994, these wages declined and have made only modest

EXHIBIT 5.6. **U.S. Households, before and after Government Transfers (1995)**

| Quintiles | Aggregate Income of U.S. Households before Government Transfers | Aggregate Income of U.S. Households after Government Transfers |
|---|---|---|
| Lowest | 3.7% | 5.2% |
| Second | 9.1% | 11.0% |
| Third | 15.2% | 16.3% |
| Fourth | 23.4% | 23.4% |
| Highest | 48.6% | 44.1% |

*Sources:* Edward Luttwak, *Turbo-Capitalism: Winners and Losers in the Global Economy* (New York: HarperCollins, 1999), pp. 86–87.

gains since then. Consequently, says Luttwak, poverty that was almost wiped out in the 1960s has returned, reaching almost 14 percent in the mid-1990s.

EXHIBIT 5.7. **Percent Distribution of Aggregate Income of the Top 5 Percent and the Bottom 40 Percent of U.S. Households, 1977–1994**

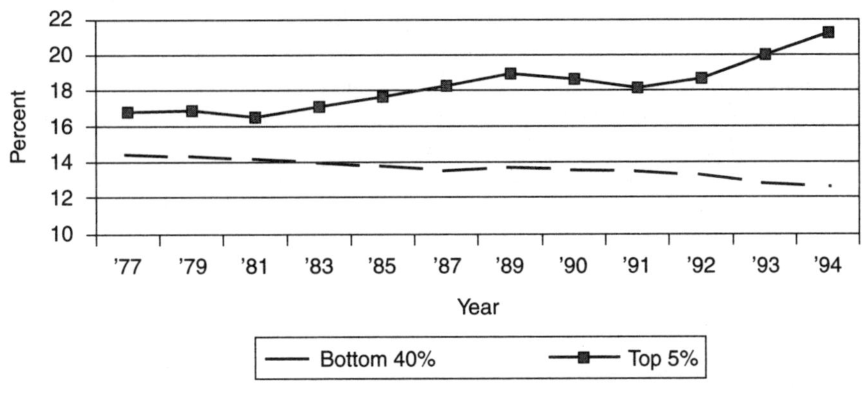


*Source:* Edward Luttwak, *Turbo-Capitalism: Winners and Losers in the Global Economy* (New York: HarperCollins, 1999), p. 89.

EXHIBIT 5.8. **Average Hourly Earnings of Nonsupervisory Personnel, 1950–1997**

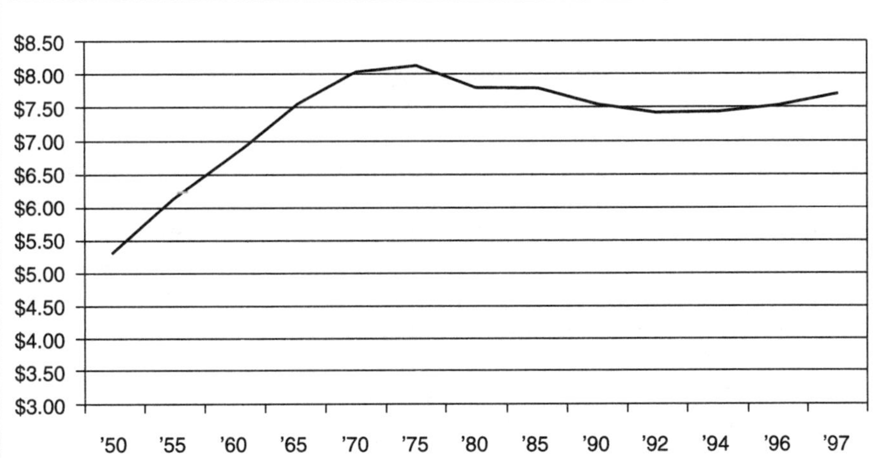


*Source:* Edward Luttwak, *Turbo-Capitalism: Winners and Losers in the Global Economy* (New York: HarperCollins, 1999), p. 96.

Although Luttwak's statistics are from the mid-1990s, more recent analysis seems to bear out many of his findings. For example, a Conference Board study released in 2000 showed that the overall poverty rate in the U.S. declined to 12.7 percent in 1998; however, the poverty rate among low-wage workers who worked more than 35 hours per week for 50 weeks per year had barely changed, remaining at about 3 percent. In contrast, between 1966 and 1978—during the controlled capitalism period—the poverty rate among the full-time working poor in the United States dropped from 4.8 percent to 2.1 percent, or by 56 percent. Between 1986 and 1998, while the United States' economy was expanding by more than 30 percent, the ranks of full-time workers living in poverty increased 40 percent.[42]

The evidence from the United States is clear, says Luttwak. When capitalism is unobstructed by such things as public ownership, government regulations, effective trade unions, or cultural inhibitions, enormous riches flow to a few while many suffer. Turbo-capitalism results in exploding incomes at the top and, if not outright exclusion, at a minimum a downward slide in pay rates for those who are less skilled.

> All countries that have undergone turbo-capitalist change, from the United Kingdom to Argentina, from Finland to New Zealand, now have their billionaires or at least centi-millionaires, as they all have their new poor. They are the unemployed or part-time employed, or poorly re-employed of no particular skill, who were once on the more generous and utterly secure payrolls of wasteful state industries and public utilities now privatized, of overstaffed bureaucracies now drastically reduced, or inefficient private businesses that could not survive the removal of the internal regulations and external trade barriers that once protected their inefficiencies from domestic and foreign competitors. Cities such as Buenos Aires, where a modest affluence was the norm, now contain hundreds of thousands of these new poor, but they are also to be found in some numbers in Helsinki or Auckland, as in the less fortunate parts of the United Kingdom.[43]

Spawned in the United States, turbo-capitalism is going global. In fact, for many of our gurus, turbo-capitalism is the very essence of globalization. If Luttwak is right, and many gurus think he is, turbo-capitalism carries with it some extremely harsh realities with all-too-human and poignant consequences.

Thomas L. Friedman compares the experience of living in a hyper-competitive turbo-capitalist world with the experience of the lion and gazelle in the jungle:

> Every night the lion goes to sleep in the jungle knowing that in the morning, when the sun comes up, if it can't outrun the slowest gazelle, it will go hungry. Every night the gazelle goes to sleep in the jungle knowing that in the morning, when the sun comes up, if it can't outrun the fastest lion, it's going to be somebody's breakfast. But the one thing that the lion and the

gazelle both know when they go to sleep is that in the morning, when the sun comes up, they had better start running.[44]

Unfortunately, Friedman notes, in the jungle of globalization, not everyone is equipped to get up every morning and run fast.

> There are a lot of turtles out there, desperately trying to avoid becoming roadkill. The turtles are all those people who got sucked into the [turbo-capitalist] fast world . . . and, for one reason or another now feel economically threatened or spurned by it. It is not because they all don't have jobs. It is because the jobs they have are being rapidly transformed, downsized, streamlined or made obsolete by globalization. And because this global competition is also forcing their governments to downsize and streamline at the same time, it means many of these turtles have no safety net to fall into.[45]

Friedman writes that the plight of the turtles of the world was brought home to him forcefully in the summer of 1998. He was taking a tour of Brazil with Conservation International to see an ecopark. It was being built with the hope of attracting tourists and providing jobs for workers in the town of Una so that they could quit logging the rain forests. The mayor of the small town, a 48-year-old by the name of Dejair Birschner, had been asked to show Friedman around and explain how globalization was affecting his town.

> The mayor was a Paul Bunyon type, whose father and grandfather had been loggers, but now the environmentalists had basically put him out of business. As we walked through the rain forest, Mayor Birschner patted every other tree. He knew each tree species in the rain forest by its Brazilian name. I took an immediate liking to this Brazilian lumberjack. There was something very solid about him. After our walk, we sat on a picnic table . . . and talked about the challenges facing the mayor. The mayor explained to me that intellectually he understood that logging was not sustainable anymore. But as much as he knew this, he also knew that his little town was not prepared for life without logging. We talked for about thirty minutes, and when I was done interviewing the mayor, I thanked him and started to pack up my IBM ThinkPad laptop, when he said to me, "Now I want to ask something."
>
> "Please," I answered, "ask anything you like."
>
> The mayor then looked me in the eye and said, "Do we have any future?"[46]

Friedman says the question hit him like a punch in the stomach because he knew what this sturdy, proud man was asking: "My villagers can't live off the forest anymore and we're not equipped to live off computers. My father and grandfather made a living off logs and my grandchildren might make a living off the Internet.

But what are all the rest of us supposed to do?"[47] Friedman cobbled together an answer having to do with making the transition from an agro- to a knowledge economy, educating the town's people, and so on but says that he felt that none of his answers were truly adequate.

What indeed will happen to the turtles of the world? Friedman thinks the poorest of the human turtles will rebel. They will quit trying to adapt to turbo-capitalism and just eat the rain forests instead—each in their own way. "In Indonesia, they will eat the Chinese merchants by ransacking their stores. In Russia, they will sell weapons to Iran and turn to crime. In Brazil, they will log the rest of the rain forest or join the peasant movement in the Brazilian countryside called 'Sem Teto' (Without Roofs), who simply steal what they need."[48]

If, as our gurus argue, global turbo-capitalism has such harsh realities for so many people, then why aren't more countries just saying No? Is this American-style souped-up, hyper-competitive, turbo-charged capitalist globalization inevitable? Yes, say our guru, it likely is inevitable for one very good reason. Countries have no other choice.

## Globalization Forces Countries into a Golden Straitjacket

In 1997 massive global speculation in Thailand's currency, the baht, led to its collapse and the bankruptcy of 56 of the country's top 58 financial institutions. The ensuing economic crisis caused tens of thousands of Thailand's workers, including some of its most wealthy, to lose their jobs. While in Thailand covering the story, Friedman arranged an interview with a prominent Thai real estate developer who had gone bankrupt during the crisis. The developer and his former employees had resorted to making and delivering sandwiches on the streets of Bangkok in order to make a living. What Friedman remembers most about the interview is "the absence of bitterness in the developer's voice, and the much more pungent air of resignation. . . . His message was that Thailand had messed up. People knew it. They would now have to tighten their belts and get with the program and there wasn't much else to say."[49]

Friedman recalls that he was incredulous. Wasn't the former real estate developer mad? Didn't he want to riot, tear down a building, or do something to express his anger at being wiped out? No, the man replied, he did not. He explained, "Communism fails, socialism fails, so now there is only capitalism. We don't want to go back to the jungle, we all want a better standard of living, so you have to make capitalism work, because you don't have a choice."[50]

Friedman finally realized that the Thai real-estate-developer-turned-sandwich-maker was right. There were no other choices. The democratizations of technology, finance, and information that came in the 1980s blew away all alternative economic forms. Capitalism was all that remained, and twenty-first-century turbo-capitalist globalization is quite different from the globalization of the nineteenth and early twentieth centuries. The Darwinian brutality of free-market capitalism had been challenged by alternatives—communism, socialism, and fascism—but each of these challengers had been discredited, often by the very people who lived under them. There was no new Engels, Marx, Lenin, or Mussolini to champion an ideological alternative that could generate a rising standard of living.

> Other systems may be able to distribute and divide income more efficiently and equitably, but none can generate income to distribute as efficiently as free-market capitalism. And more and more people know that. So, ideologically speaking, there is no more mint chocolate chip, there is no more strawberry swirl and there is no more lemon-lime. Today there is only free-market vanilla. . . . There can be different brands of free-market vanilla and you can adjust your society to it by going faster or slower. But, in the end, if you want higher standards of living, . . . the free market is the only ideological alternative left. One road. Different speeds. But one road.[51]

When a country recognizes that there is only one road to economic progress and decides to abide by free-market rules, writes Friedman, then it puts on an economic and political Golden Straitjacket. It's a one-size-fits-all garment that isn't pretty, gentle, or comfortable. It squeezes, pinches, and otherwise keeps the entire society under pressure to streamline its economy and upgrade its performance. Countries that refuse to put the Golden Straitjacket on or shuck it off get quickly left behind. Countries that squeeze into the jacket no matter how it binds get ahead quicker than ever.

The rules for wearing the Golden Straitjacket, says Friedman, are simple.[52]

- Make the private sector the primary engine of your country's economic growth.
- Maintain a low rate of inflation and price stability.
- Shrink the size of your state bureaucracy.
- Maintain as close to a balanced budget as possible, if not a surplus.
- Eliminate or lower tariffs on imported goods.
- Remove restrictions on foreign investments.
- Get rid of quotas and domestic monopolies.
- Increase exports.
- Privatize state-owned industries and utilities.
- Deregulate capital markets.
- Make your currency convertible.
- Open your industries and stock and bond markets to direct foreign investment.
- Deregulate your economy to promote domestic competition.
- Eliminate government corruption, subsidies, and kickbacks as much as possible.
- Open your banking and telecommunications systems to private ownership and competition.
- Allow your citizens to choose from an array of competing pension options and foreign-run pension and mutual funds.

Of course, writes Friedman, countries don't all put on or wear the Golden Straitjacket the same way. Some don't even put it on all the way.

> Some just go partway or a little at a time (India, Egypt). Some put it on and take it off (Malaysia, Russia). Some try to tailor it to their specific culture and wear a few of the buttons unfastened (Germany, Japan and France). Some think they can resist its pinch altogether because they have a natural resource such as oil (Iran, Saudi Arabia). And some are so poor, that they can get away with dressing their people not in a Golden Straitjacket, but in a plain old straitjacket (North Korea, Cuba, Sudan, Afghanistan). But over time, this Golden Straitjacket is becoming harder and harder for countries to avoid.[53]

To those who reject the Golden Straitjacket and argue for retaining their own culture, values, and ways of doing things, Friedman offers this response:

> I am not saying that you have to put on the straitjacket. And if your culture and social traditions are opposed to the values embodied in that jacket, I certainly sympathize with that. But I am saying this: "Today's global market system, the Fast World and the Golden Straitjacket were produced by large historical forces that have fundamentally reshaped how we communicate, how we invest and how we see the world. If you want to resist these changes, that is your business. And it should be your business. But if you think that you can resist these changes without paying an increasingly steep price, without building an increasingly high wall and without falling behind increasingly fast, then you are deluding yourself."
>
> Here's why: The democratizations of finance, technology and information . . . gave birth to a new power source in the world—what I call the Electronic Herd.
>
> The Electronic Herd is made up of all the faceless stock, bond and currency traders sitting behind computer screens all over the globe, moving their money around from mutual funds to pension funds to emerging market funds, or trading on the Internet from their basements. And it also consists of the big multinational corporations who now spread their factories around the world, constantly shifting them to the most efficient low-cost producers. The herd has grown . . . so much . . . that today it is beginning to replace governments as the primary source of capital for both companies and countries. . . . The Electronic Herd loves the Golden Straitjacket, because it embodies all the liberal, free-market rules the herd wants to see in a country. Those countries that put on the Golden Straitjacket and keep it on are rewarded by the herd with investment capital. Those that don't put it on are disciplined by the herd—either by the herd avoiding or withdrawing money from the country.[54]

Ultimately, says Friedman, most countries will find the Electronic Herd irresistible. They will put on the Golden Straitjacket and button it up tight. As they do, they will find their cultures increasingly Americanized. For most people, Golden Straitjacket globalization "wears Mickey Mouse ears, eats Big Macs, drinks Coke or Pepsi and does its computing on an IBM PC, using Windows 98, with an Intel Pentium II processor and a network link from Cisco Systems."[55]

Friedman subscribes to the theory that the world's economies boil down to five different types of gas stations, only one of which will survive:[56]

> **Japanese.** Gas is five dollars a gallon. Four men in uniforms and white gloves pump your gas, wash your windows, and give you a friendly smile and wave as you drive away.
>
> **Western European.** Gas is five dollars a gallon also, but only one grumpy man is on duty. He pumps your gas and changes your oil but reminds you that he only works 35 hours per week, closes the station 90 minutes each day for lunch, gets six weeks vacation each summer, and doesn't do windows because it isn't in his contract. He has two brothers and an uncle who haven't worked in 10 years because they can collect more in state employment insurance than they were paid in their last jobs.
>
> **Developing Country.** Gas is subsidized by the government, so it only costs 50 cents a gallon. The station is owned by a man who lives in Zurich and takes all of the profit from the station out of the country. It is so run-down that only one of the six pumps work. The others have been broken for months, waiting for parts to be flown in from Europe. The station is patronized by three types of customers: those who drive late-model Mercedes; those who drive motor scooters; and those who ride bikes and use the station's air pump to fill their tires. Fifteen people, all cousins, work at the station but are too busy talking to pay customers any attention. Half of the cousins sleep at the station and use the car wash as a shower.
>
> **Communist.** Gas is only 50 cents a gallon, but there usually isn't any because most of it has already been sold on the black market by the four people who work at the station. Of course, only one of the four employees is actually at the station. The others are working second jobs in the underground economy. They only come by to collect their paychecks.
>
> **American.** Gas costs a dollar a gallon, but you must pump it yourself. The same is true of changing your own oil and filling your own tires. Also, you have to watch your car. If you leave it for a second, four homeless people will try to steal your hubcaps.

Friedman believes that globalization is forcing everyone to use an American-type gas station, whether they like it or not. While Golden Straitjacket, turbo-capitalism globalization empowers individuals, and therefore fits perfectly with American culture, it doesn't fit so well with others. (See Exhibit 5.9 for other ways in which Friedman believes the United States is ideally suited for globalization.)

## EXHIBIT 5.9. The Ideal Country for Globalization

Thomas L. Friedman writes that the United States is ideally situated to compete and win in a global economy for several reasons:

- It has an ideal geographic position that gives it access to both the Atlantic and Pacific as well as Canada and Latin America. Therefore, it can easily interact with all three key markets of the world—Asia, Europe, and the Americas.
- It has a multicultural, multiethnic, and multilingual population that has natural connections to all parts of the world. Although diverse, this population shares a single dominant language—English—which is the language of the Internet.
- It has five different regional economies bound together by the reserve currency of the world—the dollar. The five different regions smooth out the peaks and valleys of business cycles.
- It has innovative and efficient capital markets in which venture capitalism is admired as an art. Consequently, almost anyone with an idea can get funding. Additionally, the capital markets are transparent. Because secrecy isn't tolerated by the stock markets, all companies must file timely and audited earnings reports and financial statements.
- It has the most honest legal and regulatory systems in the world. There is very little corruption and plenty of legal safeguards to keep the playing field level even for foreigners.
- It has bankruptcy laws that encourage people who fail in a business venture to try again and again. Failure is seen as an inevitable, perhaps even necessary, part of innovation.
- It readily accepts new immigrants and treats them as constitutionally equal to everyone else. Because of this, it routinely siphons off the best brains of the world to its companies, laboratories, universities, and hospitals.
- It has a democratic, federal political system that decentralizes decision making so that regions and localities can adjust to world trends without having to wait on decisions at the national level. States and regions compete to find answers to problems in education, welfare, health care, and so on, meaning that a lot of experimentation is always going on.
- It has the most flexible labor force in the world. Workers can move easily from region to region, and businesses are relatively free to hire and fire people as conditions dictate.
- It has a society and culture in which Schumpeterian creative destruction is allowed to work. (See Exhibit 5.3 for an explanation of Schumpeter's ideas.)
- It is a country in which monopolies are not tolerated and government-protected cartels are abhorred, meaning that every company must stand on its own and compete.

(continued)

## EXHIBIT 5.9. The Ideal Country for Globalization

- It is a country that tolerates the oddball on the chance that the guy with a ponytail or girl with a ring in her nose might just be the next genius who in response to the declaration "that's impossible" announces with confidence, "I just did it."
- It is a country that has already downsized, privatized, networked, deregulated, reengineered, streamlined, restructured, and done all the other things necessary to exploit the democratizations of finance, technology, and information.
- It has a deep-rooted entrepreneurial culture and a tax system that allows successful investors to keep a large share of their capital gains and thus become rich.
- It still retains lots of environmentally friendly open spaces, lush green valleys, pristine mountains, and small towns that are attractive to knowledge workers.
- It tolerates the free flow of knowledge and information even from pornographers and racists.
- It is a country in which multinational companies and small start-ups think equally big and global.
- It is a country that already excels in virtually every fast-paced, knowledge-intensive endeavor.

*Source:* Adapted from Thomas L. Friedman, *The Lexus and the Olive Tree: Understanding Globalization* (New York: Anchor Books, 2000), pp. 367–368.

The Japanese, Western European, and former Communist countries all have social contracts that are very different from the American one. In the American gas station, the customer is king, and the gas station has no social function other than to provide gas at a reasonable price. If it can do so without employees and thereby be more efficient, then so much the better. The Japanese, Western Europeans, and Communists dislike such open markets that deliver unequal benefits and rewards. They don't like the answer many Americans would give to the question Friedman says he was asked by one educated Egyptian woman: "Does globalization mean we just leave the poor to fend for themselves?"[57] For them, a "Yes" to that question is unacceptable, even inconceivable. They had designed their economic gas stations to remove some of the inequities. Now they are being forced to give up their stations for American ones, and frequently they see the Americans as responsible. Some, of course, envy the United States and see American-type globalization as "a highly attractive, empowering, incredibly tempting pathway to rising living standards."[58] (See Exhibit 5.10 for a humorous illustration of this.) Others see the situation quite differently. Friedman notes that the view many Americans have of their country is best portrayed in Grant Wood's painting *American Gothic*—the strait-laced, stoic couple standing watch outside the barn, pitchfork in hand. To much of the world, however, American Gothic means something quite different.

> [It] is actually two twenty-something American software engineers who come into your country wearing long hair, beads and sandals, with rings in their noses and paint on their toes. They kick down your front door, overturn everything in the house, stick a Big Mac in your mouth, fill your kids' heads with ideas you've never had or can't understand, slam a cable box onto your television, lock the channel to MTV, plug an Internet connection into your computer and tell you: "Download or die."[59]

And they do one other thing. They destroy your environment—the third argument against globalization.

### EXHIBIT 5.10. **The McDonald's Ambassador**

In *The Lexus and the Olive Tree,* Thomas L. Friedman tells the following story to illustrate just how much people around the world equate globalization with Americanization.

> Martin Indyk, the . . . U.S. ambassador to Israel, . . . was called upon to open the first McDonald's in Jerusalem. . . . McDonald's gave him a colorful baseball hat with the McDonald's logo on it to wear as he was invited to eat the first ceremonial Big Mac in Jerusalem's first McDonald's—with Israeli television filming every bite for the evening news. The restaurant was packed with young Israelis eager to be on hand for this historic event. While Ambassador Indyk was preparing to eat Jerusalem's first official Big Mac, a young Israeli teenager worked his way through the crowd and walked up to him. The teenager was carrying his own McDonald's hat and he handed it to Ambassador Indyk with a pen and asked, "Are you the ambassador? Can I have your autograph?"
>
> Somewhat sheepishly, Ambassador Indyk replied, "Sure, I've never been asked for my autograph before."
>
> As Ambassador Indyk took the hat and prepared to sign his name on the bill, the teenager said to him, "Wow, what's it like to be the ambassador from McDonald's, going around the world opening McDonald's restaurants everywhere?"
>
> Stunned, Ambassador Indyk looked at the Israeli youth and said, "No, no. I'm the American ambassador—not the ambassador for McDonald's!"
>
> The Israeli youth looked totally crestfallen. Ambassador Indyk . . . said to him, "Does this mean you don't want my autograph?" And the kid said, "no, I don't want your autograph," and he took his hat back and walked away.

*Source:* Thomas L. Friedman, *The Lexus and the Olive Tree: Understanding Globalization* (New York: Anchor Books, 2000), pp. 382–383.

## Globalization Destroys the Environment

Hilary French is vice president for research at the Worldwatch Institute in Washington, D.C., and author of *Vanishing Borders.* No one makes a better case for the environmental horrors of globalization than French. We can't cite all of her voluminous and depressing statistics here because we don't have the space. Instead, we will just highlight some of the more sobering numbers. Nature, says French, is under siege. She attributes all of the following devastation of the environment, in one way or another, to globalization:

- "The loss of living species in recent decades . . . represents the largest mass extinction since the dinosaurs were wiped out 65 million years ago. Globalization is a powerful force behind today's unprecedented biological implosion."[60]
- "Biologists warn that as many as one fifth of all plant and animal species could disappear within the next 30 years."[61]
- "Nearly half of the forests that once covered Earth have already been lost, and almost 14 million hectares [35 million acres] of tropical forest—an area nearly three times the size of Costa Rica—is being destroyed each year" due in part to the global timber trade.[62]
- "Mining, energy development and associated activities represent the second biggest threat to frontier forests after logging, affecting nearly 40 percent of threatened forests."[63]
- "The rapid growth in the movement of human beings and their goods and services around the world has provided convenient transportation for thousands of other species of plants and animals that are now taking root on foreign shores . . . The spread of non-native 'exotic' species, a process dubbed bioinvasion, . . . [is] a major threat to the diversity of life on Earth. Nearly 20 percent of the world's endangered species are threatened by exotics, and almost half of all species in danger of extinction in the United States are imperiled at least in part by non-native species."[64]
- "Nearly half of the world's turtle species face possible extinction, due in large part to the growing demand for turtles for both food and medicinal ingredients."[65]
- Globalization is accelerating the spread of diseases. "Over the past two decades, more than 30 infectious diseases have been identified in humans for the first time, including AIDS, Ebola, Hantavirus, and hepatitis C and E. . . . Health experts confirmed in October 1999 that at least five people in New York City and surrounding areas died from a new strain of the African West Nile virus, a rare mosquito-borne disease never before seen in the western hemisphere. They attribute the emergence of the disease to the steady rise in international trade and travel, concluding that the disease was transmitted either by a smuggled exotic bird or by an infected human who carried it into the country from abroad."[66]

- "Global trade in meat is . . . causing environmental destruction. In Central America, the lure of the export market for beef spurred a massive clearing of the rainforest for cattle ranching. . . . In Botswana, heavy dependence on beef exports has resulted in land degradation from overgrazing. . . . And in Somlia, . . . rapid growth in exports of sheep, goats, and cattle . . . contributed to . . . overgrazing, soil erosion, and the degradation of rangelands."[67]
- "The world's fisheries are under siege as a result of habitat destruction, pollution, and overexploitation, with 11 of the world's 15 major fishing grounds and 70 percent of the primary fish species either fully or overexploited. The lure of international markets is a driving force behind this growing crisis. Fish exports have climbed nearly five fold in value since 1970."[68]
- "Shrimp aquaculture has grown particularly fast in many developing countries. . . . In Thailand [for example] shrimp and prawn production surged from 61,000 tons in 1970 to a peak of 389,000 tons in 1995, with exports accounting for 60 percent of the 1995 total." Shrimp farms are a threat to mangrove ecosystems that play a critical role in protecting coastlines and serve as a spawning ground for oceanic fisheries. "In Thailand alone, some 253,000 hectares [632,500 acres] of the country's original 380,000 hectares [950,000 acres] of mangrove forests have already been destroyed by shrimp farms."[69]
- "Over the ages, farmers have relied upon diverse crop varieties as protection from pests, blights, and other forms of crop failure. . . . [However,] the last century has seen a steady erosion of genetic diversity in agriculture. . . . 75 percent of crop diversity has been lost over this century. . . . In the United States, more than 70 percent of all cornfields are now planted in just six varieties of corn. In India, farmers grew as many as 30,000 varieties of rice 50 years ago; today, three fourths of India's rice fields are planted with fewer than 10 varieties. And in Mexico, only 20 percent of the corn varieties that were cultivated in the 1930s can still be found today. The rapid pace at which plant genetic diversity is disappearing is leaving the world vulnerable to multi-billion-dollar crop losses and reducing the storehouse from which future agricultural strains can be derived."[70]
- "Despite the progress made in recent years in controlling the hazardous waste trade, the problem remains far from solved. UNEP [the United Nations Environment Program] estimates that some 440 million tons of hazardous waste are generated worldwide every year, about 10 percent of which is shipped across international borders. Illegal trade is believed to be flourishing. . . . Officials have intercepted illegal shipments originating in the United States that were bound for Ecuador, Guinea, Haiti, Malaysia, Mexico, Panama, and Sri Lanka."[71]

## Yes, No, and Maybe. . . . Is It Really as Bad as It Seems?

For the most part, Luttwak, Friedman, and French paint a very gloomy picture of globalization. According to them, globalization creates tremendous economic inequalities, destroys cultures, and devastates the planet. Does it really do all of that, or are these gurus and others who deliver such warnings simply alarmists? Even the most pessimistic of the alarmists have to acknowledge that, for all the bad associated with globalization, there are good features as well—or at least the potential for good. For example, Friedman admits that the same Electronic Herd (those faceless financial traders behind their computer screens) that Americanizes everything, locks countries into Golden Straitjackets, and forces people to given up centuries-old cultures also demands that countries become more democratic and that companies develop world-class standards for the treatment of their workers. He cites the example of a visit he made in 1999 to a factory in Sri Lanka that manufactured clothing for Victoria's Secret and Marks & Spencer.

> The factory was completely computerized and was soon to be linked by Internet to Victoria's Secret chain to handle E-commerce. About 1,400 employees, mostly women ages eighteen and older, worked on rows and rows of pneumatic sewing machines. Everyone wore a uniform, and pregnant women were identified by a red cap, and expected to keep a slower pace. The factory was air conditioned and was clean enough to eat off the floor. The workday was eight hours, but intense, as each woman had to stitch so many garments per minute. Each assembly line was tracked by computer and a certain average production had to be reached for the women to get their monthly bonuses. Wages were about \$80–\$100 a month, including breakfast, and there was a waiting list for jobs. In terms of working conditions, the factory was world-class.[72]

Friedman says that he was so impressed with the way the plant was run and how the employees were treated, with the exception of their wages, that he would have let his own daughters work there. Still, he was curious as to why the factory owners had gone to so much trouble and why they had not created a sweat shop that would make them bigger profits. The owners responded that, in fact, they would not make money that way. The only way they could compete in the textile business against even lower-waged countries such as China, they explained, was to produce goods for big name global retailers such as Victoria's Secret and Marks & Spencer, and these big-name retailers were demanding not only high quality products, but better conditions for workers. Their customers were increasingly socially conscious and wanted to know that the fancy, high-priced goods they bought were not produced under sweat-shop conditions or through the exploitation of workers. "When the buyers from Victoria's Secret and the other big brands come through now, . . . one of the first things they ask about [is working conditions]," said the factory owner. "They have to, because they have customers asking them about it."[73] In short, you might say that the customers were looking for a good story behind the products they bought (recall our discussion in Chapter 1 of the dream society), and global companies were being forced to deliver.

John Micklethwait and Adrian Woolridge have a similar perspective on the question of whether globalization is good or bad. They maintain that it is a little of both.

> Yes, it does increase inequality, but it does not create a winner-take-all society, and the winners hugely outnumber the losers. Yes, it leaves some people behind, but it helps millions more to leap ahead. Yes it can make bad government worse, but the onus should be on crafting better government, not blaming globalization. Yes, it curtails some of the power of the nation-states, but they remain the fundamental unit of modern politics. Globalization is not destroying geography, merely enhancing it. . . .
>
> The simple fact is that globalization makes us richer—or makes enough of us richer to make the whole process worthwhile. Globalization clearly benefits producers by giving them greater choice over their raw materials, production techniques, and human talent, not to mention over the markets where they sell their goods. Equally clearly, globalization benefits consumers by providing them with better goods at better prices. Globalization increases efficiency and thus prosperity.[74]

As we noted at the beginning of this chapter, globalization is a contentious and complicated subject. It is, as Friedman describes, everything and its opposite. "It can be incredibly empowering and incredibly coercive. It can democratize opportunity and democratize panic. It makes the whales bigger and the minnows stronger. It leaves you behind faster and faster, and it catches up to you faster and faster. While it is homogenizing cultures, it is also enabling people to share their unique individuality farther and farther."[75] Globalization is a lot of things, say our gurus, but the most important thing to know about it is that it is here to stay. That reality leads us to the second big globalization issue. If globalization is here to stay, how do businesses play the game? How do they succeed in a global economy?

> With all due respect to revolutionary theorists [who predict a backlash against globalization], the "wretched of the earth" want to go to Disney World—not to the barricades. They want the Magic Kingdom, not Les Misérable. And if you construct an economic and political environment that gives them half a sense that with hard work and sacrifice they will get to Disney World and get to enjoy the Magic Kingdom, most of them will stick with the game—for far, far longer than you would expect.
>
> *Thomas L. Friedman*[76]

# THE IMPACT OF GLOBALIZATION ON BUSINESS

"I would say in 2000," writes Thomas L. Friedman, "we understand as much about how today's system of globalization is going to work as we understood about how the Cold War system was going to work in 1946—the year Winston Churchill gave his speech warning that an 'Iron Curtain' was coming down, cutting off the Soviet zone of influence from Western Europe."[77] Which is to say, we don't know very much at all. After all, in 1946 no Sovietologist would have predicted that there wouldn't be a Soviet Union in the year 2000. Likewise, none of our gurus truly know how globalization is going to play out between now and 2030, but that doesn't prevent them from cooking up and ladling out tons of advice. Just remember as you read this part of the chapter that none of our globalization gurus have been cooking in this particular global kitchen for very long. They are still learning. Don't be surprised then if a few years from now some of their ideas about going global and succeeding in the global economy turn out to be—well—half-baked.

As you might expect, our gurus' advice on taking your company global is wide ranging, extending from the mystically esoteric (such as the importance of "cross-geographic arbitrage," which we will discuss later in this chapter) to the decidedly practical, such as what you should do when a Japanese businessman gives you his business card. (See Exhibit 5.11 for recommended responses to this and other intercultural business encounters.) We will concentrate on two topics:

1. Why our gurus say every company should be going global.
2. The globalization strategies our gurus say you should follow to take your company global.

### EXHIBIT 5.11. What to Do When a Japanese Businessperson Gives You His/Her Card and How to Handle 19 Other Intercultural Business Encounters

This quiz on intercultural manners is based on information in *Multicultural Management 2000* by Farid Elashmawi and Philip R. Harris. See how many responses you can get right. The correct answers, according to Elashmawi and Harris, are printed at the end of the quiz.

1. When a Japanese businessperson gives you his or her card, you should:
   a. Put it in your wallet without looking at it.
   b. Examine it carefully and acknowledge the company name.
   c. Ask how to pronounce the name in Japanese.
2. When introducing yourself to a Japanese businessperson, you should emphasize your:
   a. Individual managerial capability and/or technical know-how.

(continued)

EXHIBIT 5.11. **(continued)**

b. Interest in closing the sale before you leave.
c. Company's capabilities and long-range market share.

3. When talking to Americans, you should:
   a. Keep two-arm's length away.
   b. Keep a half-arm's length away.
   c. Put your left hand in your pocket.
4. In your first encounter with an Arab businessperson, you should:
   a. Open both arms to receive his hug.
   b. Give him your business card with your left hand and extend your right hand for a handshake.
   c. Extend your right hand for a handshake.
5. An Arab businessperson offers you a cup of Arabian coffee at his office, but you don't drink coffee. You should:
   a. Say, "No, thank you."
   b. Say, "Thank you," accept the coffee, take a small sip, and set it aside.
   c. Say, "No, thank you, coffee makes me nervous."
6. Your American business partner phones from her hotel to tell you that she has arrived from overseas and is ready to meet. You should:
   a. Tell her that you will send the company limousine to pick her up.
   b. Ask her if she needs directions to your office.
   c. Ask her where she would like to meet you.
7. You are calling an Arab distributor from your home office. You may start the conversation by:
   a. Asking if he has mailed his late payment.
   b. Saying that you hope he and his family are well.
   c. Asking how his business is doing.
8. You telephone your American business associate. After you identify yourself, she says, "What can I do for you?" You respond:
   a. "Where is my order?"
   b. "How is the weather in your city?"
   c. "How is business?"
9. At the end of your telephone discussion with your Japanese friend, you ask him if the price is acceptable. He answers, "Yes, yes," meaning:
   a. He accepts your price.
   b. He has heard and understood your offer.
   c. He is politely saying no.
10. You are attending an American business meeting. If you disagree with one of the points being discussed, you should:
    a. Bring up the disagreement immediately.

(continued)

EXHIBIT 5.11. **(continued)**

b. Write down your disagreement and pass it to the coordinator.
c. Just sit quietly until someone brings up the subject.

11. When you introduce yourself at an American meeting, you should emphasize your:
    a. Educational credentials and current responsibilities.
    b. Current salary.
    c. Latest accomplishments.
12. You are starting a meeting with a Japanese team. The team leader asks you, "What is the purpose of your visit?" You answer:
    a. "To exchange information about our products and potential market."
    b. "To present my company's product line."
    c. "To secure an agreement on a joint venture with your company."
13. You are conducting a meeting with 10 Arab managers and workers. Everyone is participating except one manager. You should:
    a. Not worry about him.
    b. Ask if anyone has any comments before the meeting ends.
    c. Look at that particular manager and ask if he has something to say.
14. You are making a presentation to executives of an American company. You should:
    a. Provide those attending the presentation with an outline of your presentation in advance and a copy of your handouts at the start of the meeting.
    b. Provide copies of your charts and handouts part-by-part as you go through your talk.
    c. Not provide a copy of your material.
15. You are conducting a presentation to Japanese managers. You should start by:
    a. Talking about your education and latest accomplishments.
    b. Apologizing for not speaking Japanese.
    c. Reminding them that you need a firm answer on your proposal by the end of the meeting.
16. It is one hour into your two-hour presentation to Arab managers and no one has asked a question. You should:
    a. Keep going.
    b. Call for a break.
    c. Look at the most senior manager and ask, "Do you have any questions?"
17. Most Americans prefer that the purpose of a business letter be stated in the:
    a. First paragraph.
    b. Middle paragraph after an extensive greeting and background information.
    c. Last paragraph.

(continued)

EXHIBIT 5.11. **(continued)**

18. You are sending a letter to an important Arab distributor, introducing your company's products. You should:
    a. Enclose a letter of recommendation from the State Department.
    b. Send him free samples of your products.
    c. Offer him a visit to your country if he distributes your products and meets sales quotas.
19. After a long communication process with a Japanese firm, you receive a letter saying, "We will keep your company name in our files, and if we need your collaboration in the future, we will contact you." You should:
    a. Send a fax thanking them for the letter.
    b. Throw the letter in the trash because you won't get their business.
    c. Ask your go-between to see what is going on.
20. During your presentation, one of the Americans in the meeting questions the data you are presenting. You should:
    a. Ask, "Why?" and justify your data.
    b. Say, "We can talk about this issue after the meeting."
    c. Ask them to put their concern in writing.

**Answers:** 1(a), 2(c), 3(a), 4(c), 5(b), 6(b), 7(b), 8(a), 9(b), 10(a), 11(c), 12(a), 13(c), 14(a), 15(b), 16(c), 17(a), 18(a), 19(a) 20 (a). For more on intercultural differences and explanations for the correct answers to these situations see *Multicultural Management 2000,* pp. 111–155.

*Source:* Adapted from Farid Elashmawi and Philip R. Harris, *Multicultural Management 2000: Essential Cultural Insights for Global Business Success* (Houston, TX: Gulf Publishing, 1998), pp. 111–155

## Reasons for Taking Your Company Global

Let's start with the most basic of questions. Why should I take my company global? Other than the fact that globalization is here to stay, why should I take my company out to play on the world stage if I'm doing just fine at home?

In an article in *Business Horizons,* gurus Anil K. Gupta and Vijay Govindarajan present five reasons why becoming global is no longer discretionary but has become imperative for most firms:

1. The growth imperative.
2. The efficiency imperative.
3. The knowledge imperative.
4. The globalization of customers.
5. The globalization of competitors.

We discuss each of these reasons in the following sections.

## Reason #1: The Growth Imperative

Everyone knows that capital markets reward growth, yet markets for most industries in developed countries are becoming quite mature. Therefore, say Gupta and Govindarajan, most companies will be forced to go global to keep growing. They cite the example of the paper industry.[78] Per capita consumption of paper in developed markets, such as North America and Western Europe, has peaked at about 600 pounds. In contrast, per capita consumption of paper in developing countries, such as China and India, is still only around 30 pounds and growing. So, if you are a paper manufacturer, what's the smart move? Should you stay at home and try to grow by taking market share away from your competitors, or should you go global and tap into a growing market? Let's say, write Gupta and Govindarajan, that per capita paper consumption in China and India grows by only one pound over the next five years. That's demand for an additional 2.2 billion pounds, which is enough to keep five state-of-the-art paper mills churning happily along at full capacity.

The global market for products and services is huge and growing. Lowell Bryan and Jane Fraser estimate that the global market for all goods and services is about $6 trillion now and will grow to as much as $73 trillion within 30 years.[79] The profit opportunities are enormous, stretching into the hundreds of billions of dollars. For example, Bryan and Fraser calculate that the global market for personal financial services (PFS), which now stands at about $300 billion, will double within 10 years. In the past, because of regulatory and technological limitations, no single company participating in the global PFS market could expect to capture more than 3 percent, or $9 billion, of it. Now, however, regulatory and technological barriers are falling, making the market much more accessible. As a result, write Bryan and Fraser, it is not inconceivable that a single company could capture as much as 10 percent of the PFS market worldwide. That would deliver as much as $60 billion to the lucky company.[80] Similar possibilities exist in other industries, say our gurus. The first reason to go global, therefore, is to take advantage of the growing global markets and make more money.

## Reason #2: The Efficiency Imperative

Gupta and Govindarajan write, "Whenever the value chain sustains one or more activities in which the minimum efficient scale (of research facilities, production centers, and so on) exceeds the sales volume feasible within one country, a company with global presence will have the potential to create a cost advantage relative to a domestic player within that industry."[81] Huh? What they are saying—we think—is that you may have to go beyond your borders to get the volume of business you need to support your investment in production facilities, research and development, and so on. For example, Mercedes-Benz gets 20 percent of its revenues from sales in North America. If it had to rely on sales from Europe alone, or worse, just from Germany, Mercedes would be much less efficient because its operating costs would be spread over fewer sales.

### Reason #3: The Knowledge Imperative

Gupta and Govindarajan point out that companies that take products and services into another country are almost always forced to adapt them in some way to the local environment. These adaptations are often cutting-edge product or process innovations that the company would not have pursued had it not expanded beyond its home country. For example, when General Electric began selling CT scanners in India, it was forced to find ways to make them simpler, more transportable, and cheaper. These innovations had worldwide application.[82]

### Reason #4: The Globalization of Customers

One reason you may be forced to go global, write our gurus, is that your customers are already there. Let's say you are an advertising agency and one of your major customers is a soft-drink manufacturer. When your client begins selling its soft drinks overseas, you had better be able to service its global needs, or you aren't likely to keep its business for very long. Ask yourself, how many executives would want to carry an American Express card if they could only use it in the United States?

### Reason #5: The Globalization of Competitors

Finally, write Gupta and Govindarajan, you may be forced to take your company global for the simple reason that your competitors are global. If they go global and you don't, they gain the advantages of a global presence (review reasons 1–4), and you don't.

Gupta and Govindarajan write that, "today, globalization is no longer an option but a strategic imperative for all but the smallest firms."[83] They may be right. Indeed, most of our gurus would argue that the benefits of going global far outweigh the risks for most firms. If you are convinced that this is true, you are probably wondering what to do next. How do you take your company global? Well, say our gurus, you need a strategy, and they just happen to have a couple of ideas. In fact, they have more than a couple of ideas about what that strategy might be.

## Strategies for Taking Your Company Global

In this section, we look at three rather different perspectives on the subject of what strategy you should follow in taking your company global. The first is that offered by Ruth Stanat and Chris West, coauthors of *Global Jumpstart.* Stanat and West take a fairly traditional approach to the topic, offering a range of options from simple exporting to overseas acquisitions. We will see what they have to say about the advantages and disadvantages of each.

The second perspective on global strategy that we present here is that offered by Booz-Allen consultant Cyrus F. Freidheim in his book *The Trillion-Dollar Enterprise.* Freidheim argues that the best globalization strategy for most companies isn't to try to become a global firm at all but rather to build global alliances. We will see why Freidheim thinks the alliance route is the way to go.

Finally, we examine the thinking of four McKinsey consultants, Lowell Bryan, Jane Fraser, Jeremy Oppenheim, and Wilhelm Rall, whom we will refer to simply as Bryan for the remainder of this chapter. Bryan says that, instead of developing strategies for expanding into foreign geographic markets, you should be preparing your company to dominate and shape a "sliver" of the global market for a particular product or service. We will sift through Bryan's frustratingly dense, jargon-filled prose to decipher their reasoning.

We begin our discussion with your basic options.

## Going Global the Traditional Way

In their book *Global Jumpstart,* Stanat and West describe a range of traditional options companies have for going global, including exporting, licensing, strategic alliances, overseas joint ventures, overseas subsidiaries, and overseas acquisitions. Here are the advantages and disadvantages they identify for each method.

### Exporting

Exporting involves selling products or services to a foreign market through an intermediary, such as a commissioned agent or trading company. It is the method of going global used most frequently by small firms. The advantages and disadvantages of exporting, according to Stanat and West, are as follows:[84]

**Advantages**

- You can gain a global presence with little commitment of staff time and company resources.
- Your intermediary, through a network of contacts, can help you establish business relationships in foreign countries that you might have difficulty accessing on your own.
- Your intermediary can guide you through the export process so you do not have to learn on your own.

**Disadvantages**

- You may lose control over how your products are marketed and serviced.
- You will lose part of your profit margin by discounting to an intermediary.
- Using an intermediary may result in a higher price being passed on to overseas buyers, which may affect your competitive position.

### *Licensing*

With international licensing, you assign your technology or products over to another party for exploitation in one or more foreign markets. The advantages and disadvantages of licensing according to Stanat and West are as follows:[35]

| ADVANTAGES | DISADVANTAGES |
|---|---|
| • Your capital requirements for entering foreign markets are low.<br>• Licensing provides you with a low-cost method for distributing your products in foreign countries.<br>• The local licensee has the knowledge of the local market and can use that knowledge to modify the product, technology, or service to better fit local needs and requirements.<br>• You can easily discontinue the license if the arrangement doesn't seem to be working. | • You may lose control of the quality of your product.<br>• You may risk patent or copyright infringement if the licensee is in a country with a less-developed legal system.<br>• You may not like the way the technology or product is adapted for the local market.<br>• You will lose hands-on control of your products and technology in foreign markets you have turned over to a licensee. |

### *Strategic alliances*

Strategic alliances can range from a handshake deal to a formal agreement with a partner or firm to act as your supplier, distributor, trading partner, or local representative in a foreign country. The advantages and disadvantages of strategic alliances, say Stanat and West, are as follows:[86]

| ADVANTAGES | DISADVANTAGES |
|---|---|
| • Your costs for developing and maintaining the relationship are low.<br>• You can easily discontinue the relationship if it doesn't work out.<br>• You can form alliances with other partners or even competitors in the same foreign markets.<br>• You can form alliances at many different levels including local, global, regional or multicountry. | • You may subject your company to patent and/or copyright infringement.<br>• You lose control over local marketing and manufacturing.<br>• Your partner may sign similar agreements with your competitors. |

### *Overseas joint ventures*

In establishing a joint venture, you identify a foreign company that has the labor force, local-market knowledge, technology, or some other advantage to your firm and develop a marketing relationship, manufacturing partnership, or technology-licensing venture to which both partners commit capital, technology, management expertise, marketing expertise, and so on to develop a business in that country. The advantages and disadvantages of joint ventures, say Stanat and West, are as follows:[87]

**ADVANTAGES**

- Although you must make at least a moderate commitment of capital, human resources, and so on, your investment is less than in some other methods of going global, such as establishing subsidiaries and making acquisitions.
- You can usually terminate joint-venture agreements in case of nonperformance, adverse market conditions, or even a change in corporate direction.
- Joint ventures are usually considered less risky than financing subsidiaries or foreign acquisitions.

**DISADVANTAGES**

- You may lack control over the management of the joint venture.
- You may lose control over the distribution of your products in countries covered by the joint-venture agreement.
- You may subject your firm to copyright or patent infringement.
- It may be difficult for you to repatriate profits if most of the goods coproduced in the joint-venture agreement are for export.

### *Overseas subsidiaries*

You set up your own local office, manufacturing plant, and/or marketing facility in a foreign country. The advantages and disadvantages of setting up a subsidiary, according to Stanat and West, are as follows:[88]

**ADVANTAGES**

- You have a local office supported by local production and distribution that can service your local customers.
- You control your product's distribution.
- You have more control over your copyrights and patents than you do with other methods of going global.
- You control local marketing, advertising, and promotion of your products.

**DISADVANTAGES**

- It may be expensive to incorporate in a foreign country.
- You may be subjected to more-stringent labor laws than in your home country.
- If the foreign country is a developing or emerging one, it may lack the infrastructure to support your manufacturing, marketing, and distribution facilities.

### *Overseas acquisitions*

Finally, you may develop a presence in a foreign country by acquiring an established local firm outright. The advantages and disadvantages of acquisitions, say Stanat and West, are as follows:[89]

| ADVANTAGES | DISADVANTAGES |
|---|---|
| • You buy your way into a successful and established market.<br>• The firm you acquire already has an established name and reputation in the local market.<br>• You can leverage off the local firm's existing strength to develop new products and services.<br>• Your start-up time in entering the local market is minimal. | • The cost of acquiring an established firm with a good reputation may be high.<br>• You will be subject to local accounting methods and local taxation.<br>• You may have difficulty merging the cultures of your existing firm and that of the one you are acquiring.<br>• You may have difficulty hiring the best talent to manage the acquired firm because the top local candidates may not want to work for a foreign-owned business in which they view their chances of advancement as limited. |

For Stanat and West, exporting, licensing, alliances, joint ventures, subsidiaries, and acquisitions all represent viable options for taking your company global. No single option is necessarily better than another. You just have to weigh the advantages and disadvantages of each and select the option that is most comfortable to you and that fits your overall business strategy. Other gurus, particularly Cyrus F. Freidheim, disagree. Freidheim sees exporting, licensing, and joint ventures as short-sighted strategies. If you want to think global, you should be thinking 30 or 40 years out, and you should not concentrate on getting your existing products into a foreign market. Instead, you should be thinking about creating a truly global, trillion-dollar enterprise. That's right. Freidheim said a "trillion-dollar" enterprise. That's "trillion" with a "T," and, says Freidheim, he and his cohorts at the consulting firm of Booz-Allen just happen to know how to do that.

## *Going Global: The Trillion-Dollar Enterprise*

Freidheim says that the idea for the trillion-dollar enterprise first came to his attention during a meeting of Booz-Allen's advisory board several years ago. A team of Booz-Allen consultants was making a presentation on the way they saw the global corporation evolving over the next decade. The team had done a lot of research, and, says Freidheim, everyone was impressed with their findings. "We had talked extensively to our clients and reviewed internal research projects on alliances and on the extended enterprise, which is a way of looking at a company and all its suppliers as one unit. As a result of this spade work, we thought we had a good idea of how companies should act during the coming decade in the increasingly competitive international arena. We presented our ideas—brilliantly, I thought."[90]

Then, writes Freidheim, the Booz-Allen team got a question. It wasn't as much a question as it was a criticism. Bob Galvin, chairman of Motorola, spoke up. "You're not asking the right questions," he said. "And you are short sighted."[91] Galvin chastised the Booz-Allen team for thinking only 10 years out instead of 40 or 50 and for focusing on how companies should react to the new environment rather than how they should move to shape the future. "You should be thinking about what having a trillion-dollar enterprise will mean,"[92] continued Galvin. The room fell silent. The Booz-Allen team was embarrassed. It was, as Freidheim recalls, like they were being spanked in public, and they were being punished in front of some of the world's most influential business leaders—people like Dick Rosenberg, CEO of BankAmerica; Yoh Kuroswa, CEO of Industrial Bank of Japan; and Larry Fuller, chairman of Amoco; not to mention the six Booz-Allen partners who were also present. Finally, Fuller broke the silence. "Don't we have trillion-dollar enterprises today?" he asked. He then went on to describe the network of alliances and relationships formed in his industry that brought together individual companies in huge, multiyear, bet-the-ranch efforts to explore for oil. The combined sales of companies engaged in such efforts had to approach a trillion dollars, speculated Fuller. Similar alliances were being formed in telecommunications, aerospace, and in other industries. The trillion-dollar enterprise wasn't a thing of the future. Indeed, said Fuller, it was becoming almost commonplace.[93]

Freidheim believes that the exchange helped to coalesce trends, ideas, and research that Booz-Allen had been monitoring for some time. "We had realized that companies were struggling to deal with a business world that was irreversibly globalizing, just as nations were forming blocs and protecting their borders. The development of huge enterprises linking independent companies together was the solution developed by business—in the main unwittingly—to deal with these two incompatible forces."[94]

It became obvious to the Booz-Allen consultants, as they looked around them, that trillion-dollar enterprises were already being built, but that they weren't being built through the creation of international, multinational, worldwide, global corporations. Instead, they were being built through alliances. That is not to say that companies weren't expanding internationally. Companies were developing global perspectives, global strategies, and global managers. But such globalization took them only so far. Although people might talk about the "global corporation," which sourced products with great efficiency worldwide and was run by a truly international band of executives at the top, few such corporations existed. The number of truly global products—like Coca-Cola, the producers of cellular telephones, and airplane manufacturers—might be growing rapidly, but 90 percent of what most countries consumed in the late 1990s was still produced within their own borders.

And while a handful of companies such as ABB, the energy equipment giant, had more than 10 percent of nonnationals in their executive suites, most companies were still run by executives from their own home country. No, concludes Freidheim, the true path to "going global" and creating the trillion-dollar enterprise is to bring together a network of companies in a strategic alliance, such as the Airbuse Industrie alliance between German, French, British, and Spanish aerospace companies, or the strategic alliance Banc One developed with Barclays Bank to service its customers in the United Kingdom. These alliances involve a long-term commitment to the partnership by all parties, as well as shared resources, funding, and/or equity. There are seven reasons, writes Freidheim, why they are a better alternative for building a global presence.[95]

***Reason #1: Enjoy the cost savings and benefits of risk sharing.***

It can cost $15 to $20 billion to develop a new super-jumbo jet for sale in the global aerospace market, $5 billion to install a transatlantic fiber-optic cable network, and equally enormous funds to explore for oil in the North Sea or Azerbajan. With alliance partners, you can share the costs and minimize the risk. It is just cheaper not to try to go it alone.

***Reason #2: Avoid acquisition barriers.***

Acquisition may take too long, be too expensive, or be totally impractical as a means of gaining the capabilities you need to succeed globally. Even if you could buy Ford, where would you get the $100 billion or so it would take? Or how are you going to get the British government to sell you the "golden" share it owns of British Aerospace? Even if you can come up with the money and negotiate a price you can afford, you may run afoul of antitrust laws. That's what happened to Boeing when it tried to acquire McDonnell Douglas. The European Community almost blocked the sale and acquiesced only after extracting painful concessions from Boeing, including its agreement to rescind some exclusive contracts it had with its customers.

***Reason #3: Achieve market-segment access and understanding of customer requirements.***

Few companies understand or have access to all of the markets for their products and services throughout the world, nor do they understand customer needs and requirements everywhere. Alliance partners can bring much-needed market presence, local infrastructure, and an understanding of local markets and customer requirements.

***Reason #4: Avoid the need for a bureaucracy to monitor subsidiary activities.***

If you own a subsidiary, then you are accountable to your stockholders for its performance and will likely have to institute controls and put in place a bureaucracy to monitor its activities. That's going to make you much less nimble, but, writes Freidheim, it may be necessary.

> If your alliance partner in Singapore violates financial and trading laws and blows $1 billion, it's nothing more than a shame (as long as they didn't blow your billion!) and you get another partner. If your Singapore subsidiary does it, your whole company goes down the tube (as happened in the case of the old-line British investment bank, Barings). If you are a U.S. company and own a subsidiary anywhere in the world, you are subject to all U.S. laws, and, consequently, you establish controls to ensure that no one steps out of line. You file taxes in the host country, worry about U.S. foreign tax credits, audit the subsidiary's operations, and set policies on everything from compensation to the environment and safety, to accounting practices, and to ethical standards. If the subsidiary has financial problems, you must explain them to Wall Street. If the managers don't measure up, you must replace them. Often, companies build complex, bureaucratic, costly corporate systems and require subsidiaries to use them. Those costs, although buried, are very real.[96]

***Reason #5: Closing technology gaps.***

Often, companies don't have all of the technology they need to compete effectively on a global basis, and they may not have the time or resources to quickly acquire that technology on their own. A strategic partner can provide immediate access to the technology you require.

***Reason #6: Gaining geographic access to markets.***

Some markets are effectively closed to you if you don't have a local partner. For example, China encourages—effectively mandates—that you have a Chinese partner to do business there.

***Reason #7: Keeping management skills.***

The best people in any company want a shot at the top jobs, but they understand a truth about foreign-owned firms, writes Freidheim:

> All corporations and managers are bound to a culture, affected by local political interests and unable to remain unbiased in the face of other-than-obvious trade-offs. Corporations will have a home country—and a home culture—whose interests they reflect even as they operate around the world. And this includes the companies that they acquire in other countries. The cultural transition from French corporation to French subsidiary of a U.S. company can be subtle, but it is always real. The Brazilian manager of the Japanese subsidiary in São Paulo will never achieve the status of her Japanese counterpart at the Tokyo headquarters, and the likelihood of her becoming a top executive in Tokyo is almost zero.[97]

The best management talent recognizes this reality, and they leave. Strategic partnerships rarely result in such a talent drain.

The answer to going global is, if not exactly simple, at least straightforward, argues Freidheim. Find a partner, or two or three or more, and develop a strategic partnership. In fact, develop a whole series of strategic partnerships. "Choose acquisition last and alliances first if you want to be global."[98] When you do, Freidheim says, all good things will flow to you:

- You will be able to serve and have access to markets wherever your products and services are relevant.
- You will understand all of your potential customers and markets worldwide, including the obstacles, opportunities, and risks of serving them.
- You will be able to meet and anticipate your customers' needs for cost, reliability, service, distribution, technology, and so on wherever they are in the world. And you will be able to do it better than anyone else in the world.
- You will be able to obtain raw materials and services from the best sources in the world.
- You will understand all the important factors and trends that will impact your business in the years ahead, including the challenges you will face from developments anywhere in the world.
- You will innovate, deliver value, have world-class processes, retain world-class people, and build world-class capabilities.
- You will reap all the benefits and economies of scale of being global while understanding the specific requirements of local markets and having access to all of the benefits differentially available to locally owned enterprises.

According to Freidheim, you will be global, set world standards, and be local, all at the same time. And, you will leap tall buildings in a single bound. . . . Okay, maybe not that, but alliances are the only way to go, right? You already know the answer to that question, because we told you earlier that McKinsey consultants Lowell Bryan, Jane Fraser, Jeremy Oppenheim, and Wilhelm Rall say that, not only are alliances not the only way to go, they actually miss the point. Winning the world isn't about building networks of alliances to open geographic markets; it is about dominating and shaping the global market—or at least a tiny piece of it.

### *Going Global: Winning the Race for the World*

The McKinsey gurus note that, in the aftermath of World War II, most companies imposed controls on capital flows, restrictions on access to markets, and other limitations on trade that made it difficult for companies to conduct business across geographic boundaries. As a consequence, local companies had privileged access to customers, capital, and technology in their own local markets that companies from other markets did not have. In other words, U.S. companies had artificially imposed advantages doing business in the U.S. market. French companies had advantages doing business in the French market, and Germany companies had advantages doing business in the Germany market. Companies that wanted to "go global" and do business in local markets, other than their own, were forced to find ways to overcome these local market advantages. In order to do so, says Bryan, most companies adopted one of three basic geographic expansion strategies:[99]

1. **Multilocal.** Companies that adopted a multilocal approach to globalization built or acquired a full business system in each country in which they wished to do business. They set up production facilities, acquired access to distribution channels, hired local talent, learned and abided by local business protocols and standards, acquired local capital, gained regulatory approval, and did all of the things in each local market that a local firm would do. In effect, they overcame local advantages by creating a local subsidiary. Bryan cites Nestlé and Shell as examples of companies that followed this approach.

2. **Global.** Companies that adopted a global strategy focused on creating global demand and setting global standards for a particular good or service. Instead of trying to build a complete business in every geographic market, they kept production and research and development largely in one country and relied on their economies of scale or patents and access to specialized proprietary technology to "buy" them access to local markets. In short, the quality of their products and cost advantages enabled them to create a demand for their products sufficient to overcome geographic restrictions. Their investment in local markets was often limited to no more than the hiring of a local sales force. Bryan cites Boeing, with its scale advantages in airframes, and Canon, with its specialized 35-millimeter camera technology, as two companies that employed a global approach.

3. **Transnational.** Finally, says Bryan, beginning in the late 1980s, some companies began to combine the multilocal and global approaches, following a globalization strategy described by Christopher A. Bartlett and Sumantra Ghoshal in their 1989 best-seller *Managing across Borders.* These companies invested in building a strong presence and management structure in each local market while simultaneously trying to share knowledge and integrate activities worldwide to gain scale and specialty advantages of companies that adopted a global approach. Bartlett and Ghoshal describe the transnational approach this way:

> Some decisions will tend to be made on a global basis, often at the corporate center (most often research priorities and financing decisions, for example); others will be the appropriate responsibility of local management (typically sales and service tasks and labor relations, for instance). But for some issues, multiple perspectives are important and shared responsibility is necessary. Product policy decisions, for example, often involve negotiation between global product division managers pushing for greater standardization to achieve scale economies, and local subsidiary managers advocating modifications to fit the product to their local market needs.[100]

Bartlett and Ghoshal cite Procter & Gamble, Philips, and NEC as examples of companies that adopted the transnational approach.

The common denominator of the multilocal, global, and transnational approaches, write the McKinsey consultants, is that each approach seeks to overcome local company advantages and open up geographic markets. But, they add, such efforts today are irrelevant and unnecessary because three powerful forces are working to lower the geographic barriers to international trade that the multilocal, global, and transnational approaches seek to overcome:

> First, national governments, under market pressure, are removing the legal and regulatory barriers to international economic interaction and welcoming those who have the ingenuity to turn possibilities into economic growth and profits. Second, a genuinely global capital market of enormous proportions has formed and is searching for returns. Participants who use capital wisely have incredible opportunities, as it has never been easier to tap into the capital markets. But this market is a harsh taskmaster. It rewards those who produce the results it demands but punishes those who don't. Third, rapid advances in digital technology are causing communication and computing costs to plunge.[101]

The practical result of these three economic forces, write the McKinsey consultants, is to expand significantly consumer choice.

> Throughout history, . . . for most customers, the interaction costs of finding better suppliers than those available in their local markets have been prohibitive, and so choice has been limited to local suppliers and companies able to overcome geographic boundaries. Now it has become far easier for customers to comparison shop outside their local markets. As a result, they now have a rapidly expanded range of choices and new price value trade-offs.[102]

Local producers who once had an advantage lose that advantage. Wherever they are in the world, customers demand greater value, and any company that isn't prepared to adopt the losing strategy of competing on price alone is forced to offer a superior value proposition. And in order to do that, argue the McKinsey consultants, every company will be forced to make the most of their intangible assets.

> As every participant worldwide loses geographically privileged access to customers, labor, capital, technology, and techniques of production, many of these historical determinants of cost and value advantage disappear. In their place come intangibles such as talent, intellectual property, brands, and networks.
>
> Intangibles "buy" you the access that used to come with geographic privilege. Because intangibles have always been at the heart of specialization, they increase in value as an integrating economy of six billion people

allows more and more specialization. And, as the world opens up, intangibles are now the differentiating capability required to generate enormous scale effects.[103]

Bryan says that, regardless of your industry, you should expect competition to get tougher and tougher, since you will now be forced to compete with the best in the world. Instead of competing in geographically bounded markets where you had protective regulations, loyal customers, known competition, and known technologies, you are now going to have to compete in a global market that is unfamiliar, complex, and uncertain.

How do you prepare to compete in such a world? Your first task, according to Bryan, is to understand the race you are going to have to run. And the first thing to understand about that race is that the world economy is currently in transition. "While all of the world's markets are *becoming* global, most are far from global today."[104] Global markets, write our gurus, are markets in which *the law of one price* rules. Consider the market for commercial airplanes. It is a global market because the cost of an airplane built by Boeing or Airbus Industries is the same worldwide. Contrast that to the market for beer. The price of a six-pack of Heineken varies greatly from country to country and between markets within the same country. Today, writes Bryan, about one-third of the world's GDP is globally defined. These global markets, in rough order from most to least global, include markets for the following:

Petroleum products.
Mineral ores.
Timber.
Aircraft engines.
Construction equipment.
Semiconductors.
Airframes.
Shipping.
Refineries.
Machine tools.
Telecommunications equipment.
Aluminum.
Specialty steel.
Bulk pharmaceuticals.
Pulp.
Specialty chemicals.
Consumer electronics.
Personal computers.
Cameras.
Automobiles.
Television.

Another group of markets have progressed part way to being globally defined. They include the following:

Beer.
Shoes.
Movie production.
Investment banking.
Legal services.
Accounting services.
Consulting services.
Personal financial services.
Telecommunications services providers.
Electric power services providers.

Finally, say our gurus, some markets are still locally defined. They include the following:

Food.
Television production.
Retail distribution.
Education.
Household services.
Medical care.
Civil servants.
National defense.

Knowing where your industry stands in the transition to global markets is important, according to Bryan, because "it is possible—and greatly advantageous—for individual companies to move into global markets at a faster pace than their industry as a whole."[105] In effect, the race to create global markets is the race for the world, and, say our gurus, three extremely attractive prizes await those companies who run the good race.

***Prize #1: A virtuous cycle of geographic expansion.***

Bryan explains, "As producers successfully expand geographically, profits increase, further enhancing their abilities to invest more into gaining greater geographic access, penetrating their existing markets more deeply, increasing scale and specialization advantages, and investing even more in intangibles such as intellectual property and talent, which further enhances their value propositions. A virtuous cycle of geographic expansion gets under way as initial advantages are used to gain even greater advantage."[106]

In short, as Coca Cola expands geographically, it becomes more profitable, and its brand name becomes more valuable, making it even easier for the company to expand into additional markets. Coke becomes "It!" in more ways than one.

***Prize #2: Increasing returns.***

You will recall from our discussion in Chapter 1 that the phenomenon of increasing returns is peculiar to the new network economy. It says, in short, that a network becomes more valuable with use. The more customers on a telephone network, the more valuable the network because there are more people you can call. It costs little, if anything, to add one additional customer to the network, but the benefits are enormous. The same is true for the globalization of markets, say our gurus.

> Throughout history, most of the relevant limits to growth have been geographically based. As geographic barriers fall, the historical limits that have constrained producers from capturing market share outside their home base are continually being relaxed. Companies with superior value propositions to offer have increasing returns on capital invested partly because they enjoy a free ride on past investments. They will not have to seek out new customers. Customers will come to them. A movie intended for a U.S. audience turns out to be popular throughout the world. A new drug for the developed world is also demanded throughout the emerging markets.[107]

***Prize #3: Cross-geographic arbitrage.***

Finally, say our gurus, companies that move into global markets can benefit from cross-geographic arbitrage, which is the practice of generating profits and/or cost advantages by leveraging differences in costs of production and efficiencies across geographic markets. It is the equivalent, in the real economy, of buying bills of exchange, stocks, and so on in one country and selling them again at a higher price in another country. Bryan explains the practice as it has been employed in the PC industry this way:

> Most of the PC industry's component manufacturers are spread over North America and the Far East. Components with high technical sophistication and proprietary knowledge advantage are concentrated in North America, the traditional engine for innovation in the industry. A good example is the microprocessor industry; almost all leading manufacturers (Intel, IBM, Motorola, DEC, etc.) are based in the United States. Components such as monitors and liquid crystal display (LCD) panels have traditionally been located in the Far East. Japan, a leader in the consumer electronics industry, was ideally suited to cost-effective manufacture of monitors. The storage industry (disk drives, CD-ROMs, etc.) moved to Southeast Asia very early as manufacturers pressed by low margins sought to take advantage of inexpensive skilled labor. Memory chips (particularly DRAMs) have become commoditized, and scale advantage is significant. Micron, a U.S.-based manufacturer, has used this to its advantage and remains a highly specialized player in the semiconductor industry. Other leading players in South Korea have sought to take advantage of access to lower factor costs (capital and labor) to become strong players in the memory market. Even in the sophisticated and capital-intensive micro-

> processor industry, Intel relies on lower labor costs in Asia to mount and encase the chips it produces, as do the DRAM manufacturers.[108]

By producing components wherever there are significant cost and/or productivity advantages, PC manufacturers have been able to manufacture their product at a lower cost than they would have experienced if all manufacturing were located in the United States.

Bryan notes that differences in factor costs—that is, the cost of labor, rent, taxes, and so on—and productivity levels vary greatly within the developed world and vary enormously between the developed world and emerging markets like Mexico, Brazil, and Argentina. A company that can put together world-class productivity with the lowest factor cost, argues Bryan, can enjoy production savings of as much as 80 percent, compared with that of an equivalent producer in the developed world. "A producer specializing in supplying goods and services where he enjoys both world-class productivity and factor cost advantages has the potential to earn extraordinary returns. Strategies built on cross-geographic arbitrage can provide lucrative and enduring advantages in specialization and scale over slower-moving geographic incumbents living within the constraints of local or national value chains."[109] In summary, say our gurus, running the race for the world involves three things:

1. Investing in intangible assets to create world-class value and then using that superior value to set in motion a virtuous cycle of geographic expansion.
2. Taking advantage of the increasing returns that result when customers with choice seek out superior value.
3. Capturing cross-geographic arbitrage.

Ultimately, writes Bryan, companies that win the world will be those that can become shapers of an industry by dominating a sliver of the global market, a sliver being a specialized product or service based on a distinctive intellectual property, talent, brand, or network. In other words, a sliver in software parlance is a "killer app" (killer application) that is highly attractive to customers throughout the world because it offers value that is overwhelmingly superior to any competing offering. Bryan cites Cisco as an example of an industry shaper:

> Cisco has come to dominate the market for routers—the critical equipment needed to facilitate the movement, at switching "hubs" of data and voice communications, between one network point in, for example, one service provider's network to another network point in another service provider's network. In particular, Cisco has specialized in the routers that facilitate global Internet-based communication.
>
> As Internet traffic has taken off, Cisco has turned its investment in intangibles in this arena into a virtuous cycle of geographic expansion while also capturing increasing returns. . . .
>
> Through astute investment in technology, by leveraging early market share, and by developing an excellent sales force, it has achieved remarkable

organic growth in revenue and earnings, riding the exponential growth of Internet-based traffic. Cisco is an industry shaper because, more than any other company in its industry, it is redefining telecommunications on its own terms through dominance of the markets for routers.[110]

Industry shapers like Cisco that dominate market slivers, say the McKinsey consultants, will win the race for the world. Of course, there is one problem. Our gurus are forced to admit that most companies don't have what it takes to become an industry shaper. "Most competitors," Bryan writes, "do not currently possess superior intangibles and, as a result, do not offer a superior value proposition. Therefore, they can neither put in place a virtuous cycle of geographic expansion nor benefit from increasing returns. Moreover, they have little capacity to capture cross-geographic arbitrage."[111] What, then, is such a company to do? The answer, say the gurus, is to pursue a temporary transitional strategy—something to get you in position to become an industry shaper at a future date. They offer two possible transitional or "midgame" strategies.

**Midgame Strategy #1: The Integrator**

In the integrator midgame, you take advantage of falling geographic barriers by acquiring or merging with similar companies in adjacent geographies. The intent is to gain the virtuous cycle effects of geographic expansion while capturing cross-geographic arbitrage through internal integration of operations. . . . As you get larger, you can acquire bigger and bigger competitors. This increases your absolute earnings and expands your geographic base, relative to others, while eliminating potential rivals.

In the integrator midgame, a company expands across geography and across the business system by either owning or controlling all parts of the value chain. Depending on the industry, integrators' strategies can be based on going from local to national, from national to regional, or from regional to global. Integrators usually connect to customers by owning or controlling direct distribution channels. They either produce the goods or services themselves or use captive suppliers for this purpose. Either way, integrators try to control how work is undertaken throughout the business's value chain, enabling them to capture cross-geographic arbitrage.[112]

Bryan points to the examples of the mergers of Daimler-Benz and Chrysler; Bank-America and NationsBank; USB and Swiss Bancorp; Bell Atlantic, NYNEX, and GTE; and British Petroleum and Amoco as companies pursuing an integrator midgame strategy.

**Midgame Strategy #2: The Specialist**

In the specialist midgame you focus on doing more business where you have relative skill advantages and less business where you lack world-class skills. The intent is to gain increasing return effects and to capture cross-geographic arbitrage opportunities through partnering with others. As you

> do more business in your specialty, you learn more, attract more talent, and find other specialists to acquire. As you gain specialization advantages, others want to work with you and help you expand your market access. As your reputation grows, more customers search you out, enabling you to capture greater intangible scale effects while increasing returns.
>
> In the specialist model, a company competes across geography by leveraging specialization advantages and intangible scale effects (i.e., leveraging the fixed costs of building intangible assets). These players work as part of an industry value chain. They do not own or control the entire value chain. They accomplish much of the work of producing and delivering their output through contractual arrangements with integrators or other specialists.[113]

Examples of companies pursuing specialist midgame strategies include automotive parts manufacturers TRW and Bosch; payments-processing specialists ADP and FDC; and telephone-equipment manufacturer Lucent.

So, there you have it. Ideally, say our gurus, be an industry shaper, or if you don't have what it takes to be a shaper, be an integrator or specialist. Of course, Bryan admits that there are some problems with these strategies. Integrators eventually run out of companies to acquire, and if they just keep getting bigger without getting better, they eventually become clumsy dinosaurs. Specialists eventually saturate the global market for their specialty. Worse, an industry shaper may come along and redefine their industry, thus making their particular expertise irrelevant. Even shapers don't get a free ride. Unfortunately, all sliver specializations have a limited life span, so shapers are constantly looking for new slivers to dominate.

It all sounds so elegant, but is the McKinsey integrator/specialist/shaper approach to going global any better than the Booz-Allen alliances alternative? Are either of them better than traditional globalization strategies?

## OUR VIEW

No one knows. As we remarked earlier, as much as they may pontificate, none of our gurus truly know how globalization is going to play out over the next 30 years—or even over the next 5 or 10 years, for that matter.

## KEY POINTS

- Globalization is about two major issues:

    1. The societal implications of the emerging global economy.
    2. The implications of globalization for business.

- There is no standard definition for the term *globalization.* It means different things to different people. Generally, it refers to the growth of global corporations, cultural and social integration, and the growing permeability of international borders.
- Ample statistical and anecdotal evidence, however, indicates that globalization as it is defined is occurring and that its affects are irreversible.
- The forces driving globalization include the following:
  - The democratization of technology that enables people around the world to communicate cheaper and faster.
  - The democratization of finance that makes investment capital more readily available to start-ups and allows more individuals to become involved in international investments.
  - The democratization of information that makes it possible for people worldwide to comparison shop for ideas, political solutions, products, and services.
- Opponents of globalization put forth these arguments:
  - Globalization creates a rough-and-tumble, winner-take-all world in which enormous income inequalities allow a fortunate few to lavish themselves in luxuries while the wretched of the earth suffer in a continual downward economic spiral.
  - It forces countries throughout the world into a kind of economic Golden Straitjacket in which ancient cultures are destroyed and the American way of life becomes the only way of life people are allowed to live.
  - It unleashes rampant exploitation of the environment that destroys the world's forests, pollutes its oceans, and endangers its species, including humans themselves.
- Proponents and defenders of globalization make these counterarguments:
  - For every evil opponents can cite about globalization, there is an offsetting benefit.
  - Although globalization can lead to economic inequalities, social safety nets can be built to protect those most endangered.
- Today, we understand the impact globalization will have on future business and society about as well as people in 1946 could anticipate the outcome of the Cold War. In other words, we don't know very much with certainty.
- The main reasons a company should go global include the following:
  - To tap new markets for their products and services.
  - To get a volume of business sufficient to support investments in production facilities, research and development, and so on that cannot realistically be sustained through sales in a single country.

- To gain knowledge from process and product changes required to adapt products and services to foreign markets.
- To service global customers.
- To avoid being disadvantaged by competitors who go global.

🗝 Traditional options for going global include exporting, licensing, strategic alliances, overseas joint ventures, overseas subsidiaries, and overseas acquisitions.

🗝 At least one guru argues that the best globalization option for most companies is to form strategic alliances. He argues that alliances are preferable to other methods of building a global presence because they allow companies to do the following:

- Enjoy the cost savings of globalization while minimizing the risks.
- Avoid barriers to acquisition that many countries erect.
- Achieve access to market segments they might not otherwise be able to reach.
- Develop a better understanding of customer requirements in different parts of the world.
- Avoid the need to create a bureaucracy to monitor activities of subsidiaries.
- Quickly close technology gaps by gaining access to a partner's technology.
- Gain geographic access to markets that otherwise might be closed.
- Retain the management skills of partner companies.

🗝 Another group of consultants argues that, instead of focusing on gaining access to geographic markets, companies should seek to become shapers of their industry who dominate a "sliver" of the global market. In order to win the "race for the world," say these consultants, companies must invest in developing and deploying world-class intangible assets (knowledge, skills, patents, proprietary technology, etc.) in order to create world-class value. The companies must then use that superior value to set in motion a virtuous cycle of self-perpetuating geographic expansion in which they can take advantage of the increasing returns that result from customers seeking superior choices and the cost saving that result from cross-geographic arbitrage.

## BUSINESS ETHICS—The Gurus

**Doug Bandow,** senior fellow at the Cato Institute and writer

**Jeffrey Coors,** president of ACX Technologies, which reformed as CoorsTek and Graphic Packaging International Corporation

**John Dalla Costa,** president of the Center of Ethical Orientation and author of *The Ethical Imperative: Why Moral Leadership Is Good Business*

**John Elkington,** cofounder of the environmental consulting group SustainAbility and author of *Cannibals with Forks: The Triple Bottom Line of Twenty-first Century Business*

**Ralph Estes,** cofounder of The Center for the Advancement of Public Policy and author of *Tyranny of the Bottom Line*

**Milton Friedman,** Nobel Prize–winning economist and senior research fellow at the Hoover Institution

**Blair Gibb,** coauthor of *When Good Companies Do Bad Things: Responsibility and Risk in an Age of Globalization*

**John M. Hood,** president of the Locke Foundation and author of *The Heroic Enterprise: Business and the Common Good*

**Michael J. D. Hopkins,** economist, cofounder of MHC International, Ltd., and author of *The Planetary Bargain: Corporate Social Responsibility Comes to Age*

**Rushworth M. Kidder,** founder of the Institute for Global Ethics and author of *How Good People Make Tough Choices*

**Tom Morris,** founder and chairman of the Morris Institute for Human Values and author of *If Aristotle Ran General Motors: The New Soul of Business*

**Peter Schwartz,** cofounder and chairman of Global Business Network and author of *When Good Companies Do Bad Things: Responsibility and Risk in an Age of Globalization*

**Jeffrey L. Seglin,** assistant professor at Emerson College and author of *The Good, the Bad, and Your Business: Choosing Right When Ethical Dilemmas Are Pulling You Apart*

**Robert C. Solomon,** professor of business and philosophy at the University of Texas, Austin, and author of *A Better Way to Think about Business: How Personal Integrity Leads to Corporate Success*

**Manuel G. Velasquez,** professor of business ethics and philosophy at Santa Clara University and author of *Business Ethics: Concepts and Cases*

6

# Business Ethics in the Knowledge Economy

In the first part of this chapter, we describe six real-life situations people have faced in the workplace. The first dilemma, reported in the August 2000 issue of *Fast Company,* challenged the chairman and CEO of a Silicon Valley start-up company. The next two situations are based on ethical cases reported by Rushworth M. Kidder in his book *How Good People Make Tough Choices.* The final three are based on cases described by Manuel G. Velasquez in *Business Ethics: Concepts and Cases.* Later in this chapter we will reveal how the people involved in each real-life situation resolved their particular ethical dilemma. For now, as a way of getting you to start thinking about the issues of corporate social responsibility and business ethics, we ask what you would do in each case.

## SIX ETHICAL DILEMMAS

### Case #1: The Case of the Hiring Decision

Sheldon Laube was the chairman and CEO of a high-tech start-up company based in Santa Clara, California. He was struggling to produce his product, win customers, and most important, attract increased funding from venture capitalists and investors. A key to his strategy was to recruit the best and brightest people for every available position, and that's just what he thought he had done. The company had made a verbal offer to someone whom everyone in the company thought was an outstanding candidate for a position that was critical to their expansion plans. Then, before the person could accept the offer, a contender with truly dazzling credentials submitted a resume. Laube had the chance to grab a true superstar for his team, but he couldn't afford to hire both people. His managers wanted him to rescind the first offer so that they could bring the superstar on board.[1]

If you were Laube, what would you do? Would you hire the candidate to whom you have already made an offer, or would you rescind the offer and hire the genuine superstar your company desperately needs?

I would ______________________________________________

______________________________________________

## Case #2: The Case of the Consultant's Report

In May 1991, a group of executives from a military defense contractor attended a meeting with U.S. Navy representatives and a private consultant hired by the navy. The purpose of the meeting was to discuss the contractor's work on an existing contract. The meeting was held in a conference room at the company's headquarters and concluded amicably and uneventfully as scheduled at 5:00 P.M.

The following morning, while cleaning the conference room, a maintenance worker discovered that the navy's consultant had accidentally left behind an envelope marked "Business Sensitive." The worker passed the envelope along to his boss, who examined the contents and quickly passed it along to his boss. Within a few hours, the envelope was deposited on the desk of the defense contractor's CEO. By now it was obvious that the envelope the consultant had inadvertently left behind contained extremely valuable information. At that time, the defense contractor was in a bidding war with a competitor for additional defense-department business. The consultant's envelope contained a complete analysis of the cost structures of both the defense contractor and its competitor. The CEO was aware that a federal law, the Procurement Integrity Act, required contractors bidding for government contracts to certify that they had never possessed proprietary information. He was also aware that the information contained in the envelope before him would be extremely helpful in bidding against his competitor.[2]

If you were the CEO, what would you do with the envelope?

I would ______________________________________________

______________________________________________

## Case #3: The Case of the Trapped Truck Driver

A state trooper, driving his normal route on a remote and lonely state highway, rounded a curve to discover that an accident had occurred. A flat-bed truck loaded with steel beams had run off the road, slammed into a tree, and caught fire. As the trooper got out of his car and approached the wreck, he could see that the driver was still alive. He could also see that the load of steel, which had broken loose on impact, had driven through the back of the cab and hopelessly pinned the driver inside. The trooper knew that he could not free the driver by himself, and he knew that the growing fire would reach the victim long before help could arrive. Then the trooper heard the trucker scream, "Shoot me!" He begged again, "Please, shoot me!"

The trooper stood still for a moment, then slowly reached for his service revolver. He paused and reconsidered as the driver continued to plead, "Shoot me! Please, shoot me!"[3]

If you were the trooper, what would you do?

I would ______________________________________________

______________________________________________

## Case #4: The Case of Malden Mills

On the night of December 11, 1995, an explosion at the Malden Mills factory in Lawrence, Massachusetts, destroyed the plant and injured 25 workers. Fourteen hundred of the plant's 3,000 employees were put out of work two weeks before Christmas.

Malden Mills was a family-owned business, founded in 1906, and it was one of the few remaining textile mills in New England. It survived by shunning low-margin commodity fabrics in favor of producing high-quality synthetic fabrics for outdoor clothing sold by companies like Patagonia, L.L. Bean, and Eddie Bauer. The company had invented and patented special high-tech equipment to produce the fabric, and its workers had been trained in the special skills required to operate the equipment and produce the product while maintaining tight tolerances for quality. Malden Mills employees were the highest-paid textile workers in the country.

The morning after the fire, Aaron Feurstein, president and majority owner of the company, faced two options. He could collect $100 million in insurance, close the factory, and rebuild in a Third World country where labor costs would be cheaper, or he could rebuild in Lawrence.[4]

If you were Feurstein, what would you do?

I would ______________________________________________

______________________________________________

## Case #5: The Case of River Blindness

River blindness is a horrible disease that afflicts millions of people living along the riverbanks of the remote tropical regions of Africa and Latin America. In his presentation of this case, Manuel Velasquez describes river blindness this way:

The disease is caused by a tiny parasitic worm that is passed from person to person by the bite of the black fly which breeds in river waters. The tiny worms burrow under a person's skin where they grow as long as two feet curled up inside ugly round nodules half an inch to an inch in diameter. Inside the nodules the worms reproduce by releasing millions of microscopic offspring called microfilaria that wiggle their way throughout the body moving beneath the skin, discoloring it as they migrate, and causing lesions and such intense itching that victims sometimes commit suicide. Eventually, the microfilaria invade the eyes and gradually blind the victim.[5]

In 1979 a research scientist at a leading U.S. drug company discovered that the drug Ivermectin, developed by his company and marketed for animals, might kill the microfilaria. Further investigation by company scientists led them to conclude that a human version of the drug might offer a low-cost, safe, and effective cure for the dreaded disease, and they recommended to the chairman of the drug company that they proceed with development. Other managers argued that the company could not afford to develop the drug for the following reasons:

- At a time when the company was experiencing increased competition, it should not spend the estimated $100 million required to develop the drug.
- Because the victims were so poor, it was unlikely that the company could ever sell the drug for enough to recover the costs of development.
- Even if the drug could be developed, distributing the drug would be almost impossible because the victims lived in remote areas with no access to doctors, hospitals, or pharmacies.
- There was a heightened risk of harmful side affects if the drug was used without qualified medical supervision, as it might be in an undeveloped nation.
- If a cheap human version of the drug was developed, it might be sold on the black market, thus undermining sales of the animal version of the drug.[6]

If you were the chairman, would you authorize your scientists to proceed with development of the drug?

I would ____________________________________________

____________________________________________

## Case #6: The Case of the "Cost-Benefit" Study

In the early 1960s, the American automotive industry was under serious attack from foreign competitors, particularly the Japanese. The race was on to develop small, fuel-efficient, and compact models of American cars to compete with imports. One American manufacturer set a goal to develop a subcompact that would weigh less than 2,000 pounds, cost less than $2,000, and could be brought to the market in half the normal time. The company succeeded, only to discover during crash tests that the new model's gas tank occasionally ruptured when the car was hit from the rear at speeds greater than 20 miles per hour. Worse, when the gas tank ruptured, gasoline sprayed into the passenger compartment, risking the possibility of fire. Although the gas tank was a problem, the company's managers were reassured by the facts that (1) government regulations at the time only required that gas tanks stay intact in rear-end collisions of *less than* 20 miles per hour, (2) the car was comparable in safety to similar models produced by other automotive companies, both domestic and foreign, and (3) an internal cost-benefit study showed that the cost of modifying the car to make the gas tank safe at higher speeds would far outweigh the benefits. The cost-benefit analysis reasoned as follows:

1. The cost of modifying the car would be $137 million, or $11 per car multiplied by the expected production of 12.5 million cars. This cost would have to be passed along to customers in the form of higher prices.
2. The benefits from modifying the car would be $49.15 million calculated as follows:

(180 expected deaths from rear-end collisions X $200,000 [the value the U.S. Government placed on a human life]) + (180 expected injuries from rear-end collisions X $67,000 [the value of a serious burn injury according to U.S. insurance companies at the time]) + (2,100 cars X $700 [the estimated residual value of a subcompact automobile]).

The study's authors argued that it was not right to spend $137 million of society's money to generate benefits that society valued at just $49.15 million.[7]

If you had been the CEO of the automotive company, would you have spent the $137 million and modified the car's gas tank?

I would ______________________________

______________________________

## One Final Question

We know this sounds like a strange question, but it is one that a guru poses and actually has the chutzpah to answer. We'll reveal his answer later in this chapter, but we thought you might like to take a stab at answering the question yourself. Here it is: *What is the meaning of life?*

You can write your answer here if you like:

______________________________

If you are complaining about the small amount of space we have allowed for your answer, you should be aware that our guru answers the question in just two words. Tough, huh? In fact, we think that all of these questions are tough. Although some may seem simple at first glance, we imagine that you discovered, as we did, that the more you thought about your answers to these questions, the less sure you were of them.

At this point, you may be asking, "Is this just an interesting intellectual parlor game, or are these questions and their answers relevant to the knowledge economy?" Let's see if we can answer that.

A note to our readers: In this chapter we will discuss both business ethics and what is commonly known as "corporate social responsibility." Michael J. D. Hopkins makes the following distinction between the two:

> [Corporate social responsibility] goes much further [than business ethics.] Social responsibility encompasses good business ethics. This is because one normally thinks of business ethics applying to what business does within its walls, that is to four of its seven stakeholders—managers, consumers, investors/owners and employees. Less concern is placed on [the other three stakeholders:] the natural environment, the community and its suppliers and their conditions of work. Social responsibility encompasses good ethics, both within the walls of the company and without. It encourages enterprises to be involved in social issues, such as community improvement, improving Third World working conditions, and so on, that are outside the walls of the enterprise.[8]

## BUSINESS ETHICS AND THE KNOWLEDGE ECONOMY

Jeffrey L. Seglin, coauthor of *The Good, the Bad, and Your Business,* writes that, when a friend of his heard that Seglin had decided to take a year off to write a book on business ethics, the friend sent him a note saying, "Good for you. . . . But let me warn you, my friend, that using the word 'ethics' in the title of a book is the kiss of death."[9] Seglin notes that his friend wasn't the first one to warn him that the reading public, especially readers of business books, seemed to be turned off or scared off by the topic of ethics. Well, say our gurus, if that's been your tendency in the past, get over it. Business ethics is more critical to your personal and business success than you may imagine. Like it or not, they warn, the world is changing and expects more from businesses than in the past. A single-minded focus on the financial bottom line isn't enough.

John Elkington, author of *Cannibals with Forks,* reflects the thinking of many of our gurus when he maintains that the knowledge economy expects—even demands—that business managers today pay attention to a "triple bottom line" consisting of the following:[10]

- Economic prosperity (the traditional financial bottom line).
- Environmental prosperity.
- Social justice.

(See Exhibit 6.1 for a slightly different perspective provided by the Global Business Responsibility Resource Center.)

### EXHIBIT 6.1. Trends Driving Interest in Corporate Social Responsibility

According to the Global Business Responsibility Resource Center, the following global trends are forcing companies worldwide to give greater attention to business ethics and corporate social responsibility.

**Changing Expectations of Stakeholders Regarding Business.** The public and various stakeholders have come to expect more of business, according to several studies. Increasingly, they are looking to the private sector to help with myriad complex and pressing social and economic issues. There is a growing ability and sophistication of activist groups to target corporations they perceive as not being socially responsible, through actions such as public demonstrations, shareholder resolutions, and even "denial of service" attacks on company websites. These efforts emphasize the issue of accountability to stakeholders when doing business.

**Shrinking Role of Government.** In many countries, national and local governments have taken a more hands-off approach to regulating business, due to the globalization of commerce and shrinking resources. As a result, companies—and multinational companies in particular—are relying less on government for guidance; instead they are adopting their own policies to govern such matters as environmental performance, working conditions and ethical marketing practices.

**Increased Customer Interest.** The growing interest in CSR [corporate social responsibility] comes both from business-to-business customers as well as consumers. In the former, there is a significant move by many companies, governments, universities and other institutions to align their purchasing decisions with social criteria, particularly those related to companies' environmental and human rights performance. In the latter, numerous studies correlate consumer purchasing preferences with ethical and socially responsible business conduct, though it is unclear the extent to which these sentiments translate into actual changes in purchasing patterns. . . .

**Supply Chain Responsibility.** As stakeholders take a growing interest in companies' corporate social responsibility, many companies are finding that they are responsible not only for their own CSR performance, but for that of the companies "upstream" and "downstream"—that is, a company's suppliers as well as its customers and even its customers' customers. The result is that some companies are imposing codes of conduct on both their suppliers and customers to ensure that other companies' policies or practices do

(continued)

EXHIBIT 6.1. **(continued)**

not reflect unfavorably on them. This has a cascading effect along the entire supply chain, encouraging suppliers to adopt socially responsible business practices.

**Growing Investor Pressure.** The growth of socially responsible investing has accelerated in recent years, with investor groups increasingly pressuring companies on social issues. . . . Many of these investors are using the shareholder resolution process to pressure companies to change policies and increase disclosure on a wide range of CSR issues, including environmental responsibility, workplace policies, community involvement, human rights practices, ethical decision-making and corporate governance. Activist groups are also buying shares in targeted companies to give them access to annual meetings and the shareholder resolution process.

**More Competitive Labor Markets.** In a tight labor market, many workers—especially professional, technical or highly skilled employees—are looking beyond paychecks and benefits to seek employers whose philosophies and operating practices align with their own beliefs. For example, some companies have found that having "family-friendly" policies or being identified as an employer of choice have given them a competitive advantage in attracting and retaining employees. At the same time, companies are finding they need to turn to nontraditional labor pools—including economically disadvantaged, non-English-speaking, and physically or mentally challenged individuals—to meet current and future demands for both skilled and entry-level employees.

**Demands for Increased Disclosure.** Customers, investors, regulators, community groups, environmental activists, trading partners and others are asking companies for more and more detailed information about their social performance. In response, leadership companies are responding with a variety of reports and/or social audits that describe and disclose their social performance on one or several fronts. As part of this move toward greater disclosure, many companies are putting increasingly detailed information about their social and environmental performance—even when it may be negative—onto their publicly accessible websites.

*Source:* "Introduction to Corporate Social Responsibility," <http://www.bsr.org>, (August 4, 2000).

Elkington enumerates seven economic, social, and technical revolutions that are driving this focus on the triple bottom line and warns that companies choosing to ignore the demands of these seven revolutions do so at their own peril: "To refuse the challenge implied by the triple bottom line is to risk extinction. Nor are these simply issues for major transnational corporations: they will increasingly be forced to pass the pressure on down their supply chains, to smaller suppliers and contractors. These changes flow from a profound reshaping of society's expectations and, as a result, of the local and global markets businesses serves."[11] In the following sections, we examine each of the seven revolutions that Elkington believes are driving this focus on the triple bottom line.

## Revolution #1: Changing Markets

According to Elkington, domestic and international markets are becoming more open to competition because public and private anticompetitive practices have been removed. (See our discussion of globalization in Chapter 5.) One undesirable side effect of removing anticompetitive practices is that rules, standards, and regulations put in place to protect people and the environment have been removed or weakened. This leaves a gap that financial markets and customers increasingly look to businesses to fill. In the past, says Elkington, business has used competition as an excuse for inaction or limited action when addressing environmental and social issues. Now, he argues, business leaders are beginning to realize that extreme solutions—environmental and social lawlessness at one extreme and government re-regulation at the other—would be disruptive to business. They have sought more open markets, and they got them at the cost of greater scrutiny. Consequently, concludes Elkington, "growing numbers of companies are already finding themselves challenged by customers and the financial markets about aspects of their triple bottom line, commitments and performance."[12] He adds that the biggest mistake business leaders could make is to assume that this heightened focus on the triple bottom line is some sort of late twentieth-century aberration when, in fact, it signals a fundamental change in societal values—the second revolution.

## Revolution #2: Changing Values

Elkington predicts that we are witnessing a worldwide shift in human and societal values:

> "I believe . . . we are seeing a profound values shift in countries around the world. For the most part this is not something that is being regulated: instead, it is happening as a natural outgrowth of people's evolving awareness and concern. And a key dimension of this shift is the way in which what would once have been seen as "soft" values (such as concern for future generations) are now coming in alongside—and sometimes even overriding—traditional "hard" values (such as the paramount importance of the financial bottom line).[13]

Increasingly, writes Elkington, companies find themselves embarrassed, if not economically damaged, when their practices clash with these new environmental, social, and ethical standards. He cites the apparel industry's painful experience in 1996 as just one example of what companies can expect when their behaviors are perceived as "out of line":

> 1996 brought into American living rooms stark images of Pakistani children stitching footballs, Haitian workers sewing Walt Disney T-shirts and tearful

celebrity confessions. If any single moment defined the new agenda, it was the confession by American talk-show host Kathie Lee Gifford that her Wal-Mart outfits were made by Honduran girls paid 31¢ an hour—but, she said, she hadn't known. Her admission was picked up by a tiny human rights organization, National Labor Committee, whose director went on to a congressional hearing on labor abuses and increased the pressure on Gifford and other celebrities who, like basketball star Michael Jordan, endorse products made in this way.

Jordan, who at the time earned $20 million a year endorsing Nike sneakers, was presumably embarrassed to find that this sum was a great deal more than the annual payroll for the thousands of Indonesians who actually made the shoes. The fundamental issue was further highlighted by a report from the International Labour Organization concluding that about 250 million children are working in developing countries—nearly twice earlier estimates. The report also documented many examples of children doing dangerous work putting them at risk of death, crippling accidents, disease, poisoning, and sexual abuse.

Rather than lying low in the hope that the storm would blow over, Gifford went on Larry King Live and launched a crusade to end child labor. . . .

As the issues hit the front-pages and TV headline news, consumers were faced with an urgent question: "How much are Americans willing to sacrifice the children of other countries to give their [own] children what they want?". . .

[In response to the crisis,] companies like Gap, Levi Strauss, and Sears pledged themselves to fight exploitative practices. Reebok called on its arch-rival Nike, the market leader in trainers, to join it in a bid to end child labor and improve working conditions in their Asian factories. Reebok, which had long taken a public stance on social issues, was edging into the lead in this new form of values-based competition. Nike, however, had already stressed that its contractors had been subject to a "memorandum of understanding" binding them to rules on child labor, worker, and environmental standards. Even so, the company became a lightning rod for protests, not least because of the extraordinary contrast between Michael Jordan's earnings and the $2.23 basic daily wage paid by Nike's Indonesian sub-contractors.

Shortly afterwards, the World Federation of the Sporting Goods Industry pledged to try to eliminate child labor in their operations worldwide by 2000. Nike, which had commissioned labor practice audits of its factories, was beginning to release selected data, while Reebok was calling upon activists to alert it to abuses. And one US importer noted that: "Virtually every retailer is asking for certification from vendors that they are complying with codes of conduct."[14]

Elkington maintains that the experience of the apparel industry increasingly will be the rule rather than the exception. And don't think that you can escape scrutiny by hiding and keeping your head down because there is a third revolution—transparency.

## Revolution #3: Increased Transparency

All companies increasingly live in a global goldfish bowl, says Elkington. New and radically different technologies such as the Internet and satellite communication (see our discussion of the knowledge economy in Chapter 1) are making it possible for a wide range of stakeholders to demand and obtain much more detailed information on what businesses are doing or planning to do than ever before. They are using that information to compare, contrast, analyze, benchmark, and rank the performance of competing companies on the new values.

> "None of your business!" was the typical reply a few decades back when environmentalists and others asked leading companies for information on their operations and plans. . . . [The values] revolution is now pushing business in a completely different direction: towards openness and disclosure. . . . [W]e now increasingly live in "a CNN world." New information technologies, coupled with employee allegiance to much broader social agendas, mean that companies can no longer count on their ability to maintain secrecy over time.[15]

Recognizing the impossibility of keeping secrets, more companies are deciding to open up—to voluntarily enter the goldfish bowl, so to speak. When competitors decide to go public with information that used to be their deepest, and sometimes darkest, secrets, it puts more pressure on you to do the same. The trend, writes Elkington, is clearly toward more transparency, and one of the things companies will be asked increasingly to disclose is what they are doing about managing the life cycles of their products. That's the fourth revolution.

## Revolution #4: A Demand That Companies Manage Product/Service Life Cycles

Elkington explains the rise of life-cycle accountability:

> Companies are being challenged about the triple bottom line implications of either industrial or agricultural activities far back down the supply chain, or of their products in transit, in use, and, increasingly, after their useful life has ended. Here we are seeing a shift from companies focusing on the acceptability of their products at the point of sale to their performance from cradle to grave and, increasingly, from cradle to cradle; i.e. from the extraction of raw materials right through to recycling or disposal. Managing the life-cycles of technologies and products as different as batteries, jumbo jets and offshore oil-rigs will become increasingly challenging, transforming key elements of R&D and product design processes.[16]

Recognizing that they will be called on to account for the life cycle of their products and services, leading-edge companies will subject some or all of their offering to some type of "needs test" or impact assessment. Life-cycle accountability will lead to clear winners and losers in the knowledge economy. Elkington continues:

> Like any revolution, the life-cycle revolution will often disrupt, or even destroy, existing commercial relationships. With many companies already trying to slim down their supply chains to a smaller number of strategic suppliers, poor life-cycle performance (actual or perceived) will become a further reason for dropping particular companies. Many companies will not even know why they have been deleted.
>
> The winners in this new world will be those companies that have already x-rayed much of their supply chain and operations for potential problems and moved to address any issues identified. The losers will include a high proportion of those who have not.[17]

Of course, it is not easy to bulletproof a product or service across its entire life cycle. The difficulty of the task will force more companies to seek out partners, even partners they might not have expected to acquire—the fifth revolution.

## Revolution #5: Partnering for Triple-Bottom-Line Performance

Elkington predicts that we can expect to see companies form new types of economic, social, and environmental partnerships as they seek to manage product and service life cycles and achieve outstanding triple-bottom-line performance. These new partnerships, which will include partnerships between long-standing enemies, will allow companies and their partners to reach goals they couldn't achieve on their own. He cites as examples the environmental group Greenpeace's "Greenfreeze" campaign with companies like DKK Scharfenstein and Calor to launch ozone-friendly refrigeration technology and the U.S. Environmental Defense Fund's work with companies like General Motors, McDonald's, and S.C. Johnson & Son to develop and deploy environmentally friendly product packaging. Companies will engage in such partnerships to gain valuable suggestions for product development and marketing. Just as frequently, says Elkington, they will seek partnerships because they need to engage stakeholders and build public credibility. The losers in the knowledge economy will be those companies that are left out of significant partnerships because of past triple-bottom-line transgressions or that, because of short sightedness, don't seek to build such partnerships in the first place. Avoiding this trap and taking the long view is the sixth revolution.

## Revolution #6: Time and the Long View

Businesspeople have become accustomed to certain refrains: "time is money," all competition is "time-based," everything must be "just-in-time." Now, says Elkington, they must become practitioners of the "long view." What is the long view? Elkington cites a distinction between "wide" time and "long" time offered by Stewart Brand, creator of *The Whole Earth Catalog* and cofounder of the Global Business Network. According to Brand, "wide time was 'everything-happening-now-and-last-week-and-next week,' while long time is a 'deep, flowing process in which centuries are minor events.' The wide view of time sees events as most influenced by what is happening at the moment, while the long view inclines to the idea that the causes of many of today's issues and challenges lie deep in the past."[18]

Elkington believes that the winners in the knowledge economy will take the long view and that the losers will cling to "the belief that the time-scales dictated by Wall Street and other financial centers are 'reality.' Instead, they are bubble environments which—as illustrated by the history of spectacular economic crashes around the world—can delude and destroy even the deepest-rooted businesses. Unless companies can balance the shortermism of most 'wide time' markets with a real sense of 'long time,' they are extremely unlikely to survive."[19]

## Revolution #7: Revolution in the Boardroom

"The profound business implications of the [triple bottom line] . . . mean that the role of the corporate board, and of company directors is rapidly moving to centre stage."[20] Elkington adds that he expects corporate boards to shift from "exclusive" to "inclusive" membership as companies feel increased pressure from stakeholder groups to be heard. Social and environmental activists now understand that the triple bottom line will not improve in most companies "if the corporate brain can not be switched on and 'locked in' to the new agenda."[21] Thus they are going to demand participation, or at least an audience. He quotes Professor Tom Gladwin of New York University, who encourages companies to "install three new chairs around the boardroom table: one for a fish, to speak for the natural world; one for the poorest person on earth, to speak for the disadvantaged; and one for a representative of the year 3001."[22]

Even Elkington admits that we are unlikely to see boardrooms equipped with fish tanks. He does predict, however, that most corporate boards will bring in individuals with triple-bottom-line interests and experience to challenge traditional thinking.

# POINT-COUNTERPOINT: THE BUSINESS ETHICS DEBATE

John Elkington's presentation of his "revolutions" and the trends cited by the Global Business Responsibility Resource Center (Exhibit 6.1) appear to presage the inevitability of business ethics as a key agenda item for all business leaders: Businesses will act ethically and pursue the triple bottom line because they will have no choice. It seems that the issue has been settled. Far from it. In fact, there is still a lively debate among our gurus about the inevitability and indeed, even advisability of corporations pursuing anything but profits. In this section, we will examine the arguments for and against corporate social responsibility, beginning with the arguments against.

## The Arguments against Corporate Social Responsibility

Most of the gurus who argue that corporate social responsibility is unwise or unnecessary echo the classic argument put forward by Nobel laureate Milton Friedman some thirty years ago. Here in part is what Friedman had to say:

> When . . . businessmen speak eloquently about the "social responsibilities of business in a free-enterprise system," . . . they are—or would be if they or anyone else took them seriously—preaching pure and unadulterated socialism. Businessmen who talk this way are unwitting puppets of the intellectual forces that have been undermining the basis of a free society these past decades.
>
> The discussions of the "social responsibilities of business" are notable for their analytical looseness and lack of rigor. What does it mean to say that "business" has responsibilities? Only people can have responsibilities. . . .
>
> Presumably, the individuals who are to be responsible are . . . corporate executives. . . .
>
> In a free-enterprise, private-property system, a corporate executive is an employee of the owners of the business. He has direct responsibility to his employers. That responsibility is to conduct the business in accordance with their desires, which generally will be to make as much money as possible while conforming to the basic rules of society, both those embodied in law and those embodied in ethical custom. . . .
>
> Of course, the corporate executive is also a person in his own right. As a person, he may have many other responsibilities that he recognizes or assumes voluntarily. . . . He may feel impelled by these responsibilities to

devote part of his income to causes he regards as worthy . . . If we wish, we may refer to these responsibilities as "social responsibilities." But in these respects he is acting as a principal, not an agent; he is spending his own money, . . . not the money of his employers. . . .

What does it mean to say that the corporate executive has a "social responsibility"? . . . It must mean that he is to act in some way that is not in the interest of his employers. For example, that he is to refrain from increasing the price of the product in order to contribute to the social objective of fighting inflation, even though a price increase would be in the best interests of the corporation. Or that he is to make expenditures on reducing pollution beyond the amount that is in the best interests of the corporation or that is required by law in order to contribute to the social objective of improving the environment. Or that, at the expense of corporate profits, he is to hire "hard-core" unemployed instead of better-qualified available workmen to contribute to the social objective of reducing poverty.

In each of these cases, the corporate executive would be spending someone else's money for a general social interest. . . .

[I]f he does this, he is in effect imposing taxes, on the one hand, and deciding how the tax proceeds shall be spent on the other. . . .[T]he imposition of taxes and the expenditure of tax proceeds are governmental functions [not the corporate executive's function, and to allow the corporate executive to undertake such responsibilities would be] . . . "taxation without representation." . . .

[T]he doctrine of "social responsibility" . . . [is] a fundamentally subversive doctrine in a free society. . . . [T]here is one and only one social responsibility of business—to use its resources and engage in activities designed to increase its profits so long as it stays within the rules of the game, which is to say, engages in open and free competition without deception or fraud.[23]

In a more recent defense of the corporation, John M. Hood, author of *The Heroic Enterprise,* reasons against corporate social responsibility this way:

By detaching management decisions from their moorings in shareholder value, corporate social responsibility would in practice leave managers with the impossible task of trying to balance competing claims from workers, consumers, lenders, social activists, and other so-called stakeholders. In juggling these claims, managers would lack the decision rule—returning the highest value to shareholders—that currently allows them to set priorities and that makes markets work. . . .Without a clear function in mind for the organization they head, managers would be left to make essentially political rather than economic decisions . . . [as Friedman said.][24]

In any case, writes Hood, advocates of corporate social responsibility have an unrealistic and a historical view of the corporation, blaming business for the world's evils while simultaneously neglecting all the good that companies do.

> Critics of corporations zero in on the stories like the *Exxon Valdez* oil spill . . . because they are well-known to the public, who have been told ceaselessly by news and entertainment media that businesses are corrupt, destructive institutions. The positive, indeed revolutionary, ways in which corporations have made the everyday lives of Americans better over the past half-century are rarely recognized. . . .
>
> American business creates jobs, treats workers fairly, supports educational innovation, trains employees, contributes to the health of cities, discovers new drugs and medical treatments, makes workplaces and products safer, conserves resources, invents ways to save energy and reduce or eliminate waste, gives women and minorities unparalleled economic opportunities, and contributes to the stability and quality of life of families. It does all these things not in spite of its search for the highest possible return to shareholders, but because of it.
>
> American businesses contribute to the progress and well-being of society because they must. If firms mistreat workers, they cannot be productive. If firms ignore issues of education and skills among young people, they will not be productive in the future. If they discriminate against women and minorities, they pay the price in the market for employees and for consumers. If they ignore the wastes they generate, they pay higher energy bills and disposal fees. Most importantly, if firms fail to take advantage of the opportunities they see to create new products or services to solve society's problems, then they will surely lose profits to their competitors.[25]

Corporate social responsibility advocates, Hood goes on, confuse the role of the corporation with the role of other institutions of society.

> Commercial activity conducted by corporations and other forms of business is fundamentally different from the type of activity conducted by coercive governments or by voluntary, philanthropic organizations. For society to function, each institution must operate according to its own unique purpose. A simple demarcation of responsibilities might go something like this:
>
> - *Businesses exist to make and sell things.* They thrive on competition, on prices, on freely negotiated contracts, on optimism, and on a search for innovation and productivity.
> - *Governments exist to take and protect things.* They thrive on a monopoly of sovereignty and authority, on providing necessary services to all without separate prices or negotiations, on realism, and on a search for justice and safety.

- *Charities exist to give things away.* They thrive on cooperation, on gifts, on volunteerism and services, on altruism or religious values, and on a search for compassion and enlightenment.[26]

Each institution has its proper role, argues Hood. Take the environment as an example. Governments have a role and responsibility to set reasonable standards for emissions of potentially hazardous substances. Charities have a role to pay in collecting donations and marshaling volunteers, for example, to protect endangered species, and businesses have a role that "is no less crucial: to find ways to produce the goods and services that individuals want and need at the lowest possible cost in resources and energy output."[27] The mistake advocates of corporate social responsibility make, maintains Hood, is expecting businesses to act like standard-setting governments or environmental charities. Not only is such mixing a mistake; it is inefficient and ultimately harmful to the common good.

Doug Bandow, a senior fellow at the Cato Institute, a libertarian public-policy research institute, makes a similar argument in a 1992 *Business and Society Review* article:

> Corporations are specialized institutions created for a specific purpose. They are only one form of enterprise in a very diverse society with lots of different organizations. Churches exist to help people fulfill their responsibilities toward God in community with one another. Governments are instituted most basically to prevent people from violating the rights of others. Philanthropic institutions are intended to do good works. Community associations are to promote one or another shared goal. And businesses are established to make a profit by meeting people's need and wants. . . .
>
> In short, businessmen should concentrate on being good businessmen. They shouldn't be charged with saving men's souls. Nor should they be expected to house the homeless, preserve the community, or do any of many other important tasks for which other institutions have been created.[28]

Finally, there is Jeffrey Coors, president of ACX Technologies, which was recently reformed as CoorsTek and Graphic Packaging International Corporation. Coors asks the question, "What is corporate responsibility?" and comes away with a quite different answer than advocates of corporate social responsibility would give: "Very simply, a business sells goods and/or services to people who want them. . . . The profits [of the business] belong to all who invest in expectation of earning a return, so shouldn't the profits of a corporation be reserved for the benefit of the owners?"[29]

Given that the profits belong to the owners, argues Coors, corporate executives have no right to engage in any form of corporate philanthropy.

> Many arguments are raised to justify corporate giving. One of them is genuine altruism. People are moved by pure motives to contribute and that is commendable. A second argument is that the needs are so great that they

> require corporate rather than individual resources. A third justification is that giving creates goodwill in the community. This view is based on the idea that it is important for corporations to be good citizens and to contribute to the community. (It sounds appealing until one realizes that it is possible to give back to the community by lowering prices.)
>
> The current buzzword in corporate giving is "enlightened self-interest." If you make the world a better place, people will buy more of what you have to sell. . . .
>
> There is a great deal of peer pressure to conform in the corporate world. If a worthy cause is in need and most of the community is giving to that organization, a company becomes conspicuous by its absence. And corporate philanthropy can help avoid trouble. Dozens of special interest groups routinely target corporations and issue the threat of a boycott in order to secure contributions. Often these contributions are in reality just like "protection money" businesses are forced to pay to the underworld.[30]

Worse, writes Coors, the "protection money" goes too often to the wrong groups. He cites a study by the Capital Research Group of the philanthropic contributions of the top 250 U.S. corporations. The study "graded" the corporations according to the ideological bent of the organizations benefiting from the companies' generosity. Gifts to conservative organizations got an "A." Contributions to nonideological organizations got a "C." And contributions to leftist/liberal groups got a "D" or "F" (presumably on the basis of just how left they leaned). Coors found the results shocking. "Since the [study] was first published in 1986, there has not been a single top corporation with a record of giving that deserved an 'A' rating. Only 13 percent in the last study had a 'B'; 24 percent had a 'C'; 52 percent had a 'D'; 11 percent had an 'F.' "[31]

Coors finds this whole leftward tilt of corporate philanthropic contributions suspicious. He writes, "I can't help but question the motives and values of companies that give shareholder profits to organizations that encourage further dependence on government."[32]

Perhaps Al Dunlap, the former CEO of Scott Paper, sums up the objections of the anticorporate social responsibility gurus best:

> The most ridiculous word you hear in boardrooms these days is "stakeholders." A stakeholder is anyone with a stake in a company's well-being. That includes its employees, suppliers, the communities in which it operates and so on. The current theory is that a chief executive has to take all these people into account in making decisions. Stakeholders! Whenever I hear that word, I ask: how much did they pay for their stake? Stakeholders don't pay for their stake. Shareholders do.[33]

(See Exhibit 6.2 for an earlier and well-known statement of the argument against social responsibility.)

## EXHIBIT 6.2. **An Excerpt from Charles Dickens's *A Christmas Carol***

They were portly gentlemen, pleasant to behold, and now stood, with their hats off, in Scrooge's office. They had books and papers in their hands, and bowed to him.

"Scrooge and Marley's, I believe," said one of the gentlemen, referring to his list. "Have I the pleasure of addressing Mr. Scrooge, or Mr. Marley?"

"Mr. Marley has been dead these seven years," Scrooge replied. "He died seven years ago, this very night."

"We have no doubt his liberality is well represented by his surviving partner," said the gentleman, presenting his credentials.

It certainly was; for they had been two kindred spirits. At the ominous word "liberality" Scrooge frowned, and shook his head, and handed the credentials back.

"At this festive season of the year, Mr. Scrooge," said the gentleman, taking up a pen, "it is more than usually desirable in that we should make some slight provision for the Poor and destitute, who suffer greatly at the present time. Many thousands are in want of common necessaries; hundreds of thousands are in want of common comforts, sir."

"Are there no prisons?" asked Scrooge.

"Plenty of prisons," said the gentleman, laying down the pen again.

"And the Union workhouses?" demanded Scrooge. "Are they still in operation?"

"They are. Still," returned the gentleman, "I wish I could say they were not."

"The Treadmill and the Poor Law are in full vigor, then?" said Scrooge.

"Both very busy, sir."

"Oh! I was afraid, from what you said at first, that some thing had occurred to stop them in their useful course," said Scrooge. "I am very glad to hear it."

"Under the impression that they scarcely furnish Christian cheer of mind or body to the multitude," returned the gentleman, "a few of us are endeavoring to raise a fund to buy the Poor some meat and drink, and means of warmth. We choose this time, because it is a time, of all others, when Want is keenly felt, and Abundance rejoices. What shall I put you down for?"

"Nothing!" Scrooge replied.

"You wish to be anonymous?"

"I wish to be left alone," said Scrooge. "Since you ask me what I wish, gentlemen, that is my answer. I don't make merry myself at Christmas, and I can't afford to make idle people merry. I help to support the establishments I have mentioned—they cost enough: and those who are badly off must go there."

"Many can't go there; and many would rather die."

(continued)

EXHIBIT 6.2. **(continued)**

"If they would rather die," said Scrooge, "they had better do it, and decrease the surplus population. Besides—excuse me I don't know that."

"But you might know it," observed the gentleman.

"It's not my business," Scrooge returned. "It's enough for a man to understand his own business, and not to interfere with other people's. Mine occupies me constantly. Good afternoon, gentlemen!"

*Charles Dickens*

*Source:* Charles Dickens, *A Christmas Carol and The Cricket on the Hearth* (New York: Platt & Peck, 1905), pp. 17–18.

## THE ARGUMENTS FOR CORPORATE SOCIAL RESPONSIBILITY

Like those who argue against corporate social responsibility, proponents base their argument on a common foundation. Opponents of corporate social responsibility argue that profit is the motive of business and that to use the profits of a business for any purpose other than rewarding stockholders is irresponsible. Supporters of corporate social responsibility argue that profits are not and never have been the primary purpose of corporations and that, even if they were, the single-minded pursuit of profits is the least-responsible thing managers can do for stockholders. In fact, say the proponents, the entire argument against corporate social responsibility is founded on a string of myths.

### *Myth # 1: Corporations Exist to Make Profits for Shareholders*

Wrong, say the proponents. The original purpose of corporations wasn't to make profits for shareholders but to serve the public interests. "Profits as primary purpose" is the result of a historical accident and represents a perversion of the original goal of incorporation. Ralph Estes, author of *Tyranny of the Bottom Line,* summarizes the history of corporations this way:

> In the beginning corporations were chartered by monarchs to serve the interests of the state. . . . Democracies later adopted this tradition. . . .
>
> Investors were allowed a return as an inducement to fund the corporation, but providing a return to financial investors was secondary to the corporation's real purpose, which was to provide a *public* return, a public benefit. . . .

> The earliest corporations to deserve the name were ecclesiastical organizations, in a time when religion was very much a concern of the state. Next came municipalities, universities, guilds, and livery companies. These were followed by corporations chartered to exploit foreign lands—the Russia or Muscovy Company, the Levant (Turkey) Company, the Jamestown Company, the East India Trading Company. . . .
>
> America's colonization was accomplished largely through corporations: the Jamestown Company, the Massachusetts Bay Company, the Plymouth Company, the London Company. . . .
>
> As the colonizing corporations metamorphosed into colonies, the weak colonial governments in turn looked to chartered private corporations to meet public needs. These early American corporations mainly provided transport, water, insurance, library, and banking services.[34]

In each case, Estes continues, the purpose of the corporation was to serve a social function for the state. For example, when Massachusetts chartered a turnpike company, it didn't do so to benefit the stockholders of the company but to benefit the citizens of the commonwealth. Later, when the concept of incorporation was extended to other types of businesses such as manufacturing that didn't have such a clearly defined public purpose, state legislatures placed severe restrictions on corporate charters. Corporate charters had time limits (usually 20 years or less), stockholders were held responsible for the company's debts, and legislatures reserved the right to amend corporate charters at any time for any reason.

How then did profits become supreme? Estes ties what he calls the "loss of accountability" of corporations to two developments. First, in the early part of the nineteenth century, states began competing with each other to attract corporations that would stimulate settlement and growth. "Soon," explains Estes, "states were prostrating themselves before corporations with inducements, benefits, and a general relaxation of restrictions. Populist concerns were swept aside; the corporation was king."[35]

The second phase in the conversion—or "perversion," as Estes describes it—of the corporate mission came in the years following the U.S. Civil War. Business exploded in size, and giant corporate empires like those of Cornelius Vanderbilt, John D. Rockefeller, Andrew Carnegie, J. Pierpont Morgan, and the other "robber barons" emerged. Estes notes that these robber barons were secretive and distrustful and wanted to be held accountable to no one. They had no formal procedures or formal structures. They oversaw their business operations personally. Eventually, however, these enterprises simply became too big for a single person to oversee, and the tycoons were forced to bring in professional managers to help them. It was then, argues Estes, that profits became king.

> The simple structure of the early corporations . . . evolved into a complex entity organized into many divisions and branches, territories, and subsidiaries. These had to be monitored, evaluated, and scored. The tycoons,

> the owner-managers, may have disdained a formal scorekeeping system; the professional managers whom they hired to run their far-flung empires were more bureaucratic. They didn't manage by "gut" feel or the seat of their pants. They believed in numbers. They wanted performance reports. But there was no mechanism in place for scoring the corporation, for assessing and reporting its performance in fulfilling its chartered purpose.
>
> There was, however, another mechanism already in place. This was the simple system that stockholders' agents had first set up to report to their principals on how well their investments were doing. It was never intended to show the performance of the corporation as a whole, in terms of chartered purpose. But it *existed.* It was on hand. And it looked reasonable. So the professional managers of these expanding corporations turned to this simplistic and inapplicable system as a measure of corporate performance.[36]

The inadequate mechanism that the early investors' agents had developed and that the professional managers turned to was profits—a simple count of what came in, what went out, and most important, what was left on hand in the end. Managers came to serve the interests of stockholders, argues Estes, not because there were no other stakeholders but because of the historical accident that stockholders were the only stakeholders with a simple and readily available measure of performance.

### *Myth #2: The Application of Moral Thinking in Business Decision Making Is an Abrogation of Fiduciary Responsibility*

Wrong again, say our gurus. When managers ignore social responsibilities, they often end up costing stockholders more than they gain them. John Dalla Costa, author of *The Ethical Imperative,* cites the case of Texaco as an example:

> The company had been embroiled for more than a year in a class action suit by black employees who felt victimized by an institutionalized prejudice. After first denying the charge and fighting the suit, Texaco was embarrassed into settlement by tapes, made pubic in 1996, in which senior executives uttered racial barbs while plotting to destroy incriminating documents relating to the suit. With apologies and promises of new training and promotional policies, Texaco promptly paid out $115 million. Ironically, the infamous tapes were made by a white manager, not out of concern about inequality toward fellow employees but as a negotiating lever to protect his job in a forthcoming reengineering. There is no doubt that this manager, arrested and prosecuted for his role in destroying evidence, did something illegal, something grossly self-serving and cynical. But it must also be acknowledged that he was behaving not unlike the way Texaco itself was behaving toward its own employees.[37]

Dalla Costa notes that Texaco's stock price dropped three dollars per share in the first few days after its race-bias scandal, which he says amounted to "a neglect or omission of fiduciary obligations on the scale of $1 billion."[38] He adds that other costs of unethical and socially irresponsible behavior never show up on the balance sheet:

> [T]he disloyalty of disgruntled employees, legal and public relations expenses to cover impropriety, and the general executive profligacy that tends to go in tandem with a self-serving corporate culture create millions of dollars in drag on potential earnings. . . .
>
> Business is complex and confusing, . . . but what is clear is that seemingly straight-line relationships between self-interest and profit involve many other factors that often impede, diminish and destroy shareholder value. Rather than harming value, an ethical orientation often creates the conditions necessary for enhancing and preserving it.[39]

### *Myth #3: Ethics and Social Responsibility Run Counter to the Pursuit of Self-interest upon Which a Free Market is Based*

Wrong once again, says Dalla Costa. Ethical behavior isn't an "either-or" proposition or a choice between one's self-interest and that of another. "Ethics essentially provide a framework for fairness that benefits both the individual pursuing self-interest and the community that must manage to stay functional. . . . We as individuals are not the opposite of our community, but its members, contributors and beneficiaries. Self and other, economy and community, competition and cooperation are not therefore antonyms but continuities of interdependent ebb and flow."[40]

Robert C. Solomon, author of *A Better Way to Think about Business,* argues that this forced polarity between ethical behavior and self-interest "betrays a lack of vision, thought, and imagination":[41]

> [O]ur self-interest is intimately tied up with *serving the interests of others.* Thus the polarity between doing what is in our interest and doing the right thing—or doing things for other people—breaks down. In serving others, we serve ourselves. The language of "self-sacrifice" is misleading, at best. The conflict between our own interests and others' interest is rare.
>
> When corporations struggle over the choice between self-interest (profitability) and doing right (treating the employees or customers fairly, paying attention to the surrounding community), it is almost always a symptom of unimaginative, nonstrategic, short-term thinking.[42]

Soloman cites Fred Reichheld, author of *The Loyalty Effect* (see our discussion of Reichheld's ideas in Chapter 4.), who believes that "it is foolish to think you can ignore employees' family demands and still get committed, energetic, long-term employees. That's fairyland."[43]

Solomon adds that the choice between self-interest, whether corporate or personal, and doing right is usually an illusion, as is the image of the autonomous, self-sustaining, self-defining individual:

> The "self-made" man or woman is a social creature, and he or she "makes it" by being an essential part of society, however innovative or eccentric he or she may be. To say that we are communal creatures is to say that we have mutual interests, that even in the most competitive community, our self-interests are parasitic on and largely defined in terms of those vital interests we hold in common. . . .
>
> Princeton anthropologist Clifford Geertz once wrote that a human being all alone in nature would not be a noble, autonomous being but a pathetic, quivering creature with no identity and few defenses or means of support. Our heroic conception of "the individual"—often exemplified by the lone (usually male) hero—is a bit of bad but self-serving anthropology. There are exceptional individuals, to be sure, but they are social creations and become exceptional just because they serve the needs of their society, more often than not by exemplifying precisely those forms of excellence most essential to that society.[44]

### *Myth #4: The Corporation Is an Autonomous Entity—Something Apart from the Community*

Nonsense, say our gurus. Rather than being an autonomous, independent entity, a corporation is part of the communities in which it operates—a "citizen"—whether it likes it or not. Our gurus argue that it is ludicrous to think otherwise. Peter Schwartz and Blair Gibb, coauthors of *When Good Companies Do Bad Things,* maintain that today's corporations can't choose whether to become involved in social issues like economic development, diversity and equal opportunity, human rights, and so on. They simply are involved.

> As soon as a company hires an employee or files a tax return or makes a capital investment, it has involved itself with social issues—it has just not made those involvements explicit. The company pays its employees what the market will bear—*or a little more or a little less.* It enforces certain health and safety practices—*to the minimum required by law or a little better.* It recruits and promotes employees—on the basis of merit, *with fewer or more exceptions for internal or external politics.*[45]

A corporation can't choose whether to be involved; it is involved. A corporation can only choose whether that involvement will be for the good or bad, whether it will be creative or destructive, and whether it will foster the interests of humankind or detract from it.

## Myth #5: Laws Are Sufficient to Protect Those Who Cannot Protect Themselves

Wrong again, say our gurus. Laws and ethics aren't the same thing, and one is not a substitute for the other. Dalla Costa explains the difference between laws and ethics this way:

> For thousands of years, as long as there have been laws, there has also been a set of ethics guiding the community's behavior. The two are complementary but not redundant. Laws emerge largely by precedent, whereas ethics derive from moral belief. Laws create authority by the threat of punishment, whereas ethics are usually an expression of principle that engages individuals at the deeper level of identity and belonging. The focus of laws is compliance, while the focus of ethics is human character and community development. History provides ample examples of widely followed, strictly enforced laws that clearly have been unethical: the laws enshrining slavery in the U.S. states; Nazi laws depriving Jewish citizens of their property; apartheid in South Africa. Nether the law nor ethics are ever perfect, since the examples just listed also involved a moral (immoral) complicity on the part of the majority. The point, however, is that justice may be served without satisfying moral right.[46]

## Myth #6: Stakeholders Don't Pay for Their Stake—Shareholders Do!

Finally, we have our gurus' response to the argument offered by Al Dunlap. Recall Dunlap's remarks: "The most ridiculous word you hear in boardrooms these days is 'stakeholders.' A stakeholder is anyone with a stake in a company's well-being. . . . The current theory is that a chief executive has to take all these people into account in making decisions. . . . Whenever I hear that word [stakeholders], I ask: how much did they pay for their stake? Stakeholders don't pay for their stake. Shareholders do."[47]

In response to Dunlap, Schwartz and Gibb recall the disaster that occurred at Union Carbide's pesticide plant in Bhopal, India, on the evening of Sunday, December 2, 1984. For reasons that were never fully determined, a deadly chemical used to make pesticides (methyl isocyanate, or MIC) escaped from the plant and spread as a toxic cloud over Bhopal and surrounding communities. The accident killed 3,800 people. Most died when their lungs filled with fluid, the equivalent of drowning. Others died of heart attacks. In addition to the deaths, up to half a million people were injured. Some of the injured were blinded; others suffered concussions or paralysis. Many had serious lesions in their bronchial and nasal passages. The Bhopal disaster became the worst industrial accident in history.[48] Schwartz and Gibb's response to Dunlap is simple: "[M]any thousands of Indians living around the Bhopal plant paid with their lives for their 'stake' in Union Carbide."[49]

> No man is an island, entire of itself; every man is a piece of the continent, a part of the main; . . . any man's death diminishes me, because I am involved in mankind; and therefore never send to know for whom the bell tolls; IT TOLLS FOR THEE.
>
> From *Devotions XVII* by John Donne[50]

## OUR VIEW

Given that we dropped in a passage from Dickens at the end of one discussion and a passage from John Donne at the end of the other, it probably will come as no surprise to you that we side with those who favor corporate social responsibility. We think corporations will be forced to be socially responsible in the knowledge economy whether they want to or not. We see increasing evidence that investors, consumers, and employees are all demanding socially responsible behavior from corporations. Here are some examples:[51]

- Between 1995 and 1999, assets in stock funds that screen investments for ethical, environmental, and other corporate social responsibility issues grew from $639 billion to over $2 trillion.
- In a 1999 survey of 25,000 people in 23 countries, 90 percent of the respondents said they wanted companies to focus on more than just profits. Seventeen percent said they would actively boycott a company that they perceived as being socially irresponsible.
- In another survey, 76 percent of consumers said that, provided price and quality were equivalent, they would switch brands or retailers to support companies that associated with good causes.
- Finally, in a 1997 survey of American workers, 42 percent said that the ethics of the business was a critical factor in their decision to work for a company.

In short, companies that don't focus on all three parts of John Elkington's triple bottom line run the risk of alienating workers, angering customers, and missing out on access to over two trillion dollars of badly needed operating capital. That's a high price to pay for "profit-motive" purity and ironically, is the ticket to destroying profits in the long-term.

We hope you agree with us, but whether you do or not, we hope you keep reading because we are just about to tackle one of the most intriguing aspects of this topic. Assuming you want to behave ethically and responsibly, how do you decide what to do or not to do? We take a look at the ways our gurus tell us we can make those decisions, and we'll get to that small matter we mentioned earlier about the meaning of life.

# CODES OF ETHICS

How do you decide what is the ethical or socially responsible thing to do or not do in a given situation? Wouldn't it be nice if there was a code or standard you could look to as a guide? Well, say our gurus, there is not just one code or standard; there are literally hundreds of them. Here are the ones most mentioned by the gurus.

## The Ten Commandments

You surely remember the ten commandments—Moses and all. For a refresher, pick up a Bible and flip to Exodus 20:1–17. You'll find the following prescriptions in various translations:

- You shall have no other gods before Me.
- You shall not make for yourself an idol.
- You shall not take the name of the Lord your God in vain.
- Remember the Sabbath day, to keep it holy.
- Honor your father and your mother.
- You shall not murder.
- You shall not commit adultery.
- You shall not steal.
- You shall not bear false witness.
- You shall not covet you neighbor's house, wife, servants, or possessions.

## The Boy Scout and Girl Scout Laws

If the Girl Scout Law printed here looks different from the one you remember from your youth, that's because it is different. The Girl Scout Law was rewritten in the mid-1990s to make it more politically correct.

| BOY SCOUT LAW | GIRL SCOUT LAW |
|---|---|
| ***A scout is:*** | ***I will do my best to be:*** |
| Trustworthy. | honest and fair, |
| Loyal. | friendly and helpful, |
| Helpful. | considerate and caring, |
| Friendly. | courageous and strong, |
| Courteous. | and |
| Kind. | responsible for what I say and do, |

(continued)

| **Boy Scout Law** (continued) | **Girl Scout Law** (continued) |
|---|---|
| Obedient. | and to |
| Cheerful. | respect myself and others, |
| Thrifty. | respect authority, |
| Brave. | use resources wisely, |
| Clean. | make the world a better place, |
| Reverent. | and be a sister to every Girl Scout. |

## The Minnesota Principles

The Minnesota Principles were developed by a group of business leaders in Minnesota who wanted to encourage fairness and integrity in the global marketplace. The principles consist of a preamble and five propositions and stakeholder principles covering relations with customers, employees, owners/investors, suppliers, communities, and competitors. The general principles are as follows:

> **Proposition #1: Stimulating economic growth is the particular contribution of business to the larger society.** We understand that profits are fundamental to the fulfillment of this function.
> **Proposition #2: Business activities must be characterized by fairness.** We understand fairness to include equitable treatment and equality of opportunity for all participants in the marketplace.
> **Proposition #3: Business activities must be characterized by honesty.** We understand honesty to include candor, truthfulness, and promise keeping.
> **Proposition #4: Business activities must be characterized by respect for human dignity.** We understand this to mean that business activities should show a special concern for the less powerful and the disadvantaged.
> **Proposition #5: Business activities must be characterized by respect for the environment.** We understand this to mean that business activities should promote sustainable development and prevent environmental degradation and waste of resources.[52]

## The CAUX Principles

The CAUX Round Table was created in 1986 by a group of business leaders from Europe, Japan, and North America who wanted to reduce trade tensions. The Round Table developed and circulated a statement of principles of business that consist of a preamble, seven general principles, and a statement of stakeholder principles covering relations with customers, employees, owners/investors, suppliers, competitors, and communities. The seven general principles are as follows:

**Principle #1: The responsibilities of business: beyond shareholders toward stakeholders.** The value of a business to society is the wealth and employment it creates and the marketable products and services it provides to consumers at a reasonable price commensurate with quality. To create such value, a business must maintain its own economic health and viability, but survival is not a sufficient goal.

Businesses have a role to play in improving the lives of all their customers, employees, and shareholders by sharing with them the wealth they have created. Suppliers and competitors as well should expect businesses to honor their obligations in a spirit of honesty and fairness. As responsible citizens of the local, national, regional and global communities in which they operate, businesses share a part in shaping the future of those communities.

**Principle #2: The economic and social impact of business: toward innovation, justice, and world community.** Businesses established in foreign countries to develop, produce or sell should also contribute to the social advancement of those countries by creating productive employment and helping to raise the purchasing power of their citizens. Businesses also should contribute to human rights, education, welfare, and vitalization of the countries in which they operate.

Businesses should contribute to economic and social development not only in the countries in which they operate, but also in the world community at large, through effective and prudent use of resources, free and fair competition, and emphasis upon innovation in technology, production methods, marketing and communications.

**Principle #3: Business behavior: beyond the letter of law, toward a spirit of trust.** While accepting the legitimacy of trade secrets, businesses should recognize that sincerity, candour, truthfulness, the keeping of promises, and transparency contribute not only to their own credibility and stability but also to the smoothness and efficiency of business transactions, particularly on the international level.

**Principle #4: Respect for rules.** To avoid trade frictions and to promote freer trade equal conditions for competition, and fair and equitable treatment for all participants, businesses should respect international and domestic rules. In addition, they should recognize that some behavior, although legal, may still have adverse consequences.

**Principle #5: Support for multilateral trade.** Business should support the multilateral trade systems of the GATT/World Trade Organization and similar international agreements. They should cooperate in efforts to promote the progressive and judicious liberalization of trade and to relax those domestic measures that unreasonably hinder global commerce, while giving due respect to national policy objectives.

**Principle #6: Respect for the environment.** A business should protect and, where possible, improve the environment, promote sustainable development, and prevent the wasteful use of natural resources.

**Principle #7: Avoidance of illicit operations.** A business should not participate in or condone bribery money laundering, or other corrupt practices: indeed, it should seek cooperation with others to eliminate them. It should not trade in arms or other materials used for terrorist activities, drug traffic or other organized crime.[53]

## The Parliament of the World's Religions Declaration toward a Global Ethic

Drafted by Han Küng, the Declaration toward a Global Ethic was signed by two hundred delegates representing the world's religions at the Parliament of the World's Religions held in Chicago in 1993. Among other things, the declaration contains four "irrevocable directives":[54]

1. A commitment to a culture of nonviolence and respect for life.
2. A commitment to a culture of solidarity and just economic order.
3. A commitment to a culture of tolerance and a life in truthfulness.
4. A commitment to a culture of equal rights and partnership between men and women.

## SA 8000

SA 8000 is a voluntary international standard developed by the Council on Economic Priority Accreditation Agency (CEPAA) to ensure the ethical sourcing of goods and services. The standard covers child labor, forced labor, health and safety, freedom of association and the right to collective bargaining, discrimination, disciplinary practices, working hours, and compensation. Companies adopting the standard must agree to respect the Universal Declaration of Human Rights and the United Nations Convention on the Rights of the Child. They must also put in place a Social Management System to ensure that the requirements of the standard are followed. You can obtain a copy of the standard from CEPAA's Internet site at www.cepaa.org or by going to www.ellipson.com/sa8000/ .

## The Golden Rule

You are probably familiar with this ethical standard, whether from the Bible, the Talmud, or other religious and cultural writings. Here is the way it is expressed in a variety of religions and cultures:[55]

**Buddhism.** Comparing oneself to others in such terms as "Just as I am so are they, just as they are so am I," he should neither kill nor cause others to kill (Sutta Nipta 705).

**Christianity.** Whatever you wish that men would do to you, do so to them (Bible, Matthew 7:12).
**Confucianism.** Try your best to treat others as you would wish to be treated yourself and you will find that is the shortest way to benevolence (Mencius VII.A4); Tsetung asked, "Is there one word that can serve as a principle of conduct for life?" Confucius replied, "It is the word shu—reciprocity: Do not do to others what you do not want them to do to you" (Analects 15.23).
**Hinduism.** One should not behave toward others in a way which is disagreeable to oneself. This is the essence of morality. All other activities are due to selfish desire (Mahabharata, Anusasana Parva 113.8).
**Islam.** Not one of you is a believer until he loves for his brother what he loves for himself (Forty Hadith of an-Nawawi 13).
**Jainism.** A man should wander about treating all creatures as he himself would be treated (Sutrakvitanga 1.11.33).
**Judaism.** When he went to Hillel, he said to him, "What is hateful to you, do not do to your neighbor: that is the whole Torah; all the rest of it is commentary; go and learn" (Talmud, Shabbat 31a).

## The Search for Universal Ethics

If you noticed some similarities in the codes of ethics we just discussed, so did two of our gurus. In fact, after reviewing the CAUX Principles and several other codes, John Dalla Costa tried his hand at developing some universal themes. He came up with five values and two essential qualities that, he says, pervade most codes. The values are declarative:

- Respect life.
- Be fair.
- Be honest.
- Strive for justice.
- Honor the environment.

Here are the essential qualities:

- Personal responsibility and accountability. "The message . . . that any action, for both persons and companies, starts with a clear recognition that 'I am responsible.'"[56]
- Reciprocity. A sense of give-and-take interdependence between the individual and community, rights and responsibilities, global and local, rational and emotional, material and spiritual, and so on.[57]

Rushworth Kidder also muses about the universality of values. He cites the work of a number of different philosophers, anthropologists, and theologians who purport to have identified universal ethical standards or principles:

There is no group that thinks it right to kill an adult, healthy member of society who has committed no crime and whose death is not required by the welfare of the group.

*Richard B. Brandt, philosopher*

[T]here is no group in which marriage or sexual intercourse is approved between members of the immediate family, with the possible exception of some royal families and with the further exception of some important ritual occasions. There is no society in which kindliness, sympathy, hospitality, or regard for others and their rights is disapproved.

*Edward Westermarck, anthropologist*

Every culture has a concept of murder, distinguishing this from execution, killing in war, and other "justifiable homicides." The notions of incest and other regulations upon sexual behavior, of prohibitions upon untruth under defined circumstances, of restitution and reciprocity, of mutual obligations between parents and children—these and many other moral concepts are altogether universal.

*Clyde Kluckholn, anthropologist*

The ten rules below . . . are the basic or fundamental rules of morality:

*The First Five*

1. Don't kill.
2. Don't cause pain.
3. Don't disable.
4. Don't deprive of freedom or opportunity.
5. Don't deprive of pleasure.

*The Second Five*

6. Don't deceive.
7. Keep your promise.
8. Don't cheat.
9. Obey the law.
10. Do your duty.

*Bernard Gert, philosopher*

[F]ive basic commands to human beings which also have countless applications in the business world and in politics, hold in *all* the great world religions:

1. Do not kill.
2. Do not lie.
3. Do not steal.

4. Do not practice immorality.
5. Respect parents and love children.

*Hans Küng, thologian*[58]

Of course, admits Kidder, the idea of universal core moral or ethical values doesn't sit well with everyone. Some people believe that ethics are "relative, situational, subjective, negotiable, and up for grabs by whoever wants to lay down the definitions."[59] This theory or position is called "ethical relativism." Here is how Manuel Velasquez explains it:

> Ethical relativism is the theory that, because different societies have different ethical beliefs, there is no rational way of determining whether an action is morally right or wrong other than by asking whether the people of this or that society believe it is morally right or wrong. Or, to put it another way: Ethical relativism is the view that there are no ethical standards that are absolutely true and that apply or should be applied to the companies and people of all societies. Instead, relativism holds, something is right for the people or companies in one particular society if it accords with their moral standards, and wrong for them if it violates their moral standards. The people of certain Arab societies, for example, hold that business bribery is morally acceptable, although Americans believe it is immoral. The ethical relativist will conclude that while it is wrong for an American company to bribe in America, it is not wrong for Arabs or their companies to bribe in their own society. The company or the businessperson who operates in several different countries, then, and who encounters societies with many different moral standards will be advised by the theory of ethical relativism that in one's moral reasoning one should always follow the moral standards prevalent in whatever society one finds oneself. After all, since moral standards differ and since there are no other criteria of right and wrong, the best one can do is to follow the old adage "When in Rome, do as the Romans do."[60]

Kidder says he likes the way Stanford University professor Ronald A. Howard responds to ethical relativism when he hears it from his students.

> When Howard's students took up this line, he would engage them in a little thought experiment. Imagine, he told them, that I'm going to parachute you into a country somewhere in the world, and you haven't any idea where it is. As soon as you get out of your parachute, I want you to walk up to the first person you see, take away whatever he or she is holding, and run away with it. Then see what happens.
>
> With the possible exception, he explains, that you have landed in front of a Buddhist monk and taken away his begging bowl—and that his only

response is to sigh, "Ah! That's karma!"—you will run squarely into the universal concept of property rights, codified in the Western world through the commandment "Don't steal." You didn't bring that precept with you. You didn't impose it on the culture from the perspective of your Judeo-Christian, free-enterprise, democratically individualistic heritage. You found it. And you will find it in any culture in which you land.[61]

Certainly, if we believe that any one moral standard is as good as any other, we are likely to be more tolerant. We shall tolerate widow-burning, human sacrifice, cannibalism, slavery, the infliction of physical torture, or any other of the thousand and one abominations which are, or have been, from time to time approved by one moral code or another. But this is not the kind of toleration we want, and I do not think its cultivation will prove "an advantage to morality."

*Walter T. Stace, British philosopher*[62]

## The Small Problem of the Values-Tactics Ladder

It would seem, given this discussion, that business ethics and corporate social responsibility largely boil down to selecting the right code of ethics, or maybe just grabbing hold of some truly universal values. We could print them in the annual report, post them on office walls, recite them in meetings, and be done with it. In one respect, that is exactly what our gurus propose that you do. You should develop, adopt, preach, and most important, try to abide by some code of ethics. But, they warn us, don't think that is going to be enough. There is an inherent weakness in codes when it comes to guiding you in resolving dilemmas such as the ones we presented at the beginning of this chapter. Kidder refers to it as the "Values-Tactics Ladder."

Kidder lists four words that bubble up in conversation without much definition in any organization—values, goals, plans, and tactics. Yet, he claims, these terms reveal a lot about the strengths and weaknesses of ethical codes. He explains:

Suppose we've established a code of ethics for our local high school and nailed it above the door. It has on it the word honesty. Along the way to establishing that code, nearly everyone in our community has bought into the importance of putting that word on our list. But how does it translate? What does it mean? How can we make it operational in our school?

Well, we might observe that there is far too much cheating in the school and propose that our goal the second step down on our ladder ought to be to reduce cheating dramatically. Most of the community would probably buy into that, too. Some might demur, of course, asking whether it is really the most important goal we could address. But the consensus would probably be fairly broad.

So, moving down still another rung on the ladder, we ask what plan or strategy might best reach that goal. How do we reduce cheating? The answer that comes back might be, "Throw the book at cheaters! Clamp down on them with fierce determination—detentions, expulsions, letters home, failing grades, and all, the rest!" Here consensus will get seriously frayed, as perhaps up to half the community says, "Wait a minute: The kids who are the real problem cheaters have already been hammered in all kinds of ways. More punishment won't do it. They need care, counsel, and attention."

But you persist, moving down to the bottom, tactical rung. Through what tactic, you ask, can we fulfill our plan of getting tough on cheaters? Why not close down all the public schools since they have wimpy attitudes on punishment, anyway and force all kids to attend private schools, where we can really control them? Here consensus dissolves as the vast majority flees to other options.[63]

That's the problem with codes of ethics. They are excellent at the level of values, pretty good at the level of goals, and useful at the level plans. But when you get down to tactics, particularly when it comes to resolving the kind of dilemmas we mentioned at the beginning of this chapter, they often fail as guides to ethical and socially responsible behavior. You need something more than these simple codes. You need an approach to making ethical decisions. Well, don't worry. Our gurus have some suggestions.

## THREE APPROACHES TO ETHICAL DECISION MAKING

Rushworth Kidder lists two major types of ethical dilemmas that people face: choices between right and wrong and choices between right and right. The dilemma faced by the CEO in Case #2: The Case of the Consultant's Report was a case of right versus wrong. Recall what happened:

**Case #2: The Case of the Consultant's Report**

In May 1991, a group of executives from a military defense contractor attended a meeting with U.S. Navy representatives and a private consultant hired by the navy. The purpose of the meeting was to discuss the contractor's work on an existing contract. The meeting was held in a conference room at the company's headquarters and concluded amicably and uneventfully as scheduled at 5:00 P.M.

The following morning, while cleaning the conference room, a maintenance worker discovered that the navy's consultant had accidentally left

> behind an envelope marked "Business Sensitive." The worker passed the envelope along to his boss, who examined the contents and quickly passed it along to his boss. Within a few hours, the envelope was deposited on the desk of the defense contractor's CEO. By now it was obvious that the envelope the consultant had inadvertently left behind contained extremely valuable information. At that time, the defense contractor was in a bidding war with a competitor for additional defense-department business. The consultant's envelope contained a complete analysis of the cost structures of both the defense contractor and its competitor. The CEO was aware that a federal law, the Procurement Integrity Act, required contractors bidding for government contracts to certify that they had never possessed proprietary information. He was also aware that the information contained in the envelope before him would be extremely helpful in bidding against his competitor.

The CEO had a choice. He could abide by the law—do what was right—or he could break the law by reading the report and using its contents to put together a more competitive bid. What did you decide you would do?

**Here's what really happened.** In the actual case, the CEO had his staff photocopy the document and return the original to the conference room. Company employees then began entering information from the report into computer spreadsheets and analyzing the data. Later that day, the CEO had a change of mind and ordered that the photocopies and computer files be destroyed. He retrieved the report from the conference room and returned it to a local navy official and informed him that "no copies of the report existed." He did not tell the navy official that a copy had been made and then destroyed. After an official investigation in which it was determined that employees of the company had seen the contents of the report, the navy concluded that "no material damage" had been done and that the company could participate in the bidding process provided those who had seen the report were sequestered. Several months later, the CEO resigned in disgrace. His decision to read and copy the report had been a career-ending move.

Kidder names three types of wrongs that you can commit in right versus wrong dilemmas: (1) violating the law—like the CEO did, (2) departing from the truth—you tell a lie, or (3) deviating from moral rectitude—for example, you claim someone else's work as your own. Codes of ethics usually steer you in the proper direction when it comes to right versus wrong: don't lie, don't cheat, don't steal. As Kidder notes, "There may be ways to weasel around the wrongness. And there will surely be temptations to overlook it. But the issue clearly does not involve two rights. One side is wrong."[64]

The other type of ethical dilemma, right versus right, isn't so simple to resolve. Here are some examples of right-versus-right dilemmas provided by Kidder:

> - It is right to protect the endangered spotted owl in the old-growth forests of the American Northwest and right to provide jobs for loggers. . . .

- It is right to provide our children with the finest public schools available—and right to prevent the constant upward ratcheting of state and local taxes.
- It is right to extend equal social services to everyone regardless of race or ethnic origin—and right to pay special attention to those whose cultural backgrounds may have deprived them of past opportunities.
- It is right to refrain from meddling in the internal affairs of sovereign nations and right to help protect the undefended in warring regions where they are subject to slaughter. . . .
- It is right to resist the importation of products made in developing nations to the detriment of the environment—and right to provide jobs, even at low wages, for citizens of those nations.
- It is right to condemn the minister who has an affair with a parishioner—and right to extend mercy to him for the only real mistake he's ever made.
- It is right to find out all you can about your competitors' costs and price structures—and right to obtain information only through proper channels.
- It is right to take the family on a much-needed vacation—and right to save that money for your children's education. . . .
- It is right to support the principle of creative and aesthetic freedom for the curator of a photography exhibition at a local museum—and right to uphold the community's desire to avoid displaying pornographic or racially offensive works.
- It is right to "throw the book" at good employees who make dumb decisions that endanger the firm—and right to have enough compassion to mitigate the punishment and give them another chance.[65]

Our gurus provide us with three approaches to resolving right-versus-right dilemmas:

1. Ends-based thinking.
2. Rule-based thinking.
3. Care-based thinking.

We discuss each of these in the following sections.

## Ends-Based Thinking

The ends-based approach to resolving ethical dilemma is sometimes called the "consequentialist" or "utilitarian" approach. In summary, it goes like this:

> An action is right from an ethical point of view if and only if the sum of utilities produced by that act is greater than the sum total of utilities produced by any other act the agent could have performed in its place.[66]

Utilitarianism is derived from the writings of Jeremy Bentham (1748–1832), John Stuart Mill (1806–1873), and Henry Sidgwick (1838–1900). It assumes that, in arriving at a decision, you have some way of measuring outcomes so that you can add up the benefits that would be derived from each course of action you could take and subtract out the harm (or costs) of each action. The action that produces the greatest sum total of utility is the ethical action.

Velasquez cautions that it is easy to misunderstand utilitarianism.

> When the utilitarian principle says that the right action for a particular occasion is the one that produces more utility than any other possible action, it does not mean that the right action is the one that produces the most utility for the person performing the action. Rather, an action is right if it produces the most utility for *all* persons affected by the action (including the person performing the action.) Nor does the utilitarian principle say that an action is right so long as it benefits outweigh its costs. Rather, utilitarianism holds that in the final analysis only one action is right: that one action whose net benefits are greatest by comparison to the net benefits of all other possible alternatives. A third misunderstanding is to think that the utilitarian principle requires us to consider only the direct and immediate consequences of our actions. Instead, both the immediate and all foreseeable future costs and benefits that each alternative will provide for each individual must be taken into account as well as any significant indirect effects.[67]

Case #6: The Case of the "Cost Benefit" Study is an example of a utilitarian approach. You will recall the case as follows:

**Case #6: The Case of the "Cost-Benefit" Study**

In the early 1960s, the American automotive industry was under serious attack from foreign competitors, particularly the Japanese. The race was on to develop small, fuel-efficient, and compact models of American cars to compete with imports. One American manufacturer set a goal to develop a subcompact that would weigh less than 2000 pounds, cost less than $2,000, and could be brought to the market in half the normal time. The company succeeded, only to discover during crash tests that the new model's gas tank occasionally ruptured when the car was hit from the rear at speeds greater than 20 miles per hour. Worse, when the gas tank ruptured, gasoline sprayed into the passenger compartment, risking the possibility of fire. Although the gas tank was a problem, the company's managers were reassured by the facts that (1) government regulations at the time only required that gas tanks stay intact in rear-end collisions of *less than* 20 miles per hour, (2) the car was comparable in safety to similar models produced by other automotive companies, both domestic and foreign, and (3) an internal cost-benefit study showed that the cost of modifying the car to make the gas tank safe at higher speeds would far outweigh the benefits. The cost-benefit analysis reasoned as follows:

> The cost of modifying the car would be $137 million, or $11 per car multiplied by the expected production of 12.5 million cars. This cost would have to be passed along to customers in the form of higher prices.
>
> The benefits from modifying the car would be $49.15 million calculated as follows: (180 expected deaths from rear-end collisions X $200,000 [the value the U.S. Government placed on a human life]) + (180 expected injuries from rear-end collisions X $67,000 [the value of a serious burn injury according to U.S. insurance companies at the time]) + (2,100 cars X $700 [the estimated residual value of a subcompact automobile]).

The study's authors argued that it was not right to spend $137 million of society's money to generate benefits that society valued at just $49.15 million.

Velasquez notes that the study's authors took a classic utilitarian approach. First, they determined the alternative course of action—modify the car or not modify the car. Second, they calculated the costs and benefits of each course of action. Finally, they arrived at the conclusion that the course of action that would impose the lowest costs and generate the greatest benefits would be to *not* make the modification. What did you decide to do?

**Here's what really happened.** This is the famous case of the Ford Pinto. Ford managers decided not to make the modification. Velasquez reports that, during the decade following the decision not to modify the Pinto, an estimated 60 people died in fiery crashes involving the unmodified cars and at least twice that many were severely burned.

Velasquez notes that, regardless of your feelings about the utilitarian answer the Ford employees reached, a number of aspects of the utilitarian approach make it attractive to many people.

- Utilitarianism fits nicely with the approach most people take to making public-policy decisions—the greatest good for the greatest number.
- Utilitarianism fits in with the criteria most people use when discussing moral conduct. "When people explain, for example, why they have a moral obligation to perform some action, they will often proceed by pointing to the benefits or harms the action will impose on human beings."[68] The moral obligation is to pursue the course of action that has the greatest net utility, which of course is what utilitarianism says.

- Utilitarianism explains why some things like lying, cheating, and killing are consider morally wrong while others like telling the truth, fidelity, and respect for life are considered morally right. For example, "the utilitarian can say that lying is generally wrong because of the costly effects lying has on our human welfare. When people lie to each other, they are less apt to trust each other and to cooperate with each other. And the less trust and cooperation, the more our welfare declines."[69]
- Utilitarianism supports a value that most people hold dear—efficiency. "[A]n efficient operation is one that produces a desired output with the lowest resource input. Such efficiency is precisely what utilitarianism advocates since it holds that one should always adopt that course of action that will produce the greatest benefit at the lowest cost."[70]

Critics of utilitarianism, however, point to two deficiencies. First, they point to problems with measurement. How can one possibly find adequate and reliable ways of measuring the utility and cost of different courses of action as utilitarianism requires? For example, in the case of the Ford Pinto, the report writers valued a human life at $200,000. Critics of utilitarianism argue that such a valuation is entirely arbitrary. Second, say the critics, utilitarianism can lead to conclusions that are at odds with the notions most people have about *rights* and *justice.* Velasquez provides the following illustration:

> [S]uppose that your uncle had an incurable and painful disease, so that as a result he was quite unhappy but does not choose to die. Although he is hospitalized and will die within a year, he continues to run his chemical plant. Because of his misery he deliberately makes life miserable for his workers and has insisted on not installing safety devices in his chemical plant, although he knows that as a result one worker will certainly lose his life over the next year. You, his only living relative, know that on your uncle's death you will inherit his business and will not only be wealthy and immensely happy, but also intend to prevent any future loss of life by installing the needed safety devices. You are cold-blooded, and correctly judge that you could secretly murder your uncle without getting caught and without your happiness being in any way affected by it afterwards. If it is possible for you to murder your uncle without in any way diminishing anyone else's happiness, then according to utilitarianism you have a moral obligation to do so. By murdering your uncle, you are trading his life for the life of the worker, and you are gaining your happiness while doing away with his unhappiness and pain: The gain is obviously on the side of utility.[71]

Velasquez points out that, in this case, utilitarianism ends up saying that the act of murder is morally right. Yet the act of murder would violate one of the most important *rights* an individual has—the right to life.[72]

## Rule-Based Thinking

An alternative to the ends-based/utilitarian approach to resolving ethical dilemmas is an approach based on the ethical theory developed by Immanuel Kant in the eighteenth century. Kant's theory is founded on a moral principal called the *categorical imperative,* which Velasquez explains as follows:

> [T]he *categorical imperative* . . . requires that everyone should be treated as a free person equal to everyone else. That is, everyone has a moral right to such treatment, and everyone has a correlative duty to treat others in this way. Kant provides at least two ways of formulating this basic moral principle; each formulation serves as an explanation of the meaning of this moral right and correlative duty.
>
> Kant's first formulation . . . is as follows: "I ought never to act except in such a way that I can also will that my maxim should become a universal law." . . . Kant's first version . . . comes down to the following principle:
>
> *An action is morally right for a person in a certain situation if, and only if, the person's reason for carrying out the action is a reason that he or she would be willing to have every person act on, in any similar situation.*[73]

Velasquez uses the example of an employer wanting to fire someone because he doesn't like that person's race. Kant's first formulation says that, in deciding whether such an action would be morally right, the employer must ask himself whether he would be prepared to have all employers act in such a fashion and whether he would be prepared to be fired because of his race. If he is not prepared for everyone to fire employees because of their race and to be fired because of his race, then the act is not moral and he can't do it.

In short, says Velasquez, Kant's first formulation of the categorical imperative incorporates two criteria:

1. Universalizability. The person's reasons for acting must be reasons that everyone *could* act on at least in principle.
2. Reversibility. The person's reasons for acting must be reasons that he or she would be *willing* to have all others use, even as a basis of how they treat him or her.[74]

Kant's second formulation of the categorical imperative is as follows: "Act in such a way that you always treat humanity, whether in your own person or in the person of any other, never simply as a means, but always at the same time as an end."[75] Velasquez explains:

> What Kant means by "treating humanity as an end" is that I should treat each human being as a being whose existence as a free rational person should be

promoted. For Kant this means two things: (1) respecting each person's freedom by treating people only as they have freely consented to be treated beforehand and (2) developing each person's capacity to freely choose for him or herself the aims he or she will pursue. On the other hand, to treat a person only as a means is to use the person only as an instrument for advancing my own interests and involves neither respect for, nor development of, the person's capacity to choose freely. Kant's second version of the categorical imperative can be expressed in the following principle:

*An action is morally right for a person if, and only if, in performing the action, the person does not use others merely as a means for advancing his or her own interests, but also both respects and develops their capacity to choose freely for themselves.*[76]

In short, the second formulation states that people should not be tricked, deceived, or exploited because to do so would be morally wrong. For example, writes Velasquez, it is morally acceptable under Kant's second formulation for you to ask an employee to perform difficult (even dangerous) work, but only if the employee is aware of the health risks and freely chooses to perform the task. If you deceive, force, or coerce the employee into performing the work, then you are behaving unethically.

Velasquez points out that critics of Kant's theory tend to focus on three problems. First, they contend that, in many situations, it is too vague to be useful. "Suppose, for example, " writes Velasquez, "that Ms. Jones, an employer pays only minimum wages to her employees and refuses to install the safety equipment they want, yet she says she is 'respecting their capacity to freely choose for themselves' because she is willing to let them work elsewhere if they choose. Is she then treating them merely as means or also as ends?"[77] Kant's critics maintain that his theory offers no way to answer such a question.

Second, say the critics, Kant's theory doesn't help when rights are in conflict. For example, people have a right to freely associate and we all have a right not to be injured by others. But, writes Velasquez, what should happen when the two rights are in conflict? For example, what is the morally right thing to do when a group of freely associating musicians are playing their music so loud that they are disturbing their next-door neighbors? Kant's critics claim that his theory doesn't provide guidance concerning how to resolve such a dilemma.

Finally, say the critics, Kant's theory can lead to the conclusion that a course of action that is clearly morally wrong is the ethical thing to do. Velasquez gives this example: "Suppose an employer can get away with discriminating against blacks by paying them lower wages than whites for the same work. And suppose also that he is so fanatical in his dislike of blacks that he is willing to accept the proposition that if his own skin were black, employers should also discriminate against him. Then, according to Kant's theory, the employer would be acting morally. But this, according to the critics, is wrong, since discrimination is obviously immoral."[78]

## Care-Based Thinking

Our gurus' final approach to resolving ethical dilemmas is illustrated by Case #4: The Case of Malden Mills. You will recall the case as follows:

**Case #4: The Case of Malden Mills**
On the night of December 11, 1995, an explosion at the Malden Mills factory in Lawrence, Massachusetts, destroyed the plant and injured 25 workers. Fourteen hundred of the plant's 3,000 employees were put out of work two weeks before Christmas.

Malden Mills was a family-owned business, founded in 1906, and it was one of the few remaining textile mills in New England. It survived by shunning low-margin commodity fabrics in favor of producing high-quality synthetic fabrics for outdoor clothing sold by companies like Patagonia, L.L. Bean, and Eddie Bauer. The company had invented and patented special high-tech equipment to produce the fabric, and its workers had been trained in the special skills required to operate the equipment and produce the product while maintaining tight tolerances for quality. Malden Mills employees were the highest-paid textile workers in the country.

The morning after the fire, Aaron Feurstein, president and majority owner of the company, faced two options. He could collect $100 million in insurance, close the factory, and rebuild in a Third World country where labor costs would be cheaper, or he could rebuild in Lawrence.

What did you decide to do?
**Here's what really happened.** Not only did Feurstein decide to rebuild the factory in Lawrence; he announced the morning after the fire that every worker would be paid their full wages and receive full medical benefits for the entire time it took to rebuild the plant. Also, they would all be guaranteed a job when the plant began operating again. It cost Feurstein $300 million to rebuild the plant in Lawrence and another $20 million to pay the wages of workers forced out of work by the fire. When asked why he had responded as he did, Feurstein said: "I have a responsibility to the worker, both blue-collar and white-collar. . . . I have an equal responsibility to the community. It would have been unconscionable to put 3,000 people on the streets and deliver a death blow to the cities of Lawrence and Methen. Maybe on paper our company is [now] worthless to Wall Street, but I can tell you it's [really] worth more."[79]

Velasquez notes that Feuerstein's resolution of the dilemma concerning the burned-down plant was significantly different from the resolution we would have expected from a utilitarian or an advocate of Kant's rule-based approach. The utilitarians would have argued that Feuerstein was under no obligation to rebuild the plant, much less pay workers who weren't working. Additionally, they would have argued, Feuerstein would produce more utility by moving jobs to the Third World, where they were desperately needed, rather than spending money to preserve jobs in Lawrence.

From a rights standpoint, Kantians would have argued that Lawrence workers certainly had no *right* to have the factory rebuilt or to get paid when they weren't working. Similarly, from the standpoint of justice, failing to rebuild the plant and pay for work that wasn't performed was not unjust. In fact, the Kantians would argue that it conceivably would be more just to move the plant to the Third World to help people who are more needy than Americans.

Why do the utilitarians and Kantians reach such different conclusions? Velasquez explains that it has to do with impartiality. The utilititarian ends-based approach and the Kantian rule-based approach both assume that ethical issues should be resolved impartially. They do not allow special treatment for friends, relatives, or employees. In fact, writes Velasquez, "some utilitarians have claimed . . . that if a stranger and your parent were both drowning and you could save only one of them, and if saving the stranger would produce more utility than saving your parent (perhaps the stranger is a brilliant surgeon who would save lives), then you would have a moral obligation to save the stranger and let your parent drown."[80]

The care-based approach to ethics takes a decidedly different position. Rather than treating people impartially, the care-based approach says that you have an obligation to care for those with whom you have valuable and close relationships. The care-based approach, Velasquez explains, has two moral demands:

1. We each exist in a web of relationships and should preserve and nurture those concrete and valuable relationships we have with specific persons.
2. We each should exercise special care for those with whom we are concretely related by attending to their particular needs, values, desires, and concrete well-being as seen from their own personal perspective, and by responding positively to these needs, values, desires, and concrete well-being, particularly of those who are vulnerable and dependent on our care.[81]

Velasquez adds that one must keep several points in mind when considering the care-based approach:[82]

1. The relationships referred to in the approach include relationships between two people (such as between a parent and child) and relationships between a person and a group (such as between Feuerstein and his employees). They also include relationships between a people and the larger community.
2. The caring involved in the care-based approach involves "caring for someone," as distinguished from "caring about someone" or "caring after someone." The caring referred to in the care-based approach is the kind of caring that a mother gives to her child.
3. The relationships that are deserving of care are those characterized by compassion, concern, love, friendship and loyalty. Relationships that involve hatred, violence, disrespect, viciousness, domination, oppression, harmful intent, and so on don't qualify.

Critics of the care-based approach to ethics argue that it can degenerate into unjust favoritism and can lead to "burnout" as people sacrifice their own needs to care for children, parents, siblings, spouses, friends, and a host of other members of the community with whom they have valuable close relationships.

So, there you have it—three significantly different approaches to resolving ethical dilemmas.

## A Test Case: Outcomes of the Three Approaches

By way of review, let's take a single case and see how advocates of each approach would respond. Recall Case #3: The Case of the Trapped Truck Driver:

> **Case #3: The Case of the Trapped Truck Driver**
> A state trooper, driving his normal route on a remote and lonely state highway, rounded a curve to discover that an accident had occurred. A flat-bed truck loaded with steel beams had run off the road, slammed into a tree, and caught fire. As the trooper got out of his car and approached the wreck, he could see that the driver was still alive. He could also see that the load of steel, which had broken loose on impact, had driven through the back of the cab and hopelessly pinned the driver inside. The trooper knew that he could not free the driver by himself, and he knew that the growing fire would reach the victim long before help could arrive. Then the trooper heard the trucker scream, "Shoot me!" He begged again, "Please, shoot me!"
>
> The trooper stood still for a moment then slowly reached for his service revolver. He paused and reconsidered as the driver continued to plead, "Shoot me! Please, shoot me!"

Here is what Rushworthy Kidder has to say about the way ends-based, rules-based, and care-based advocates would have responded to the troopers dilemma.

### *Ends-Based Approach: Shoot the Driver*

According to Kidder, the utilitarian would ask, "What's the greatest good for the greatest number?"

> On first blush, there don't seem to be many numbers here: It's just the trooper and the driver on an isolated stretch of highway. So the "greatest number" may strike us as one—the driver alone. After all, the ends-based thinker will ask what are his prospects of survival? The cab is on fire and could blow up any moment. And even if the trooper had the tools to extricate the driver, to try to do so would endanger his own life as well—raising the probability that the "greatest number" could suddenly become two, not

> one. If, then, the greatest number is indeed two, what is the greatest benefit? To save one is better than losing both. And to reduce the misery of the one who is probably going to be lost in any case is better than to prolong his agony. Utilitarianism, then, would argue for shooting him.[83]

### *Rule-Based Approach: Don't Shoot the Driver*

Kidder says that Kantian thinkers would object mightily to the utilitarian's reasoning. You are just speculating, they would say. You can't be certain that the cab will blow up. Because you can't be certain about the outcome, it's better to stick with the rule you would want every trooper to follow—Don't kill. The utilitarian would undoubtedly be incredulous: "You want the trooper just to stand there and watch the guy suffer the consequences?" To which, the Kantian would probably retort:

> Consequences! . . . Let me tell you about consequences. You've told the trooper to shoot him, and he's done so. And now, with the smoke still lingering in the gun-barrel and the sound of the shot still reverberating in the trees, he hears another sound: a siren. Within half a minute a fire truck has pulled up beside the wreck—how it got there he has no idea. In another half minute the fire is out. And there lies the driver dead, because the trooper shot him. So much for your silly efforts of trying to foresee all possible consequences.[84]

### *Care-Based Approach: Shoot Him, If You Believe That's What He Really Wants*

Kidder believes that the care-based ethicist would reason this way. "Here the 'other' is clearly the driver. If you were caught in the cab, what would you want a trooper to do to you? If you were pleading for him to shoot you, wouldn't that be pretty powerful evidence of what you want? Shouldn't the trooper respect your wishes?"[85] Of course, says Kidder, the trooper would have to be confident that being shot is what the driver really wants. Given the situation, maybe the driver can't think clearly. "Lifeguards understand that drowning swimmers will often strike out and attack their rescuers. Should lifeguards, therefore, interpret, that behavior as a clear signal whose meaning is: 'Please leave me alone: I prefer to drown'? Hardly," says Kidder, "They're taught to knock such persons out, if necessary, and drag them ashore against what seems to be their will. Should the trooper here assume that 'Shoot me!' means what it says?"[86] The trooper needs to be confident that he does.

So, what did you decide? If you were in the trooper's place, would you shoot the driver or not?

**Here's what really happened.** The trooper took out his service revolver and pointed it at the driver, then he put it back in his holster. The driver continued to scream, "Shoot me!" Again the trooper withdrew his revolver only to put it back in the holster. Suddenly, the trooper turned and ran to his patrol car. He grabbed a small carbon tetrachloride fire extinguisher from the front seat. The extinguisher was much too small to extinguish the fire, but the trooper ran back to the truck with it anyway. When he got there, he sprayed the driver, full in the face, with the chemical. The trooper knew that the chemical in the extinguisher would not kill the driver but that it would put him to sleep. It did.

The trooper found a third way out of his dilemma. It wasn't just a choice between killing the driver and ending his suffering or not killing him and letting him suffer. Kidder explains that sometimes a third way out of dilemmas will present itself, but not always. So, what do you do when there isn't a third way out? How do you choose between approaches?

No guru has a definitive answer to this question. When it comes to which approach to apply, argue our gurus, your best approach may be to try all three. For example, Velasquez suggests that you ask yourself a series of questions:

1. Does the action, as far as possible, maximize social benefits and minimize social injuries?
2. Is the action consistent with the moral rights of those whom it will affect?
3. Will the action lead to a just distribution of benefits and burdens?
4. Does the action exhibit appropriate care for the well-being of those who are closely related to or dependent upon oneself?[87]

In addition, Rushworth Kidder suggests nine steps you should follow in deciding how to respond to an ethical dilemma. We present them in Exhibit 6.3.

### EXHIBIT 6.3. Rushworth Kidder's Nine Steps for Dealing with Ethical Issues

1. **Recognize that there is a moral issue.** It is important that you distinguish moral issues from issues dealing with manners or social conventions. You need to find a balance between being a self-righteous hypermoralist who sees sin everywhere and an apathetic cynic who dismisses even the most-compelling ethical challenge as not requiring a response.
2. **Determine the actor.** You need to determine who will be affected by the decision. Most important, you need to determine your role. Are you responsible? Are you morally obligated and empowered to do something about the moral issue that has been raised?
3. **Gather the facts.** You need to find out how events have unfolded, what happened, who did what to whom, and so on. In addition, you need to peer into the future. What is likely to happen? What scenarios can you image in terms of how things may turn out?

(continued)

EXHIBIT 6.3. **(continued)**

4. **Test for right-versus-wrong issues.** Ask yourself if lawbreaking is involved. If it is, then the issue has to do with obeying the laws of the land. If the answer to "Is it illegal?" is less obviously "yes," then there are three more tests.

   ***The stench test:*** What does your gut tell you? Does something not smell right?

   ***The front-page test:*** How would you feel if what you are about to do ended up on the front page of the nation's papers tomorrow morning?

   ***The mom test:*** Would your mom do it? (Notice that the test is not: Would your dad do it?)
5. **Test for right-versus-right paradigms.** There are four common types of ethical dilemma paradigms: truth versus loyalty, self versus community, short-term versus long-term, and justice versus mercy.
6. **Apply the resolution principles.** Work through all three approaches to resolving the dilemma: ends-based, rule-based, and care-based. Your goal is not to arrive at a vote—three to nothing, two against one, etc.—but to find the line of reasoning that seems to be most relevant to the issue and that seems most persuasive given the dilemma you are facing.
7. **Investigate the "trilemma" options.** See if there is a third way out of the situation such as the option the trooper found in the case of the trapped driver.
8. **Make the decision.** Move to action. Don't be surprised if this step requires moral courage; it will.
9. **Revisit and reflect on the decision.** Go back over your decision-making process. What lessons can you learn?

*Source:* Adapted from Rushworth M. Kidder, *How Good People Make Tough Choices: Resolving the Dilemmas of Ethical Living* (New York: William Morrow, 1995), pp. 183–186.

What our gurus are offering here in response to the question of which approach you should use is called moral pluralism, the view that no single moral theory of what is right and wrong can be applied to all situations. Advocates of moral pluralism generally give you two options: (1) you can apply each approach every time you face a moral dilemma, or (2) you can pick and choose, using one approach under certain situations (they don't tell you which) and other approaches under different situations. We know that's not much help, but look at it this way: The nice thing about having so many different approaches to resolving ethical dilemmas is that, if the first approach you try doesn't yield permission for you to do what you want to do, then you can just try another and another until you get the answer you are seeking. Or would that be unethical?

Anyway, try Velasquez's four questions or, if you prefer, Kidder's nine steps on the remaining cases that we presented at the beginning of the chapter: Case #1: The Case of the Hiring Decision and Case #5: The River Blindness Case.

### Case #1: The Case of the Hiring Decision

Sheldon Laube was the chairman and CEO of a high-tech start-up company based in Santa Clara, California. He was struggling to produce his product, win customers, and most important, attract increased funding from venture capitalists and investors. A key to his strategy was to recruit the best and brightest people for every available position, and that's just what he thought he had done. The company had made a verbal offer to someone whom everyone in the company thought was an outstanding candidate for a position that was critical to their expansion plans. Then, before the person could accept the offer, a contender with truly dazzling credentials submitted a resume. Laube had the chance to grab a true superstar for his team, but he couldn't afford to hire both people. His managers wanted him to rescind the first offer so that they could bring the superstar on board.

**Here's what really happened.** Laube decided to stick by the original offer. When asked why, he said: "We made a promise to the first candidate. . . . If we're going to be the kind of company that people trust, we've got to keep our promises."[88]

### Case #5: The River Blindness Case

River blindness is a horrible disease that afflicts millions of people living along the riverbanks of the remote tropical regions of Africa and Latin America. In his presentation of this case, Manuel Velasquez describes river blindness this way:

> The disease is caused by a tiny parasitic worm that is passed from person to person by the bite of the black fly which breeds in river waters. The tiny worms burrow under a person's skin where they grow as long as two feet curled up inside ugly round nodules half an inch to an inch in diameter. Inside the nodules the worms reproduce by releasing millions of microscopic offspring called microfilaria that wiggle their way throughout the body moving beneath the skin, discoloring it as they migrate, and causing lesions and such intense itching that victims sometimes commit suicide. Eventually, the microfilaria invade the eyes and gradually blind the victim.[89]

In 1979 a research scientist at a leading U.S. drug company discovered that the drug Ivermectin, developed by his company and marketed for animals, might kill the microfilaria. Further investigation by company scientists led them to conclude that a human version of the drug might offer a low-cost, safe and effective cure for the dreaded disease, and they recommended to the chairman of the drug company that they proceed with development. Other managers argued that the company could not afford to develop the drug for the following reasons:

1. At a time when the company was experiencing increased competition, it should not spend the estimated $100 million required to develop the drug.
2. Because the victims were so poor, it was unlikely that the company could ever sell the drug for enough to recover the costs of development.
3. Even if the drug could be developed, distributing the drug would be almost impossible because the victims lived in remote areas with no access to doctors, hospitals, or pharmacies.
4. There was a heightened risk of harmful side affects if the drug was used without qualified medical supervision, as it might be in an undeveloped nation.
5. If a cheap human version of the drug was developed, it might be sold on the black market, thus undermining sales of the animal version of the drug.

**Here's what really happened.** The drug company in this case was Merck and Company. It not only went ahead with development of the drug but working with the World Health Organization, it set up the infrastructure to distribute the drug safely. Asked why the company had invested so much in developing a drug it would only have to give away, Merck's chairman, Dr. P. Roy Vagelos, said that the company had no choice. Once it suspected that it had a drug that might cure a human disease, the only ethical thing to do was to develop it.

(For more information about river blindness, visit the Merck Web site at http://www.merck.com/overview/philanthropy/9.htm/.)

## THE VIRTUES ALTERNATIVE

Let's say that you have examined all of the three approaches to resolving ethical dilemmas that our gurus offer and find none of them to your liking. Is there an alternative, a different way to approach business ethics? Yes, there is, say our gurus. Why not just try being a morally virtuous person?

"A moral virtue," writes Manuel Velasquez, "is an acquired disposition that is valued as part of the character of a morally good human being and that is exhibited in the person's habitual behavior. A person has a moral virtue when the person is disposed to behave habitually in the way, and with the reasons, feelings, and desires, that are characteristic of a morally good person."[90] In search of these characteristics, our gurus point to the theories of the Greek philosopher Aristotle and the Christian philosopher of the Middle Ages Saint Thomas Aquinas. Aristotle identified four cardinal moral virtues: courage, temperance, justice, and prudence. He argued that each of these was the middle ground between two vices: excess and deficiency. Thus courage is the middle ground between fear and cowardliness. Temperance is the middle ground between indulging too much or too little. Justice is the middle ground between giving people either more or less than they deserve. Finally, prudence is the virtue that enables one to find the middle ground. It enables a person to determine what was reasonable in any given situation.

Thomas Aquinas added three more virtues: faith, hope, and charity. These were "theological" virtues that enabled one to get closer to God. Also, Aquinas added some moral virtues that Aristotle had not included. For example, he held that humility was a virtue and that pride was a vice. (Interestingly, Aristotle had it the other way around. According to him pride was a virtue and humility was a vice. Go figure.)

In addition to the moral and theological virtues identified by Aristotle and Aquinas, our gurus add many more that they claim are important in the new age. For example, Tom Morris, author of *If Aristotle Ran General Motors,* includes such virtues as these:

| Kindness. | Decency. | Honesty. | Modesty. | Loyalty. | Sincerity. |
|---|---|---|---|---|---|
| Openness. | Reliability. | Amiability. | Tolerance. | Sensitivity. | Tactfulness. |
| Helpfulness. | Boldness. | Creativity. | Altruism. | Harmony. | Balance. |
| Integrity. | Dignity. | Humor. | Thrift. | Resiliency. | Empathy. |

The implication of virtue ethics, says Velasquez, is this:

> An action is morally right if in carrying out the action the agent exercises, exhibits, or develops a morally virtuous character, and it is morally wrong to the extent that by carrying out the action the agent exercises, exhibits, or develops a morally vicious character.[91]

Therefore, according to virtue ethics, the key question to ask when faced with a dilemma is, Will I be exhibiting or developing courage, temperance, justice, prudence, and so on by taking a course of action? If you will, then the action is ethical. If not, then it is morally wrong.

It struck us as we were reviewing Aristotle's and Aquinas's virtues, particularly those of temperance, prudence, faith, hope, and charity, that boys are rarely given virtuous names while girls are. Why is that?

## GLOBAL MORALITY

One final note before we leave the topic of ethics. Our gurus raise an issue that is important, given the global economy. When you are operating in a country other than your own, where the laws, culture, and customs are quite different from your home country, what ethical practices should you follow? Velasquez notes that people have taken two extreme positions in response to this question. Some argue that you should always adopt the practices of the host country: When in Rome, do as the Romans do. (Recall our earlier discussion of ethical relativism.) Others argue that, when you are operating in a country less developed than your own, the only ethical thing to do is to always follow the practices that are deemed ethical in the more-developed country. The counterargument to always following local practices, writes Velasquez, is that you may end up supporting policies such as apartheid or engaging in practices such as environmental pollution that in your own country would be considered unethical and maybe even illegal. On the other hand, the counterargument to always imposing the standard of the more-developed country, he says, is that you may end up doing more harm than good, thus violating the utilitarian standard. Velasquez offers the following example: "If an American company operating in Mexico pays local workers U.S. wages, it may draw all the skilled workers away from local Mexican companies that cannot afford to pay the same high salaries. As a consequence, Mexico's efforts to develop local companies may be crippled, while havoc is wreaked in local labor markets."[92]

It is clear that there are no simple solutions or easy choices, but that is the nature of ethical dilemmas. The choices must and will be made since not choosing is, in reality, a choice. That's why we felt it was important to include a chapter on ethics in this *Guru Guide*™.

In previous chapters, we discussed how we are moving increasingly into a free-market global economy in which the commodity that is sold is less a product or service than an idea and perhaps even an emotion. Business, as Bill Gates says, is now moving at the speed of thought, and the collection, storage, analysis, and use of the most-sensitive customer data is becoming not only commonplace but increasingly essential to business success. Today, all businesses, even the smallest ones, are instantly and inexpensively global and largely freed from nation-state oversight. The protection of workers that was built up over decades has been greatly diminished. These and other dramatic changes we have discussed in this *Guru Guide*™ make one thing clear: The potential for abuse and illicit behavior is greater than ever before. That makes business ethics and corporate social responsibility essential. We hope you agree.

## THE MEANING OF LIFE

You thought we had forgotten, didn't you? You want to know the meaning of life, don't you? Okay, here it is.

Tom Morris, who used to teach philosophy at Notre Dame, recalls that, at the conclusion of the very first session of his Introduction to Philosophy course one semester, he was approached by a fresh-faced 18-year-old coed who had just one question for her professor: She wanted to know what the meaning of life was. Morris says that he told her that it might take until later in the semester for him to answer that question, so if she would just hang in there for a while, he'd get back to her. Later, says Morris, he thought about the answer to that question. After all, wasn't it the most basic of all questions? As a philosopher, he knew that thoughtful people had given three possible answers.

For nihilists, the answer was that there was no meaning. Life was the outcome of an accidental collection of atoms. So, get over it. Get used it. And by the way, have a nice day.

Relativists answered the question somewhat differently. Yes, there is meaning to life, and you give it that meaning. This, says Morris, is a sort of "do-it-yourself" approach. "You want meaning? Then quit whining and give your life meaning. You don't need to worry about philosophy or cosmology or theology. It's all up to you."[93]

Finally, says Morris, there were the Absolutists. Was there a meaning to life? Absolutely, they responded. An all-powerful God endowed every life with meaning, and it was an absolute, objective level of meaning that was not dependent upon what the person did, thought, or valued. Of course, writes Morris, the Absolutist never got around to actually answering the question—What exactly was the meaning of life? He couldn't find any direct, succinct answers in their writings. Therefore, Morris decided to propose one.

Morris decided to do what others had not. He would state clearly and straightforwardly, "The meaning of life is ________________," and fill in the blank. His answer:

> The meaning of life is *creative love* [our emphasis]. Not love as an inner feeling, as a private sentimental emotion, but love as a dynamic power moving out into the world and doing something good.
>
> Loving creativity. In business and in life it means the creative building of new structures, new relationships, and new solutions, new possibilities for our world that are rooted in love, a concern for the dignity and integrity and value of others in this life. This is the bedrock, the foundation on which any meaningful life must be built. It runs through the proclamations of the great religious traditions. It defines the lives of the saints. It's the attractive force within the scope of any genuine heroism. This is the absolute standard against which the relativities of our lives all must be measured.[94]

## OUR VIEW

Is Morris right? Is creative love really the meaning of life? Naaah. Do you want to know what we think the meaning of life really is? It's finishing a book. That's the real meaning of life. Do we believe that? Naaah, but that is what we have just done. We finished a book. And by the way, so did you.

E-mail us a boyett@jboyett.com and let us know what you think. In the meantime, we wish you good ethics.

## KEY POINTS

- Business ethics encompass the way businesses treat their managers, customers, investors/owners, and employees. Corporate social responsibility encompasses business ethics and extends the concern to the way businesses treat the environment, the communities in which they operate, and their suppliers.
- Businesses today must pay attention to a triple bottom line—economic prosperity, environmental prosperity, and social justice.
- Seven revolutions are driving businesses to focus on the triple bottom line:

  1. Changing markets. Markets are more open to competition with less governmental oversight. This has given companies greater freedom of action but has also brought greater scrutiny from financial markets and customers who want businesses to pay attention to the triple bottom line.
  2. Changing values. "Soft" values such as concern for future generations are becoming as important as "hard" values such as financial performance.
  3. Increased transparency. Stakeholders today have access to much more information about the behavior of companies. Companies now live in a goldfish bowl.
  4. A demand that companies manage the product/service life cycle. Companies are being held accountable for the life cycle performance of their products and services.
  5. Partnering for triple-bottom-line performance. Companies are being forced to partner with each other and with nongovernmental organizations such as the environmental group Greenpeace to find ways to improve the life-cycle performance of their products and services.
  6. Time and the long view. Companies are being forced to manage for the long term.
  7. Revolution in the boardroom. Social and environmental activists are increasingly demanding to be heard by the board of directors of companies.

- Critics of corporate social responsibility argue that it is inappropriate for managers of businesses to use the money of stockholders to further environmental and social agendas. They say the role of business is to generate profits for shareholders.

- Proponents of corporate social responsibility argue the following:

  - The original purpose of corporations wasn't to make money for stockholders but rather to serve the public good.
  - When managers ignore social responsibilities, they end up costing stockholders more than they gain.
  - Ethical behavior and the pursuit of profits are not incompatible.
  - A corporation cannot choose whether to be part of the community. It is part of the community from the time it hires its first employee.
  - Laws are not sufficient by themselves to protect those who cannot protect themselves.
  - All stakeholders have a "stake" in companies because they can be harmed if a company behaves unethically.

- A number of international codes of ethics exist to guide corporate behavior. The most prominent are the Minnesota Principles, the CAUX Principles, the Parliament of the World's Religions Declaration toward a Global Ethic, and SA 8000.

- Although codes of ethics are helpful as general guides to proper corporate behavior, they are less useful as guides to proper behavior in specific daily situations.

- There are three classical approaches to resolving ethical dilemmas: ends-based thinking (also called utilitarianism), rule-based thinking (Kantian theory), and care-based thinking.

- No single approach to ethics is appropriate in all situations.

- Virtue ethics is an alternative to applying ends-based, rule-based, or care-based thinking to ethical situations. In virtue ethics, an action is considered morally right if in carrying out the action the person performing the action exercises, exhibits, or develops a morally virtuous character.

- People have taken two extreme positions concerning how managers should behave when conducting business in a country other than their own. Some argue that local customs and practices should always be followed even if they would be considered unethical or even illegal in one's home country. Others argue that the ethical and legal standards of the most-developed country should always be applied. The ethics gurus say neither extreme position is entirely correct.

# The Gurus

**Verna Allee** is the founder and president of Integral Performance Group and consults in the areas of knowledge management, benchmarking, and strategic development. She developed the HoloMapping™ process for understanding complex systems and served on the executive committee for the Special Interest Group for the Learning Organization of ASTD (American Society for Training and Development).

Allee is the author of *The Knowledge Evolution,* coeditor of *Elegant Solutions: The Power of Systems Thinking,* and coauthor of the *Quality Tools Matrix.* She can be reached as follows: Integral Performance Group, 500 Ygnacio Valley Road, Suite 250, Walnut Creek, CA, 94596; telephone: (925) 825-2663; fax: (925) 825-1515; e-mail: VernaAllee@compuserve.com; Internet: http://www.vernaallee.com.

**Daniel Amor** is an e-business consultant for Hewlett-Packard in Germany and author of *The E-Business (R)evolution: Living and Working in an Interconnected World.*

**Douglas Armstrong,** who received a master's degree in business administration from the University of Illinois, Urbana-Champaign, is director of marketing and digital communications at Arthur Andersen Knowledge Enterprises, where he directs the development of The Virtual Learning Network and Knowledge-Space (www.knowledgespace.com). He is also coauthor of *The Clickable Corporation.*

**Doug Bandow** is senior fellow at the Cato Institute in Washington, D.C., and a writer. He holds a bachelor of science degree in economics from Florida State University and a law degree from Stanford. He worked in the Reagan administration as a special assistant to the president. He can be contacted by e-mail at dbandow@cato.org.

**Christopher A. Bartlett** holds the MBA Class of 1996 Chair at the Harvard Business School and is chairman of the Program for Global Leadership. At Harvard since 1979, Bartlett focuses on general management issues, particularly those relating to multinational corporations. He served as chairman of the school's International Senior Management Program from 1990 to 1993. Prior to his association with Harvard, he was a marketing manager, a management consultant at McKinsey & Company's London office, and a general manager at a Baxter laboratory subsidiary in France. He continues to maintain relationships with large corporations, both as a board member and consultant.

Bartlett is the author and coauthor of numerous books, including *Transnational Management: Text, Cases, and Readings in Cross Border Management* and *Managing across Borders: The Transnational Solution,* which has been translated into nine language and produced as a video. Additional biographical information is available at http://www.hbs.edu/bios/cbartlett.html.

**Michael Berry** is the coauthor of *Data Mining Techniques: For Marketing, Sales, and Customer Support* and *Mastering Data Mining: The Art and Science of Customer Relationship Management.* He specializes in the areas of advanced data-mining techniques, data warehousing design, Internet and Intranet solutions, and the design and implementation of software applications. Berry, who holds both U.S. and E.U. citizenship, received a bachelor of arts degree in mathematics from Oberlin College.

Berry maintains an Internet site, Data Miners, at http://www.data-miners.com. He can be reached through Data Miners' Boston office at 147 Sherman Street, Suite 200, Cambridge, MA, 02140; telephone: (617) 576-0292; fax: (617) 576-0295; e-mail: info@data-miners.com. The Data Miners' New York office is located at 16 West Sixteenth Street, #12C-S, New York, NY, 10011; telephone: (212) 929-0050.

**Keki R. Bhote** is president of Keki R. Bhote Associates, a consulting company specializing in quality and productivity improvement. He received a bachelor of science in engineering from the University of Madras and a master of science in applied physics and engineering sciences from Harvard University before joining Motorola as a development engineer. He was eventually promoted to senior consultant on quality and productivity and participated in Motorola's applying for and winning the Malcolm Baldrige National Quality Award. He retired as consultant emeritus with Motorola.

Bhote's numerous publications include: *Next Operation as Customer (NOAC: How to Improve Quality, Cost, and Cycle Time in Service Operations), World Class Quality: Using Design of Experiments to Make It Happen, Beyond Customer Satisfaction to Customer Loyalty: The Key to Greater Profitability,* and *Strategic Supply Management: A Blueprint for Revitalizing the Manufacturer-Supplier Partnership.*

**Annie Brooking** specializes in the areas of strategic marketing, management, strategic planning, intellectual capital, and knowledge management. Prior to founding The Technology Broker, Brooking held executive marketing positions at Sun Microsystems and Symbolics. She also founded The Knowledge Based Systems Centre, Europe's first artificial intelligence research and consulting group and has consulted for the European Economic Community in Brussels.

Brooking is the author of *Corporate Memory: Strategies for Knowledge Management* and *Intellectual Capital: Core Assets for the Third Millennium.* She can be contacted in the United Kingdom through The Technology Broker as follows: telephone: +441-954-261199; fax: +441-954-260291; e-mail: annie@tbroker.co.uk. She maintains a Web site for The Technology Broker at http://www.tbroker.co.uk.

**Stanley A. Brown** is the leader for the Pricewaterhouse Centre of Excellence in Customer Care. His publications include *Customer Relationship Management: Linking People, Process, and Technology, Strategic Customer Care: An Evolutionary Approach to Increasing Customer Value and Profitability,* and *Breakthrough Customer Service: Best Practices of Leaders in Customer Support.* He can be reached by e-mail at stan.a.brown@ca.pwcglobal.com or through the Centre for Excellence at (416) 869-2990.

**Lowell Bryan** has been a consultant with McKinsey & Company since 1975 and leads their Global Financial Institutions practice. His publications include *Bankrupt: Restoring the Health and Profitability of Our Banking System, Market Unbound: Unleashing Global Capitalism,* and *Race for the World: Strategies to Build a Great Global Firm.*

Bryan holds a bachelor of arts degree from Davidson College and a master of business administration degree from the Harvard Business School.

**Jeffrey Coors,** of the Coors Brewery family, was president of ACX Technologies, which recently split into CoorsTek and Graphic Packaging International Corporation.

**Jay Curry** is an independent consultant in the area of direct marketing and chairman of the Customer Marketing Institute. Born and raised in New York State, Curry received a bachelor's degree from Bates College and a master of science from Boston University School of Public Communication. He is the cofounder of the Amsterdam-based consulting company MSP Associates (see http://mspassociates.com), author of *Know Your Customer* and *Customer Marketing: How to Increase the Profitability of Your Customer Base,* and coauthor of *The Customer Marketing Method.* He can be reached as follows: MSP Associates bv, Oranje Nassaulaan 35, 1075 AJ Amsterdam; telephone: +31 20-6793077; telefax: +31 20-6792224; e-mail: info@MSPAssociates.com.

**John Dalla Costa** is president of the Center of Ethical Orientation, a consulting firm that specializes in global business ethics. In addition to his regular contributions to *The Financial Post Magazine* in Canada and *Marketing Weekly* in the United Kingdom, he is the author of *Working Wisdom: The Ultimate Value in the New Economy* and *The Ethical Imperative: Why Moral Leadership Is Good Business.*

**Thomas H. Davenport** is the Curtis Mathes Fellowship Professor and director of the Information Management Program at the University of Texas at Austin. Prior to joining the faculty at the University of Texas, he was a partner in Ernst & Young's Center for Information Technology and Strategy and served as director of information technology research at McKinsey & Company and at CSC Index. He also taught at Boston University, Harvard Business School, Harvard University, and the University of Chicago. He is currently a professor in the information systems department of the Boston University School of Management, through which he can be reached as follows: Boston University School of Management, 595 Commonwealth Avenue, Boston, MA, 02215; telephone: (617) 353-4155; fax: (617) 353-5244; e-mail: tdav@bu.edu.

Davenport's publications include *The Information Imperative: Managing the Impact of Technology on Businesses and People, Process Innovation: Re-engineering Work through Information Technology, Information Ecology: Mastering the Information and Knowledge Environment,* and *Working Knowledge: How Organizations Manage What They Know*. His articles have been published in the *Harvard Business Review, Management Review,* and *Sloan Management Review*. He is also a regular contributor to *CIO* and *Information Week* magazines, and he is one of the founding editors of *Knowledge Inc*.

**Frank W. Davis Jr.,** coauthor of *Customer Responsive Management: The Flexible Advantage,* is a professor of marketing, logistics, and information technology at the University of Tennessee, Knoxville. He can be reached as follows: 316 SMC, College of Business Administration, The University of Tennessee, Knoxville, TN, 37996; telephone: (423) 974-1648; fax: (423) 974-1932; e-mail: fsdavis@utk.edu.

**Stan Davis** is senior research fellow with Ernst & Young's Center for Business Innovation in Cambridge, Massachusetts. He is the author of eight books, including *Blur: The Speed of Change in the Connected Economy,* which he coauthored with Christopher Meyer, *2020 Vision, The Monster under the Bed,* and *Future Perfect,* which received the Tom Peter's Book of the Decade Award. He can be reached by e-mail at stanmdavis@aol.com.

**George S. Day** is the Geoffrey T. Boisi Professor of Marketing at the Wharton School of Management of the University of Pennsylvania. He is also director of the Huntsman Center for Global Competition and Innovation and director of the Emerging Technologies Management Research Program. He received a bachelor of science degree from the University of British Columbia, Canada, a master of business administration from the University of Western Ontario, Canada, and a doctorate from Columbia University. Prior to joining the Wharton faculty in 1991, he taught at the University of Toronto, the International Management Development Institute (IMEDE), Switzerland, Stanford University, and the University of Western Ontario. He also held visiting appointments at the Massachusetts Institute of Technology; Harvard University; and the London Business School.

Day's publications include *Wharton on Managing Emerging Technologies, The Market Driven Organization: Understanding, Attracting, and Keeping Valuable Customers, Wharton on Dynamic Competitive Strategy, Market Driven Strategy: Processes for Creating Value,* and *Marketing Research.*

**Peter Drucker** is the Marie Rankin Clarke Professor of Social Science and Management at The Claremont Graduate School. He has served as a consultant to government, public-sector organizations, and corporations. His 20-plus books have been translated into more than 20 languages.

Drucker's extensive publication list includes two novels, an autobiography, several volumes of essays, and numerous magazine and journal articles, in addition to his well-known books. They include *Management: Tasks, Responsibilities, Practices, The Practice of Management, Concept of the Corporation,* and *Management Challenges for the Twenty-first Century.* He can be reached by e-mail at druckerp @cgs.edu.

**Leif Edvinsson,** coauthor of *Intellectual Capital: Realizing Your Company's True Value by Finding Its Hidden Brainpower,* is vice president and corporate director of Intellectual Capital at Skandia of Stockholm, Sweden. The University of California, Berkeley, graduate also served as senior vice president for training and development of S-E Bank and president and chairman of Consultus AB, a Stockholm-based consulting company.

**Farid Elashmawi,** coauthor of *Multicultural Management 2000,* is president of Global Success, a San Jose–based consulting company that specializes in multicultural management and corporate culture reengineering. He has consulted with multinational corporations around the world, including Sony, Hitachi, NEC, Apple Computer, Hewlett-Packard, and others. He holds a bachelor of science degree in electrical engineering from Alexandria University, a master of business administration from Santa Clara University, and a doctorate in nuclear engineering from North Carolina State University. Elashmawi can be reached through Global Success as follows: Global Success, 111 West St. John Street, Suite 706, San Jose, CA, 95113; telephone: (408) 286-8013; fax: (408) 286-3468; e-mail: farid@ix.netcom.com.

**John Elkington** is a cofounder of the environmental consulting group SustainAbility and an acknowledged expert in the areas of sustainable development and environmental strategies in business. In addition to his work with SustainAbility, Elkington is a member of numerous environmental committees and advisory boards. For a detailed description of his environmental activities, see the Internet site http://www.sustainability.co.uk.

Elkington is the author or coauthor of more than 30 books, including the bestselling *Green Consumer Guide* and *Cannibals with Forks: The Triple Bottom Line of Twenty-first Century Business.*

**Juanita Ellis** holds a bachelor of science degree in business and management and a master's degree in information systems and is working on a doctorate in electrical engineering and communications at George Washington University. She has lectured at the University of Maryland and Southern Methodist University (SMU), worked with Lotus Consulting, and is the coauthor of *The E-Commerce Book.*

Ellis and her coauthor Steffano Korper founded SMU's Networking Technologies Program and developed the E-Commerce Program, consisting of six courses that focus on Web/commerce server, back-end integration, credit-card verification integration, firewall security, and Java technology.

**Ralph Estes,** an accounting professor emeritus at the American University, is also a cofounder of the Center for the Advancement of Public Policy. His extensive publication list includes *Tyranny of the Bottom Line* and *Corporate Social Accounting.* He can be reached through the center as follows: Center for Advancement in Public Policy, 1735 S Street, NW, Washington, DC, 20009; telephone: (202) 797-0606; fax: (202) 265-6245.

**Philip Evans** was educated at Cambridge University and the Harvard Business School, where he later became a Harkness Fellow in the Economics Department. He is now a senior vice president and consultant with the Boston Consulting Group, serving as a coleader of its Media and Convergence Practice, and is coauthor of *Blown to Bits: How the New Economics of Information Transforms Strategy.*

**Walter Forbes** is a venture capitalist and author of *The Future of the Electronic Marketplace.*

**Jane Fraser** has been a consultant with McKinsey & Company since 1994, focusing on global strategic issues for financial institutions. Born and raised in Scotland, she holds a master's degree in economics from Girton College, Cambridge, and a master of business administration from the Harvard Business School. Prior to joining McKinsey, she worked for Goldman, Sachs in the United Kingdom and for Asesores Bursatiles in Spain. She is the coauthor of *Race for the World: Strategies for Building a Global Firm.*

**Cyrus F. Freidheim,** a consultant with Booz-Allen, is the author of *The Trillion-Dollar Enterprise: How the Alliance Revolution Will Transform Global Business.*

**Hilary F. French** is vice president for research at the nonprofit policy research organization Worldwatch Institute, where she focuses on the role of international institutions in environmental protection and sustainable development. In addition to her book, *Vanishing Borders: Protecting the Planet in the Age of Globalization,* she has written six Worldwatch Papers and coauthored nine of the institute's annual *State of the World* reports.

French holds degrees from Dartmouth College and from the Fletcher School of Law and Diplomacy. Prior to joining the Worldwatch Institute, she interned with the United Nations Development Programme in Côte d'Ivoire and with the United Nations Institute for Disarmament Research in Geneva.

**Milton Friedman** is a Nobel Prize–winning economist and senior research fellow at the Hoover Institution at Stanford University. He is also a professor emeritus of economics at the University of Chicago and worked as a member of the research staff of the National Bureau of Economic Research. Friedman has written widely on the subject of preserving and extending individual freedom. He holds a bachelor's degree from Rutgers University, a master's degree from the University of Chicago, and a doctorate from Columbia University.

**Thomas L. Friedman** is a Pulitzer Prize–winning foreign-affairs correspondent for the *New York Times* and author of the two best-selling books: *From Beirut to Jerusalem,* winner of the National Book Award in 1988, and *The Lexus and the Olive Tree.* He was educated at Brandeis University and St. Anthony's College, Oxford.

**Richard Gascoyne** is coauthor of *The Corporate Internet Planning Guide.*

**Bill Gates** is cofounder of Microsoft, Inc., and author of numerous books on management and technology, including *Business @ the Speed of Thought: Using a Digital Nervous System, Business @ the Speed of Thought: Succeeding in the Digital Economy, What Will Be: How the New World of Information Will Change Our Lives,* and *The Road Ahead.*

**J. Russell Gates** is a partner in Arthur Andersen LLP. He leads that company's computer risk-management practice in North America and the worldwide electronic commerce risk consulting and assurance initiative. He is coauthor of *The Clickable Corporation.*

**Sumantra Ghoshal** is the Robert P. Bauman Professor of Strategic Leadership at the London Business School, where his research concentrates on global strategy, corporate entrepreneurship, and corporate renewal. Formerly professor of business policy at INSEAD (European Institute of Business Administration) in Fontainebleau, France, Ghoshal is a member of the editorial boards of many journals, including the *Strategic Management Journal,* the *Academy of Management Review,* the *European Management Journal,* and the *Journal of International Business.* His most recent books include *The Individualized Corporation, The Differentiated Network, Organization Theory and the Multinational Corporation,* and *Managing across Borders: The Transnational Solution,* which he coauthored with Christopher Bartlett. Ghoshal can be reached by e-mail at sghoshal@london.edu.

**Blair Gibb,** coauthor of *When Good Companies Do Bad Things: Responsibility and Risk in an Age of Globalization,* is a principal at the Global Business Network (GBN) and former planning officer for Amnesty International. She can be reached through GBN as follows: Global Business Network, 5900-X Hollis

Street, Emeryville, CA, 94608; telephone: (510) 547-6822; fax: (510) 547-8510; Internet site: http://www.gbn.org.

**James H. Gilmore,** a graduate of the Wharton School of Management of the University of Pennsylvania, began his career with Procter & Gamble, the Cleveland Consulting Associates, and Computer Science Corporation, where he led CSC Consulting's process innovation practice. He serves on the faculty of The Institutes for Organization Management for the U.S. Chamber of Commerce and works with various organizations to foster innovative thinking. He is a cofounder of Strategic Horizons LLP, and coauthor with B. Joseph Pine II of numerous articles on business strategy and innovation. The writing team has published articles in the *Harvard Business Review,* the *Wall Street Journal, Strategy and Leadership,* the *Journal of Cost Management, CIO,* and *Chief Executive.* They are also coauthors of *The Experience Economy: Work Is Theater and Every Business a Stage,* and *Markets of One: Creating Customer-Unique Value through Mass Customization.*

**Seth Godin** is vice president of direct marketing at Yahoo! He is also the founder of Yoyodyne, the first company to use on-line direct-mail marketing, which Yahoo! subsequently bought. Godin, who graduated from Tufts University with a degree in computer science and philosophy and from Stanford Business School, worked as a brand manager at Spinnaker Software along with Arthur C. Clarke and Michael Crichton.

Godin's publications include: *Permission Marketing: Turning Strangers into Friends, and Friends into Customers, The Guerrilla Marketing Handbook, Guerilla Marketing for the Home-Based Business, Emarketing,* and *Get What You Deserve! How to Guerrilla Market Yourself.* He can be reached by e-mail at Seth@permission.com.

**Ian Gordon** is a management consultant and director of TCI Convergence Management Consultants in Toronto. Prior to helping found TCI, he held senior management positions with consumer products and software-marketing companies, and he was a senior partner with Ernst & Young, Toronto. Gordon has written more than 40 articles. His books include *Beat the Competition: How to Use Competitive Intelligence to Develop Winning Business Strategies, Relationship Marketing: New Strategies, Techniques and Technologies to Win the Customers You Want and Keep Them Forever,* and *Competitor Targeting: A Strategic Approach to Winning the Battle for Market Share.* He can be reached as follows: telephone: (416) 920-8883; fax: (416) 515-2097; or e-mail: Rel82ian@aol.com.

**Vijay Govindarajan** is Earl C. Daum 1924 Professor of International Business at the Amos Tuck School of Business Administration at Dartmouth College. He can be reached by e-mail at Vijay.Govindarajan@dartmouth.edu.

**C. Jackson Grayson Jr.** is founder and chairman of the American Productivity & Quality Center (APQC) and coauthor with Carla O'Dell of *American Business: A Two Minute Warning* and *If Only We Knew What We Know.* He can be contacted through the APQC offices as follows: APQC, 123 North Post Oak Lane, 3rd Floor, Houston, TX, 77024; telephone (inside US): (800) 776-9676; (outside US): (713) 681-4020; fax: (713) 681-8578; e-mail: apqcinfo@apqc.org. Also see http://www.apqc.org.

**Alan Greenspan,** chairman of the Federal Reserve Board, showed an early propensity for numbers and music. His mother reportedly showed off her five-year-old son's mathematical ability by having him add three-digit numbers in his head. While in high school, Greenspan played clarinet and tenor saxophone. He later attended the Julliard School of Music in New York, then played with the Henry Jerome swing band for one year before entering New York University's School of Commerce. After graduating summa cum laude with a degree in economics, he received a master's degree and doctorate from New York University.

Greenspan and bond trader William Townsend opened an economic consulting company in the mid-1950s, but it was a chance encounter with an old swing-band friend, Leonard Garment, that set him on his journey in government service. In 1966 Garment, an adviser to Richard Nixon's presidential campaign, introduced Greenspan to the candidate. Greenspan subsequently became Nixon's director of policy research and chairman of the Council of Economic Advisers.

During the Carter administration, Greenspan returned to his consulting firm, but he was recalled to public service as Ronald Reagan's chairman of the Commission on Social Security Reform. He was tapped in 1987 to replace Federal Chairman Paul Volcker and has continued to serve in that position since.

**Anil K. Gupta** is professor of strategy and international business at the University of Maryland, College Park. He can be reached by e-mail at agupta@mbs.umd.edu.

**John Hagel III** is a principle in McKinsey & Company, where he serves as leader of the company's Global Electronic Commerce Practice. Prior to joining McKinsey, Hagel was senior vice president for strategic planning at Atari, president of a turnkey computer systems company (Sequoia Group), and a consultant with Boston Consulting Group. He has published articles in the *Harvard Business Review* and the *Wall Street Journal* and is the author of both legal and business books, including *Net Gain: Expanding Markets through Virtual Communities* and *Net Worth: Shaping Markets When Customers Make the Rules.* He holds a bachelor's degree from Wesleyan University, a master's degree in business administration from Harvard Business School, a law degree from Harvard Law School, and a graduate degree from Oxford University. Hagel can be reached through McKinsey & Company's Internet site: http://www.mckinsey.com.

**Philip R. Harris** is a management and organizational psychologist and president of Harris International. He has written or edited more than 40 books and published over 200 journal articles and is coauthor of *Multicultural Management 2000.* He can be reached through Harris International as follows: Harris International, 2702 Costebelle Drive, La Jolla, CA, 92037; telephone: (619) 453-2271; Internet: http://www.simplenet.com/harris.

**John M. Hood,** author of *The Heroic Enterprise: Business and the Common Good,* is president of the Locke Foundation and a former fellow at the Heritage Foundation. He holds a graduate degree in journalism from the University of North Carolina, Chapel Hill, and worked as a reporter for the *New Republic*. Hood can be reached as follows: The John Locke Foundation, P.O. Box 17822, Raleigh, NC, 27619; telephone: (919) 847-2690; fax: (919) 847-8371; e-mail: jhood@johnlocke.org.

**Michael J. D. Hopkins,** author of *The Planetary Bargain: Corporate Social Responsibility Comes to Age,* is an economist and cofounder of MHC International, Ltd., a research and consulting company that focuses on the measurement of corporate social responsibility. He can be reached by e-mail at mjdhopkins@mhcinternational.com.

**Frances Horibe** is president of VisionArts, Inc., a consulting company that specializes in the area of intellectual capital. She has also served as director-general of strategic planning and international marketing for Transport Canada and as vice president for quality and customer care for the TQM consulting firm Achieve International. She holds a bachelor's degree in psychology from McGill University and a master's degree in psychology from the University of Western Ontario and is the author of *Managing Knowledge Workers.* She can be reached through her Web site at http://www.magma.ca/~fhoribe/.

**Joel Hyatt** is a member of the California Public Utilities Commission and teaches entrepreneurship at the Stanford University Graduate School of Business. He was a cofounder and senior partner of Hyatt Legal Services and CEO of Hyatt Legal Plans, Inc. Hyatt also coauthored *The Long Boom: A Vision for the Coming Age of Prosperity.*

**Jean-Pierre Jeannet,** author of *Managing with a Global Mindset,* is F. W. Olin Distinguished Professor of Global Business and director of the W. F. Glavin Center for Global Entrepreneurial Management at Babson College and holds a dual appointment at IMD (formerly IMEDE) in his native Switzerland. He holds a master of business administration and doctorate from the University of Massachusetts, concentrating his research in the areas of international and global marketing, global strategies, global and strategic thinking, market orientation, and competitive marketing strategies.

**Rolf Jensen** is the director of the future-oriented think tank The Copenhagen Institute for Future Studies and advisor to The Futures Council of the Conference Board, Europe. He is a member of the World Future Society and author of *The Dream Society: How the Coming Shift from Information to Imagination Will Transform your Business.*

**Thomas O. Jones** is the president of Elm Square Technologies and a former senior lecturer in the Harvard Business School's service management interest group. He can be reached through the Internet site: http://www.elmsquare.com.

**Bruce Judson** is the founder and editor of *Bruce Judson's Grow Your Profits* and cofounder of Time Warner's Pathfinder Web site. He is a graduate of Dartmouth College and holds degrees from the Yale Law School and the Yale School of Management. Judson's publications include *NetMarketing: How Your Business Can Profit from the Online Revolution* and *Hyper Wars: Eleven Strategies for Survival and Profit in the Era of Online Business.* He can be contacted through his Internet site: http://www.growyourprofits.com.

**Ravi Kalakota** is the founder and CEO of e-Business Strategies, director of the Center for Digital Commerce, and a chaired professor of information systems at Georgia State University. He received a doctorate in information systems from the University of Texas at Austin, a master's degree in computer science from the University of Hawaii, and a bachelor of technology in computer science from Osmania University, India. Kalakota is the coauthor of *Frontiers of Electronic Commerce, Electronic Commerce: A Manager's Guide,* and *E-Business: Roadmap for Success,* and the editor of *Readings in Electronic Commerce.*

**Rosabeth Moss Kanter** is a chaired professor of business administration at the Harvard Business School and author or coauthor of 13 books, including the bestsellers *Men and Women of the Corporation, The Change Masters, When Giants Learn to Dance,* and *World Class: Thriving Locally in the Global Economy.* She served as editor of the *Harvard Business Review* from 1989 until 1992, holds 19 honorary doctoral degrees, and was named to the lists of "100 most important women in America" and "50 most powerful women in the world."

In addition to her teaching and research responsibilities, Kanter has consulted with such prominent international companies as IBM, Monsanto, British Airways, Bell Atlantic, and GAP, Inc. She can be reached by e-mail at rkanter@hbs.edu.

**Guy Kawasaki** is founder, CEO, and chairman of garage.com, an Internet site that helps entrepreneurs and investors create, build, and fund promising early-stage technology companies. Prior to founding garage.com in 1997, he served as chief evangelist of Apple Computer (1995–1998) and as CEO of Fog City Software, Inc. He holds a bachelor's degree from Stanford University and a master of business administration from the University of California, Los Angeles.

Kawasaki is a columnist for *Forbes Magazine* and author or coauthor of seven books, including *Rules for Revolutionaries, New Rules for the New Economy: Ten Radical Strategies for a Connected World,* and *How to Drive Your Competition Crazy: Creating Disruption for Fun and Profit.* He can be reached through the Internet site http://www.garage.com or through garage.com's corporate offices at 420 Florence Avenue, Palo Alto, CA, 94301; telephone: (650) 470-0950; fax: (650) 470-0940.

**Kevin Kelly** is executive editor of *Wired Magazine,* which won the National Magazine Award for General Excellence in 1994 and the National Magazine Award for Design in 1996. Prior to his association with *Wired,* he was the editor and publisher of the *Whole Earth Review* (1984–1990) and was a founding board member of WELL, a teleconferencing system. Kelly is also the author of *Out of Control: The New Biology of Machines, Social Systems and the Economic World* and *New Rules for the New Economy.* For more information, see his Web site, http://www.well.com/user/kk. He can be reached at *Wired* as follows: Wired, 520 Third Street, San Francisco, CA, 94107; telephone: (415) 222-6242; fax: (415) 222-6249; e-mail: kk@well.com.

**Rushworth M. Kidder** is the founder of the Institute for Global Ethics. He is also a former columnist for the *Christian Science Monitor* and author of *Shared Values for a Troubled World: Conversations with Men and Women of Conscience* and *How Good People Make Tough Choices.* Kidder can be reached as follows: Institute for Global Ethics, 11 Main Street, P.O. Box 563, Camden, ME, 04843; telephone: (207) 236-6658; fax: (207) 236-4014; e-mail: webethics@globalethics.org.

**Philip J. Kitchen,** coauthor of *Communicating Globally,* is the Martin Naughton Professor of Business Strategy at the Queen's University School of Management, Belfast, and specializes in marketing. Before joining the faculty at Queen's, he worked at Strathclyde and Keele Universities in the United Kingdom.

**Steffano Korper,** who holds a bachelor's degree in business and management and a master's degree in information systems, is an adjunct professor of electrical engineering at Southern Methodist University (SMU). He has also lectured for networking and telecommunications courses at the Universities of Texas and Maryland.

Korper coauthored *The E-Commerce Book: Building the E-Empire* with Juanita Ellis, with whom he founded SMU's Networking Technologies Program and developed the E-Commerce Program, consisting of six courses that focus on Web/commerce server, back-end integration, credit-card verification integration, firewall security, and Java technology.

Afterward, he accepted a position as director of MIS with Wyndham Hotels and Resorts. He is currently vice president of e-commerce solutions at Going Beyond E-commerce Technologies LLC.

**David Kosiur** is a freelance writer and networking consultant. His articles have appeared in such publications as *PC Week, Sunworld Online, ZD Internet Magazine,* and *Inter@ctive Week.* He is also the author of *Understanding Electronic Commerce* and *Ip Multicasting: The Complete Guide to Interactive Corporate Networks.*

**Philip Kotler** is the S.C. Johnson & Son Distinguished Professor of International Marketing at Northwestern University's Kellogg Graduate School of Management. Professor Kotler received a master's degree in economics from the University of Chicago and a doctorate in economics from the Massachusetts Institute of Technology. Among his many awards are the American Marketing Association's Distinguished Marketing Educator Award and being chosen Leader in Marketing Thought by the Academic Members of the American Management Association.

Kotler's extensive publications list includes *Marketing Management and Strategy, Kotler on Marketing: How to Create, Win, and Dominate Markets, Value-Added Public Relations: The Secret Weapon of Integrated Marketing, Principles of Marketing,* and *The New Marketing Era: Marketing to the Imagination in a Technology-Driven World.* He can be reached by e-mail at p-kotler@nwu.ed or through the graduate school at Kellogg Graduate School of Management, 2001 Sheridan Road, Leverone/Andersen Complex, Evanston, IL, 60208-2001; telephone: (847) 491-3300.

**Dorothy Leonard** is the William J. Abernathy Professor of Business Administration at the Harvard Business School and a faculty member of Harvard Programs on Enhancing Corporate Creativity and Managing International Collaboration. Prior to accepting her position at Harvard, Leonard taught at the Sloan School of Management at the Massachusetts Institute of Technology. She has also conducted executive courses at and consulted with such organizations and governments as Harvard, the Massachusetts Institute of Technology, Digital, AT&T, Johnson & Johnson, Kodak, and Monsanto and the governments of Sweden, Jamaica, and the United States.

Leonard has written numerous articles for books and journals and is the author of *The Wellsprings of Knowledge* and *When Sparks Fly.* She can be reached by e-mail at dleonard@hbs.edu.

**Peter Leyden** is the former managing editor of *Wired Magazine,* was a special correspondent in Asia for *Newsweek,* and has written about technology, economics, politics, and contemporary history since the mid-1980s. He is a coauthor of *The Long Boom: A Vision for the Coming Age of Prosperity.*

**Gordon Linoff** is a founder of Data Miners, a data-mining consulting company, and coauthor of *Data Mining: The Art and Science of Customer Relationship Management* and *Data Mining Techniques: For Marketing, Sales, and Customer Support.* He can be reached through the Data Miner's Internet site: http://www.data-miners.com.

**Alex Lowy,** managing partner and cofounder of the Alliance for Converging Technologies, now Digital 4Sight, is a recognized management consultant and educator. This coauthor of *Digital Capital: Harnessing the Power of Business Webs* and *Blueprint to the Digital Economy: Wealth Creation in the Era of E-Business* received a bachelor's degree in psychology from McGill University, a bachelor's degree in applied social science and philosophy from Concordia University, and a master's degree in environmental studies from York University. He can be reached through Digital 4Sight at 360 Adelaide Street W, 4th Floor, Toronto, ON, M5V 1R7; telephone: (416) 979-7899; fax: (416) 979-7616; Internet site http://www.actnet.com.

**Edward Luttwak,** a senior fellow at the Center for Strategic and International Studies in Washington, D.C., is a well-known strategy consultant and writer. Born in Transylvania and educated in Italy, England, and the United States, he is the author of the best-selling book *Turbo-Capitalism: Winners and Losers in the Global Economy.*

**Michael S. Malone** is an accomplished high-tech reporter and coauthor of *Intellectual Capital: Realizing Your Company's True Value by Finding Its Hidden Brainpower* and *The Virtual Corporation*. In addition, he has written for the *Wall Street Journal,* the *New York Times, Upside,* and *Fast Company,* and he hosts *Malone,* an interview series on public television.

**Karl B. Manrodt** is an assistant professor of logistics at the University of Tennessee, Knoxville, and coauthor of *Customer Responsive Management: The Flexible Advantage*. He can be reached by mail as follows: 315 SMC, College of Business Administration, The University of Tennessee, Knoxville, TN, 37996. He can also be reached as follows: telephone: (423) 974-5311; fax: (423) 974-8898; e-mail: kmanrodt@utk.edu.

**Chuck Martin** was the founding publisher and chief operating officer of *Interactive Age,* the first publication to be launched electronically. Prior to that venture, he was an associate publisher of *Information Week* and editor-in-chief of *Personal Computing*. He was also corporate technology editor for Time, Inc., worked for five daily newspapers, and hosted a daily television show on the Financial News Network (FNN).

Following the establishment of *Interactive Age,* Martin became vice president for publishing and advertising in IBM's telecommunications and media industry solution unit, after which he became president of the Net Future Institute, which focuses on the future of electronic commerce. He is an associate of the Alliance for Converging Technologies, now Digital 4Sight, president of the Digital Estate Group LLC, and author of *The Digital Estate: Strategies for Competing, Surviving, and Thriving in an Internetworked World* and *Net Future: The Seven Cybertrends That Will Drive Your Business, Create New Wealth, and Define Your Future.* He can be reached by e-mail at chuckmartin@worldnet.att.net; through the Internet site http://www.netfutureinstitute.com; or through the Institute at (603) 964-3930.

**Regis McKenna** is chairman of the management and marketing consulting firm the McKenna Group. He is also an independent investor in Web start-ups such as Weblogic (www.weblogic.com), Graham Technologies (www.graham.com), and Real Time Knowledge Systems (www.rtks.com). McKenna worked in several entrepreneurial start-ups including America Online, Apple, Compaq, Genentech, Intel, Lotus, and Microsoft.

McKenna's books include *The Regis Touch: Who's Afraid of Big Blue?, Relationship Marketing: Successful Strategies for the Age of the Customer,* and *Real Time: Preparing for the Age of the Never Satisfied Customer.* He can be reached as follows: The McKenna Group International, 5587 School Road, West Bend, WI, 53095; telephone: (800) 562-4536; voice mail: (262) 306-7355; fax: (262) 306-7357; e-mail: Regis@mckenna-group.com. The company also maintains an Internet site at http://www.mckennagroup.com.

**Christopher Meyer** is director of the Ernst & Young Center for Business Innovation and president of the Ernst & Young subsidiary Bios GP, Inc., Ernst & Young's attempt to apply complexity theory to business. Meyer's expertise is in the area of the evolution of the information economy and its impact on business. He is a coauthor of *Blur: The Speed of Change in the Connected Economy* and *Future Wealth* and author of *Fast Cycle Time: How to Align Purpose, Strategy, and Structure for Speed* and *Relentless Growth: How Silicon Valley Innovative Strategies Can Work in Your Business.*

**John Micklethwait** is in charge of coverage of the United States for *The Economist,* where he previously worked as New York bureau chief and business editor. He is a coauthor of *A Future Perfect: The Challenge and Hidden Promise of Globalization* and has written for the *Los Angeles Times,* the *Boston Globe,* and the *New York Times.* He can be reached by e-mail at http://www.afutureperfect.com or http://www.johnmicklethwait.com.

**Mary Modahl** is vice president of marketing at Forrester Research, Inc., and author of *Now or Never: How Companies Must Change Today to Win the Battle for Internet Consumers.* She can be contacted through Forrester's Internet site at http://www.forrester.com.

**James Moore** is founder and chairman of GeoPartners Research, a strategy consulting and investment firm known for scenario development, strategic planning, and technology assessment. He is the author of *The Death of Competition: Leadership and Strategy in the Age of Business Ecosystems* and writes a regular column for tech-oriented *Upside.* Moore received his doctorate in human development from Harvard University and conducted research on strategy and technology at

Stanford and the Harvard Business School. He is a visiting professor at the University of Virginia Darden Graduate School of Business.

**Tom Morris,** a former professor of philosophy at the University of Notre Dame, is the founder and chairman of the Morris Institute for Human Values. In addition to his schedule as a public speaker, he is the author of *True Success: A New Philosophy of Excellence* and *If Aristotle Ran General Motors: The New Soul of Business.* He is a graduate of the University of North Carolina, Chapel Hill, and holds a doctorate in both philosophy and religious studies from Yale University. He can be reached as follows: Morris Institute for Human Values, PMB 210, 1319 Military Cutoff Road, Wilmington, NC, 28405; telephone: (910) 256-6119; fax: (910) 256-6575; e-mail: tmorris@morisinstitute.com.

**Walid Mougayar** is president of the management consulting firm CYBERManagement, Inc., and author of *Opening Digital Markets: Battle Plans and Business Strategies for Internet Commerce.* He earned a bachelor's degree from the University of Washington, Seattle, and is a graduate of the Executive Management Program at the University of Western Ontario, Canada. Before founding CYBERManagement, he was national sales manager, national marketing manager, business process reengineering manager, and information highways program manager for Hewlett-Packard (1982–1995). His other publications include *The Business Internet and Intranets: A Manager's Guide to Key Terms and Concepts* and *How to Be a Successful Computer Consultant.* He can be reached as follows: CYBERManagement, Inc., 151 Bloor Street West, Suite 470, Toronto, ON, M5S 1S4; telephone: (416) 929-1014; fax: (416) 929-1552; e-mail: walid@cyberm.com.

**Frederick Newell** is a pioneer in the field of database marketing and a partner in the international consulting firm Seklemian/Newell. His books include *Loyalty.com: Customer Relationship Management in the New Era of Internet Marketing* and *The New Rules of Marketing: How to Use One-to-One Relationship Marketing to Be the Leader in Your Industry.*

**Ikujiro Nonaka** is a professor at Hitotsubashi University and coauthor of *The Knowledge-Creating Company: How Japanese Companies Create the Dynamics of Innovation.* His other works include *Enabling Knowledge Creation: How to Unlock the Mystery of Tacit Knowledge and Release the Power of Innovation, Knowledge Creation: A Source of Value,* and *Relentless: The Japanese Way of Marketing.*

**Carla O'Dell** is president of the American Productivity & Quality Center (APQC) and director of the center's International Benchmarking Clearinghouse. She is coauthor of *American Business: A Two Minute Warning* and *If Only We Knew What We Know.* She can be contacted through the APQC offices as follows: APQC, 123 North Post Oak Lane, 3rd Floor, Houston, TX, 77024; telephone (inside US):

(800) 776-9676; (outside US): (713) 681-4020; fax: (713) 681-8578; e-mail: apqcinfo@apqc.org. Also see http://www.apqc.org.

**Jeremy Oppenheim,** a coauthor of *Race for the World: Strategies to Build a Great Global Firm,* is a consultant in the London offices of McKinsey & Company, specializing in globalization. He holds a master's degree in law and economics from Trinity College, Cambridge, and a master's degree from the Kennedy School of Government. Before joining McKinsey, Oppenheim worked as a senior economist with the World Bank.

**Jeff Papows** is the former CEO of Lotus Development Corporation and author of *Enterprise.com: Market Leadership in the Information Age.*

**Don Peppers** is an independent consultant and speaker in the areas of marketing technology, business development, and customer retention and cofounder of Peppers and Rogers Group. His publications include *Enterprise One-to-One: Tools for Competing in the Interactive Age, The One-to-One Fieldbook: The Complete Toolkit for Implementing a One-to-One Marketing Program, The One-to-One Future: Building Relationships One Customer at a Time,* and *The One-to-One Manager: Real-World Lessons in Customer Relationship Management.*

Peppers can be contacted through his Web site, http://www.1to1.com. He can also be contacted as follows: Peppers and Rogers Group / Marketing 1to1, 470 West Avenue, Stamford, CT, 06902; telephone: (203) 316-5121; fax: (203) 316-5126; e-mail: Peppers@1to1.com.

**Jeffrey Pfeffer** is Thomas D. Dee Professor of Organizational Behavior in the Graduate School of Business, Stanford University. He holds bachelor's and master's degrees from Carnegie-Mellon University and a doctorate in business from Stanford. Prior to joining the faculty at Stanford, he taught at the Universities of Illinois and California, Berkeley, and was a visiting professor at the Harvard Business School. He is the author of *The Human Equation, New Directions for Organization Theory, Organizations and Organization Theory, Power in Organizations,* and *Organizational Design* and coauthor of *The External Control of Organizations* and most recently *The Knowing-Doing Gap.* His complete publications list includes more than a hundred articles and book chapters. Pfeffer can be reached through Stanford University as follows: Graduate School of Business, Mail Code 5015, GSB L351, Stanford, CA, 94305-5015; telephone: (650) 723-2915; e-mail: pfeffer_Jeffrey@gsb.stanford.edu.

**B. Joseph Pine II** is a cofounder of Strategic Horizons LLP, guest lecturer, award-winning author of *Mass Customization: The New Frontier in Business Competition,* and coauthor of *The Experience Economy: Work Is Theater and Every Business a Stage.* Prior to founding Strategic Horizons, he held several positions with IBM and contributed to IBM Rochester's (Minnesota) winning application for the Malcolm Baldrige National Quality Award.

Pine is a member of the faculty of the Penn State Executive Education Program and the Executive Education faculty of the Anderson Graduate School of Management, University of California, Los Angeles. In addition, he is an adjunct faculty member with the IBM Advanced Business Institute and a frequent guest lecturer at the Sloan School of Management, Massachusetts Institute of Technology, from which he graduated.

**Laurence Prusak** is a managing principal with the IBM Consulting Group. Prior to joining IBM, he was a principal in the Ernst & Young Center for Business Innovation, an instructor of social and economic history, and a researcher and librarian at the Baker Library, Harvard Business School. He is published in such journals as the *International Journal of Information Management, Sloan Management Review,* and *California Management Review,* edited *Knowledge in Organizations,* and is the coauthor of *Managing Information Strategically* and *Working Knowledge.*

**James Brian Quinn** is professor emeritus at the Amos Tuck School, Dartmouth College, and an international consultant. He is a three-time McKinsey award winner for the best *Harvard Business Review* article and winner of the Academy of Management's 1994 George R. Terry Award. Quinn's publications include *The Innovation Explosion: Intellect and Software to Revolutionize Growth Strategies, FutureWork: Putting Knowledge to Work in the Knowledge Economy,* and *Intelligent Enterprise: A Knowledge and Service Based Paradigm for Industry.*

**Wilhelm Rall,** a coauthor of *Race for the World: Strategies to Build a Great Global Firm,* is a consultant for McKinsey & Company. Before joining McKinsey, he was an assistant professor of economics at the University of Tübingen.

**Frederick Reichheld** is a director of the consulting firm Bain & Company and leads the firm's loyalty practice. He is coauthor of *The Loyalty Effect: The Hidden Force behind Growth, Profits, and Lasting Value* and editor of *The Quest for Loyalty: Creating Value through Partnerships.* Reichheld can be reached through the Boston offices of Bain & Company at Two Copley Place, Boston, MA, 02116; telephone: (617) 572-2000; fax: (617) 572-2427.

**Marcia Robinson** is president of e-Business Strategies and coauthor of *E-Business: Roadmap for Success.* Prior to joining e-Business Strategies, she held management positions at EDS (Electronic Data Systems), Frontier Corporation, and SunTrust Bank.

**Martha Rogers** is an associate professor in marketing at Bowling Green State University and partner in the Peppers and Rogers Group. She has also worked as a copywriter and advertising executive and served on the National Advertising

Review Board. Her publications include *The One-to-One Fieldbook: The Complete Toolkit for Implementing a One-to-One Marketing Program, The One-to-One Manager: Real-World Lessons in Customer Relationship Management,* and *Enterprise One-to-One: Tools for Competing in the New Age of Interactivity.* She can be contacted through her Web site, http://www.1to1.com and can also be contacted as follows: Peppers and Rogers Group / Marketing 1to1, 470 West Avenue, Stamford, CT, 06902; telephone: (203) 316-5121; fax: (203) 316-5126; e-mail: Rogers@1to1.com.

**Jonathan Rosenoer** is a director in Arthur Andersen's national computer risk-management practice. In 1992 he founded the CyberLaw section of America Online and later produced the first accredited on-line legal education program for Counsel Connect. An attorney, Rosenoer is the author of *CyberLaw: The Law of the Internet* and coauthor of *The Clickable Corporation.* He has also published articles in such periodicals as *Wired Magazine, Ethics and Behavior, Policy Options,* and *The Computer Lawyer.*

**W. Earl Sasser** is the UPS Foundation Professor of Service Management at the Harvard Business School and coauthor of *Service Breakthroughs: Changing the Rules of the Game* and *The Service Profit Chain: How Leading Companies Link Profit and Growth to Loyalty, Satisfaction, and Value.* He received a bachelor's degree in mathematics from Duke University, a master of business education from the University of North Carolina, and a doctorate in economics from Duke University. He can be reached through the Harvard Business School as follows: telephone: (617) 495-6439; fax: (617) 496-7379; e-mail: wsasser@hbs.edu.

**Don E. Schultz,** coauthor of *Communicating Globally,* is president of the consulting firm Agora, Inc., and a senior partner with Targetbase Marketing International and the Targetbase Institute. He is also a communications professor in Northwestern University's journalism school and author or coauthor of several other books, including *Strategic Brand Communication Campaigns, Essentials of Advertising Strategy,* and the best-selling *Integrated Marketing Communications.*

**Evan I. Schwartz** is a former editor at *Business Week* and a contributor to *Wired Magazine* and the *New York Times.* He is also the author of *Digital Darwinism: Seven Breakthrough Business Strategies for Surviving in the Cutthroat Web Economy.* An earlier book, *Webonomics,* was a finalist for both the Computer Press Award and the Booz-Allen Global Business Book Award. He can be reached through his Web site, http://www.digataldarwinism.com, or by e-mail at evan@webonomics.com.

**Peter Schwartz** is a cofounder and chairman of Global Business Network, author of *The Long View,* and coauthor of *The Long Boom: A Vision for the Coming Age of Prosperity* and *When Good Companies Do Bad Things: Responsibility and Risk in* *an Age of Globalization*. He can be reached through the offices of Global Business Network as follows: 5900-X Hollis Street, Emeryville, CA, 94662; telephone: (510) 547-6822; fax: (510) 547-810. E-mail for general information at info@gbn.com or see http://www.gbn.com.

**Jeffrey L. Seglin** is an assistant professor at Emerson College in Boston and editor-at-large for *Inc. Magazine*. He writes a monthly business ethics column for the Sunday *New York Times* and a quarterly column for *Inc. Technology.* He has written more than a dozen business books, including *The Good, the Bad, and Your Business: Choosing Right When Ethical Dilemmas Are Pulling You Apart,* which he wrote while a fellow at the Center for the Study of Values in Public Life at Harvard University.

Professor Seglin holds an undergraduate degree from Bethany College and a graduate degree from Harvard Divinity School. He can be reached by e-mail at jeffrey_seglin@emerson.edu.

**Patricia Seybold** is the founder and CEO of the Patricia Seybold Group, a strategic e-business and technology consulting firm. She is also the author of *Customers.com: How to Create a Profitable Business Strategy for the Internet and Beyond.*

Seybold can be reached through the Web site http://www.psgroup.com or through the offices of the Patricia Seybold Group as follows: 85 Devonshire Street, 5th Floor, Boston, MA, 02109-3504; telephone: (800) 826-2424; fax: (617) 742-1028.

**Carl Shapiro** is the Transamerica Professor of Business Strategy at the Haas School of Business, University of California, Berkeley, and the director of the Institute of Business and Economic Research and professor of economics at the University of California, Berkeley. He holds a doctorate in economics from the Massachusetts Institute of Technology and taught at Princeton University during the 1980s.

Shapiro served as a Deputy Assistant Attorney General for Economics in the Antitrust Division of the U.S. Department of Justice and later founded the Tilden Group, an economic consulting group. His publications include *Information Rules: A Strategic Guide to the Network Economy* and *Business in the New Millennium Set.* He can be reached through his home page, http://www.haas.berkeley.edu/~shapiro.

**David Siegel** is author of *Creating Killer Web Sites* and *Futurize Your Enterprise: Business Strategy in the Age of the E-Customer.* He is chairman of Studio Verso, a Web-design firm, and president of the e-commerce strategy firm Siegel Vision. He can be reached through the Siegel Vision offices as follows: 461 Second Street #207, San Francisco, CA, 94107; telephone: (415) 777-9911; fax: (415) 777-5575.

**Marc Singer** is a principal at McKinsey & Company and works with the firm's Continuous Relationship Marketing practice. He is a coauthor of *Net Worth: Shaping Markets When Customers Make the Rules* and has published articles in the *McKinsey Quarterly* and *Harvard Business Review.*

**Robert C. Solomon** is a professor of business and philosophy at the University of Texas, Austin, where he specializes in post-Kantian continental philosophy. His more than 30 books include *A Better Way to Think about Business: How Personal Integrity Leads to Corporate Success.* Prior to joining the faculty at the University of Texas, he taught at Princeton, the University of California, Los Angeles, and the University of Pittsburgh. He is also a yearly visitor at the University of Auckland in New Zealand. He can be contacted by e-mail at rsolomon@mail.utexas.edu.

**Ruth Stanat** is founder and president of SIS International Research, a consulting firm that provides organizations with strategic planning, market research reports, and business development studies. She also held marketing and planning positions with Chase Manhattan Bank, Mars Corporation, International Paper Company, Spring Mills, and United Airlines.

Stanat is the author or coauthor of *Global Jumpstart, The Intelligent Corporation,* and *Global Gold.* She holds degrees from Ohio University and New York University.

**Thomas A. Stewart,** author of *Intellectual Capital,* is member of the board of directors of *Fortune Magazine.* He joined *Fortune* after an 18-year career with Atheneum Publishers at which he held editorial and managerial positions. The Harvard College graduate has written articles on a wide range of topics, including an influential series on intellectual capital that resulted in his receiving the 1996 International Knowledge Management Awareness Award. Stewart can be contacted through the Web site http://members.aol.com/thosstew/bio.html.

**Robert I. Sutton** is a professor of organizational behavior in the Stanford Engineering School, codirector of the Center for Work, Technology, and Organization, and research director of the Stanford Technology Ventures Program. Sutton, who holds a doctorate in organizational psychology from the University of Michigan, has also taught at the University of California at Berkeley's Haas Business School and been a fellow at the Center for Advanced Study in the Behavioral Sciences. He has published numerous articles and book chapters and is the coauthor of *The Knowing-Doing Gap.* He also published *Research in Organizational Behavior 1999: An Annual Series of Analytical Essays and Critical Reviews.* He can be reached at Stanford University as follows: Department of Management Science and Engineering, Mail Code 4026, Terman Engineering B, Stanford, CA, 94305-4026; telephone: (650) 723-0480; fax: (650) 725-8799; e-mail: bobsut@leland.stanford.edu.

**Karl Erik Sveiby**'s interest and subsequent career in the field of knowledge management began when he and his partners bought the business journal *Affärsvärlden* in 1979. The owners outsourced everything except the editorial work and soon owned a company that had only intangible assets. Sveiby set out to develop a new way to view his company as a knowledge organization. His first book, entitled *Kunskapsföretaget* (*The Know-How Company*) became a best-seller in Scandinavia, and his efforts to develop a method for measuring intangible assets resulted in *Den Osynliga Balansräkningen* (*The Invisible Balance Sheet*).

After selling their company in 1993, Sveiby completed his doctorate at Stockholm University and now consults as an independent advisor to knowledge organizations. His most recent work is *The New Organizational Wealth: Managing and Measuring Knowledge-Based Assets.*

**Hirotaka Takeuchi** is a professor at Hitotsubashi University and coauthor of *The Knowledge-Creating Company: How Japanese Companies Create the Dynamics of Innovation.*

**Scott I. Tannenbaum** is president of the Executive Consulting Group, Inc. His research in the field of human resources has won awards from the National Academy of Management and the American Society of Training and Development. He holds a doctorate in industrial/organizational psychology from Old Dominion University and has a part-time faculty position as a tenured professor in the School of Business at the State University of New York at Albany. He can be reached at Scott.Tannenbaum@ecgweb.com.

**Don Tapscott** is president of New Paradigm Learning Corporation and cofounder and chairman of Digital 4Sight, formerly the Alliance for Converging Technologies. His publications include several journal articles and books such as *Creating Value in the Network Economy, Growing Up Digital: The Rise of the Net Generation, The Digital Economy: Promise and Peril in the Age of Networked Intelligence, Who Knows: Safeguarding Your Privacy in a Networked World, Paradigm Shift: The New Promise of Information Technology,* and *Digital Capital: Harnessing the Power of Business Webs* (coauthor). Mr. Tapscott, who holds a bachelor's degree in psychology and statistics and a master of education degree specializing in research methodology, is a regular contributor to *Computerworld.* He can be reached through Digital 4Sight at 360 Adelaide Street W, 4th Floor, Toronto, ON, M5V 1R7; telephone: (416) 979-7899; fax: (416) 979-7616; Internet site http://www.actnet.com.

**David Ticoll** is president and cofounder of Digital 4Sight, formerly the Alliance for Converging Technologies. His earlier experience included establishing the Canadian program of Gartner Group and six years as director at DMR Group. Ticoll has a bachelor's degree from McGill University in sociology and political science and is the coauthor of *Digital Capital: Harnessing the Power of Business Webs.* He can be reached through Digital 4Sight at 360 Adelaide Street W, 4th Floor, Toronto, ON, M5V 1R7; telephone: (416) 979-7899; fax: (416) 979-7616; Internet site http://www.actnet.com.

**Amrit Tiwana** is a professor of information technology at Georgia State University and an independent consultant. He writes a monthly column for *IT Magazine* and is the author of *The Knowledge Management Toolkit* and *Web Security.*

**Hal R. Varian** is dean of the School of Information Management and Systems at the University of California, Berkeley, and a professor in the Haas School of Business and in the economics department. He also holds the Class of 1944 Chair at the University of California, Berkeley. He has a bachelor's degree from Massachusetts Institute of Technology (MIT), and a master's degree in mathematics and doctorate in economics from the University of California, Berkeley. He has taught at MIT, Stanford, Oxford, the University of Michigan, and other international universities.

In addition to teaching responsibilities, Varian is a fellow of the Guggenheim Foundation, the Econometric Society, and the American Academy of Arts and Sciences. He has served as an associate editor of the *Journal of Economic Perspectives* and the *Journal of Economic Literature,* and as coeditor of the *American Economic Review.* In addition to his two major economics textbooks, he is coauthor of *Information Rules: A Strategic Guide to the Network Economy.* Varian's home page is http://www.sims.berkeley.edu/~hal.

**Manuel G. Velasquez,** author of *Business Ethics: Concepts and Cases,* is a professor of business ethics in the management department and a professor of philosophy in the philosophy department at Santa Clara University. He holds bachelor's and master's degrees in philosophy from Gonzaga University and a doctorate in philosophy from the University of California, Berkeley. He can be reached by e-mail at mvelasquez@scu.edu or by mail at Department of Organizational Analysis and Management, Leavey School of Business and Administration, Santa Clara University, Santa Clara, CA, 95053.

**Chris West** is the founder and managing director of Marketing Intelligence Services, Ltd. A graduate of the London School of Economics, West worked for Shell International, Eurofinance, and Industrial Market Research, Ltd., a consulting firm that specializes in the analysis of industrial, commercial, and professional markets. In addition to coauthoring *Global Jumpstart,* he is a contributor to *Global Gold* and author of *Marketing Research.*

**Adrian Woolridge** is a correspondent for *The Economist,* coauthor of *A Future Perfect: The Challenge and Hidden Promise of Globalization,* and author of *Measuring the Mind: Education and Psychology in England, 1860–1990.* He has also written for the *Wall Street Journal,* the *New Republic,* and the *Times of London.*

**Thomas S. Wurster** is a vice president of the Boston Consulting Group (BCG), working with BCG's Media and Convergence Practice. He holds a bachelor's degree in economics and mathematics from Cornell University, a master of business administration from the University of Chicago, and a doctorate in economics from Yale University. Wurster is a coauthor of *Blown to Bits: How the New Economics of Information Transforms Strategy.*

# Notes

### *Chapter 1*

[1] Alan Greenspan and James A. Wilcox, "Is There a New Economy?" *California Management Review,* September 1998, p. 74.
[2] Ibid.
[3] Kevin Kelly, *New Rules for the New Economy: Ten Radical Strategies for a Connected World* (New York: Viking, 1998), p. 1.
[4] Carl Shapiro and Hal R. Varian, *Information Rules: A Strategic Guide to the Network Economy* (Boston: Harvard Business School Press, 1998), p. 1.
[5] Peter Schwartz, Peter Leyden, and Joel Hyatt, *The Long Boom: A Vision for the Coming Age of Prosperity* (Reading, MA: Perseus Books, 1999), pp. 14–15.
[6.] Ibid, p. 20.
[7] Ibid., pp. 19–20.
[8] Ibid., pp. 22–23.
[9] Ibid., p. 23.
[10] Ibid., p. 43.
[11] Ibid., pp. 43–44.
[12] Philip Evans and Thomas S. Wurster, *Blown to Bits: How the New Economics of Information Transforms Strategy* (Boston: Harvard Business School Press, 1999), p. 9.
[13] Ibid., p. 10.
[14] Ibid., p. 13.
[15] Charles L. Martin, *The Digital Estate: Strategies for Competing and Thriving in an Internetworked World* (New York: McGraw-Hill, 1997), p. 127.
[16] Evans and Wurster, *Blown to Bits,* p. 17.
[17] Ibid., pp. 23–24.
[18] Ibid., p. 28.
[19] Ibid., pp. 36–37.
[20] K. Kelly, *New Rules for the New Economy,* p. 97.
[21] Ibid.
[22] Ibid.
[23] Ibid., p. 98.
[24] Evans and Wurster, *Blown to Bits,* pp. 44–48.
[25] Jeff Papows, *Enterprise.com: Market Leadership in the Information Age* (Reading, MA: Perseus Books, 1998), p. 97.
[26] William Gates, *Business @ the Speed of Thought: Using a Digital Nervous System* (New York: Time Warner Books, 1999), p. 78.

27 K. Kelly, *New Rules for the New Economy,* pp. 102–103.
28 Ibid., p. 24.
29 Ibid., p. 23.
30 Ibid, p. 10.
31 Shapiro and Varian, *Information Rules,* use the term *positive feedback,* while most of our other gurus use the term *increasing returns* and refer to positive feedback as the force that leads to increasing returns. To avoid confusion, we will use the term *increasing returns* to mean the virtuous cycle by which the stronger get stronger.
32 Shapiro and Varian, *Information Rules,* p. 174.
33 Ibid., p. 13.
34 K. Kelly, *New Rules for the New Economy,* p. 26.
35 Ibid.
36 Ibid.
37 Ibid., pp. 42–43.
38 Ibid., p. 43.
39 Ibid., pp. 45–46.
40 Don Tapscott, David Ticoll, and Alex Lowy, eds., *Blueprint to the Digital Economy: Wealth Creation in the Era of E-Business* (New York: McGraw-Hill, 1998), p. x.
41 Don Tapscott, David Ticoll, and Alex Lowy, "The Rise of the Business Web," *Business 2.0,* November 1999, p. 199.
42 James F. Moore, "The New Corporate Form," in *Blueprint to the Digital Economy: Wealth Creation in the Era of E-Business,* edited by Don Tapscott, Alex Lowy, and David Ticoll (New York: McGraw-Hill, 1998), pp. 77–78.
43 Tapscott, Ticoll, and Lowy, "Rise of the Business Web," p. 201. Even Tapscott, Ticoll, and Lowy have difficulty placing knowledge-economy companies in their model. For example, at one point in their article, they cite America Online as an aggregation B-Web. Elsewhere in a table, they show it as an example of an alliance B-Web. Presumably, America Online is a little bit of both.
44 Ibid., pp. 201–208.
45 Tapscott, Ticoll, and Lowy refer to this B-Web as Agora, taking the name of a marketplace in ancient Greece. Later in *Blueprint to the Digital Economy,* they refer to this type of B-Web as open market. We use the term *open market* because we believe it is easier to understand.
46 Tapscott, Ticoll, and Lowy, "Rise of the Business Web," p. 206.
47 Ibid., pp. 207–208.
48 Stan Davis and Christopher Meyer, *Blur: The Speed of Change in the Connected Economy* (Reading, MA: Addison-Wesley, 1998), p. 84.
49 Ibid., pp. 85–86.
50 Ibid., p. 85.
51 Ibid., p. 86.
52 Davis and Meyer, *Blur,* p. 87.
53 Tapscott, Ticoll, and Lowy, "Rise of the Business Web," p. 208.

[54] Davis and Meyer, *Blur,* p. 90.
[55] Ibid., p. 91.
[56] Rolf Jensen, *The Dream Society: How the Coming Shift from Information to Imagination Will Transform Your Business* (New York: McGraw-Hill, 1999), p. 1.
[57] Ibid., p. 3.
[58] Ibid., p. 6.
[59] Ibid., pp. 6–7.
[60] Ibid., p. 7.
[61] Ibid.
[62] Ibid., p. 56.
[63] Ibid., p. 65.
[64] Ibid., p. 87.
[65] Ibid., pp. 100–101.
[66] B. Joseph Pine and James H. Gilmore, *The Experience Economy: Work Is Theater and Every Business a Stage* (Boston, MA: Harvard Business School Press, 1999), p. 3.
[67] Ibid., p. 22.
[68] Ibid., p. 25.
[69] Ibid., p. 35.
[70] Ibid., pp. 39–40.
[71] Jensen, *Dream Society,* p. 49.
[72] Pine and Gilmore, *Experience Economy,* p. 166.

### Chapter 2

[1] Peter F. Drucker, "Beyond the Information Revolution," *Atlantic Monthly,* October 1999, p. 47.
[2] Ibid., p. 48.
[3] Ibid.
[4] Ibid., p. 50.
[5] Ibid.
[6] Ibid.
[7] Steffano Korper and Juanita Ellis, *The E-Commerce Book: Building the E-Empire* (San Diego, CA: Academic Press, 2000), p. 10.
[8] Ibid., pp. 6–7.
[9] David R. Kosiur, *Understanding Electronic Commerce* (Redmond, WA: Microsoft Press, 1997), p. 4.
[10] Ravi Kalakota and Marcia Robinson, *E-Business: Roadmap for Success* (Reading, MA: Addison-Wesley 1999), p. xvi.
[11] Daniel Amor, *The E-Business (R)evolution* (Upper Saddle River, NJ: Prentice Hall, 1999), p. 7.
[12] Ibid., pp. 24–32.
[13] Walid Mougayar, "E-Commerce? E-Business? Who E-Cares?" *Computerworld,* November 2, 1998, p. 33.

[14] Patricia B. Seybold, with Ronni Marshak, *Customers.com: How to Create a Profitable Business Strategy for the Internet and Beyond* (New York: Times Business, 1998), p. 4.
[15] Drucker, "Beyond the Information Revolution," p. 50.
[16] Bruce Judson and Kate Kelly, *Hyperwars: Eleven Strategies for Survival and Profit in the Era of Online Business* (New York: Scribner, 1999), p. 30.
[17] Ibid., p. 50.
[18] David Siegel, *Futurize Your Enterprise: Business Strategy in the Age of the E-Customer* (New York: Wiley, 1999), p. 2.
[19] Walter Forbes, "A Store as Big as the World." In *The Future of the Electronic Marketplace,* edited by Derek Leebaert (Cambridge, MA: MIT Press, 1998), pp. 67–70.
[20] Judson and Kelly, *Hyperwars,* p. 46.
[21] Ibid., pp. 46–47.
[22] Guy Kawasaki, "Bricks to Bits," *Forbes,* May 31, 1999, p. 248.
[23] Jonathan Rosenoer, Douglas Armstrong, and J. Russell Gates, *The Clickable Corporation* (New York: Free Press, 1999), pp. 18–21. Although the authors list "Entertainment" and "Trust" as two additional advantages, we don't include them here because we don't see them as distinct to e-commerce. Many traditional companies use games, contests, music, and other forms of entertainment to attract customers and enhance their shopping experience. If anything, e-commerce companies have a more difficult time establishing trust with customers because of privacy and security concerns. Thus, we would view "trust" as a disadvantage rather than an advantage for on-line shoppers.
[24] Ibid., p. 26.
[25] Ibid., p. 55.
[26] Ibid., p. 75.
[27] Ibid., p. 20.
[28] Evan I. Schwartz, *Digital Darwinism: Seven Breakthrough Business Strategies for Surviving in the Cutthroat Web Economy* (New York: Broadway Books, 1999), p. 56.
[29] Ibid., pp. 56–57.
[30] Mary Modahl, *Now or Never: How Companies Must Change Today to Win the Battle for Internet Consumers* (New York: HarperBusiness, 1999), p. 82.
[31] Ibid., pp. 82–84.
[32] Ibid., p. 84.
[33] Ibid., p. 88.
[34] Ibid.
[35] John Hagel III and Marc Singer, *Net Worth: Shaping Markets When Customers Make the Rules* (Boston: Harvard Business School Press, 1999), pp. 233–234.
[36] Ibid, p. 234.
[37] Ibid., p. 235.
[38] Ibid.

[39] Richard J. Gascoyne and Koray Ozcubukcu, *Corporate Internet Planning Guide: Aligning Internet Strategy with Business Goals* (New York: Van Nostrand Reinhold, 1997), p. 108.
[40] Ibid., pp. 108–109.
[41] Ibid., p. 109.
[42] This discussion is adapted from Ranjay Gulati and Jason Garino, "Get the Right Mix of Bricks and Clicks," *Harvard Business Review,* May–June 2000, p. 114.
[43] Gascoyne and Ozcubukcu, pp. 32–34. This summary of Internet capabilities is adapted from Table 2.2.
[44] Ibid., p. 122.
[45] Ibid., p. 124.
[46] Ibid., p. 129.
[47] Ibid., p. 130.
[48] Ibid., pp. 136–137.
[49] This discussion of myths is adapted from Seth Godin, *Permission Marketing: Turning Strangers into Friends, and Friends into Customers* (Simon & Schuster, 1999), pp. 149–154.
[50] In *Customers.com,* Seybold actually lists eight critical success factors. In our summary, we combine two of her eight. We grouped streamlining business processes that impact the customer with providing a 360-degree view to the customer relationship because we feel these two factors are very similar.
[51] Seybold with Marshak, *Customers.com,* pp. 69–70.
[52] Ibid., p. 106.
[53] Ibid., pp. 135–136.
[54] Ibid., p. 34.
[55] Ibid., p. 33.
[56] Ibid., p. 42.
[57] Ibid., pp. 43–44.
[58] Ibid., p. 214.
[59] Ibid., pp. 149–150.
[60] Ibid., p. 252.
[61] Ibid., p. 254.
[62] Ibid., p. 280.
[63] Ibid., p. 281.
[64] Ibid., p. 311.
[65] Ibid., p. 313.
[66] Judson and Kelly, *Hyperwars,* pp. 75–76.
[67] Ibid., p. 209.

### Chapter 3

[1] Joseph H. Boyett and Jimmie T. Boyett, *The Guru Guide: The Best Ideas of Top Management Thinkers* (New York: Wiley, 1998), pp. 83–84.

[2] Scott I. Tannenbaum, "Knowledge Management: So, What Is It Anyway?" *IHRIM Journal,* September 1998, pp. 7–8.

[3] Ibid., p. 8.

[4] Jay Liebowitz, *Building Organizational Intelligence: A Knowledge Management Primer* (Boca Raton, FL: St. Lucie Press, 1998), pp. 37–38.

[5] Verna Allee, *The Knowledge Evolution: Expanding Organizational Intelligence* (Boston: Butterworth-Heinemann, 1997), p. xiii.

[6] Thomas A. Stewart, *Intellectual Capital: The New Wealth of Organizations* (New York: Doubleday, 1998), p. ix.

[7] Ibid., p. 6.

[8] Ibid., p. 12.

[9] Ibid., p. 18.

[10] Ibid., p. 33.

[11] Ibid., p. 16.

[12] Ibid., p. x.

[13] Ibid., p. 67.

[14] Leif Edvinsson and Michael S. Malone, *Intellectual Capital: Realizing Your Company's True Value by Finding Its Hidden Roots* (New York: HarperBusiness, 1997). Their book is based on pioneering work on the identification and measurement of intellectual capital conducted at Skandia, the largest insurance and financial-services company in Scandinavia. Skandia released the first public Intellectual Capital annual report in 1995. Edvinsson led that company's efforts.

[15] Ibid., p. 11.

[16] Stewart, *Intellectual Capital,* p. 56.

[17] Thomas Davenport and Laurence Prusak, *Working Knowledge: How Organizations Manage What They Know* (Boston: Harvard Business School Press, 1997), p. 2.

[18] Ibid., pp. 3–4.

[19] Ibid., p. 5.

[20] Ibid., p. 8.

[21] Ibid., p. 12.

[22] Stewart, *Intellectual Capital,* pp. 69–70.

[23] Ibid., p. 70.

[24] Ikujiro Nonaka and Hirotaka Takeuchi, *The Knowledge-Creating Company* (New York: Oxford University Press, 1995), p. 8.

[25] Ibid.

[26] Ibid., p. 63.

[27] Ibid.

[28] Ibid., pp. 69–71.

[29] Dorothy Leonard and Sylvia Sensiper, "The Role of Tacit Knowledge in Group Innovaton," *California Management Review,* Spring 1998, p. 112.

[30] Davenport and Prusak, *Working Knowledge,* p. 25.

[31] Ibid., p. 39.

32 Stewart, *Intellectual Capital,* p. 56.
33 Ibid., p. 57.
34 Ibid., pp. 60–61.
35 Frances Horibe, *Managing Knowledge Workers: New Skills and Attitudes to Unlock the Intellectual Capital in Your Organization* (New York: Wiley, 1999), p. 21.
36 Stewart, *Intellectual Capital,* p. 222.
37 Amrit Tiwana, *The Knowledge Management Toolkit: Practical Techniques for Building a Knowledge Management System* (Upper Saddle River, NJ: Prentice Hall PTR, 2000), p. 103.
38 Ibid., p. 129.
39 Ibid., p. 148.
40 Morten T. Hansen, Nitin Nohria and Thomas Tierney, "What's Your Strategy for Managing Knowledge?" *Harvard Business Review,* March–April 1999, p. 112.
41 Tiwana, *Knowledge Management Toolkit,* pp. 209–210.
42 Ibid., p. 589.
43 Ibid., p. 590.
44 Ibid., pp. 216–217.
45 Ibid., pp. 217–218.
46 Ibid., pp. 223–224.
47 Ibid., p. 227.
48 Ibid. p. 230.
49 See Tiwana, *Knowledge Management Toolkit,* pp. 241–271, for a full description of the audit.
50 Ibid., pp. 296–297.
51 Ibid. p. 373.
52 Ibid., p. 383.
53 Ibid., p. 384.
54 Ibid., p. 394.
55 Ibid., p. 410.
56 See Boyett and Boyett, *Guru Guide,* pp. 257–263, for a discussion of the balanced scorecard.
57 Edvinsson and Malone, *Intellectual Capital,* p. 41.
58 Ibid., p. 11.
59 Sveiby, Karl Erik, *The New Organizational Wealth: Managing and Measuring Knowledge-Based Assets,* (San Francisco: Berrett-Koehler, 1997), p. 12.
60 Dorothy Leonard, *Wellsprings of Knowledge: Building and Sustaining the Sources of Innovation* (Boston: Harvard Business School Press, 1998), pp. 19, 27.
61 Ibid., p. 30.
62 Ibid.
63 Ibid., p. 62.
64 Ibid., pp. 63–64.
65 Ibid., pp. 64–65.

[66] Ibid., p. 83.
[67] Ibid., p. 86.
[68] Ibid., pp. 93–94.
[69] Ibid., p. 103.
[70] Ibid., p. 125.
[71] Ibid., pp. 124–125.
[72] Ibid., p. 127.
[73] Ibid., p. 158.
[74] Ibid., p. 160.
[75] Ibid., pp. 21–44.
[76] Etienne C. Wenger and William M. Snyder, "Communities of Practice: The Organizational Frontier," *Harvard Business Review,* January–February 2000, p. 139.
[77] Etienne C. Wenger, "Communities of Practice: Where Learning Happens," *Benchmark,* Fall 1991, p. 7. Also see Etienne C. Wenger, *Communities of Practice: Learning, Meaning, and Identity* (New York: Cambridge University Press, 1998). For a more lengthy discussion of communities of practice, including another researcher's experience with them, see John Seely Brown and Paul Duguid, "Organizational Learning and Communities-of-Practice: Toward a Unified View of Working, Learning, and Innovation," *Organizational Science* 2, February 1991, pp. 40–57.
[78] Frances Dale Horibe, *Managing Knowledge Workers: New Skills and Attitudes to Unlock the Intellectual Capital in Your Organization* (New York: Wiley, 1999), pp. 157–158.
[79] Jeffrey Pfeffer and Robert I. Sutton, *The Knowing-Doing Gap: How Smart Companies Turn Knowledge into Action* (Boston: Harvard Business School Press, 1999), p. 3.
[80] Ibid., p. 10.
[81] Ibid., pp. 248–249.
[82] Ibid., p. 251.
[83] Ibid., pp. 256–257.
[84] Ibid., p. 259.
[85] Ibid., p. 260.
[86] Ibid., p. 261.
[87] Ibid., p. 16.
[88] Ibid., p. 22.

### Chapter 4

[1] Don Peppers and Martha Rogers, eds., *The One-to-One Manager: Real-World Lessons in Customer Relationship Management* (New York: Doubleday, 1999), p. 1.
[2] See Don Peppers and Martha Rogers, *The One-to-One Future: Building Relationships One Customer at a Time* (New York: Currency/Doubleday, 1993),

pp. xi–xviii, for more information on Peppers and Rogers during the early 1990s. At least one guru, Frederick Newell, author of *Loyalty.com: Customer Relationship Management in the New Era of Internet Marketing* (New York: McGraw-Hill, 2000), argues that the idea of managing relationships (a core principle of Customer Relationship Management) predates Peppers by at least half a decade. According to Newell, the idea was first mentioned by Lester Wunderman, chair of the direct marketing advertising agency, Wunderman, Cato, in a speech to the Annual Conference of the Direct Marketing Association in 1983.

3 "A Crash Course in Customer Relationship Management," *Harvard Management Update,* March 2000, pp. 5–6.

4 Peppers and Rogers, *One-to-One Future,* pp. 10–11.

5 Ibid., pp. 15–17.

6 See Frederick F. Reichheld and Thomas Teal, *The Loyalty Effect: The Hidden Force behind Growth, Profits, and Lasting Value* (Boston: Harvard Business School Press, 1996), pp. 36–39.

7 Ibid., p. 37.

8 Ibid., pp. 37–38.

9 Ibid., p. 35.

10 Ibid., p. 43.

11 Ibid., pp. 44–45.

12 Ibid., p. 45.

13 Ibid., p. 47.

14 Ibid., p. 48.

15 Ibid., pp. 48–49.

16 Ibid., pp. 49–50.

17 We provide here only the simplest form of this calculation. See Reichheld and Teal, *The Loyalty Effect,* pp. 50–62, for a more complete description and some cautions about the calculation.

18 Frederick F. Reichheld, "Learning from Customer Defections," *Harvard Business Review,* March–April 1996, pp. 58–59.

19 Keki R. Bhote, *Beyond Customer Satisfaction to Customer Loyalty: The Key to Greater Profitability* (New York: AMACON, 1996), p. 31.

20 Jay Curry and Adam Curry, *The Customer Marketing Method: How to Implement and Profit from Customer Relationship Management* (New York: Free Press, 2000), p. 8.

21 Ibid., p. 122.

22 Adapted from Seth Godin, *Permission Marketing: Turning Strangers into Friends, and Friends into Customers* (New York: Simon & Schuster, 1999), p. 58.

23 Ibid., p. 38.

24 Ibid., pp. 44–45.

25 Ibid., p. 46.

26 Ibid.

27 Ibid., pp. 46–47.

[28] Ibid., p. 131.
[29] Ibid., p. 136.
[30] Ibid., p. 142.
[31] This discussion is based on Don Peppers and Martha Rogers, *Enterprise One-to-One: Tools for Competing in the Interactive Age* (New York: Currency/Doubleday, 1997), pp. 55–78, 191–194; and Don Peppers and Martha Rogers, "Is Your Company Ready for One-to-One Marketing?" *Harvard Business Review,* January–February 1999, pp. 151–160.
[32] Don Peppers, Martha Rogers and Bob Dorf, *The One-to-One Fieldbook: The Complete Toolkit for Implementing a One-to-One Marketing Program* (New York: Bantom Doubleday Dell, 1999), p. 25.
[33] Ibid.
[34] Ibid., pp. 28–29.
[35] Curry and Curry, *Customer Marketing Method,* p. 51.
[36] Ibid., pp. 51–52.
[37] This list of topics to cover was suggested by Jay Curry and Adam Curry in *Customer Marketing Method,* p. 111.
[38] Peppers, Rogers, and Dorf, *One-to-One Fieldbook,* p. 95.
[39] Ibid.
[40] This discussion is adapted from James H. Gilmore and B. Joseph Pine II, "The Four Faces of Mass Customization," *Harvard Business Review,* January–February 1997, pp. 91–101; and B. Joseph Pine II and James H. Gilmore, *The Experience Economy: Work Is Theater and Every Business a Stage* (Boston: Harvard Business School Press, 1999), pp. 86–94.
[41] Frederick Newell, *Loyalty.com: Customer Relationship Management in the New Era of Internet Marketing* (New York: McGraw-Hill, 2000), p. 138.
[42] Michael Berry and Gordon Linoff, *Data Mining Techniques: For Marketing, Sales, and Customer Support* (New York: Wiley, 1997), p. 3.
[43] Ibid., pp. 51–56.
[44] Ibid., pp. 47–49.
[45] Ibid., pp. 286–287.
[46] Peppers and Rogers, *One-to-One Manager,* p. 92.
[47] Peppers, Rogers, and Dorf, *One-to-One Fieldbook,* p. 203.
[48] George S. Day, *The Market Driven Organization: Understanding, Attracting, and Keeping Valuable Customers* (New York: Free Press, 1999), pp. 232–233.
[49] Ibid., p. 235.
[50] Ibid., p. 237.
[51] Ibid., pp. 237–238.
[52] Curry and Curry, *Customer Marketing Method,* p. 58.
[53] Ibid., p. 59.
[54] Ibid.
[55] Ibid., p. 60.
[56] Peppers and Rogers, *One-to-One Future,* pp. 195–196.
[57] Day, *Market Driven Organization,* p. 244.

58 Peppers and Rogers, *One-to-One Future,* pp. 197–198.
59 Peppers, Rogers and Dorf, *One-to-One Fieldbook,* pp. 201–202.
60 Ibid., p. 202.
61 Philip Kotler, *Kotler on Marketing: How to Create, Win, and Dominate Markets* (New York: Free Press, 1999), pp. 14–15.

### Chapter 5

1 The description of globalization as "a hollow word" is credited to Jacques Manardo, European chairman of Delotte Touche Thomatsu at a meeting of the World Economic Forum in Davos, Switzerland, in 1999. See Thomas A. Stewart, "Staying Smart/Managing: The Leading Edge—A Way to Measure Worldwide Success, Going Global, Part II," *Fortune,* March 15, 1999, p. 196.
2 John Micklethwait and Adrian Woolridge, *A Future Perfect: The Challenge and Hidden Promise of Globalization* (New York: Crown Business Books, 2000), p. viii.
3 Jean-Pierre Jeannet, *Managing with a Global Mindset* (London: Financial Times Prentice Hall, 2000), p. xi.
4 Hilary French, *Vanishing Borders: Protecting the Planet in the Age of Globalization* (New York: Norton, 2000), p. 4.
5 Ibid.
6 Robert H. Rosen, Patricia Digh, Marshall Singer, and Carl Phillips, *Global Literacies: Lessons on Business Leadership and National Cultures* (New York: Simon & Schuster, 2000), p. 37.
7 Ibid.
8 Ibid.
9 Lowell Bryan, Jane Fraser, Jeremy Oppenheim, and Wilhelm Rall, *Race for the World: Strategies to Build a Great Global Firm* (Boston: Harvard Business School Press, 1999), p. 3.
10 French, *Vanishing Borders,* p. 6.
11 Jeffrey A. Rosensweig, *Winning the Global Game: A Strategy for Linking People and Profits* (New York: Free Press, 1998), p. 2.
12 French, *Vanishing Borders,* p. 5.
13 Rosensweig, *Winning the Global Game,* p. 14.
14 French, *Vanishing Borders,* p. 5.
15 Ibid., p. 6.
16 Micklethwait and Woolridge, *A Future Perfect,* p. vii.
17 Thomas L. Friedman, *The Lexus and the Olive Tree: Understanding Globalization* (New York: Anchor Books, 2000), p. 36.
18 Ibid., 36–37.
19 Ibid., p. 47.
20 Ibid., p. 46.
21 Ibid., p. 50.
22 Ibid.

23 Ibid., pp. 50–51.
24 Ibid., p. 51.
25 Ibid., p. 53.
26 Ibid., p. 54.
27 Ibid., p. 57.
28 Ibid.
29 Ibid.
30 Ibid., p. 61.
31 Ibid., pp. 69–70.
32 Ibid., p. 71.
33 "Strategies for Success in the New Global Economy: An Interview with Rosabeth Moss Kanter," *Strategy and Leadership,* November–December 1997, p. 20.
34 Ibid.
35 For more information on the Seattle talks see "The Battle of Seattle: Don't Let Protest Discourage Global Trade Deals," *Newsday,* November 28, 1999, p. B1; Jim Landers and Paul Pringle, "Violent Protests Rock Trade Talks: National Guard Called In after Seattle Ceremonies Are Halted," *Dallas Morning News,* December 1, 1999, p. 1A; Greg Wright, "World Trade Meeting Likely to Be a Contentious Affair: Variety of Groups Planning Protests inside Hall and Out," *Arizona Republic,* November 28, 1999, p. A22; Bob Deans, "Trade Protest Turns Violent: Talks Affected; Seattle under Curfew," *Palm Beach Post,* December 1, 1999, p. 1A; Les Blumenthal, "WTO Hears from Its Critics: Day of Sharp Contrasts as Trade Talks Set to Open," *Minneapolis Star Tribune,* November 30, 1999, p. 1A; and Stuart Laidlaw, "Demonstrations Scuttle Talks," *Toronto Star,* December 1, 1999, p. 1A.
36 Quoted in French, *Vanishing Borders,* pp. 3–4.
37 Edward Luttwak, *Turbo-Capitalism: Winners and Losers in the Global Economy* (New York: HarperCollins, 1999), p. 27.
38 Ibid., pp. 181–186.
39 Ibid., pp. 187–203.
40 Ibid., p. 208.
41 Ibid., p. 206.
42 Gene Koretz, "A New Economy, but No New Deal," *Business Week,* July 10, 2000, p. 34.
43 Luttwak, *Turbo-Capitalism,* p. 5.
44 Friedman, *Lexus and the Olive Tree,* p. 331.
45 Ibid.
46 Ibid., p. 330.
47 Ibid.
48 Ibid., p. 335.
49 Ibid., p. 102.
50 Ibid.
51 Ibid., p. 104.
52 Ibid., p. 105.

53 Ibid., p. 108.
54 Ibid., pp. 109–110.
55 Ibid., p. 382.
56 Ibid., pp. 378–379.
57 Ibid., p. 341.
58 Ibid., p. 383.
59 Ibid., p. 384.
60 French, *Vanishing Borders,* p. 15.
61 Ibid., p. 18.
62 Ibid., p. 19.
63 Ibid., p. 26.
64 Ibid., pp. 34–35.
65 Ibid., p. 40.
66 Ibid., p. 45.
67 Ibid., p. 56.
68 Ibid., p. 57.
69 Ibid., p. 60.
70 Ibid., p. 61.
71 Ibid., p. 75.
72 Friedman, *Lexus and the Olive Tree,* p. 177.
73 Ibid., p. 178.
74 Micklethwait and Woolridge, *A Future Perfect,* p. 355.
75 Friedman, *Lexus and the Olive Tree,* p. 406.
76 Ibid., p. 364.
77 Ibid., p. 15.
78 Anil K. Gupta and Vijay Govindarajan, "Managing Global Expansion: A Conceptual Framework," *Business Horizons,* March–April 2000, p. 45.
79 Lowell L. Bryan and Jane N. Fraser, "Getting to Global," *McKinsey Quarterly,* no. 4, 1999, p. 68.
80 Ibid.
81 Gupta and Govindarajan, "Managing Global Expansion," p. 45.
82 Ibid., p. 47.
83 Ibid., p. 47.
84 Adapted from Ruth Stanat and Chris West, *Global Jumpstart: The Complete Resource Guide for Expanding Small and Medium Size Businesses* (Reading, MA: Perseus Books, 1999), pp. 105–106.
85 Ibid., p. 111.
86 Ibid., p. 114.
87 Ibid., pp. 115–116.
88 Ibid., pp. 116–117.
89 Ibid., pp. 117–118.
90 Cyrus F. Freidheim, *The Trillion-Dollar Enterprise: How the Alliance Revolution Will Transform Global Business* (Reading, MA: Perseus Books, 1998), p. ix.
91 Ibid.

[92] Ibid.
[93] Ibid., p. x.
[94] Ibid.
[95] Ibid., pp. 6–12, 43.
[96] Ibid., p. 9.
[97] Ibid., p. 11.
[98] Ibid., p. 59.
[99] Bryan, Fraser, Oppenheim, and Rall, *Race for the World,* pp. 12–14.
[100] Christopher A. Bartlett and Sumantra Ghoshal, *Managing across Borders: The Transnational Solution* (Boston: Harvard Business School Press, 1998), pp. 294–295.
[101] Bryan, Fraser, Oppenheim, Rall, *Race for the World,* pp. 14–15.
[102] Ibid., p. 28.
[103] Ibid., p. 29.
[104] Ibid., p. 40.
[105] Ibid., p. 53.
[106] Ibid., p. 54.
[107] Ibid., p. 56.
[108] Ibid., p. 240.
[109] Ibid., pp. 58–59.
[110] Ibid., p. 93.
[111] Ibid., p. 65.
[112] Ibid., pp. 70–71.
[113] Ibid., pp. 71–72.

## Chapter 6

[1] George Anders, "Honesty Is the Best Policy," *Fast Company,* August 2000, pp. 262–266.
[2] Rushworth M. Kidder, *How Good People Make Tough Choices: Resolving the Dilemmas of Ethical Living* (New York: William Morrow, 1995), pp. 35–38.
[3] Ibid., pp. 57–58.
[4] Manuel G. Velasquez, *Business Ethics: Concepts and Cases* (Upper Saddle River, NJ: Prentice Hall, 1998), pp. 120–121.
[5] Ibid., p. 2.
[6] Ibid., pp. 2–7.
[7] Ibid., pp. 70–72.
[8] Michael Hopkins, *The Planetary Bargain: Corporate Social Responsibility Comes of Age* (New York: St. Martin's Press, 1999), p. 20.
[9] Jeffrey L. Seglin and Norman R. Augustine, *The Good, the Bad, and Your Business: Choosing Right When Ethical Dilemmas Pull You Apart* (New York: Wiley, 2000), p. 1.
[10] John Elkington, *Cannibals with Forks: The Triple Bottom Line of Twenty-first Century Business* (Oxford: Capstone, 1997), pp. 2, 69–96.

[11] Ibid., p. 2.
[12] Ibid., p. 4.
[13] Ibid., pp. 124–125.
[14] Ibid., pp. 132–133.
[15] Ibid., pp. 160–161.
[16] Ibid., p. 9.
[17] Ibid., p. 213.
[18] Ibid., p. 250.
[19] Ibid., p. 12.
[20] Ibid., p. 276.
[21] Ibid., p. 278.
[22] Ibid., p. 297.
[23] Milton Friedman, "Milton Friedman's Case against Corporate Social Responsibility," in *Business Ethics,* ed. Tamara L. Roleff (San Diego, CA: Greenhaven Press, 1996), pp. 11–17.
[24] John M. Hood, *The Heroic Enterprise: Business and the Common Good* (New York: Free Press, 1996), p. 191.
[25] Ibid., pp. 194–195.
[26] Ibid., pp. 196–197.
[27] Ibid., p. 197.
[28] Doug Bandow, "Corporations Are Responsible Only to Their Owners," in *Business Ethics,* ed. Tamara L. Roleff (San Diego, CA: Greenhaven Press, 1996), p. 74.
[29] Jeffrey H. Coors, "Corporate Philanthropy Is Counterproductive," in *Business Ethics,* ed. Tamara L. Roleff (San Diego, CA: Greenhaven Press, 1996), p. 77.
[30] Ibid., pp. 77–78.
[31] Ibid., p. 78.
[32] Ibid.
[33] Quoted in Peter Schwartz and Blair Gibb, *When Good Companies Do Bad Things: Responsibility and Risk in an Age of Globalization* (New York: Wiley, 1999), p. 105.
[34] Ralph W. Estes, *Tyranny of the Bottom Line: Why Corporations Make Good People Do Bad Things* (San Francisco: Berrett-Koehler, 1996), pp. 22–24.
[35] Ibid., p. 25.
[36] Ibid., p. 28.
[37] John Dalla Costa, *The Ethical Imperative: Why Moral Leadership Is Good Business* (Reading, MA: Addison-Wesley, 1998), p. 87.
[38] Ibid., p. 101.
[39] Ibid., p. 102.
[40] Ibid., p. 103.
[41] Robert C. Solomon, *A Better Way to Think about Business: How Personal Integrity Leads to Corporate Success* (New York: Oxford University Press, 1999), p. 32.
[42] Ibid.

43 Ibid.
44 Ibid., pp. 43–45.
45 Schwartz and Gibb, *When Good Companies Do Bad Things,* p. 97.
46 Dalla Costa, *Ethical Imperative,* pp. 107–108.
47 Schwartz and Gibb, *When Good Companies Do Bad Things,* p. 105.
48 Rogene A. Buchholz and Sandra B. Rosenthal, *Business Ethics: The Pragmatic Path beyond Principles to Process* (Upper Saddle River, NJ: Prentice Hall, 1998), pp. 211–215; and Schwartz and Gibb, *When Good Companies Do Bad Things,* pp. 48–51.
49 Schwartz and Gibb, *When Good Companies Do Bad Things,* p. 105. Schwartz and Gibb go on to say that, "to the extent that Dunlap is demanding more rigor in the discussion of stakeholder responsibility, raising the question of legitimacy is fair."
50 A. L. Alexander, compiler. *Poems That Touch the Heart* (New York: Doubleday, 1956), p. 176.
51 "Business Ethics," <http://www.bsr.org>, (August 4, 2000).
52 "The Minnesota Principles," <http://www.cebcglobal.org/MN_PRIN.htm>, (August 4, 2000).
53 "The Caux Principles," <http://astro.temple.edu/~dialogue/Codes/caux.htm/>, (August 4, 2000).
54 <http://astro.temple.edu/~dialogue/Antho/kung.htm>, (August 4, 2000).
55 Adapted from Dalla Costa, *Ethical Imperative,* pp. 141–142.
56 Ibid., 138.
57 Ibid.
58 Kidder, *How Good People Make Tough Choices,* pp. 89–91.
59 Ibid., p. 93.
60 Velasquez, *Business Ethics,* p. 22.
61 Kidder, *How Good People Make Tough Choices,* p. 272.
62 Ibid., p. 96.
63 Ibid., p. 100.
64 Ibid., p. 45.
65 Ibid., pp. 16–17.
66 Velasquez, *Business Ethics,* p. 73.
67 Ibid.
68 Ibid., p. 74.
69 Ibid., p. 74.
70 Ibid., p. 77.
71 Ibid., pp. 80–81.
72 *Rights* refer to individual entitlements to freedom of choice and well-being. *Justice* refers to how benefits and burdens are distributed among people within a society. In respect to justice, critics of utilitarianism would say that it can often lead to an unjust distribution of costs and benefits. For example, they would argue that, in the Ford Pinto case, if the design was changed, all buyers of the car would share equally in the cost of the change. However, if the design

were not changed, the 180 people who die would absorb all of the costs of the faulty design. Such unequal distribution of costs, say the critics, is unjust. Velasquez points out that utilitarians have responded to the *justice/rights* criticism by proposing an alternative to utilitarianism called *rule-utilitarianism,* which has two parts: (1) An action is right from an ethical point of view if and only if the action would be required by those moral rules that are correct, and (2) A moral rule is correct if and only if the sum total of utilities produced if everyone were to follow that rule is greater than the sum total utilities produced if everyone were to follow some alternative rule. Critics remain unimpressed and argue that *rule-utilitarianism* is nothing more than utilitarianism in disguise. See Velasquez, *Business Ethics,* pp. 82–85, for a further discussion of rule-utilitarianism and its critics.

73 Ibid., p. 94.

74 Ibid., p. 95.

75 Ibid., p. 96.

76 Ibid.

77 Ibid., p. 99.

78 Ibid., p. 100.

79 Ibid., p. 121.

80 Ibid., p. 122.

81 Ibid., pp. 122–123.

82 Ibid., pp. 123–124.

83 Kidder, *How Good People Make Tough Choices,* p. 165.

84 Ibid., p. 166.

85 Ibid.

86 Ibid.

87 Velasquez, *Business Ethics,* p. 128.

88 Anders, "Honesty Is the Best Policy," p. 264.

89 Ibid., p. 261.

90 Velasquez, *Business Ethics,* pp. 132–133.

91 Ibid., p. 137.

92 Ibid., p. 141.

93 Thomas V. Morris, *If Aristotle Ran General Motors: The New Soul of Business* (New York: Henry Holt, 1997), p. 88.

94 Ibid., pp. 94–95.

# Bibliography


Aaker, David A., and Erich Joachimsthaler. "The Lure of Global Branding." *Harvard Business Review,* November 1999, pp. 137–146.

Adams, David M. *Business Ethics for the Twenty-first Century.* Mountain View, CA: Mayfield, 1998.

Albert, Steven, and Keith Bradley. *Managing Knowledge: Experts, Agencies, and Organizations.* New York: Cambridge University Press, 1997.

Albrecht, Karl. *At America's Service: How Your Company Can Join the Customer Service Revolution.* New York: Warner Books, 1995.

————. *Service Advantage: How to Identify and Fulfill Customer Needs.* Homewood, IL: Dow Jones-Irwin, 1990.

Albrow, Martin. *Do Organizations Have Feelings?* New York: Routledge, 1997.

Aldrich, Douglas F. *Mastering the Digital Marketplace: Practical Strategies for Competitiveness in the New Economy.* New York: Wiley, 1999.

Allee, Verna. "Adaptive Organizations." *Executive Excellence,* March 1996, p. 20.

————. "Intellectual Capital and Value Creation." <http://www.vernaallee.com/page8.html> (March 13, 2000).

————. "Knowledge and Self-Organization." *Executive Excellence,* January 1997, p. 7.

————. *The Knowledge Evolution: Expanding Organizational Intelligence.* Boston: Butterworth-Heinemann, 1997.

————. "Tenets of Knowledge." *Executive Excellence,* September 1998, p. 4.

————. "Transformational Learning." *Executive Excellence,* April 1995, p. 13.

————. "Twelve Principles of Knowledge Management." *Training and Development* November 1997, pp. 71–74.

Allen, Cliff, Deborah Kania, and Beth Yaeckel. *Internet World Guide to One-to-One Web Marketing.* New York: Wiley, 1998.

Alvarez, Jose Luis, ed. *The Diffusion and Consumption of Business Knowledge.* New York: St. Martin's Press, 1998.

"Amid the Euphoria, a Note of Caution." *Business Week,* December 27, 1999, p. 220.

Amidon, Debra M. "Blueprint for Twenty-first Century Innovation Management." *Journal of Knowledge Management,* September 1, 1998, pp. 23–31.

————. *Innovation Strategy for the Knowledge Economy.* Boston: Butterworth-Heinemann, 1997.

————. "New Measures of Success." *Journal of Business Strategy,* January–February 1998, pp. 20–24.

Amor, Daniel. *The E-Business (R)evolution: Living and Working in an Interconnected World.* Upper Saddle River, NJ: Prentice Hall, 1999.

Anders, George. "Honesty Is the Best Policy." *Fast Company,* August 2000, pp. 262–266.

Anderson, Kristin. *Knock Your Socks Off Answers: Solving Customer Nightmares and Soothing Nightmare Customers.* New York: American Management Association, 1995.

Anderson, Kristin, and Ron Zemke. *Delivering Knock Your Socks Off Service.* New York: AMACOM, 1997.

Anton, Jon, and Debra Perkins. *Listening to the Voice of the Customer: Sixteen Steps to a Successful Customer Satisfaction Measurement Program.* New York: Customer Service Group, 1998.

Applbaum, Arthur Isak. *Ethics for Adversaries: The Morality of Roles in Public and Professional Life.* Princeton, NJ: Princeton University Press, 1999.

Applehans, Wayne. *Managing Knowledge: A Practical Web-Based Approach.* Reading, MA: Addison-Wesley, 1998.

Argyris, Chris. *On Organizational Learning*. 2nd ed. Malden, MA: Blackwell, 1999.

Arthur, Michael B. "Broken Ladders: Managerial Careers in the New Economy." *Administrative Science Quarterly,* March 1998, pp. 193–196.

Axtel, Roger E. *Do's and Taboos of Humor around the World: Stories and Tips from Business and Life.* New York: Wiley, 1994.

Badaracco, Joseph. *Business Ethics: Roles and Responsibilities.* Chicago: Irwin Professional, 1995.

————. *Defining Moments: When Managers Must Choose between Right and Right.* Boston: Harvard Business School Press, 1997.

Balasubramanyam, V. N. "Transnational Corporation." *Business History,* Vol. 36, no. 2, 1994, pp. 83–89.

Baldwin, Carliss Y., and Kim B. Clark. "Managing in an Age of Modularity." *Harvard Business Review,* September–October 1997, pp. 84–93.

Bandow, Doug. "Corporations Are Responsible Only to Their Owners." In *Business Ethics,* ed. Tamara L. Roleff, pp. 72–75. San Diego, CA: Greenhaven Press, 1996.

Barclay, Rebecca O., and Philip C. Murray. "What Is Knowledge Management?" <http://media-access.com/whatis.html> (March 31, 2000).

Barlow, Janelle, and Claus Moller. *A Complaint Is a Gift: Using Customer Feedback as a Strategic Tool.* San Francisco: Berrett-Koehler, 1996.

Barnard, William, and Thomas F. Wallace. *Innovation Edge: Creating Strategic Breakthroughs Using the Voice of the Customer.* Essex Junction, VT: Omne, 1995.

Barnevik, Percy, and Rosabeth Moss Kanter. *Global Strategies: Insights from the World's Leading Thinkers.* Boston: Harvard Business School Press, 1994.

Baron, David P. *Business and Its Environment.* Upper Saddle River, NJ: Prentice Hall, 2000.

Barrier, Michael. "A Global Reach for Small Firms," *Nation's Business,* April 1994, p. 66.

Barry, Norman. *Business Ethics.* West Lafayette, IN: Purdue University Press, 2000.

Barsky, Jonathan. *Finding the Profit in Customer Satisfaction: Translating Best Practices into Bottom-Line Results.* Lincolnwood, IL: Contemporary Books, 1999.

Bartholomew, Doug. "Going Out on an E-Limb." *Industry Week,* October 4, 1999, p. 38.

Bartlett, Andrew, and David Preston. "Can Ethical Behaviour Really Exist in Business?" *Journal of Business Ethics,* January 2000, pp. 199–209.

Bartlett, Christopher A., and Sumantra Ghoshal. "Going Global: Lessons from Late Movers." *Harvard Business Review,* March–April 2000, pp. 132–142.

————. *Managing across Borders: The Transnational Solution.* Boston: Harvard Business School Press, 1998.

————. *Transnational Management: Text, Cases, and Readings in Cross-Border Management.* Homewood, IL: Richard D. Irwin, 1995.

————. "What Is a Global Manager?" *Harvard Business Review,* September–October 1992, pp. 124–132.

"The Battle of Seattle: Don't Let Protest Discourage Global Trade Deals." *Newsday,* November 28, 1999, p. B1.

Bauman, Zygmunt. *Globalization: The Human Consequences.* New York: Columbia University Press, 1998.

Baumard, Philippe. *Tacit Knowledge in Organization.* London: Sage, 1999.

Bayne, Kim M. *The Internet Marketing Plan: A Practical Handbook for Creating, Implementing, and Assessing Your Online Presence.* New York: Wiley, 1997.

Beauchamp, Tom L. *Case Studies in Business, Society, and Ethics.* Upper Saddle River, NJ: Prentice Hall, 1997.

Beck, Nuala. *Shifting Gears: Thriving in the New Economy,* Toronto: HarperCollins, 1995.

Beck, Ulrich. *What Is Globalization?* Cambridge, England: Polity Press, 2000.

Becker, Hal M. *At Your Service: Calamities, Catastrophes, and Other Curiosities of Customer Service.* New York: Wiley, 1998.

Beckwith, Harry. *The Invisible Touch: The Four Keys to Modern Marketing.* New York: Warner Books, 2000.

———. *Selling the Invisible: A Field Guide to Modern Marketing.* New York: Warner Books, 1997.

Bemowski, Karen. "Americans' Nostalgic Affair with Loyalty." *Quality Progress,* February 1996, p. 33.

Bernstein, Peter L. "Are Networks Driving the New Economy?" *Harvard Business Review,* November–December 1998, pp. 159–166.

Berry, Leonard L., A. Parasuraman, and Valarie A. Zeithaml. "Improving Service Quality in America: Lessons Learned." *Academy of Management Executive,* August 1994, pp. 32–52.

Berry, Michael, and Gordon Linoff. *Data Mining Techniques: For Marketing, Sales, and Customer Support.* New York: Wiley, 1997.

Bhote, Keki R. *Beyond Customer Satisfaction to Customer Loyalty: The Key to Greater Profitability.* New York: AMACON, 1996.

———. "Determining Customer Requirements." *Management Review,* March 1997, p. 39.

———. "What Do Customers Want, Anyway?" *Management Review,* March 1997, pp. 36–40.

Blanchard, Kenneth H., Harvey MacKay, and Sheldon Bowles. *Raving Fans: A Revolutionary Approach to Customer Service.* New York: Morrow, 1993.

Blattberg, Robert C., and John Deighton. "Manage Marketing by the Customer Equity Test." *Harvard Business Review,* July–August 1996, pp. 136–144.

Blumenthal, Les. "WTO Hears from Its Critics: Day of Sharp Contrasts as Trade Talks Set to Open." *Minneapolis Star Tribune,* November 30, 1999, p. 1A.

Blumentritt, Rolf, and Ron Johnston. "Towards a Strategy for Knowledge Management." *Technology Analysis and Strategic Management,* September 1999, pp. 287–300.

Boatright, John Raymond. *Ethics and the Conduct of Business.* Englewood Cliffs, NJ: Prentice Hall, 1993.

Boisot, Max H. *Knowledge Assets: Securing Competitive Advantage in the Information Economy.* New York: Oxford University Press, 1999.

Bollier, David. *Aiming Higher: Twenty-five Stories of How Companies Prosper by Combining Sound Management and Social Vision.* New York: AMACOM, 1996.

Boswell, Terry, and Christopher Chase-Dunn. *The Spiral of Capitalism and Socialism: Toward Global Democracy.* Boulder, CO: Lynne Rienner, 2000.

Bowie, Norman E. *Business Ethics: A Kantian Perspective.* Malden, MA: Blackwell, 1999.

———. "Companies Are Discovering the Value of Ethics." *USA Today,* January 1998, pp. 22–24.

———. "A Kantian Theory of Meaningful Work." *Journal of Business Ethics,* July 1998, pp. 1083–1092.

Boyett, Joseph H., and Jimmie T. Boyett. *The Guru Guide: The Best Ideas of Top Management Thinkers.* New York: Wiley, 1998.

Bradley, Stephen P., and Richard L. Nolan, eds. *Sense and Respond: Capturing Value in the Network Era.* Boston: Harvard Business School Press, 1998.

Brake, Terence, Danielle Medina Walker, and Thomas Walker. *Doing Business Internationally: The Guide to Cross-Cultural Success.* Burr Ridge, IL: Irwin Professional, 1994.

Brooking, Annie. *Corporate Memory: Strategies for Knowledge Management.* New York: International Thomson Business Press, 1999.

Brown, John Seeley, and Paul Duguid. "Organizational Learning and Communities-of-Practice: Toward a Unified View of Working, Learning, and Innovation." *Organizational Science,* February 1991, pp. 40–57.

Brown, Lester R., and Christopher Flavin. "A New Economy for a New Century." *Humanist,* May 1999, pp. 23–28.

Brown, Stanley A. "Breakthrough Service." *Executive Excellence,* April 1998, p. 15.

————. "Honing Our Focus on Customer Service." *Canadian Business Review,* Winter 1994, pp. 29–31.

————. "Managing Customer Relationships." *Executive Excellence,* July 1997, p.11.

————. *Strategic Customer Care: An Evolutionary Approach to Increasing Customer Value and Profitability.* Toronto: Wiley, Canada, 1999.

————. "Technology and Customer Satisfaction: Myths and Facts." *Canadian Business Review,* June 22, 1996, pp. 29–31.

————. *What Customers Value Most: How to Achieve Business Transformation by Focusing on Processes That Touch Your Customers.* New York: Wiley, 1995.

————, ed. *Breakthrough Customer Service: Best Practices of Leaders in Customer Support.* Toronto: Wiley, Canada, 1998.

Bryan, Lowell L., and Jane N. Fraser. "Getting to Global." *McKinsey Quarterly,* no. 4, 1999, pp. 68–81.

Bryan, Lowell, Jane Fraser, Jeremy Oppenheim, and Wilhelm Rall. *Race for the World: Strategies to Build a Great Global Firm.* Boston: Harvard Business School Press, 1999.

Bryan, Lowell L., Timothy G. Lyons, and James Rosenthal. "Corporate Strategy in a Globalizing World: The Market Capitalization Imperative." *McKinsey Quarterly,* no. 3, 1998, pp. 6–19.

Buchholz, Rogene A. "The Ethics of Consumption Activities: A Future Paradigm?" *Journal of Business Ethics,* June 1998, pp. 871–882.

Buchholz, Rogene A., and Sandra B. Rosenthal. *Business Ethics: The Pragmatic Path beyond Principles to Process.* Upper Saddle River, NJ: Prentice Hall, 1998.

Budman, Matthew. "New Rules for the New Economy." *Across the Board,* October 1998, p. 60.

Bukowitz, Wendi R., and Ruth L. Williams. *Knowledge Management Fieldbook.* London: Financial Times Prentice Hall, 1999.

Burge, Frank. "Loyalty and the New Economy." *Electronic Engineering Times,* April 12, 1999, p. 100.

"Business Ethics," <http://www.bsr.org> (August 4, 2000).

Carlson, John B., and Mark E. Schweitzer. "Productivity Measures and the New Economy." *Economic Commentary,* June 1998, p. 1.

Carr, Nicholas G. "Being Virtual: Character and the New Economy." *Harvard Business Review,* May–June 1999, p. 181.

Carroll, Archie B. "Models of Management Morality for the New Millennium." *Vital Speeches of the Day,* November 1, 1999, pp. 48–50.

Cartwright, Roger, and George Green. *In Charge of Customer Satisfaction.* Cambridge, MA: Blackwell Business, 1997.

Castells, Manuel. *The Rise of the Network Society.* Mauldin, MA: Blackwell Publishers, 1996.

"The Caux Principles." <http://astro.temple.edu/~dialogue/Codes/caux.htm/> (August 4, 2000).

Cavanagh, Gerald F. *American Business Values: With International Perspectives.* Upper Saddle River, NJ: Prentice Hall, 1998.

Chambers, Nancy. "Does the Bell Toll for Your Living Company? Interview with Arie de Geus." *HR Focus,* October 1997, pp. 1–4.

Chander, P. G., and T. Radhakrishnan. "Design Schemes for Rule-Based Systems." *International Journal of Expert Systems,* Vol. 10, No. 1, 1997, pp. 36–41.

Chase, Larry. *Essential Business Tactics for the Net.* New York: Wiley, 1998.

————. "Web Marketers Beware: Ten Traps You Want to Miss." *Advertising Age's Business Marketing,* January 1997, p. M10.

Chesher, James, and Tibor R. Machan. *Business of Commerce: Examining an Honorable Profession.* Stanford, CA: Hoover Institution Press, 1999.

Ciulla, Joanne B., ed. *Ethics, the Heart of Leadership.* New York: Quorum Books, 1998.

Cohen, Don. "Toward a Knowledge Context: Report on the First Annual U.C. Berkeley Forum on Knowledge and the Firm." *California Management Review,* Spring 1998, pp. 22–39.

————. *Managing Knowledge for Business Success.* New York: Conference Board, 1997.

Cohen, Sheldon, and James Moore. "Today's Buzzword: CRM (Customer Relationship Management)." *Public Management (US),* April 2000, pp. 10–13.

Coleman, Zach. "Rosensweig: Firms Must Expand Their World View." *Atlanta Business Chronicle,* November 14, 1997, p. 7C.

Collins, James C. "Letters to the Editor: Review of The Living Company." *Harvard Business Review,* May–June 1997, pp. 182–183.

Colvin, Geoffrey. "Changing Art of Becoming Unbeatable." *Fortune,* November 24, 1997, pp. 299–300.

*The Complete MBA Companion in Global Business.* London: Financial Times Pitman, 1999.

Conaway, Roger N., and Thomas L. Fernandez. "Ethical Preferences among Business Leaders: Implications for Business Schools." *Business Communication Quarterly,* March 2000, pp. 23–38.

Conhaim, Wallys W. "New Rules for the New Economy: Ten Radical Strategies for a Connected World." *Link-Up,* May–June 1999, p. 26.

Coors, Jeffrey H. "Corporate Philanthropy Is Counterproductive," in *Business Ethics,* ed. Tamara L. Roleff, pp. 76–79. San Diego, CA: Greenhaven Press, 1996.

Copacino, William C. "The Emergence of 'Value Networks.'" *Logistics Management and Distribution Report,* August 1999, p. 38.

Coy, Peter. "A New Calculus for the New Economy." *Business Week,* November 8, 1999, pp. 34–35.

Craig, C. Samuel and Susan P. Douglas. "Globalization." *Columbia Journal of World Business,* Spring 1996, pp. 70–81.

Crainer, Stuart. "Shared Values Break Down Borders." *Management Today London,* March 1999, p. 109.

Cram, Tony. *The Power of Relationship Marketing: How to Keep Customers for Life.* London: Financial Times/Pitman, 1994.

"A Crash Course in Customer Relationship Management." *Harvard Management Update,* March 2000, pp. 3–6.

Crocket, Roger O. "A Web That Looks Like the World." *Business Week E.Biz,* March 22, 1999, pp. EB46–EB47.

Crook, Clive. "Confused about the Economy? That's OK. So Is Alan Greenspan." *National Journal,* July 3, 1999, pp. 1934–1935.

Cross, Richard, and Janet Smith. *Customer Bonding: Pathway to Lasting Customer Loyalty.* Lincolnwood, IL: NTC Business Books, 1994.

Curry, Jay, and Adam Curry. *The Customer Marketing Method: How to Implement and Profit from Customer Relationship Management.* New York: Free Press, 2000.

Cvetkovich, Ann, ed. *Articulating the Global and the Local: Globalization and Cultural Studies.* Boulder, CO: Westview Press, 1997.

Dahle, Cheryl. "Can an Old School Learn to Love New Media?" *Fast Company,* October 1999, pp. 98–100.

Dalla Costa, John. *The Ethical Imperative: Why Moral Leadership Is Good Business.* Reading, MA: Addison-Wesley, 1998.

Danaher, Kevin, ed. *Corporations Are Gonna Get Your Mama: Globalization and the Downsizing of the American Dream.* Monroe, ME: Common Courage Press, 1997.

Davenport, Thomas H. "Building the Perfect Workforce." *Workforce,* July 1999, pp. 56–58.

————. "Improving Knowledge Work Processes." *Sloan Management Review,* Summer 1996, pp. 53–65.

————. *Information Ecology: Mastering the Information and Knowledge Environment.* New York: Oxford University Press, 1997.

————. "Managing Customer Support Knowledge." *California Management Review,* Spring 1998, pp. 195–208.

Davenport, Thomas H., David W. DeLong, and Michael C. Beers. "Successful Knowledge Management Projects." *Sloan Management Review,* Winter 1998, pp. 43–57.

Davenport, Thomas H., Robert G. Eccles, and Laurence Prusak. "Information Politics." *Sloan Management Review,* Fall 1992, pp. 53–65.

Davenport, Thomas H., and Laurence Prusak. *Working Knowledge: How Organizations Manage What They Know.* Boston: Harvard Business School Press, 1997.

Davis, Frank W. Jr., and Karl B. Mandrodt. *Customer Responsive Management: The Flexible Advantage.* Cambridge, MA: Blackwell Business, 1996.

Davis, Stan, and Christopher Meyer. *Blur: The Speed of Change in the Connected Economy.* Reading, MA: Addison-Wesley, 1998.

————. "An Economy Turned on Its Head." *Strategy and Leadership,* November–December 1997, pp. 16–19.

Day, George S. *The Market Driven Organization: Understanding, Attracting, and Keeping Valuable Customers.* New York: Free Press, 1999.

de Geus, Arie. *The Living Company.* Boston: Harvard Business School Press, 1997.

de Jonge, Peter. "Riding the Wild, Perilous Waters of Amazon.com." *New York Times Magazine,* March 14, 1999, pp. 36, 38–41, 54, 68, 79, 81.

De Long, J. Bradford. "What 'New' Economy?" *Wilson Quarterly,* Fall 1998, pp. 14–20.

Deans, Bob. "Trade Protest Turns Violent: Talks Affected; Seattle under Curfew." *Palm Beach Post,* December 1, 1999, p. 1A.

DeGeorge, Richard T. *Business Ethics.* Upper Saddle River, NJ: Prentice Hall, 1999.

Demars, Nan. *You Want Me to Do What? When, Where, and How to Draw the Line at Work.* New York: Fireside, 1997.

Deresky, Helen. *International Management: Managing across Borders and Cultures.* Reading, MA: Addison-Wesley, 1997.

Devlin, Keith J. *InfoSense: Turning Information into Knowledge.* New York: W.H. Freeman, 1999.

Dickens, Charles. *A Christmas Carol and The Cricket on the Hearth.* New York: Platt & Peck, 1905.

"Distance Management." *Training and Development,* January 1999, p. 69.

Donaldson, Thomas, and Thomas W. Dunfee. *Ties That Bind.* Boston: Harvard Business School Press, 1999.

Donaldson, Thomas, and Patricia Hogue Werhane, eds. *Ethical Issues in Business: A Philosophical Approach.* Upper Saddle River, NJ: Prentice Hall, 1998.

Doney, Patricia M., Joseph P. Cannon, and Michael R. Mullen. "Understanding the Influence of National Culture on the Development of Trust." *Academy of Management Review,* July 1, 1998, pp. 601–621.

Donnelly, James H. Jr. *Twenty-five Management Lessons from the Customer's Side of the Counter.* Chicago: Irwin, 1996.

Doremus, Paul N., William W. Keller, Simon Reich, and Louis W. Pauly. *The Myth of the Global Corporation.* Princeton, NJ: Princeton University Press, 1998.

Downes, Larry, and Chunka Mui. *Unleashing the Killer App: Digital Strategies from Market Dominance.* Boston: Harvard Business School Press, 1998.

Drucker, Peter F. "Beyond the Information Revolution." *Atlantic Monthly,* October 1999, pp. 47–57.

———. "The Emerging Theory of Manufacturing." *Harvard Business Review,* May–June 1990, pp. 94–102.

———. *Management Challenges for the Twenty-first Century.* New York: HarperBusiness, 1999.

Dutka, Alan. *AMA Handbook for Customer Satisfaction: A Complete Guide to Research, Planning, and Implementation.* Lincolnwood, IL: NTC Business Books, 1995.

———. *Competitive Intelligence for the Competitive Edge.* Lincolnwood, IL: NTC Business Books, 1999.

Dyson, Esther. *Release 2.0: A Design for Living in the Digital Age.* New York: Broadway Books, 1997.

Eckhouse, John Linkages. "Fuel the Economy." *Informationweek,* February 1, 1999, p. 110.

"The Economist Review: Internet Economics." *Economist,* December 12, 1998, p. R7.

Edmondson, Gail, Marsha Johnston, Neil Gross, Seanna Browder, and Kathy Rebello. "Silicon Continent." *Business Week,* May 6, 1996, pp. 131, 135–136.

Edvinsson, Leif, and Michael S. Malone. *Intellectual Capital: Realizing Your Company's True Value by Finding Its Hidden Brainpower.* New York: HarperBusiness, 1997.

Edvinsson, Leif, Grant Miles, Raymond E. Miles, and Vincenzo Perrone. "Some Conceptual and Research Barriers to the Utilization of Knowledge." *California Management Review,* Spring 1998, pp. 281–288.

Einhorn, Bruce, Pete Engardio, and Manjeet Kripalani. "In Search of New Growth Engines." *Business Week,* November 29, 1999, pp. 68–71.

Elashmawi, Farid. "How to Manage across Cultures." *People Management,* March 30, 2000, pp. 52–53.

Elashmawi, Farid, and Philip R. Harris. *Multicultural Management 2000: Essential Cultural Insights for Global Business Success.* Houston, TX: Gulf Publishing, 1998.

Elkington, John. *Cannibals with Forks: The Triple Bottom Line of Twenty-first Century Business.* Oxford: Capstone, 1997.

———. "From the Top." *The Guardian,* October 2, 1999, p. 24.

———. "Management: From the Top." *The Guardian,* April 8, 2000, p. 33.

———. "The Triple Bottom Line Revolution: Reporting for the Third Millennium." *Australian CPA,* December 1999, pp. 75–76.

Epstein, Marc J., and Bill Birchard. *Counting What Counts: Turning Corporate Accountability to Competitive Advantage.* Reading, MA: Perseus Press, 1999.

Estes, Ralph W. *Tyranny of the Bottom Line: Why Corporations Make Good People Do Bad Things.* San Francisco: Berrett-Koehler, 1996.

Evans, Philip, and Thomas S. Wurster. *Blown to Bits: How the New Economics of Information Transforms Strategy.* Boston: Harvard Business School Press, 1999.

————. "Strategy and the New Economics of Information." *Harvard Business Review,* September 1997, pp. 71–82.

Farrell, Robert Jr. "Quality Function Deployment: Helping Business Identify and Integrate the Voice of the Customer." *Industrial Engineering,* October 1994, pp. 44–45.

Ferguson, Andrew Lewis, and Clark. "Find the New Economy." *Fortune,* November 22, 1999, p. 83.

"Finance and Economics: Economics Focus—Lock and Key." *Economist,* September 18, 1999, p. 88.

Fine, Charles H. *Clockspeed: Winning Industry Control I the Age of Temporary Advantage.* Reading, MA: Perseus Books, 1998.

Fisher, Anne. "A Guide for the Globally Clueless." *Fortune,* May 15, 2000, p. 498.

Fites, Donald V. "Make Your Dealers Your Partners." *Harvard Business Review,* March–April 1996, pp. 84–95.

Flanigan, James. "Knowledge Powers New Economy." *Caribbean Business,* April 15, 1999, p. 19.

Forbes, Walter. "A Store as Big as the World." In *The Future of the Electronic Marketplace,* edited by Derek Leebaert. Cambridge, MA: MIT Press, 1998.

Forrest, Edward, and Richard Mizerski, eds. *Interactive Marketing: The Future Present.* Lincolnwood, IL: NTC Business Books, 1996.

Foulkes, Rowland A. "Developing the Global Organization." *Columbia Journal of World Business,* Winter 1994, pp. 90–95.

Fox, Justin. "Just What Is Holding This Economy Up?" *Fortune,* July 20, 1998, pp. 24–25.

Freeman, Chris. "Feature Review: The Information Age." *New Political Economy,* November 1998, pp. 461–466.

Freeza, Bill. "The New Economy and the End of Innocence." *Internetweek,* November 2, 1998, p. 33.

Freidheim, Cyrus F. "The Battle of the Alliances." *Management Review,* September 1999, pp. 47–52.

————. *The Trillion-Dollar Enterprise: How the Alliance Revolution Will Transform Global Business.* Reading, MA: Perseus Books, 1998.

French, Hilary. *Vanishing Borders: Protecting the Planet in the Age of Globalization.* New York: Norton, 2000.

Friedman, Milton. "Milton Friedman's Case against Corporate Social Responsibility." In *Business Ethics,* ed. Tamara L. Roleff, San Diego, CA: Greenhaven Press, 1996. pp. 11–17.

Friedman, Milton, and Rose D. Friedman. "Our Backward Schooling." *Across the Board,* June 1999, p. 10.

Friedman, Thomas L. "How Globalization Hit the High Street." *Global Finance,* June 1999, pp. 23–24.

————. *The Lexus and the Olive Tree: Understanding Globalization.* New York: Anchor Books, 2000.

Fritzsche, David J. *Business Ethics: A Global and Managerial Perspective.* New York : McGraw-Hill, 1997.

Galbraith, Jay A. *Designing the Global Corporation.* San Francisco: Jossey-Bass, 2000.

Ganguly, Ashok S. *Business-Driven Research and Development: Managing Knowledge.* West Lafayette, IN: Ichor Business Books, 1999.

Garten, Jeffrey E. "What Could Go Wrong in the New Economy." *Business Week,* December 13, 1999, p. 28.

———, ed. *World View: Global Strategies for the New Economy.* Boston: Harvard Business School Press, 2000.

Gascoyne, Richard J. "Adapt to the Internet." *Informationweek,* May 5, 1997, pp. 89–100.

Gascoyne, Richard J., and Koray Ozcubukcu. *Corporate Internet Planning Guide: Aligning Internet Strategy with Business Goals.* New York: Van Nostrand Reinhold, 1997.

Gates, William. *Business @ the Speed of Thought: Using a Digital Nervous System.* New York: Time Warner Books, 1999.

Gera, Surendra, and Kurt Mang. "The Knowledge-Based Economy: Shifts in Industrial Output." *Canadian Public Policy,* June 1998, pp. 149–184.

Gerstner, John. "The Other Side of Cyberspace: Interview with Manuel Castells." *Communication World,* March 1999, pp. 11–18.

Ghoshal, Sumantra, and Christopher A. Bartlett. *The Individualized Corporation: A Fundamentally New Approach to Management.* New York: HarperBusiness, 1997.

Gibb, Blair. "Human Rights: Global Aspirations, Local Gospels." *Whole Earth,* Summer 1999, pp. 20–23.

Gilmore, James H., and B. Joseph Pine II. "The Four Faces of Mass Customization." *Harvard Business Review,* January–February 1997, pp. 91–101.

———, eds. *Markets of One: Creating Customer-Unique Value through Mass Customization.* Boston: Harvard Business School Press, 2000.

Gilpin, Robert. *The Challenge of Global Capitalism: The World Economy in the Twenty-first Century.* Princeton, NJ: Princeton University Press, 2000.

Gitomer, Jeffrey. *Customer Satisfaction Is Worthless, Customer Loyalty Is Priceless: How to Make Customers Love You, Keep Them Coming Back, and Tell Everyone They Know.* Austin, TX: Bard Press, 1998.

Godin, Seth. "Permission Is Key to Successful Marketing." *Advertising Age,* November 10, 1997, p. 31.

———. "Permission Marketing: The Way to Make Advertising Work Again." *Direct Marketing,* May 1999, pp. 40–43.

———. "Permission Marketing: The Way to Make Advertising Work Again." *Direct Marketing,* June 1999, pp. 60–63.

———. *Permission Marketing: Turning Strangers into Friends, and Friends into Customers.* New York: Simon & Schuster, 1999.

Goldman, Steven L. *Agile Competitors and Virtual Organizations: Strategies for Enriching the Customer.* New York: Van Nostrand Reinhold, 1997.

Gomme, Paul. "What Labor Market Theory Tells Us about the New Economy." *Economic Review,* July 1998, p. 16.

Gordon, Ian. *Relationship Marketing: New Strategies, Techniques, and Technologies to Win the Customers You Want and Keep Them Forever.* Etobicoke, Ontario: Wiley, Canada, 1998.

Gouillart, Francis J., and Frederick D. Sturdivant. "Spend a Day in the Life of Your Customers." *Harvard Business Review,* January–February 1994, pp. 116–125.

Greco, Susan, Christopher Ciggiano, and Marc Ballon. "I Was Seduced by the New Economy." *Inc.,* February 1999, p. 34.

Green, Heather. "Throw Out Your Old Business Model," *Business Week E.Biz,* March 22, 1999, pp. EB22–EB23.

Greenspan, Alan, and James A. Wilcox. "Is There a New Economy?" *California Management Review,* September 1998, p. 74.

Greider, William. *One World, Ready or Not: The Manic Logic of Global Capitalism.* New York: Simon & Schuster, 1997.

Gross, Neil. "Building Global Communities." *Business Week E.Biz,* March 22, 1999, pp. EB42–EB43.

Gross, T. Scott. "'Outrageous Service' Keeps Them Laughing." *Nation's Business,* March 1992, p. 6.

————. *Outrageous! Unforgettable Service . . . Guilt-free Selling.* New York: AMACON, 1998.

————. *Positively Outrageous Service.* New York: Warner Books, 1994.

Gulati, Ranjay, and Jason Garino. "Get the Right Mix of Bricks and Clicks." *Harvard Business Review,* May–June 2000, pp. 107–114.

Gupta, Anil K., and Vijay Govindarajan. "Managing Global Expansion: A Conceptual Framework." *Business Horizons,* March–April 2000, pp. 45–54.

Hackett, Brian. "The Intellectual Capital Manifesto." *Across the Board,* June 1997, pp. 59–61.

Hackman, Sandra. "Building a Better Economy." *Public Management (US),* September 1997, pp. 4–8.

Hagel, John III. "1999 McKinsey Awards." *Harvard Business Review,* January 2000, p. 137.

————. "Collaborate and Conquer." *Informationweek,* September 14, 1998, pp. 274–277.

————. "The Coming Battle for Customer Information." *Harvard Business Review,* January 1, 1997, p. 53.

————. "Guru Watch." *Inc.,* July 1997, p. 22.

————. *Net Gain: Expanding Markets through Virtual Communities.* Boston: Harvard Business School Press, 1997.

————. "Net Gain: Expanding Markets through Virtual Communities." *Journal of Interactive Marketing,* Winter 1999, pp. 55–65.

————. "Private Lives." *McKinsey Quarterly,* 1999, pp. 6–15.

————. "Unbundling the Corporation." *Harvard Business Review,* March 1, 1999, p. 133.

Hagel, John III, and Marc Singer. *Net Worth: Shaping Markets When Customers Make the Rules.* Boston: Harvard Business School Press, 1999.

Halal, William E., ed. *The Infinite Resource: Creating and Leading the Knowledge Enterprise.* San Francisco: Jossey-Bass, 1998.

Hallberg, Garth, and David Ogilvy. *All Consumers Are Not Created Equal: The Differential Marketing Strategy for Brand Loyalty and Profits.* New York: Wiley, 1995.

Hamel, Gary, and Jeff Sampler. "E-Corporation: More Than Just Web-Based, It's Building a New Industrial Order." *Fortune,* December 7, 1998, pp. 80–92.

Hamm, Steve, Andy Reinhardt, and Peter Burrows. "Builders of the New Economy." *Business Week,* June 21, 1999, p. 118.

Hamm, Steve, and Marcia Stepanek. "From Reengineering to E-Engineering." *Business Week E.Biz,* March 22, 1999, pp. EB14–EB15.

Hammer, Michael, and Steven Stanton. "How Process Enterprises Really Work." *Harvard Business Review,* November 1999, pp. 108–118.

Hammonds, Keith H. "Good News: It's a Small World." *Fast Company,* May 2000, pp. 90–94.

Hansen, Fay. "Compensation in the New Economy." *Compensation and Benefits Review,* January–February 1998, p. 7.

Hansen, Morten T., Nitin Nohria, and Thomas Tierney. "What's Your Strategy for Managing Knowledge?" *Harvard Business Review,* March–April 1999, pp. 106–116.

*Harvard Business Review on Business and the Environment.* Boston: Harvard Business School Press, 2000.

*Harvard Business Review on Knowledge Management.* Boston: Harvard Business School Press, 1998.

Hayes, Bob E. *Measuring Customer Satisfaction: Survey Design, Use, and Statistical Analysis Methods.* New York: McGraw-Hill, 1998.

Haylock, Christina Ford, and Len Muscarella. *Net Success: Twenty-four Leaders in Web Commerce Show You How to Put the Internet to Work for Your Business.* Holbrook, MA: Adams Media, 1999.

Henderson, Hazel. *Beyond Globalization: Shaping a Sustainable Global Economy.* West Hartford, CT: Kumarian Press, 1999.

Heskett, James L., Thomas O. Jones, Gary W. Loveman, and W. Earl Sasser. "Putting the Service-Profit Chain to Work." *Harvard Business Review,* March–April 1994, pp. 164–174.

Heskett, James L., W. Earl Sasser, and Leonard A. Schlesinger. *The Service-Profit Chain: How Leading Companies Link Profit and Growth to Loyalty, Satisfaction, and Value.* New York: Free Press, 1997.

Hiebeler, Robert. *Best Practices: Building Your Business with Customer-Focused Solutions.* New York: Arthur Andersen/Simon & Schuster, 1998.

Hill, Sam, and Glenn Rifkin. *Radical Marketing: From Harvard to Harley, Lessons from Ten That Broke the Rules and Made It Big.* New York: HarperBusiness, 1998.

Hodge, Sheida. *Global Smarts: The Art of Communicating and Deal Making Anywhere in the World.* New York: Wiley, 2000.

Hof, Robert D. "The Buyer Always Wins." *Business Week E.Biz,* March 22, 1999, pp. EB26, EB28.

————. "What Every CEO Needs to Know about Electronic Business." *Business Week E.Biz,* March 22, 1999, pp. EB9–EB12.

Hof, Robert D., Heather Green, and Linda Himelstein. "Now It's Your Web." *Business Week,* October 5, 1998, pp. 164–176.

Holt, Jim. "Gone Global?" *Management Review,* March 2000, p. 13.

Hood, John M. *The Heroic Enterprise: Business and the Common Good.* New York: Free Press, 1996.

Hoover, Judith D., ed. *Corporate Advocacy: Rhetoric in the Information Age.* Westport, CT: Quorum Books, 1997.

Hope, Jeremy, and Tony Hope. *Competing in the Third Wave: The Ten Key Management Issues of the Information Age.* Boston: Harvard Business School Press, 1997.

Hopkins, Michael. *The Planetary Bargain: Corporate Social Responsibility Comes of Age.* New York: St. Martin's Press, 1999.

Hopkins, Michael, and Tom Richman. "The Culture Wars." *Inc.,* May 18, 1999, pp. 107–108.

Horibe, Frances Dale. *Managing Knowledge Workers: New Skills and Attitudes to Unlock the Intellectual Capital in Your Organization.* New York: Wiley, 1999.

"How Nordstrom Became the Leader in Customer Service." *Bottom Line/Business,* October 15, 1995, pp. 7–8.

"How the U.S. Can Shape the Global Economy." *Corporate Board,* January–February 1999, p. 28.

"In a Knowledge-Based Economy, the Race Belongs to the Smartest." *Business News New Jersey,* July 28, 1997, p. 17.

"Internet Economics." *Economist,* December 12, 1998, p. 7.

"Introduction to Corporate Social Responsibility." <http://www.bsr.org> (August 4, 2000).

Jeannet, Jean-Pierre. *Managing with a Global Mindset.* London: Financial Times Prentice Hall, 2000.

Jeffrey, Jaclyn R. "Preparing the Front Line." *Quality Progress,* February 1995, pp. 79–82.

Jennings, Lane. "Building a Business for the Long Term." *Futurist,* April 1998, pp. 45–46.

Jennings, Marianne. *Business Ethics: Case Studies and Selected Readings.* Cincinnati, OH: West Educational Publishing, 1999.

Jensen, Rolf. *The Dream Society: How the Coming Shift from Information to Imagination Will Transform Your Business.* New York: McGraw-Hill, 1999.

Jeurissen, Ronald. "Cannibals with Forks: The Triple Bottom Line of Twenty-first Century Business." *Journal of Business Ethics,* January 2000, pp. 229–231.

Jones, Thomas M., and Norman E. Bowie. "Moral Hazards on the Road to the 'Virtual' Corporation." *Business Ethics Quarterly,* April 1998, pp. 273–292.

Jones, Thomas O., and W. Earl Sasser Jr. "Why Satisfied Customers Defect." *Harvard Business Review,* November–December 1995, pp. 88–99.

Judson, Bruce, and Kate Kelly. *Hyperwars: Eleven Strategies for Survival and Profit in the Era of Online Business.* New York: Scribner, 1999.

Kalakota, Ravi. "Intranets: The SAP Killer?" *Computerworld,* March 11, 1996, p. 37.

Kalakota, Ravi, and Ralph A. Oliva. "Move Over, E-Commerce." *Marketing Management,* Fall 1999, pp. 22–32.

Kalakota, Ravi, and Marcia Robinson. *E-Business: Roadmap for Success.* Reading, MA: Addison-Wesley, 1999.

Kalakota, Ravi, and Andrew B. Whinston. *Electronic Commerce: A Manager's Guide.* Reading, MA: Addison-Wesley, 1997.

———. *Frontiers of Electronic Commerce.* Reading, MA: Addison-Wesley, 1996.

———. "Payment Schemes Needed." *Computerworld,* February 27, 1995, p. 66.

Kanter, Rosabeth Moss. "Change Is Everyone's Job: Managing the Extended Enterprise in a Globally Connected World." *Organizational Dynamics,* Summer 1999, pp. 6–23.

———. "Collaborative Advantage: The Art of Alliances." *Harvard Business Review,* July–August 1994, pp. 96–108.

———. "Thriving Locally in the Global Economy." *Harvard Business Review,* September–October 1995, pp. 151–160.

———. *World Class: Thriving Locally in the Global Economy.* New York: Simon & Schuster, 1997.

Kanter, Rosabeth Moss, and Thomas D. Dretler. "'Global Strategy' and Its Impact on Local Operations: Lessons from Gillette Singapore." *Academy of Management Executive,* November 1998, pp. 60–68.

Kantrow, Alan M. "Intelligent Enterprise and Public Markets." *McKinsey Quarterly,* 1994, No. 2, pp. 83–89.

Karake, Zeinab A. *Organizational Downsizing, Discrimination, and Corporate Social Responsibility.* Westport, CT: Quorum Books, 1999.

Katz, Bruce, and Katherine Allen. "Help Wanted." *Brookings Review,* Fall 1999, pp. 31–35.

Kawasaki, Guy. "The Beauty of Metaphor." *Forbes,* August 25, 1997, p. 84.

———. "Bricks to Bits." *Forbes,* May 31, 1999, p. 248.

———. "Geek Speak" *Forbes,* August 24, 1998, p. 96.

———. "Needbucks.com." *Forbes,* January 10, 2000, p. 188.

———. "Put Up a Soapbox." *Forbes,* June 15, 1998, p. 136.

———. "Time to Money." *Forbes,* March 22, 1999, p. 136.

———. "Who Cares about Sex?" *Forbes,* October 20, 1997, p. 296.

———. "Why Newspapers Are in Trouble." *Forbes,* February 9, 1998, p. 102.

Kawasaki, Guy, and Michele Moreno. Rules for Revolutionaries: The Capitalist Manifesto for Creating New Products and Services. New York: HarperBusiness, 1999.

Kelly, Eileen P. "A Better Way to Think about Business: How Personal Integrity Leads to Corporate Success." *Academy of Management Executive,* May 2000, pp. 127–128.

Kelly, Kevin. *New Rules for the New Economy: Ten Radical Strategies for a Connected World.* New York: Viking, 1998.

Kennedy, Carol. "New Rules for the New Economy." *Directory,* November 1998, p. 121.

Kets de Vries, Manfred F. R. *The New Global Leaders: Richard Branson, Percy Barnevik, and David Simon.* San Francisco: Jossey-Bass, 1999.

Khan, Azizur Rahman, ed. *Employment Expansion and Macroeconomic Stability under Increasing Globalization.* New York: St. Martin's Press, 1997.

Kidder, Rushworth M. "Guiding Responsible Discussion about Ethics." *Association Management,* October 1999, pp. 88–98.

———. *How Good People Make Tough Choices: Resolving the Dilemmas of Ethical Living.* New York: William Morrow, 1995.

———. "What Ever Happened to Honesty?" *Boston Globe,* November 20, 1998, p. A27.

Kilmann, Ralph H. *Producing Useful Knowledge for Organizations.* San Francisco: Jossey-Bass, 1994.

Kim, W. Chan, and Renée A. "Mauborgne Making Global Strategies Work." *Sloan Management Review,* Spring 1993, pp. 11–27.

Kindley, Randall W., and David F. Good, ed. *Challenge of Globalization and Institution Building: Lessons from Small European States.* Boulder, CO: Westview Press, 1997.

Kinni, Theodore. "New Rules for the New Economy." *Training,* January 1999, pp. 94–96.

Kirkpatrick, David. "E-Ware War: Competition Comes to Enterprise Software." *Fortune,* December 7, 1998, pp. 102–104, 106, 108, 110,112.

Klein, David A. *The Strategic Management of Intellectual Capital.* Boston: Butterworth-Heinemann, 1997.

"Know What You Know." <http://www.cio.com/archive/021598_exerpt_content.html> (March 13, 2000).

"The Knowledge Gurus." *New Statesman,* September 27, 1999, pp. xix–xxi.

*Knowledge Management: A New Competitive Asset.* Washington, DC: Special Libraries Association, 1998.

Kogut, Bruce. "What Makes a Company Global?" *Harvard Business Review,* January 1999, pp. 165–174.

Koretz, Gene. "A New Economy, but No New Deal." *Business Week,* July 10, 2000, p. 34.

Korper, Steffano, and Juanita Ellis. *The E-Commerce Book: Building the E-Empire.* San Diego: Academic Press, 2000.

Kosiur, David R. *Understanding Electronic Commerce.* Redmond, WA: Microsoft Press, 1997.

Kotler, Philip. "A Generic Concept of Marketing." *Marketing Management,* Fall 1998, pp. 48–54.

———. *Kotler on Marketing: How to Create, Win, and Dominate Markets.* New York: Free Press, 1999.

———, ed. *Marketing Management and Strategy: A Reader.* Englewood Cliffs, NJ: Prentice Hall, 1980.

Koulopoulos, Thomas M. "Make Knowledge Accessible to All." *Informationweek,* April 26, 1999, pp. 17ER–20ER.

———. "The Portal Landscape." *Informationweek,* April 26, 1999, p. 20ER.

———. *Smart Companies, Smart Tools: Transforming Business Processes into Business Assets.* New York: Van Nostrand Reinhold, 1997.

———. *Smart Things to Know about Knowledge Management.* New York: Van Nostrand Reinhold, 1999.

Koulopoulos, Thomas M., Richard Spinello, and Wayne Toms. *Corporate Instinct: Building a Knowing Enterprise for the Twenty-first Century.* New York: Van Nostrand Reinhold, 1997.

Krebs, Valdis. "Knowledge Networks: Mapping and Measuring Knowledge Creation in Your Organization." *IHRIM Journal,* September 1998, pp. 17–21.

Krugman, Paul. "Requiem for the New Economy." *Fortune,* November 10, 1997, pp. 32–36.

Kruth, Joseph. "Sustainable Communities, Globalization and Increasing Complexity." *Futures Research Quarterly,* Summer 1998, pp. 23–40.

Kulik, Todd. *Expanding Parameters of Global Corporate Citizenship.* New York : Conference Board, 1999.

Labarre, Polly. "The New Face of Office Politics." *Fast Company,* October 1999, pp. 80–82.

Laidlaw, Stuart. "Demonstrations Scuttle Talks." *Toronto Star,* December 1, 1999, p. 1A.

Landers, Jim, and Paul Pringle. "Violent Protests Rock Trade Talks: National Guard Called In after Seattle Ceremonies Are Halted." *Dallas Morning News,* December 1, 1999, p. 1A.

Ledgerwood, Grant, and Arlene Idol Broadhurst. *Environment, Ethics, and the Corporation.* New York: St. Martin's Press, 2000.

Leebaert, Derek. "A Strategic Approach to Electronic Transaction Conversion." *Telecommunications (American Edition),* January 1999, pp. 49–52.

————. "Transaction Interoperability: The Key to Electronic Commerce." *Telecommunications (American Edition),* June 1996, pp. 58–62.

————, ed. *The Future of the Electronic Marketplace.* Cambridge, MA: MIT Press, 1998.

Leonard, Dorothy. *Wellsprings of Knowledge: Building and Sustaining the Sources of Innovation.* Boston: Harvard Business School Press, 1998.

Leonard-Barton, Dorothy. "Managing Creative Abrasion in the Workplace." *Harvard Business Review,* July–August 1995, pp. 2–3.

Leonard, Dorothy, and Sylvia Sensiper. "The Role of Tacit Knowledge in Group Innovation." *California Management Review,* Spring 1998, pp. 112–132.

Lewicki, Roy J., Daniel J. McAllister, and Robert Bies. "Trust and Distrust: New Relationships and Realities." *Academy of Management Review,* July 1, 1998, pp. 438–459.

Lieber, Ronald B. "Storytelling: A New Way to Get Close to Your Customer." *Fortune,* February 3, 1997, pp. 102–110.

Liebowitz, *Jay. Building Organizational Intelligence: A Knowledge Management Primer.* Boca Raton, FL: St. Lucie Press, 1998.

————. *Knowledge Management and Its Integrative Elements.* Boca Raton, FL: St. Lucie Press, 1997.

————. *Knowledge Management Handbook.* Boca Raton, FL: St. Lucie Press, 1999.

————. *Knowledge Organizations: What Every Manager Should Know.* Boca Raton, FL: St. Lucie Press, 1998.

*The Link between Corporate Citizenship and Financial Performance.* New York: Conference Board, 1999.

Linton, Ian. *Building Customer Loyalty.* London: Pitman, 1993.

Lippke, Richard L. *Radical Business Ethics.* Lanham, MD: Rowman & Littlefield, 1995.

Littrell, Mary Ann, and Marsha Ann Dickson. *Social Responsibility in the Global Market: Fair Trade of Cultural Products.* Thousand Oaks, CA: Sage, 1999.

Locke, Christopher, Rick Levine, Doc Searls, and David Weinberger. *The Cluetrain Manifesto: The End of Business as Usual.* Reading, MA: Perseus Books, 2000.

Lowenstein, Michael W. *The Customer Loyalty Pyramid.* Westport, CT: Quorum Books, 1997.

Luttwak, Edward. *Turbo-Capitalism: Winners and Losers in the Global Economy.* New York: HarperCollins, 1999.

Maas, Judith. "The Search for Meaning in Organizations: Seven Practical Questions for Ethical Managers." *Sloan Management Review,* Winter 2000, pp. 101–102.

Machan, Tibor R. *Business Ethics in the Global Market.* Stanford, CA: Hoover Institution Press, 1999.

Madsen, Hunter. "Survival Rules." *Management Today,* August 1999, p. 40.

Mandel, Michael J. "How Fast Can This Hot-Rod Go?" *Business Week,* November 29, 1999, pp. 40–42.

———. "How Most Economists Missed the Boat." *Business Week,* November 15, 1999, pp. 100–102.

———. "New Economy Starts to Hit Home." *Business Week,* March 23, 1998, p. 34.

———. "The New Economy: For Better or Worse." *Business Week,* October 19, 1998, p. 42.

———. "The Prosperity Gap." *Business Week,* September 27, 1999, pp. 90–96.

———. "Taking the Measure of the New Economy." *Business Week,* October 19, 1998, p. 22.

———. "Yes, But for Now, Let the New Economy Run." *Business Week,* June 21, 1999, p. 39.

Mandel, Michael J., and Laura Cohn. "New Math for the New Economy." *Business Week,* September 20, 1999, p. 35.

March, James G. *The Pursuit of Organizational Intelligence.* Malden, MA: Blackwell, 1999.

Marquardt, Michael J. *Action Learning in Action: Transforming Problems and People for World-Class Organizational Learning.* Palo Alto, CA: Davies-Black, 1999.

———. *The Global Advantage: How World Class Organizations Improve Performance Through Globalization.* Houston, TX, Gulf Publishing Company, 1998.

———. *Technology-based Learning: Maximizing Human Performance and Corporate Success.* Boca Raton, FL: St. Lucie Press, 1999.

Martin, Charles L. *The Digital Estate: Strategies for Competing, Surviving, and Thriving in an Internetworked World.* New York: McGraw-Hill, 1997.

———. *Net Future: The Seven Cybertrends That Will Drive Your Business, Create New Wealth, and Define Your Future.* New York: McGraw-Hill, 1999.

McCallum, John S. "The New Economy: Fact or Fantasy?" *Ivey Business Journal,* November–December 1999, pp. 75–77.

McCauley, Lucy. "Voices: The State of the New Economy." *Fast Company,* September 1999, pp. 111–152.

McClenaen, John S. "Working the World." *Industry Week,* August 15, 1996, pp. 80–86.

McDermott, Lynda, Bill Waite, and Nolan Brawley. "Putting Together a World-Class Team." *Training and Development,* January 1999, pp. 47–51.

McDermott, Richard. "Why Information Technology Inspired but Cannot Deliver Knowledge Management." *California Management Review,* Summer 1999, pp. 103–117.

McDonald, Gael. "Business Ethics: Practical Proposals for Organisations." *Journal of Business Ethics,* May 2000, pp. 169–284.

McIntosh, Malcolm. *Corporate Citizenship: Successful Strategies for Responsible Companies.* London: Financial Times, Pitman, 1998.

McKenna, Regis. *Real Time: Preparing for the Age of the Never Satisfied Customer.* Boston: Harvard Business School Press, 1997.

———. *Relationship Marketing: Successful Strategies for the Age of the Customer.* Reading, MA: Perseus Press, 1993.

"Memories of the Future: Interview with Arie de Geus." *Across the Board,* July–August 1997, pp. 39–44.

Michaels, James W. "How New Is the New Economy?" *Forbes,* October 11, 1999, pp. 48–49.

Micklethwait, John, and Adrian Woolridge. *A Future Perfect: The Challenge and Hidden Promise of Globalization.* New York: Crown Business Books, 2000.

Mies, Maria, and Veronika Bennholdt-Thomsen. *The Subsistence Perspective: Beyond the Globalized Economy.* New York: Zed Books, 1999.

"The Minnesota Principles." <http://www.cebcglobal.org/MN_PRIN.htm/> (August 4, 2000).

Modahl, Mary. *Now or Never: How Companies Must Change Today to Win the Battle for Internet Consumers.* New York: HarperBusiness, 1999.

Modahl, Mary, Bill Doyle, and Ben Abbott. "What Advertising Works." *Mediaweek,* May 5, 1997, pp. 38–42.

Molitor, Graham T. T. "The Next 1,000 Years: The 'Big Five' Engines of Economic Growth." *Futurist,* December 1999, pp. 13–18.

Moore, Geoffrey A. *Inside the Tornado: Marketing Strategies from Silicon Valley's Cutting Edge.* New York: Simon & Schuster, 1995.

Moore, James F. "The New Corporate Form." In *Blueprint to the Digital Economy: Wealth Creation in the Era of E-Business,* edited by Don Tapscott, Alex Lowy, and David Ticoll. New York: McGraw-Hill, 1998.

Morris, Michael H., Duane L. Davis, and Jeffrey W. Allen. "Fostering Corporate Entrepreneurship: Cross-Cultural Comparisons of the Importance of Individualism versus Collectivism." *Journal of International Business Studies,* 1994, first quarter, pp. 65–89.

Morris, Thomas V. *If Aristotle Ran General Motors: The New Soul of Business.* New York: Henry Holt, 1997.

———. *True Success: A New Philosophy of Excellence.* New York: G. P. Putnam's Sons, 1995.

Mougayar, Walid. "E-Commerce? E-Business? Who E-Cares?" *Computerworld,* November 2, 1998, p. 33.

———. "The Next Generation of Affiliations." *Business 2.0,* August 1999, p. 66.

———. *Opening Digital Markets: Battle Plans and Business Strategies for Internet Commerce.* New York: McGraw-Hill, 1997.

———. "Seeing beyond the Main Web Site." *Ivey Business Quarterly,* Fall 1998, pp. 21–22.

———. "What You Can Learn from the Portals." *Computerworld,* August 31, 1998, p. 32.

Muhammad, Tariq K. "Leaders of the Digital Economy." *Black Enterprise,* March 1999, pp. 72–77.

Myers, Paul S., ed. *Knowledge Management and Organizational Design.* Boston: Butterworth-Heinemann, 1996.

Myron, Monique Reece. "Expert Discusses One-to-One Strategy." *Denver Business Journal,* February 26, 1999, p. 19A.

Naisbitt, John. *High Tech, High Touch: Technology and Our Search for Meaning.* New York: Broadway Books, 1999.

Nalebuff, Barry J., and Adam M. Brandenburger. "Co-opetition: Competitive and Cooperative Business Strategies for the Digital Economy." *Strategy and Leadership,* November–December 1997, pp. 28–35.

Narus, James A., and James C. Anderson. "Rethinking Distribution: Adaptive Channels." *Harvard Business Review,* July–August 1996, pp. 112–120.

Naumann, Earl. *Customer Satisfaction Measurement and Management: Using the Voice of the Customer.* Cincinnati, OH: Thomson Executive Press, 1995.

Naumann, Earl, and Donald W. Jackson Jr. "One More Time: How Do You Satisfy Customers?" *Business Horizons,* May–June 1999, pp. 71–76.

Neuborne, Ellen, and Kathleen Kerwin. "Generation Y: Today's Teens—The Biggest Bulge since the Boomers—May Force Marketers to Toss Their Old Tricks." *Business Week,* February 15, 1999, pp. 81–88.

Newell, Frederick. *Loyalty.com: Customer Relationship Management in the New Era of Internet Marketing.* New York: McGraw-Hill, 2000.

———. *New Rules of Marketing: How to Use One-to-One Relationship Marketing to Be the Leader in Your Industry.* New York: McGraw-Hill, 1997.

Nohria, Nitin, and Sumantra Ghoshal. *Differentiated Network: Organizing Multinational Corporations for Value Creation.* San Francisco: Jossey-Bass, 1997.

Nonaka, Ikujiro, and Noboru Konno. "The Concept of 'ba': Building a Foundation for Knowledge Creation." *California Management Review,* Spring 1998, pp. 40–54.

Nonaka, Ikujiro, and Hirotaka Takeuchi. *The Knowledge-Creating Company: How Japanese Companies Create the Dynamics of Innovation.* New York: Oxford University Press, 1995.

"Now You Know." *Economist,* May 27, 1995, p. 58.

Nykiel, Ronald A. *Keeping Customers in Good Times and Bad.* Stamford, CT: Longmeadow Press, 1992.

O'Dell, Carla. "Is KM a Fad?" *Training,* March 1999, pp. 36–42.

O'Dell, Carla, and C. Jackson Grayson Jr. *If Only We Knew What We Know.* New York: Free Press, 1998.

O'Dell, Susan M., and Joan A. Pajunen. *The Butterfly Customer: Capturing the Loyalty of Today's Elusive Customer.* New York: Wiley, 1997.

Ohmae, Kenichi. *Evolving Global Economy: Making Sense of the New World Order.* Boston: Harvard Business School Press, 1995.

Oliver, Richard W. *The Shape of Things to Come: Seven Imperatives for Winning in the New World of Business.* New York: McGraw-Hill, 1998.

Olson, Margi. "Practical Solutions for Managing Knowledge." *IHRIM Journal,* December 1998, pp. 11–17.

Omae, Kenichi. *The Borderless World: Power and Strategy in the Interlinked Economy.* New York: HarperBusiness, 1999.

———. *The End of the Nation State: The Rise of Regional Economics.* New York: Free Press, 1995.

Ormerod, Paul. *Butterfly Economics: A New General Theory of Social and Economic Behavior.* New York: Pantheon Books, 2000.

Owen, Geoffrey. "Capitalising on Knowledge." *Management Today,* July 1999, p. 43.

Pan, Shan L., and Harry Scarbrough. "Knowledge Management in Practice: An Exploratory Case Study." *Technology Analysis and Strategic Management,* September 1999, pp. 359–374.

Papows, Jeff. "Comdex Keynote: Lotus President Jeff Papows—It's All about the Internet." *Computer Reseller News,* June 16, 1997, p. 36.

———. Enterprise.com: Market Leadership in the Information Age. Reading, MA: Perseus Books, 1998.

Parker, Barbara. *Globalization and Business Practice.* London: Sage, 1998.

Pascarella, Perry. "Management: Technique." *Management Review,* October 1997, pp. 37–41.

Pasternack, Bruce A., and Albert J. Viscio. *The Centerless Corporation: A New Model for Transforming Your Organization for Growth and Prosperity.* New York: Simon & Schuster, 1998.

Pava, Moses L. "Religious Business Ethics and Political Liberalism: An Integrative Approach." *Journal of Business Ethics,* November 1998, pp. 1633–1652.

———. *Search for Meaning in Organizations: Seven Practical Questions for Ethical Managers.* Westport, CT: Quorum Books, 1999.

Peacock, Peter R. "Data Mining in Marketing: Part 1." *Marketing Management,* Winter 1998, pp. 8–18.

Peppers, Don, and Martha Rogers. "Do You Really Know Your Customers?" *Sales and Marketing Management,* January 1999, pp. 26–27.

———. "Don't Drown Customers in Choices." *Sales and Marketing Management,* December 1998, pp. 24–25.

———. "Don't Put Customer Relationships on Hold." *Sales and Marketing Management,* September 1999, pp. 26–27.

———. *Enterprise One-to-One: Tools for Competing in the Interactive Age.* New York: Currency/Doubleday, 1997.

———. "Growing Revenues with Cross-Selling." *Sales and Marketing Management,* June 1999, p. 24.

————. "Is Your Company Ready for One-to-One Marketing?" *Harvard Business Review,* January–February 1999, pp. 151–160.

————. "Lessons from the Front: Five Companies That Have What It Takes to Become a 1:1 Enterprise." *Marketing Tools,* January 11, 1998, p. 3842.

————. *The One-to-One Future: Building Relationships One Customer at a Time.* New York: Currency/Doubleday, 1993.

————. "The Price of Customer Service. *Sales and Marketing Management,* April 1999, pp. 20–21.

————. "The Short Way to Long-Term Relationships." *Sales and Marketing Management,* May 1999, pp. 24–25.

————, eds. *The One-to-One Manager: Real-World Lessons in Customer Relationship Management.* New York: Doubleday, 1999.

Peppers, Don, Martha Rogers, and Bob Dorf. *The One-to-One Fieldbook: The Complete Toolkit for Implementing a One-to-One Marketing Program.* New York: Bantam Doubleday Dell, 1999.

Peppers, Don, Martha Rogers, Steve Munday, and Jay Winchester. "Marketing's New Direction." *Sales and Marketing Management,* March 1999, pp. 48–53.

Petreley, Nicholas. "Talkin' about a Revolution: Support Is Key to the New Open-Source Economy." *InfoWorld,* May 10, 1999, p. 126.

Petzinger, Thomas. *The New Pioneers: The Men and Women Who Are Transforming the Workplace and Marketplace.* New York: Simon & Schuster, 1999.

Pfeffer, Jeffrey, and Robert I. Sutton. *The Knowing-Doing Gap: How Smart Companies Turn Knowledge into Action.* Boston: Harvard Business School Press, 1999.

Pine, B. Joseph. "Joe Pine's Secret for Keeping Customers: Mass Customization." *Bottom Line/Business,* July 15, 1995, pp. 3–4.

Pine, B. Joseph, and James H. Gilmore. *The Experience Economy: Work Is Theater and Every Business a Stage.* Boston: Harvard Business School Press, 1999.

Pine, B. Joseph, Don Peppers, and Martha Rogers. "Do You Want to Keep Your Customers Forever?" *Harvard Business Review,* March–April 1995, pp. 102–114.

Pink, Daniel H. "What Happened to Your Parachute?" *Fast Company,* September 1999, pp. 238–246.

Porter, Michael E. "Location, Competition, and Economic Development: Local Clusters in a Global Economy." *Economic Development Quarterly,* February 2000, pp. 15–34.

————. *On Competition.* Boston: Harvard Business School Press, 1998.

Porter, Michael E., and Anne Habiby. "A Window on the New Economy." *Inc.,* May 1999, pp. 49–50.

Pospisil, Vivian. "New Rules, Old Lessons." *Industry Week,* October 19, 1998, p. 126.

Prahalad, C. K., and Kenneth Lieberthal. "The End of Corporate Imperialism." *Harvard Business Review,* July–August 1998, pp. 69–79.

Probst, Gilbert. *Managing Knowledge: Building Blocks for Success.* New York: Wiley, 2000.

Probst, Gilbert, and Bettina S. T. Büchel. *Organizational Learning: The Competitive Advantage of the Future.* New York: Prentice Hall, 1997.

Prokesch, Steven E. "Competing on Customer Service: An Interview with British Airways' Sir Colin Marshall." *Harvard Business Review,* November–December 1995, pp. 101–116.

Prusak, Laurence. "The Knowledge Advantage." *Strategy and Leadership,* March–April 1996, pp. 6–8.

————, ed. *Knowledge in Organizations.* Boston: Butterworth-Heinemann, 1997.

Prusak, Laurence, and Liam Fahey. "The Eleven Deadliest Sins of Knowledge Management." *California Management Review,* Spring 1998, pp. 265–276.

Pukszta, Helen. "Forget Knowledge Management: Back to Information." *Computerworld,* May 3, 1999, p. 32.

Quazi, Ali M., and Dennis O'Brien. "An Empirical Test of a Cross-National Model of Corporate Social Responsibility." *Journal of Business Ethics,* May 2000, pp. 33–51.

Quinn, James Brian. "Appraising Intellectual Assets." *McKinsey Quarterly,* 1994, No. 2, pp. 90–95.

———. *Innovation Explosion: Intellect and Software to Revolutionize Growth Strategies.* New York: Free Press, 1997.

———. "The Intelligent Enterprise: A New Paradigm." *Academy of Management Executive,* November 1992, pp. 48–63.

———. "Leveraging Intellect." *Executive Excellence,* October 1993, pp. 7–8.

———. "Managing the Intelligent Enterprise: Knowledge and Service-Based Strategies." *Planning Review,* September–October 1993, pp. 13–16.

Quinn, James Brian, Philip Anderson, and Sydney Finkelstein. "Leveraging Intellect." *Academy of Management Executive,* August 1996, pp. 7–27.

Qureshi, Anique A., Jae K. Shim, and Joel G. Siegel. "Artificial Intelligence in Accounting and Business." *National Public Accountant,* September 1998, pp. 13–18.

Ransdell, Eric. "Network Effects." *Fast Company,* September 1999, pp. 208–224.

Raymond, Joan. "2020 Vision." *American Demographics,* December 1999, pp. 46–55.

"Readjusting the Lens." *Economist,* November 20, 1999, pp. 29–30.

Reder, Alan. *In Pursuit of Principle and Profit: Business Success through Social Responsibility.* New York: G. P. Putnam's Sons, 1994.

Reichheld, Frederick F. "Business Loyalty." *Executive Excellence,* June 1997, p. 19.

———. "Learning from Customer Defections." *Harvard Business Review,* March–April 1996, pp. 56–69.

———. "Loyalty and the Renaissance of Marketing." *Marketing Management,* 1994, pp. 10–21.

———. "Loyalty-Based Management." *Harvard Business Review,* March–April 1993, pp. 64–73.

———. "Wrong Move." *Inc.,* March 1996, pp. 19–20.

Reichheld, Frederick F., and Thomas Teal. *The Loyalty Effect: The Hidden Force behind Growth, Profits, and Lasting Value.* Boston: Harvard Business School Press, 1996.

Reingold, Jennifer. "The Power of Cosmic Thinking." *Business Week,* June 7, 1999, p. 17.

Riahi-Belkaoui, Ahmed. *Corporate Social Awareness and Financial Outcomes.* Westport, CT: Quorum Books, 1999.

Richman, Tom. "Service Industries: Why Customers Leave." *Harvard Business Review,* January–February 1996, pp. 9–10.

Ries, Laura, and Al Ries. *The Twenty-two Immutable Laws of Branding: How to Build a Product or Service into a World-Class Brand.* New York: HarperCollins, 1998.

Roos, Johan. *Managing Knowledge: Perspectives on Cooperation and Competition.* Thousand Oaks, CA: Sage, 1996.

Roos, Johan, and Georg von Krogh. "Figuring Out Your Competence Configuration." *European Management Journal,* December 1992, pp. 422–427.

———. "Perspective on Knowledge, Competence and Strategy." *A Personnel Review,* 1995, pp. 56–76.

Roos, Johan, et al., eds. *Intellectual Capital: Navigating in the New Business Landscape.* New York: New York University Press, 1997.

"Rosabeth Moss Kanter: World-Class Thinker." *Management Review,* December 1995, pp. 25–27.

Rosen, Robert. "Enter the Brave New World." *Workforce,* April 2000, pp. 76–77.

———. "The New Rules of Business." *Workforce,* April 2000, p. 80.

Rosen, Robert H., Patricia Digh, Marshall Singer, and Carl Phillips. *Global Literacies: Lessons on Business Leadership and National Cultures.* New York: Simon & Schuster, 2000.

Rosenoer, Jonathan, Douglas Armstrong, and J. Russell Gates. *The Clickable Corporation.* New York: Free Press, 1999.

Rosensweig, Jeffrey A. *Winning the Global Game: A Strategy for Linking People and Profits.* New York: Free Press, 1998.

Rosenthal, Sandra B. *Rethinking Business Ethics: A Pragmatic Approach.* New York: Oxford University Press, 2000.

Rousseau, Denise M., and Michael B. Arthur. "The Boundaryless Human Resource Function: Building Agency and Community in the New Economic Era." *Organizational Dynamics,* Spring 1999, pp. 6–18.

Royal, Weld F. "Keep Them Coming Back." *Sales and Marketing Management,* September 1995, pp. 50–52.

Sagawa, Shirley, and Eli Segal. *Common Interest, Common Good: Creating Value through Business and Social Sector Partnerships.* Boston: Harvard Business School Press, 1999.

————. "Common Interest, Common Good: Creating Value through Business and Social Sector Partnerships." *California Management Review,* Winter 2000, pp. 105–122.

Sager, Ira. "Go Ahead, Farm Out Those Jobs." *Business Week E.Biz,* March 22, 1999, p. EB35.

Sahlman, William A. "The New Economy Is Stronger Than You Think." *Harvard Business Review,* November–December 1999, pp. 99–106.

Sanchez, Ron, and Aime Heene. *Strategic Learning and Knowledge Management.* New York: Wiley, 1998.

Sassen, Saskia. "Women's Burden: Counter-Geographies of Globalization and the Feminization of Survival." *Journal of International Affairs,* Spring 2000, pp. 503–524.

Sassen, Saskia, and Kwame Anthony Appiah. *Globalization and Its Discontents.* New York: New Press, 1998.

Sawhney, Mohanbir, and Sumant Mandal. "Go Global." *Business 2.0,* May 2000, pp. 178–215.

Schmitt, Bernd H. *Experiential Marketing: How to Get Customers to Sense, Feel, Think, Act, Relate to Your Company and Brands.* New York: Free Press, 1999.

Schmitt, Bernd, and Alex Simonson. *Marketing Aesthetics: The Strategic Management of Brands, Identity, and Image.* New York: Free Press, 1997.

Schofield, Jack. "Lords of the New Economy." *Management Today,* September 1998, p. 72.

Schöllhammer, Hans. "Strategies and Methodologies in International Business and Comparative Management Research." *Management International Review,* Special Issue, 1994, pp. 5–20.

Schonfeld, Erick. "Schwab Puts It All Online." *Fortune,* December 7, 1998, pp. 94–96, 98, 100.

Schrage, Michael. "E-Mail or E-Sting? Your Boss Knows, But He's Not Telling." *Fortune,* March 20, 2000, p. 240.

Schultz, Don E., and Philip J. Kitchen. *Communicating Globally: An Integrated Marketing Approach.* Lincolnwood, IL: NTC Business Books, 2000.

Schwandt, David R. *Organizational Learning: From World-Class Theories to Global Practice.* Boca Raton, FL: St. Lucie Press, 2000.

Schwartz, Evan I. *Digital Darwinism: Seven Breakthrough Business Strategies for Surviving in the Cutthroat Web Economy.* New York: Broadway Books, 1999.

————. *Webonomics: Nine Essential Principles for Growing Your Business on the World Wide Web.* New York: Broadway Books, 1997.

Schwartz, Peter, and Blair Gibb. *When Good Companies Do Bad Things: Responsibility and Risk in an Age of Globalization.* New York: Wiley, 1999.

Schwartz, Peter, Peter Leyden, and Joel Hyatt. *The Long Boom: A Vision for the Coming Age of Prosperity.* Reading, MA: Perseus Books, 1999.

Schwerin, David A. *Conscious Capitalism: Principles for Prosperity.* Boston: Butterworth-Heinemann, 1998.

Sears, David. "Staffing the New Economy: Shortage or Myth?" *HR Magazine,* June 1998, p. 130.

Seglin, Jeffrey L. "As Office Snooping Grows, Who Watches the Watchers?" *New York Times,* June 18, 2000, pp. 3–4.

———. "Boys on the Brand." *Inc.,* June 13, 2000, pp. 145–146.

———. "The Ethics Policy: Mind-Set over Matter." *New York Times,* July 16, 2000, p. 4.

———. "Ethics Requires Revealing the Whole Truth: Trust, Rather Than Selective Disclosure, by Its Nature Is an Act of Reasonable Faith." *Houston Chronicle,* May 28, 2000, p. 5.

———. "The Future of Business." *Inc.,* May 1999, p. 102.

———. "Writing the Book on Managing Employees." *Inc.,* June 1999, p. 111.

Seglin, Jeffrey L., and Norman R. Augustine. *The Good, the Bad, and Your Business: Choosing Right When Ethical Dilemmas Pull You Apart.* New York: Wiley, 2000.

Sellers, Patricia. "Inside the First E-Christmas." *Fortune,* February 1, 1999, pp. 70–73.

Sennett, Richard. *The Corrosion of Character: The Personal Consequences of Work in the New Capitalism.* New York: Norton, 2000.

———. "How Work Destroys Social Inclusion." *New Statesman,* May 31, 1999, pp. 25–27.

———. "Why Good Workers Make Bad People." *New Statesman,* October 9, 1998, pp. 25–27.

———. "The Wonder of Work." *Los Angeles Times,* September 5, 1999, p. 3.

Seybold, Patricia B. "Death of the Computer Salesman." *Computerworld,* April 7, 1997, p. 35.

———. "How to Succeed in E-Business." *Computerworld,* November 9, 1998, pp. 85–86.

———. "Privacy, Individual Services Are in the Smart Cards." *Computerworld,* July 21, 1997, p. 37.

Seybold, Patricia B., with Ronni Marshak. *Customers.com: How to Create a Profitable Business Strategy for the Internet and Beyond.* New York: Times Business, 1998.

Shapiro, Carl, and Hal R. Varian. *Information Rules: A Strategic Guide to the Network Economy.* Boston: Harvard Business School Press, 1998.

———. "Versioning: The Smart Way to Sell Information." *Harvard Business Review,* November–December 1998, pp. 106–114.

Shaw, William H. *Business Ethics.* Belmont, CA: Wadsworth, 1999.

Shelton, Ken. *Best of Class: Building a Customer Service Organization.* Provo, UT: Executive Excellence, 1998.

Sheridan, John H. "What Do You Really Know about . . . Customer Satisfaction?" *Industry Week,* November 11, 1994, pp. 63–66.

Siebel, Thomas M. "Supersalesman Siebel." *Business Week,* January 10, 2000, p. 78.

———. "A Web of Misperceptions." *Across the Board,* June 1999, pp. 11–12.

Siebel, Thomas M., Pat House, and Charles R. Schwab. *Cyber Rules: Strategies for Excelling at E-Business.* New York: Doubleday, 1999.

Siegel, David. *Futurize Your Enterprise: Business Strategy in the Age of the E-Customer.* New York: Wiley, 1999.

———. "Letters to the Editor." *Harvard Business Review,* March 1999, pp. 178–179.

Siegel, David, and Candice Carpenter. "How Should Rachel Relaunch Her Upgraded, Internet-Friendly Product Line? What Role Should the Web Site Play?" *Harvard Business Review,* March 1999, pp. 28–32.

Slywotzky, Adrian J. *Profit Zone: How Strategic Business Design Will Lead You to Tomorrow's Profits.* New York: Times Business, 1997.

———. *Value Migration.* Boston: Harvard Business School Press, 1996.

Smith, Patrick. "The Trouble with Globalism." *Business Week,* March 29, 1999, pp. 15–16.

Solomon, Robert C. *A Better Way to Think about Business: How Personal Integrity Leads to Corporate Success.* New York: Oxford University Press, 1999.

————. "Is It Ever Right to Lie? The Philosophy of Deception." *Chronicle of Higher Education,* February 27, 1998, p. A60.

Stalk, George Jr., David K. Pecaut, and Benjamin Burnett. "Breaking Compromises, Breakaway Growth." *Harvard Business Review,* September 1, 1996, p. 131.

Stanat, Ruth, and Chris West. *Global Jumpstart: The Complete Resource Guide for Expanding Small and Medium Size Businesses.* Reading, MA: Perseus Books, 1999.

Stepanek, Marcia. "You'll Wanna Hold Their Hands." *Business Week E.Biz,* March 22, 1999, pp. EB30–EB31.

Stevens, Tim. "Managing across Boundaries." *Industry Week,* March 6, 1995, pp. 24–30.

Stewart, Thomas A. "After All You've Done for Your Customers, Why Are They Still Not Happy?" *Fortune,* December 11, 1995, pp. 178–194.

————. "Brain Power: Who Owns It . . . How They Profit from It." *Fortune,* March 17, 1997, pp. 104–110.

————. "The Case for Managing Structural Capital." *Health Forum Journal,* May–June 1999, pp. 30–33.

————. "Getting Real about Going Global." *Fortune,* February 15, 1999, pp. 170–172.

————. "Grab the Knowledge and Squeeze." *Fortune,* November 8, 1999, p. 322.

————. *Intellectual Capital: The New Wealth of Organizations.* New York: Doubleday, 1998.

————. "Knowledge, the Appreciating Commodity." *Fortune,* October 12, 1998, pp. 199–200.

————. "On the Job: The Leading Edge—Three Rules for Managing in the Real-Time Economy." *Fortune,* May 1, 2000, p. 196.

————. "Packaging What You Know." *Fortune,* November 9, 1998, pp. 253–254.

————. "A Satisfied Customer Isn't Enough." *Fortune,* July 21, 1997, pp. 112–114.

————. "Staying Smart/Managing: The Leading Edge—A Way to Measure Worldwide Success, Going Global Part II." *Fortune,* March 15, 1999, p. 196.

————. "Telling Tales at BP Amoco." *Fortune,* June 7, 1999, pp. 220–224.

————. "A Way to Measure Worldwide Success." *Fortune,* March 15, 1999, pp. 196–198.

————. "Why Dumb Things Happen to Smart Companies." *Fortune,* June 23, 1997, pp. 159–160.

————. "Your Company's Most Valuable Asset: Intellectual Capital." *Fortune,* October 3, 1994, pp. 68–74.

Stiroh, Kevin. "Is There a New Economy?" *Challenge,* July–August 1999, pp. 82–101.

"Strategies for Success in the New Global Economy: An Interview with Rosabeth Moss Kanter." *Strategy and Leadership,* November–December 1997, pp. 20–26.

Struebing, Laura. "Customer Loyalty: Playing for Keeps." *Quality Progress,* February 1996, pp. 25–30.

"Study Reveals Technology's Role in Customer Satisfaction." *Quality Progress,* June 1996, pp. 22–23.

Sveiby, Karl Erik. "The Balanced Score Card (BSC) and the Intangible Assets Monitor." <http://203.147.220.66/BSCandIAM.html> (March 13, 2000).

————. "The Intangible Assets Monitor." <http://203.147.220.66/IntangAss/CompanyMonitor.html> (March 13, 2000).

————. "Knowledge Works: Managing Intellectual Capital at Toshiba." *Administrative Science Quarterly,* December 1998, pp. 936–938.

————. "The New Organizational Wealth: Managing and Measuring Knowledge-Based Assets." <http://s1.webtrax.com.au/BB/971001Sveiby.bbd> (March 13, 2000).

———. *The New Organizational Wealth: Managing and Measuring Knowledge-Based Assets.* San Francisco: Berrett-Koehler, 1997.

———. "What Is Knowledge Management?" <http://www.sveiby.com.au/KnowledgeManagement.html> (March 13, 2000).

———. "Why Should We Use Non-Monetary Measures." <http://203.147.220.66/IntangAss/WhyNonMonetary.html> (March 13, 2000).

Sviokla, John J., and Benson P. Shapiro, eds. *Keeping Customers.* Boston: Harvard Business School Press, 1993.

Tannenbaum, Scott I. "Knowledge Management: So, What Is It Anyway?" *IHRIM Journal,* September 1998, pp. 7–10.

———. "Knowledge Management: Understanding the Complete Picture." *IHRIM Journal,* December 1998, pp. 6–10.

———. "On the Knowledge Frontier: Ownership of Knowledge Management—Point/Counterpoint." *IHRIM Journal,* June 1999, pp. 6–10.

Tapscott, Don. "Beyond Brand: The Future of Marketing." *Computerworld,* February 9, 1998, p. 101.

———. "Business Transformation: The Ten Commandments of Multimedia—Here's How to Get Ready for Interactive Media Now. *InformationWeek,* September 2, 1996, p. 53.

———. *The Digital Economy: Promise and Peril in the Age of Networked Intelligence.* New York: McGraw-Hill, 1996.

———. "E-Businesses Break the Mold." *Internetweek,* September 14, 1998, p. 80.

———. *Growing Up Digital: The Rise of the Net Generation.* New York: McGraw-Hill, 1998.

———. "Strategy in the New Economy." *Strategy and Leadership,* November–December 1997, pp. 8–14.

———, ed. *Creating Value in the Network Economy.* Boston: Harvard Business School Press, 1999.

Tapscott, Don, David Ticoll, and Alex Lowy. "Relationships Rule: Anywhere, Anytime." *Business 2.0,* May 2000, pp. 300–319.

———. "The Rise of the Business Web." *Business 2.0,* November 1999, pp. 198–208.

———, ed. *Blueprint to the Digital Economy: Wealth Creation in the Era of E-Business.* New York: Mc-Graw Hill, 1998.

Tauhert, Christy. "The Web's a Must for Document Management: An Interview with Thomas Koulopoulos." *Insurance and Technology,* April 1998, pp. 11–12.

Taylor, Jim, Watts Wacker, and Howard Means. *The Five Hundred Year Delta: What Happens after What Comes Next.* New York: HarperBusiness, 1997.

Teece, David J. "Capturing Value from Knowledge Assets: The Economy, Markets for Know-How, and Intangible Assets." *California Management Review,* Spring 1998, pp. 55–79.

Thernstrom, Stephan, Abigail Thernstrom, Richard Sennett, and J. Evert Green. "Exchange: Historians: Good, Bad, and Ugly." *Nation,* May 18, 1998, p. 2.

Thierauf, Robert J. *Knowledge Management Systems for Business.* Westport, CT: Quorum Books, 1999.

Thompson, John A. "The Contingent Workforce: The Solution to the Paradoxes of the New Economy." *Strategy and Leadership,* November–December 1997, pp. 44–45.

Thompson, Leigh L., ed. *Shared Cognition in Organizations: The Management of Knowledge.* Mahwah, NJ: L. Erlbaum, 1999.

Thomson, James. "Will Globalization Be Good for Americans?" *Futures Research Quarterly,* Fall 1998, pp. 5–18.

Thurow, Lester C. *Building Wealth: The New Rules for Individuals, Companies, and Nations.* New York: HarperCollins, 1999.

———. "Gray Matter." *Worldbusiness,* September–October 1996, p. 56.

———. "Power to the Person: Success Secret for the Future—Human Capital." *Worldbusiness,* January–February 1996, p. 5.

———. "The Rise and Fall of Brain Power." *Industry Week,* June 9, 1997, pp. 114–117.

Tiwana, Amrit. *The Knowledge Management Toolkit: Practical Techniques for Building a Knowledge Management System.* Upper Saddle River, NJ: Prentice Hall PTR, 2000.

Triplett, Jack. E. "Economic Statistics, the New Economy, and the Productivity Slowdown." *Business Economics,* April 1999, p. 13.

Trompenaars, Alfons, and Charles Hampden-Turner. *Riding the Waves of Culture: Understanding Cultural Diversity in Global Business.* Burr Ridge, IL: Irwin Professional, 1998.

Tucker, Robert B. *Customer Service for the New Millennium: Winning and Keeping Value-Driven Buyers.* Franklin Lakes, NJ: Career Press, 1997.

"The Twenty-first Century Economy." *Business Week,* August 31, 1998, pp. 58–59.

Tyler, Gus. "The Nation-State versus the Global Economy." *Challenge,* March–April 1993, pp. 26–32.

Tyson, Laura D'Andrea. "Just How New Is the New Economy?" *Business Week,* June 1, 1998, p. 30.

Van Buren, Mark E. "A Yardstick for Knowledge Management." *Training and Development,* May 1999, pp. 71–78.

Vaught, Bobby C., Raymond E. Taylor, and Steven F. Vaught. "The Attitudes of Managers Regarding the Electronic Monitoring of Employee Behavior: Procedural and Ethical Considerations." *American Business Review,* January 2000, pp. 107–114.

Vavra, Terry G. *Aftermarketing: How to Keep Customers for Life through Relationship Marketing.* Burr Ridge, IL: Irwin Professional, 1995.

———. "The Database Marketing Imperative." *Marketing Management,* 1993, pp. 46–57.

———. "Is Your Satisfaction Survey Creating Dissatisfied Customers?" *Quality Progress,* December 1997, pp. 51–57.

———. "Just Listen to Yourself." *Marketing News,* October 26, 1998, pp. 37, 43.

Velasquez, Manuel G. *Business Ethics: Concepts and Cases.* Upper Saddle River, NJ: Prentice Hall, 1998.

Vila, Juan. "People and Knowledge: Two Sides of the Same Coin." *IHRIM Journal,* September 1998, pp. 11–13.

Von Krogh, Georg. *Knowing in Firms: Understanding, Managing, and Measuring Knowledge.* London: Sage, 1999.

———. *Knowledge Creation: A Source of Value.* New York: St. Martin's Press, 1999.

Wagner, Cynthia G. "Digital Engine Powers New Economy." *Futurist,* April 1999, p. 20.

Wall, Stephen J., and Shannon Rye Wall. "Precious Commodity: Customer Feedback—How to Collect It, How to Use It." *Bottom Line/Business,* January 1, 1996, pp. 3–4.

Wartick, Steven Leslie, and Donna J. Wood. *International Business and Society.* Malden, MA: Blackwell Business, 1998.

Weidenbaum, Murray. "Isolationism in a Global Economy." *Management Review,* December 1995, pp. 43–46.

Weintraub, Sandra. *The Hidden Intelligence: Innovation through Intuition.* Boston: Butterworth-Heinemann, 1998.

Weiss, Michael J. *Clustered World: How We Live, What We Buy, and What It All Means about Who We Are.* Boston: Little Brown, 2000.

Wenger, Etienne C. *Communities of Practice: Learning, Meaning, and Identity.* New York: Cambridge University Press, 1998.

———. "Communities of Practice: Where Learning Happens." *Benchmark,* Fall 1999, pp. 6–8.

Wenger, Etienne C., and William M. Snyder. "Communities of Practice: The Organizational Frontier." *Harvard Business Review,* January–February 2000, pp. 139–145.

Whinston, Andrew B., Sulin Ba, and Han Zhang. "Small Business in the Electronic Marketplace." *Texas Business Review,* December 1999, pp. 1–3.

Whinston, Andrew B., Soon-Yong Choi, and Dale O. Stahl. *Economics of Electronic Commerce: The Essential Economics of Doing Business in the Electronic Marketplace.* Indianapolis, IN: MacMillan Technical, 1997.

Whinston, Andrew B., P. K. Kannan, and Al-Mei Chang. "Marketing Information on the I-Way." *Communications of the ACM,* March 1998, pp. 35–40.

Whiteley, Richard. "Building a Customer-Driven Company: The Saturn Story." *Managing Service Quality,* 1994, pp. 16–20.

———. "Fix the Customer First." *Sales and Marketing Management,* August 1994, pp. 49–50.

Whiteley, Richard, and Diane Hessan. *Customer Centered Growth: Five Proven Strategies for Building Competitive Advantage.* Reading, MA: Addison-Wesley, 1996.

Whitman, Marina V. N. *New World, New Rules: The Changing Role of the American Corporation.* Boston: Harvard Business School Press, 1999.

Wiley, Carolyn. "Ethical Standards for Human Resource Management Professionals: A Comparative Analysis of Five Major Codes." *Journal of Business Ethics,* May 2000, pp. 93–114.

Wilson, Ian. *New Rules of Corporate Conduct: Rewriting the Social Charter.* Westport, CT: Quorum, 2000.

Wing, Michael J. *Arthur Andersen Guide to Talking with Your Customers: What They Will Tell You about Your Business—When You Ask the Right Questions.* Chicago: Upstart, 1997.

Woodall, Pam. "Survey: The World Economy—A New Economy for the New World?" *Economist,* September 25, 1999, pp. S6–S10.

Woods, John A., and James W. Cortada. *The Knowledge Management Yearbook 1999–2000.* Boston: Butterworth-Heinemann, 1999.

Woolf, Brian. *Customer Specific Marketing: The New Power in Retailing.* Greenville, SC: Teal Books, 1996.

Wright, Greg. "World Trade Meeting Likely to Be a Contentious Affair: Variety of Groups Planning Protests inside Hall and Out." *Arizona Republic,* November 28, 1999, p. A22.

Yip, George S. *Total Global Strategy: Managing for Worldwide Competitive Advantage.* Englewood, NJ: Prentice Hall Trade, 1992.

Zemke, Ron, and Kristin Anderson. *Coaching Knock Your Socks Off Service.* New York: AMACOM, 1996.

Zemke, Ron, and John A. Woods, eds. *Best Practices in Customer Service.* New York: AMACOM, 1998.

Zyman, Sergio. *The End of Marketing as We Know It.* New York: HarperBusiness, 1999.

# Index